Complete Guide to
Wood Carving

Complete Guide to
Wood Carving

♦ ♦ ♦

E. J. Tangerman

 Sterling Publishing Co. Inc. New York

on page 1

Fig. 1. Medium relief on the surface of a log. This seems like in-the-round carving. Carved by Bogosav Zivkovic, it is now in a gallery in Yugoslavia.

The material in this compendium has been excerpted from the following books by E. J. Tangerman, copyrighted and published by Sterling Publishing Co., Inc.: "Capturing Personality in Woodcarving" © 1981; "Carving Birds in Wood" © 1984; "Carving Faces and Figures in Wood" © 1980; "Carving Flora and Fables in Wood" © 1981; "Carving Religious Motifs in Wood" © 1980; "Carving the Unusual" © 1982; "Carving Wooden Animals" © 1980; "Relief Woodcarving" © 1981; and "Tangerman's Basic Whittling and Woodcarving" © 1983.

Second Printing, 1985

Library of Congress Cataloging in Publication Data

Tangerman, E. J. (Elmer John), 1907–
  Complete guide to woodcarving.

  Includes index.
  1. Wood-carving—Technique. I. Title.
TT199.7.T345   1984   731.4'62   84-2756
ISBN 0-8069-5532-5
ISBN 0-8069-7922-4 (pbk.)

Additional material and arrangements © 1984 by
Sterling Publishing Co., Inc.
Two Park Avenue, New York, N.Y. 10016
Distributed in Australia by Oak Tree Press Co., Ltd.
P.O. Box K514 Haymarket, Sydney 2000, N.S.W.
Distributed in the United Kingdom by Blandford Press
Link House, West Street, Poole, Dorset BH15 1LL, England
Distributed in Canada by Oak Tree Press Ltd.
% Canadian Manda Group, P.O. Box 920, Station U
Toronto, Ontario, Canada M8Z 5P9
Manufactured in the United States of America
All rights reserved
Library of Congress Catalog Card No.: 00-00000
Sterling ISBN 0-8069-5532-5 Trade 5532-5
                          Paper 7922-4

Table of Contents

1. Before You Carve   7
2. Something About Tools   10
3. Sharp Tools Are Vital   24
4. The Right Size   28
5. What Wood to Use   32
6. Some Finishing Suggestions   44
7. Small Pieces   58
8. Carving Animals   65
9. Why Not Carve Flowers?   126
10. Carving Fabulous Creatures   141
11. Portraying Buildings   156
12. Carving Models   163
13. Carving Faces and Heads   172
14. Carving the Human Figure   189
15. Portraits   216
16. Why Not Carve a Mask?   222
17. Relief Carving   231
18. How to Carve Lettering   287
19. You Can Whittle Ivory   296
    Appendix I   313
    Appendix II   335
    Index   347

Part I

1

Before You Carve

IN PAPEETE, a New York hotel designer met with a Tahitian woodcarver to negotiate a price for thirty tikis (Polynesian wood images). The first, they agreed, would cost 2,000 Tahitian francs. "And for the next twenty-nine tikis?" asked the designer. "They will be more than 3,000 francs each," the carver said. "But why?" "Because only the first one is fun."

Neil Morgan told the story in *Saturday Review*. Sharing that carver's sentiments, I have spent whatever time I have had available for fifty years, seeking out what for me were new ideas for carvings, simple or complex. I have less interest in the familiar and traditional European patterns, and much more in the things that primitive, and often self-taught, carvers make purely for the love of it. Somehow, such carvings are less rigid, less standardized, and far more imaginative—full of verve and of life. I bought those carvings I could afford and that were for sale, and photographed or sketched others. Retirement has made it possible for me to visit many of the less well-known parts of the world where carving is still respected and admired.

Prepackaged vs. hand carvings

IN RECENT YEARS relatively high incomes and early retirement have provided many people with leisure time as well as the finances to do with it what they want. Out of this and an increasing disaffection with pre-packaged, all-alike products—which many of us have spent our working lifetimes helping to make—has risen a tremendous craft movement, the desire to do one's own thing. As a result, what was once dismissed as primitive, folk, or naive art is coming to be recognized, because of its strength and originality, as fully comparable with the often slavish and more rigid productions of academic art.

My effort in this volume is to capture not only examples of American folk art but those typical of faraway places, to give you a source for new and different ideas upon which to build. This volume is devoted to subjects quite familiar to most primitive carvers but less familiar to Americans—the world of mammals, birds and fishes, and even a saurian or two. Ancient man respected, feared and admired the inhabitants of that world; the development of cities and highways has tended to take us out of it, even to destroy it, at an accelerating rate.

I have tried to maintain logical groupings of the designs presented here. The first few sections include carvings that can be made with the knife alone, while most of the remainder can be done with relatively few and inexpensive tools. This grading is based upon my own experience in carving them; indeed, many of my own designs and carvings are scattered through the book. I have provided such patterns as are

Fig. 2. Carving a horse's head with a chisel.

usually homemade and cherished, not for their number or variety but for their necessity. His "shop" is portable. In fact, only in Europe and America have all the devices for saving time been introduced, and in both places we also have duplicating machines, profilers and plastic-and-sawdust moulded fakes.

How to carve more than shavings

WHEN MY SON was learning to whittle, he would say, "Now I'm going to make a dog." After he had by mistake cut off a leg or two, he would settle for a fish, but the final admission would be, "I guess it's going to be another knife!" "Knife" was a euphemism for the pointed stick that country-store whittlers are always shown making. Wade Martin, when complimented on the latest of his excellent country carvings, would say shyly, "I'd ruther be whittlin' *somethin'* than just be whittlin' whittlin's!"

There should and can be more than just shavings for an end product in carving. What's more, the end product should vary; constant output of the same thing is too much like Detroit and automobiles. That is why I have spent as much time as I could spare this past half century hunting up new designs to carve. In recent years, many of these have been from faraway places, because the nearby ones are described in my own and other books. I am still amazed at how good and free many primitive designs are, and how well they are executed, usually without the tools and equipment we consider necessary. You do not need a fancy shop to be a good woodcarver—which is one of its attractions for me.

This book includes extensive summaries of basic information on tools, sharpening, finishing in color or natural wood, and changing drawing size. It has some simple, but different, projects for beginning whittlers and carvers, then some more advanced ones, first for whittling with the knife alone, then for carving with a variety of tools. I have added Appendix II on sharpening. The sections on knives and

necessary, and detailed instructions where difficulty might be encountered, plus tips, shortcuts and suggestions. There are also answers to the basic questions of the neophyte, to make this volume complete in itself. I have also included examples of recent original work of other Americans who are more concerned with the enjoyment to be gotten from carving than with possible income from it, and who whittle or carve as an avocation or leisure-time pursuit. They understand the Tahitian carver's reluctance to turn himself into a production machine. If you are also reluctant, this book was written for you.

All this tends to obscure the fact that woodcarving and whittling can be and are being done with very limited numbers of tools—and no other equipment whatsoever. The carver in Bali or Easter Island, in both of which woodcarving is the only industry, rarely has more than four or five tools and probably uses a shaped club for a mallet and his knees for a vise. His tools are chisels are as up-to-date and complete as I can make them. Wood selection and finishing are included piece by piece, but there is also a complete section on wood and its characteristics. All in all, I have tried to provide here a complete handbook for experienced as well as beginning carvers. May your tools stay sharp and your wood and your ideas be unchecked!

Carving personality

CALL SOMEONE AN ARTIST and the layman will ask, "Oil or watercolor?" He forgets that there were nine Muses, and the so-called fine arts include sculpture, poetry, prose, and dance, among others. Use the word "portrait" and your listener will ask, "Of whom?" Even Webster's supports this view with the definition, "a pictorial representation of a person." The use of that word for "a picture of an object" is now called obsolete. There's a similar problem with the word "image."

What we are seeking to capture is a *personality*, whether it be of a person, some other animal, or of an inanimate object. What this book deals with are individual likenesses, representations of specific animals, flora and inanimate objects so that they are distinct and recognizable.

We have a chapter or two on depicting the general shape of things other than people, then progress to attaining likenesses of such diverse subjects as a house, a barn, other models, a hobby, a dog or two, and ultimately portraits of people. Included are such ideas as how to copy a statue in miniature and how to make masks of animals and people.

In short, I've tried to explain how to carve a likeness of just about anything. This is a frequent challenge to any woodcarver, whether he be amateur or professional, neophyte or skilled. Many of the examples here described were commissions, because many customers want likenesses, if they can get them, particularly of something near and dear to them.

I have tried to arrange the text in order of difficulty, the easiest first and so on. I have shown some projects in more detail than others, depending upon the number of rough spots I encountered. Some pieces are shown in step-by-step photos; where I felt they would be useful I have provided patterns. I have avoided specialized language and specialized tools, and tried to select examples that cover a wide range of subjects.

What to carve

IN KOWLOON ONE DAY, I ASKED A SALESMAN in a carved-ivory shop what *he* carved.

"Elephants," he said.

"Horses are selling better," I offered. "Have you ever tried to carve one?"

He shook his head. "No," he replied, "I only carve elephants."

Indeed, there are whittlers who make only old boots or wooden chains, and carvers who make only decoys, signs, or furniture with traditional motifs. I've met professional cabinetmakers who never tried carving at all until they retired.

This book is not for any of the above. It is an effort to assemble a number of attractive and unusual ideas in materials, subjects, techniques and treatments that I have found refreshing alternatives to typical woodcarving and predetermined commissions. Finish is indicated piece-by-piece, and I have also provided traceable patterns for a number of them. Because many of my carvings are unusual, I have already sold some, and could have sold more.

Many of the designs are not American, because some of the most unusual of carvings are foreign in origin. Most are, however, folk art rather than formal art, because the latter usually follows traditional patterns available from many sources, and mostly utilitarian in application. These designs are largely for fun and "for a change." Go to it!

2

Something about Tools . . .

ANCIENT MAN CARVED the materials he had with whatever tools he could devise. His incentives were undoubtedly to placate the gods or worship them, to make a tool easier to hold and to make an image for himself or his children. Wood was abundant in most areas and could be cut by stone, so the stone knife and chisel found early use, followed by the axe and the adze when someone discovered how to make and bind on a handle. The point is, that ancient man got along with relatively few tools. So can you, until you know what you need.

The carver's pocketknife

THE MOST UNIVERSAL tool is the knife, particularly the pocketknife, because it is so portable and adaptable. A good one can cut a wide variety of materials, certainly those mentioned in this book. Because man is so inventive, he has developed an extraordinary number of variations on the knife, each with its own special purpose and advantages. You can buy any number of blade and handle shapes, even blades with blank handles you can carve to fit your hand. But it is better to start with a good pocketknife, with a maximum of two or three carbon-steel blades (stainless won't hold an edge as well) and no belt clips, can openers or corkscrews to chafe your palm. Because the knife will change position in your hand for various cuts, it should have an essentially smooth and uniform handle, comfortable to grip. Blades should include at least one with a sabre point, usually the big one—known as a B-clip. The other one or two

should be pen, spear or an equivalent. Be sure blades open and close easily, yet do not wobble, and do open out straight and firmly.

Fixed-blade knives

IF YOU FIND carving a particular material or subject preferable, you can branch out and get specially shaped fixed-blade knives to suit what you're doing. These are easier and safer to use at home—the blade won't snap shut on your finger—but they aren't as portable. However, I know tool enthusiasts who have made their own knives from old saw-blades or straight razors and have special cases to carry them in, just as I carry a roll with a number of chisels. Mine includes sharpening aids, and so should yours. Have at least one narrow and thin blade to get into concavities and tight corners, and one wide, heavy blade for roughing. I also find that a blade with a concave cutting edge (which I call a hook), originally developed for leatherworking, is helpful in carving details. Blades should be short—not over 1½ in (3.8 cm) long for most work—kept sharp, and oiled to avoid rust.

Many sources are eager to sell you a *set* of carving tools, a mixture of types supposedly put together by an "expert" that includes some you may never use, as was the case with the 9-tool set I bought originally. Further, you don't have to buy the finest tools available; buy cheap ones until you find out what you really need, then supplement with better quality. With a little care, you'll find that cheap tools work al-

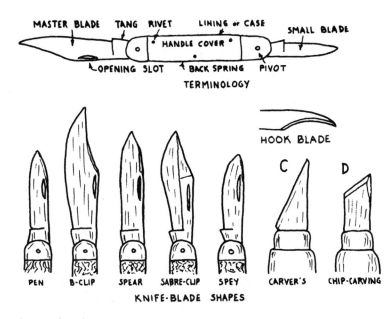

Fig. 3. Knives for woodcarving.

How to choose knives

IF YOU ARE JUST STARTING to carve, you can't beat a knife and a piece of pine or basswood. The great convenience of the pocketknife or clasp knife is that you can take it with you and set up shop whenever you're so inclined. A knife with a fixed handle is safer for cutting (the blade won't snap shut on your finger) but a nuisance to carry; its edge must be protected against all things hard or soft. Its handle is bigger and more comfortable, but you need a sheath to carry it. The knife should be of good quality and have a carbon-steel blade, rather than stainless. It will rust if you don't keep it lightly oiled, but it will also hold an edge longer, which is important unless you long to carry a hone and a lap with you as well.

As to blade shape and size, you'll find that you seldom need a blade longer than 1½ in (4 cm); a longer blade will bend and your hand is too far back to control it as well. A knife with one long blade with a sharp point (*sabre* or *B-clip*) and a smaller one with a stubbier tip (*pen*) is the basic answer. It can have three blades, but shouldn't have more than that or the knife becomes too clumsy. I usually carry two knives—one with pen, spear, and B-clip, the other with pen and B-clip. The three-bladed knife is larger and has wider blades, so will take heavier cuts; the small blade handles the delicate and hard-to-get-at spots and shallow concavities. The small blade is more likely to break and harder to control, as well as slower, but the big blades get in their own way on occasion.

Grain

WOOD HAS GRAIN and tends to splinter and split along it. It is much easier to cut *with* the grain than across it, of course (those long curling chips are cut with the grain), but a tree is a living thing and its grain may not be straight, or it may veer around damage or a knot. The first thing you must learn is to keep the grain in mind at all times. If you cut with it, it's easy; if you cut squarely across it, it's harder work but no problem

  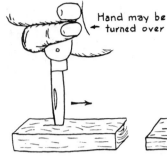 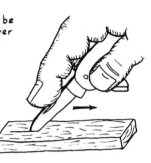

POINTING CUT
No control - hence danger.
Force from arm muscles

PARING CUT
Good cut control - watch thumb!
Force from hand clenching

DRAW CUT
Poor control - tends to
follow grain. Arm force

SLICING CUT
Close control - may tend
to follow grain. Arm force

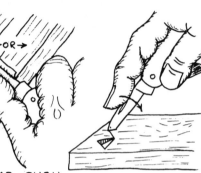 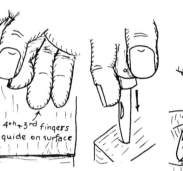 

THUMB PUSH
Short cuts -
    greater pressure
Close control -
    Arm force

ROCKING CUT
Chip carving - good
across grain - Arm force

CHAMFER or **CURL CUT**
Close control - must cut with
grain. Arm rotation + force

STAB or **DRILL CUT**
Series of hand pushes.
Danger of blade closing

HOLLOW CUT
Tip cuts concave.
Watch grain!!!

Fig. 4. Typical knife cuts done with one hand.

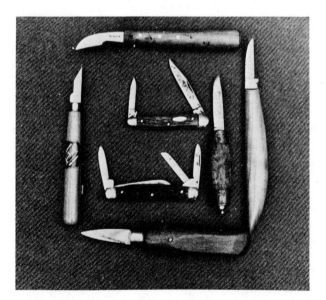

Fig. 5. Typical knives for woodcarving include: A, a penknife with pen and B-clip blades, and B, a slightly larger one with pen, spear, and cut-off pen. Both are German-made. Below them is C, an inexpensive fixed-blade knife, and to the right is a Swedish sloyd, D. The others are specialized shapes: E and F are used for chip carving; G is a German fixed-blade knife.

with splitting; but watch out if you cut *into* the grain, because even the thin wedge of a knife blade may cause splitting and will certainly cause some roughness. The problem varies with the wood: basswood and white pine offer fewer problems than ash or mahogany, teak less than walnut. You will learn about grain quickly and soon appreciate the necessity for cutting in the opposite direction on the into-grain side of even a slightly diagonal groove.

How to cut with the knife

THE STANDARD CARTOON of a whittler shows him paring off big chips with bold strokes going away from himself. That is very safe but produces only chips. The most important cut for the knife is exactly like that used by someone peeling a potato: the knife caught in the curve of the four fingers, the thumb on the work, and the cut made by closing the hand. That gives the greatest control because it is finger rather than arm muscle that does the work. (While you're learning this cut, be careful of your thumb.) Other frequent cuts are made with the thumb or the forefinger extended along the heel of the blade to provide added force just behind the cut itself. Or the knife may be gripped like a dagger and drawn or pushed to make a slice—this is an arm-muscle cut, so control is poorer. Another type of cut is that in which the point of the knife is pushed into the wood, then the knife is rocked or rotated, in the first case to make a triangular incision and in the second to make a cone-shaped depression.

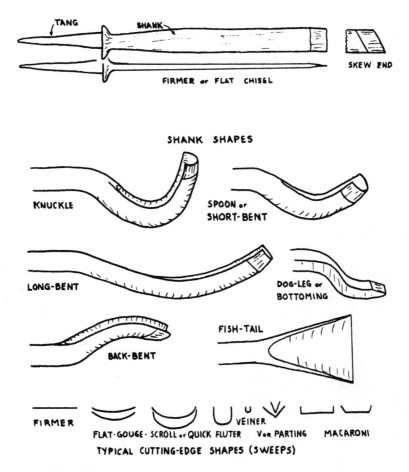

Fig. 6. Chisel shapes.

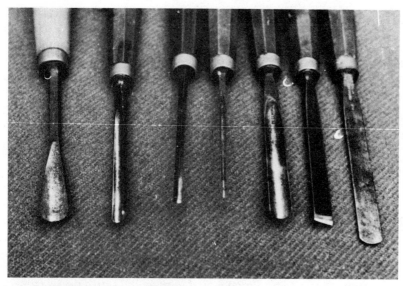

Fig. 7. Typical chisel shapes: A, 1-in (25.4-mm) No. 9 spade gouge; B, ½-in (12.7-mm) No. 10 gouge; C, ¼-in (6.3-mm) V-tool; D, veiner; E, ½-in (6.3-mm) No. 7 gouge; F, ½-in (12.7-mm) firmer; G, ⅝-in (16-mm) bullnose firmer.

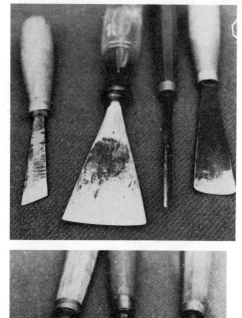

Fig. 8. Shorter tools include: A, 1-in (25.4-mm) skew firmer with homemade spade shank; B, 2½-in (6-cm) No. 5 spade gouge; C, ½-in (12.7-mm) bullnose No. 7 gouge; D, 1½-in (3-cm) No. 5 gouge.

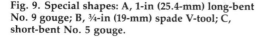

Fig. 9. Special shapes: A, 1-in (25.4-mm) long-bent No. 9 gouge; B, ¾-in (19-mm) spade V-tool; C, short-bent No. 5 gouge.

Some cuts are better done by using the thumb or forefinger of the other hand to push and guide the blade. This is very helpful with harder woods and ivory because the actual cutting force can be so exactly controlled. The cut, in any case, is very short because the hand itself will be gripping or resting on the work.

Chisels

WOODCARVING TOOLS have a long history and, thus, a vocabulary all their own. The straight chisel, like a carpenter's chisel but lighter, is called a *firmer*. It is sharpened from both sides so it doesn't dig in. If the edge is at an angle to the blade length it is called a *skew*, and is used for getting into corners, much as a knife would be (I use the knife). The rounded chisels are called *gouges*, as in carpentry, but come in a wide range of widths and curvatures or *sweeps* from almost flat to U-shaped. The very U-shaped ones are called *fluters*, particularly in small sizes. One of the most useful of gouges is a very small half-round one called a *veiner*, because it's used to carve veins, hair and any other very small grooves. Its alternate is the *V-tool* (or parting tool, from wood-turning), also used for grooving. This is essentially two firmers put together in a vee; it is difficult to sharpen because of this, but it cuts two sides at once. There are also more specialized tools such as the *macaroni*, which cuts a 3-sided groove with a flat bottom and square corners, and a *fluteroni*, which cuts a similar groove with rounded corners. These are very difficult to sharpen and of almost no use to amateur carvers.

You may have a choice of handle on the chisels. Usual ones are round or octagonal, tapering towards the cutting edge, the better ones with brass ferrules at the tang end to inhibit splitting. Round ones are usually maple, ash, beech or boxwood. The octagonal ones may be dogwood (preferred in Germany). Octagonal handles are less likely to turn in your hand or roll off a bench. There are now plastic handles also, but I prefer the octagonal wood ones with ferrules. (You can, incidentally, turn your own handles and use short sections of pipe for ferrules.) Some tools, particularly short ones, are available with palm-fitting handles, like an engraver's burin. I prefer the longer handle because it gives more clearance for the mallet and less chance for barked knuckles.

The rear of a chisel ends in a tang, a pointed end that goes into a hole in the handle as far as its collar will allow, while a ring on the handle prevents it from splitting under the wedging action of the tang. Obviously, larger chisels must have tapered shanks to end in a tang, which leads to the *spade* or *fishtail* design where the blade is wider than the shank. This is also done on many smaller tools because it gives greater clearance in carving and lightens the tool. Also, because straight tools are of limited use when entering certain areas, tools are made with bent shanks, ranging from a very short and half-circular bend called a *knuckle*, through a short bend (*spoon*) and on to a long bend. Some tools are made with similar bends backwards, and are called *back-bent* tools, but are of lesser value.

There are also *dog-leg* tools, in which a double bend offsets the cutting edge from the line of the shank. (Fig. 6)

Carving tools may be driven by the hands alone on small work in soft woods. On hand-held work, the palm tools are easy because they require only one hand. But they are very slow in material removal (as is a pocketknife), though they work well on ivory and bone. If the piece can be held or secured in any way, the long-handled tools are preferable, since one hand can supply push while the other guides and restrains the tool. The method I use is to hold the chisel in one hand and drive it with a mallet of suitable weight for the work being done. This way, I get more precise control of the cut with less danger of splitting—a problem with hand pushing because it is difficult to control arm-muscle force accurately.

Mallets and adzes

MALLETS CAN BE designed to your specifications, or bought ready-made. I prefer the traditional potato-masher type, and in recent years have used those with plastic or

MALLETS

ADZES

Fig. 10. Mallets and adzes.

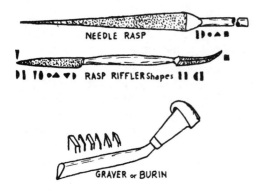

Fig. 11. Rasps and burin.

is always increased danger, and with some it is advisable to wear goggles and mask, and to work in an area where noise, dust and possible vapors (from such woods as cocobola or rosewood) will not affect others. These power tools remind me too much of mass production, so I shy away from using them unless I have a large block with a great deal of roughing to be done or a piece in which the contour permits me to cut out and save a smaller section. Rotary tools tend to chew the wood away, and small burrs tend to burn the surface.

rubber faces to reduce shock in my arthritic shoulders. Other carvers prefer babbitt-faced mallets or even copper or brass ones, but these tend to split tool handles, as an ordinary hammer would. Further, their diameter is small, so more attention must be paid to hitting the handle end squarely.

In addition to these specialized carving tools, there are also a great number of auxiliary tools used by specialty carvers. These include various kinds of saws, such as sabre and scroll saws, rasps of various sizes (much used for decoy carving in soft woods), riffler files in various shapes to smooth tight corners, scrapers, hand routers and the usual carpenter's tools, including planes and chisels. Carpenter's chisels, incidentally, are cheaper and heavier than equivalent woodcarving tools and, thus, good for roughing. The hand axe, shingling hatchet and adze are also used, particularly on larger and rougher work, like wooden Indians and totem poles. Indians of the American northwest coast, Africans and Italians use adzes for most carving. (Fig. 10)

Power tools

AMERICANS, who are accustomed to mechanizing everything, have added a whole series of power tools to this list, including chain saws, band saws, circular saws, sanders of various types—including hand-held ones that take cutters or burrs as well as grinding shapes—and even pneumatic or electric hammers. With power tools, there

Vises and benches

FOR CONVENTIONAL AMATEUR WORK, particularly with chisels, you may want to have some form of holding device. I have used a machinist's vise, opening about 4½ in (11 cm), for years, and a long-leg carpenter's vise for larger pieces. In recent years, I have also used the carver's screw—which screws through a bench or table into the base of the workpiece and holds it with a tightened wingnut. Mine are hand-made by a friend from lag bolts or threaded steel rod. If the piece is relatively large, no clamping will be necessary as its own weight will hold it. Panels can be held by nailing through scrap areas, by holding with a benchplate (a square of plywood with a stopboard), or just placing them on a section of discarded ribbed-rubber door-mat.

You can, of course, have a carver's bench, a 4-legged stand or even a stand of the type sketched here, but they take up room and begin to require a shop or studio. I do most of my carving seated next to the fireplace in my living room, with the work on my knees or lying on a card table. When clamping is needed, I adjourn to my cellar workbench or to a picnic table on the terrace, both of which can take clamps, vises or carver's screws, as well as any amount of shock from mallet blows.

The "proper" way to carve is to stand at a high bench or stand that is heavy enough so it doesn't shift under the mallet blows.

Some sculptors have four-legged stands that are weighted with a rock towards the bottom, with the top adjustable for height, possibly even incorporating a lockable lazy Susan so it can be rotated. Panel carvers, like those who work on cuckoo-clock frames, have sloping tables with 2-in (5-cm) tops and pins to index and hold the work. When I work on a trestle table on the terrace, a basement bench, and on a card table, I sit down whenever possible. The main thing is to have a stable surface that will absorb mallet blows, with some sort of adjacent surface on which your tools may be placed. For any given job, you rarely need more than ten or a dozen tools. You can have whatever sort of bench or stand that suits your ego, and as many tools as you like, but a solid surface and good light, plus some air, suit me best.

Personally, I don't need a studio.

Tool sizes and names

CARVING TOOLS are sized by the width of the cutting edge, in inches from 1/16 in (1.6 mm) to 3/8 in (9.5 mm) in sixteenths, on up to 1 in (25.4 mm) in eighths, and in larger steps to the maximum, usually about 2½ in

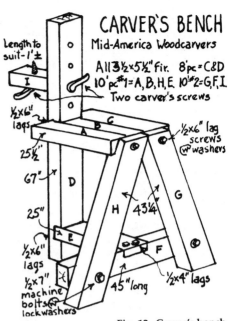

Fig. 12. Carver's bench.

(6.4 cm) for flat gouges. European tools are sized in millimetres: 1, 2, 3, 4, 5, 6, 7, 8, 10, 12, 16, 20, 25, 30, 35 and so on (1 mm = 0.039 in).

Gouges are usually numbered also by the "London" system that measures arc or radius of the sweep. A firmer is No. 1, a skew No. 2, a flat gouge No. 3 and a U-shaped one No. 11 or 12, with the other arcs in between.

Some suppliers use other numbers for the special tools, from this series or their

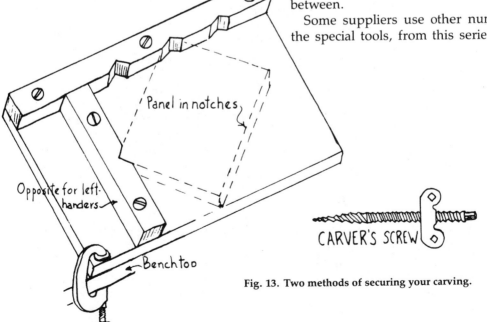

Fig. 13. Two methods of securing your carving.

own catalogue numbers. Charles M. Sayers, who taught panel carving, suggested four tools with which to start: ½-in (13-mm), or ⅜- to ⅝-in (9.5- to 16-mm V-tool or parting tool [No. 39]); ⅝-in (16-mm) No. 5 straight gouge; 1-in (25.4-mm) No. 3, or ⅞-in (22-mm) straight gouge; and a ⅜-in (9.5-mm) No. 7 straight gouge. For relief carving, he added a ⅜-in (9.5-mm) No. 5 straight gouge. (See Figs. 7, 8, 9)

H. M. Sutter, who has taught panel carving for over 30 years, starts his students—often teachers themselves—with five tools: ⅜-in (9.5-mm) No. 3 and ⅝-in (16-mm) No. 5 straight gouges (these two preferably fishtail); ⅜-in (9.5-mm) No. 9 straight gouge; ¹⁄₃₂-in (.79-mm) No. 11 veiner and a ⅜-in (9.5-mm) No. 41 parting or V-tool, plus an all-purpose carver's knife. Note that neither suggests fancy shapes or skew chisels, at least to start. Begin small, then buy with the guidance of an experienced carver—or you're likely to end up with heavy patternmakers' chisels or worse.

To carve the harder materials included in this book, try small chisels, particularly the veiner and V-tool. I find engraver's burins (solid chisels) of little help, though engraver's palm tools can work well. Riffler files will help on occasion, as will power grinders; Eskimo and German ivory carvers are both using these now. Also of help will be a chamois-skin or leather pillow filled with sand. The work can be nestled in it with less danger of rolling and slipping. Further, most of the hard materials are difficult to hold in a vise or clamp because they are rounded in shape and brittle.

Chisel vs. knife

I FIND CHISELS easier to learn to use than the knife. The cutting edge is narrower and less versatile and it is pushed directly instead of being used in an arc by finger or arm power. If you use a mallet, you must obviously learn to watch the chisel edge, not the head of the mallet. You must learn to take it easy and not try to remove all the waste wood on the first pass. You must learn to adjust the angle of the tool as you cut so it doesn't run in and stick or run out and slip. You start cutting at an edge and work towards the middle; if you cut to an edge, the chisel will break out and tear the wood.

As cutting begins, it is necessary to adjust the angle of the tool so it cuts through the wood at the desired level—too high an angle will cause it to cut deeper and deeper, too shallow an angle will cause it to run out. This is particularly important with the high-sweep or U-shaped gouges. If the cut is too deep, the edges of the gouge can get below the wood surface and cause edge tearing of fibres.

In relief cutting, it is important to outline the desired shape by "setting in"—driving the firmer or gouge into the wood to the desired depth along the line, so that cuts made to remove background wood will stop at the cut line instead of splitting or running into the design. When a chisel is driven vertically into wood, it obviously must wedge the fibres aside, so it will cause crushing and splintering of fibres along the edge of the outline. This can be avoided by cutting a groove just outside the outline with a veiner, fluter or V-tool, so the edge of the groove touches the line. Then, when the firmer or gouge is driven in along the line, the groove provides relief for the tool wedge at the surface. As a matter of fact, in shallow-relief carving, particularly in green wood, it is often possible to get the required depth of background (called "bosting") with a deep fluter alone, leaving a desirable small arc at the bottom edge of the upstanding portion.

Your constant challenge will come from the grain of the wood. In any diagonal cut, for example, one edge of the gouge will cut cleanly, the other will drag and tear the wood slightly because it is cutting into the grain. You'll learn how to cope with this and soon will be adjusting automatically for it. The other major point is to keep your tools razor-sharp, particularly for cutting soft woods—so you'll have to learn how to sharpen.

LEFT-INDEX DRAW CUT
Shaving + detailing. Gives
close control with more force

LEFT-THUMB ASSIST
Close control - more force
Short, precise cuts or shaving

GUILLOTINE CUT
Adds force at blade tip.
Left index finger- or thumb push

LEFT INDEX-FINGER ASSIST
Shaving cuts. Work must be
clamped or held by left hand

Fig. 14. Two-hand knife cuts.

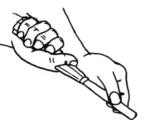

Heavy & straight cuts
Heel of back hand pushes handle end
Near hand guides, prevents overcuts & slips

Light & curving cuts
Back hand presses forward & steers
Near hand restrains, rests on work

Side cuts & V-tool cuts
Back hand presses
Near hand pulls, rests on work

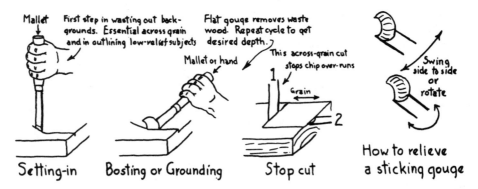

Mallet First step in wasting out backgrounds. Essential across grain
and in outlining low-relief subjects

Flat gouge removes waste
wood. Repeat cycle to get
desired depth.

Mallet or hand

This across-grain cut
stops chip over-runs

Grain

Swing
side to side
or
rotate

Setting-in   **Bosting or Grounding**   **Stop cut**   **How to relieve
a sticking gouge**

Fig. 15. How to handle chisels.

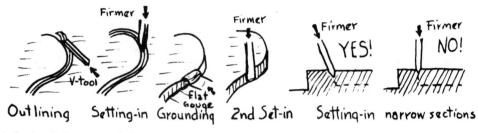

Fig. 16. Setting-in is an extended stop cut.

Some general hints

WHEN YOU ARE USING either knife or chisel, try to avoid wedging out the chip; you may break the tool or split the wood. Obviously, tools are not to be used for cutting newspaper clippings, paring nails, or peeling electrical insulation; all these destroy the cutting edge. The old professionals laid their chisels out with the edges towards themselves, so they could select the right chisel easily. I find this hard to do because it requires reversal of the tool when you pick it up and when you lay it down. Some carvers put distinguishing marks on handles for rapid identification of frequently used tools.

Leave a light film of oil on the tools after use—it will reduce rusting. This is particularly true of pocketknifes: sweat can be very corrosive. Keep tools very sharp. Store them out of reach of the curious, old and young, and keep the edges protected if you carry them about.

If you nick yourself, protect the cut, because you may find you'll repeat the nicking. This is particularly true of the ball of the thumb when you make small carvings with paring cuts. It may be advisable to use a fingerstall initially; stationery stores sell rubber ones that are used by people who sort papers.

Starting to whittle

IF YOU ARE STARTING to whittle, and intend to make hand-size items in soft wood, use a first-class pocketknife with carbon-steel blades, one pen and one B-clip. A third blade can be a spear, a cutoff pen or a sheepfoot. The straight-cutting edge of the latter

shapes has some advantages in rounding convex surfaces and attaining flatness, but tends to drag at the heel in any hollow cutting. No blade should be longer than about 1½ in (3.81 cm). Be sure the pivots are tight and the springs strong, so the blade opens and stays open, without wobbling. Beware of excrescences like corkscrews and clevises (for belt hooks); they will cause sore palms and blisters.

As you progress, add fixed-blade knives for protracted use—avoid the straight blade and rounded tip of some such knives. Or add a chuck handle with several shapes of blades, but be certain the handle fits your hand well and the chuck can be screwed up tightly on sturdy blades. The thin blades are useful only for extremely delicate work.

Be conscious all the time that the knife has a fairly long cutting edge, and never get anything in front of that edge unless you intend to cut it. This is meant particularly to apply to the hand holding the work and to the cutting-hand thumb on paring cuts. You can't whittle and talk or watch television.

Beware of sticking the blade tip into the wood and exerting pressure; the blade may close on your fingers. For the same reason, always hold the body of the knife in your fingertips when closing a blade, and make the final closure with the palm of your hand. Never have two blades open at once. On a folding blade, there is a boss that prevents a finger from slipping onto the cutting edge; many of the special knives are not thus protected.

It is obvious that a blade should not be hammered, or used for miscellaneous cutting, like paper or fingernails, or for skinning electric wire. Also, it should not be sharpened on a wheel unless it is nicked or chipped; then it should be cooled twice as often as you consider necessary. Cutting newly sanded areas or scraping a surface takes off a newly honed edge faster than a half day of cutting.

Chips

CHIP SIZE should be adjusted to the wood and the design. It is a delight to cut big chips in soft wood, but they tend to be hard to control, so you may cut beyond your intended lines or generate a split. It is advisable to make a stop cut *across* the grain before you attempt to make a cut to that point *with* the grain. The harder the wood or the greater its tendency to split, the smaller the chips should be. Also, chip size should be reduced as you approach finishing dimensions.

Rough all areas before any one is finished; this way a gash or nick can still be corrected. Chips should be cut out, not wedged out; wedging may break the blade tip and will certainly bruise or dent the wood fibres against which the knife is pressed.

Stop cuts

IN CUTTING A SLOT or a V-groove, it is advisable to make the end stop cuts first, then cut down the center with the knife tip, before cutting the two sides in towards the center. This gives better control of groove shape. It is important to cut *with* the grain whenever possible because any angling cut will be clean on the side *running out* of the grain, but tends to tear and run in on the side *entering* the grain. Thus, grain should always be considered when laying out a design and when its outlines are being carved. (In some woods, cuts with the grain in one direction may cause trouble which can be avoided by reversing the cutting direction.)

When possible, cuts across-grain should be made first. Across-grain cuts take more force than those with the grain, so there is increased chance of error. Also, when across-grain cuts and with-grain cuts are alternated, the difference in force required and the fact that an across-grain chip tends to crumble must always be kept in mind. The "hollow cut" provides a good example of this.

When the blade enters the grain, it tends to tear and split the wood ahead of it, while on the exiting portions it cuts smoothly; thus a conical cut is best made with four quarter cuts, each with the grain, rather than one continuous one. A pointed blade can be used directly as a drill by simply rotating it, but the same danger of tearing exists in that case. In general, when it is necessary to whittle across the grain or around knots or other likely grain variations, it is advisable to make very light cuts and observe the action of the blade constantly to determine when cutting direction should be changed. (In this kind of situation, the woodcarver reaches for a riffler file.)

If you keep your knife sharp and cut accurately and cleanly, sanding should not be necessary. With occasional exceptions, a whittled piece is the better for having the slight planes left by the knife; they catch the light and show that the piece is not formed plastic. Further, sanding tends to smear the surface, and, particularly on harder woods, will dull the clean gloss surface left by the tool. If you must sand, use worn fine sandpaper sparingly.

The whittler needs only one tool

"WHITTLING" MEANS to work with one tool to pare away wood, so it could be applied, for example, to a totem pole made with a shingling hatchet or to a figure carved with an adze, or even an axe handle shaped with a spokeshave. But the common understanding is that whittling is done with a knife, to produce a one-piece object usually small enough to be held in the hand. Most whittlers saw out the blank, and sand it

Fig. 17. This one-piece daisy is a variation of the old whittling trick—the fan. It is cut across grain so that the petals can later be split and spread. In this case, the petals were not interlocked, but held in place with thread.

when finished, so they have actually used at least three tools, but they only count the knife.

If your idea is to produce likenesses, you'll want more than a knife before you're through, because a knife, although it is the most versatile tool, creates problems in carving concave surfaces and shaping details.

There are many strokes or methods of cutting suited to particular purposes; you'll learn them as you go, as I did, but here are some pointers: A pushing cut with the arm, as you'd make when cutting a point on a stick, is safe but not very effective, except for roughing, because it is hard to control; a draw cut, in which you hold the knife like a stiletto and draw it towards you, is good for outlining, but tends to run with the grain. This tendency can be reduced by holding the knife the opposite way, with index finger extended along the blade heel and the knife sloped in the direction of the cut, rather than vertical. I find that I often use either thumb or a finger on the back of the blade to apply greater force to a cut, and use a thumb or forefinger of the opposite hand on the heel to combine force and control on precise cuts.

Relief carvings

"Setting-in" is really an extended stop cut, and applies particularly to relief carving. This procedure makes it possible to cut away the background. After the design is drawn on a panel, the first step is to outline it with a small V-groove just outside the outer limits of the design all around. This cuts the surface fibres and provides a guide. Then appropriate firmers and gouges are driven vertically into the wood all along the V-groove to make an extended stop cut. This is usually easier with a mallet, and the chisel should be driven in only a short depth initially to avoid crushing the fibres on each side or starting an incipient split or breakout. About ⅛ in (3.2 mm) is safe in hard woods, double that in pine or basswood. When setting in around a projection or other thin section be very careful—slope the chisel *away* from the section. The background is cut away up to the setting-in, and the procedure repeated until the desired depth of background is reached.

The usual tool for *bosting* or *grounding* (cutting away) the background is a relatively flat gouge, because it does not catch or stick at the corners as a firmer does. (Some carvers intentionally round the corners of the cutting edge on firmers to avoid this, but such a bullnosed tool cannot cut square and flat surfaces so well.) Gouges are also the primary tool for in-the-round roughing; the gouge cuts a trench and does not normally cause splitting at the edges, as a firmer may if in deep. The gouge is very versatile in such shaping. The firmer is primarily a finishing tool, used to obtain a flat surface or a curved surface without tool marks and scallops. The rough shape of the subject is obtained with gouges; final *modelling* of convex surfaces is done with a firmer.

Particularly on backgrounds, it may be desirable to texture the surface—this breaks up impinging light and makes that surface look darker and more remote. There are many ways to texture, but I usually do it with a small fluter, cutting random scallops. The East Indian carvers almost uniformly use pattern stamps, which crush the surface into star or other patterns. Such stamps can be made of spikes by grinding off the points and filing on a star or other design, or leather-working stamps can be used. The same techniques can be used for texturing parts of a modelled carving—to suggest clothing, for example. Hair and beards and fur require more specific attention, and instructions have been provided in the chapters where such attention is needed.

In my opinion, it is easier and faster to use chisels than knives for most carving, although the knife is my favorite tool and I rely on it in a pinch. The skilled carver can accomplish miracles with sweep cuts—swinging free on any surface. It goes almost without saying that you should learn to watch the chisel cutting edge, not the handle top, when using a mallet, and that you should not try to cut off all the wood on the first pass. On cross-grain cutting, start at an edge and work in; do not work towards the edge or you will split it off. Keep your tools very sharp, particularly on soft woods, do not pry out chips or you will break the tool, and do not use chisels to open paint cans or strip insulation; that is what screwdrivers are for. Protect the edges, particularly when tools are stored.

3

Sharp Tools Are Vital

Hand methods

THE NECESSITY for keeping tools sharp turns off more embryo carvers than anything else. People don't like to take the time to sharpen tools, so they do not learn to do it properly, or they leave it until there are a number of tools to be sharpened. I can sympathize with all this because I hate sharpening, myself, and I do not do it well. The edge of a cutting tool is really a microscopic saw backed by two wedges, the first just behind the edge and the second extending back at the accepted included angle of 30 degrees, more or less. I say "more or less" because a thinner angle and sharper edge work better on softer woods, and a blunter angle is necessary to hold the edge when hard woods are cut or a mallet is used.

The objective is to reduce the number of microscopic feathery teeth and to reduce their length, then to keep them as nearly aligned as possible. This is done by a series of sharpening steps, particularly when sharpening is done by hand. The first step is the rough grinding of the edge to an approximate angle; this is usually done by the manufacturer on a production basis and need not be repeated by the user unless the tool is broken or badly nicked. In fact, it is inadvisable for the user to sharpen a tool on a conventional grinding wheel under any circumstances, because he is almost certain to burn the edge, thus removing the temper. If you must grind, have a water-cooled wheel, or wet and cool the tool at least twice as often as you think necessary.

Whetting, honing and stropping

THERE ARE THREE additional steps to sharpening, and these should be your primary concern. They are whetting, honing and stropping. The first two are really fine-grinding operations, but done on a flat stone by hand rather than on a wheel under power.

Whetting is done on "Washita," a yellowish or greyish natural stone; honing, on "Arkansas," a white, very hard, uniform and fine-grained white stone, or their manufactured equivalents. Some makers now have the two (whetting and honing grains) on opposite sides of the same piece. "Slips," the small shaped stones for honing the burr off the insides of gouges and V-tools, are also made of "Arkansas," or should be—beware of the coarse reddish "slips" that are sometimes offered. In day-to-day carving, honing is a frequent operation, one that pros do subconsciously while planning the next cut; whetting is much less frequent unless the wood is very hard or abrasive.

The final operation is stropping—the same operation a barber does with a straight razor. Properly done, it is two operations (about three strokes each), one on rough leather with an oily surface containing a somewhat rough or other fine abrasive, the other on a smooth leather surface containing only a little oil. All the operations on stones are done by pushing the tool edge *towards* the abrasive as you would in cutting; stropping is done by pulling the

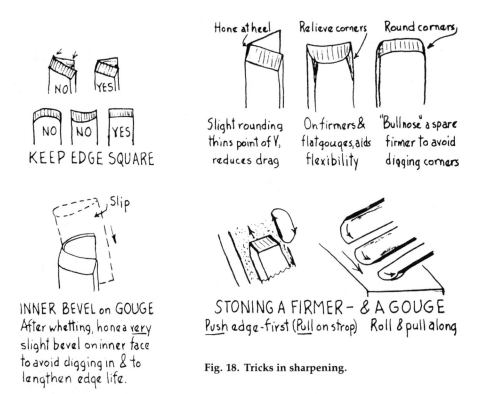

Fig. 18. Tricks in sharpening.

edge backwards. This aligns the tiny feather edges on the blade.

Nowadays, most tools are sold ground and whetted, and with a proper included angle, generally speaking. (It will be worthwhile for you to eventually experiment with an included angle, particularly if you get into carving very hard woods, bone, ivory and stone, as I do frequently.) Knives are ground so that the blade itself has the proper angle; firmers have an included angle of 30 degrees, 15 each side of center; and gouges have a straight interior and 30-degree bevel ground on the *outside*. (Beware of patternmaker's chisels with the bevel on the inside—they tend to dig in and are very difficult to resharpen by hand.) All that you should have to do is a little honing and stropping.

Some carvers, by the way, swear by a hollow-ground edge, one that repeats the curvature of a small-diameter grinding wheel, the sort of edge that is exaggerated in a straight razor. They claim that this makes honing and whetting easier because the angle behind the cutting edge is less than it should be, reducing drag. It is also claimed to make the cutting edge stay sharp longer, which may be true on soft woods but I doubt it on hard ones; my experience is that it may make the edge turn or nick. I should point out, in all fairness, that these are matters of opinion, and "experts" differ.

I have tried to sketch the motions used in sharpening tools, both to maintain their edges and to keep from wearing hollows in the stones. (Many stones become channelled from excessive center wear and this may result in dullness in the center of the cutting edge on a firmer as well as rounding or "bullnosing" of the outer corners, which we will discuss a bit later.)

Stones should be kept lubricated with thin machine oil, or even a 50:50 mixture of machine oil and kerosene. This coating should be wiped off and replaced when it turns grey and gummy from included metal particles. Periodically, also, natural stones should be washed with benzine or gasoline, or boiled in water containing a

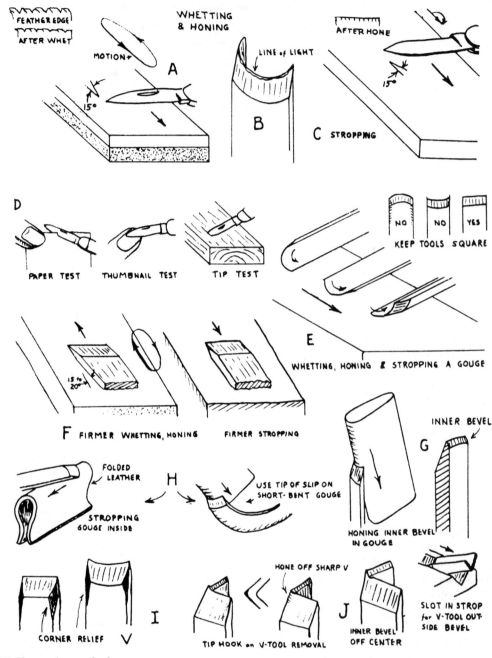

Fig. 19. Sharpening methods.

little soda. This lifts out soaked-in oil and grit. The manufactured stones are different in structure, and can be cleaned just by warming them in an oven, then wiping them off; the heating causes the oil to exude and bring the grit with it.

Testing sharpness

TO SHARPEN A KNIFE, I use a rotary or figure-eight motion (A), (Fig. 19), bearing down a bit harder as the edge is moving forward and lifting the handle a bit for part of the time to be sure I touch up the tip, which usually dulls first. Unless the knife is very dull, a few swirls on the hone should do it, followed by stropping. (Some of the time, unless the wood is very soft, I even skip the strop.)

Sharpness can be tested by trying the edge on a fingernail or on paper—it should stick on the former and slice the latter when drawn across (B), and any variation in the sticking or cutting rate will show dull or nicked spots. Test tip sharpness on a piece of soft wood. Then the blade is drawn for a stroke or two over each side of the strop, which for knife-stropping is usually on two sides of a paddle. Watch how a barber turns the razor over heel-first at the end of a stroke—it saves a second or two.

Carving chisels are sharpened in much the same way, particularly the firmer (D). However, because the gouge edge is rounded, it must be rolled as it goes over the stone, so all parts of the edge are stoned uniformly. This is tricky. Some carvers do it by sliding the tool sidewise (E), others do it by a more difficult straight push along the stone, rotating the gouge as it moves forward. Too much roll will bullnose or round the corners; too little will leave them dull so they tear the wood. Dullness in an area may be seen as a line of light (F), a reflection from a flat surface, along the edge.

Because all sharpening is done from the outer side, a wire edge or burr forms on the inside; it can be felt with the fingernail. It must be removed by passing a slip through (G), adjusting the passes so the entire inner edge is covered. The same operation is done in stropping with a piece of folded leather (H). Some carvers believe in making a very small bevel on the inside as well (G), to relieve drag. The tool can be tested with a fingernail as with the knife or by trying it on a piece of soft wood.

Note the sketches in (E); the edge of a tool should be square, not hollow in the middle or rounded at the outside corners. This ensures cleaner cuts. However, some carvers prefer to ease the corners a little to reduce their tendency to catch along an inner angle. I don't; I like them square, unless I make a real rounded bullnose to use the firmer as a flat gouge. Note the corner-relief trick in (I)—it may help.

The parting or V-tool is a special problem in sharpening—which is why many neophyte carvers do not or cannot use it well. Inevitably, the lower point of the "V" will be slightly thicker than the side walls, both because of the shape itself and because a slight curvature will be left inside in manufacture. Thus, when the tool is sharpened, there is a tendency for a small tit to form at the V-bottom (J). Either one side or the other will have a small indentation near the bottom because of manufacturing inaccuracies or because you have been a bit too enthusiastic with a right-angle slip or stone on the inside. If the edge is square and sharp, as it should be, the tit can be removed by a bit of honing *outside* (J) as well as inside—and you will have one of the most versatile chisels in your kit.

All this is merely an outline of the intricacies of sharpening, but it should help to keep you from the habit of idle whacking or mistreatment of a tool while carving. It also helps to explain why so many carvers, hyperconscious of time as Americans are, have gone to mechanical sharpening, whetting and honing on sanding belts or buffing wheels, or even shaped wheels. There is danger that these methods will result in bullnosed tools, but many carvers do not mind slight radii at inner edges and on flat surfaces of carvings, although they do take away some of the crispness of the carving.

There are a number of tricks to sharpening. Several are shown in Fig. 18. In addition, makers of stones, such as Norton, frequently provided detailed instructions.

(More on sharpening tools in the appendix)

4

The Right Size

What size should a carving be?

IN MOST CASES, there is no real reason why a carving must be of a particular size, unless it is part of an assembly. Size is usually dictated by other factors, like the available wood, convenience in carving, or the size of the tools available. A miniature can be harder to carve than a larger piece, simply because your tools are too large, or the amount of detail you plan to include is too great for the grain or texture of the wood. Further, a miniature is hard and dangerous to handle, as well as fragile. Similarly, a piece that is overly large adds to the problems of handling and removal of excess wood—you may find it difficult to hold the work as well as find a place to display it when completed.

The patterns in this book can be enlarged as desired by any of the several methods described here (see Figs. 20, 21, 22); only in rare instances is it practical to reduce size and retain all the detail shown. As a general rule, it is advisable to reduce, rather than increase, detail; it is a tendency, particularly for whittlers, to include so much detail that it tends to overpower the subject itself. What you are seeking is an image of a bear, not a texture that suggests a bearskin coat; or a rhinoceros, not a complex pattern of plates and wrinkles. A carving should be readily identifiable, unless you intend it as a puzzle. If a portrait of a person includes too much prominent detail, we are immediately conscious of it, because we are ac-customed to the soft curves in the faces and figures of people we know, not hard lines. A sculptor uses a live model or good pictures of his subject; even a tyro must do the same if his design is to be believable. You must do your homework!

So: Be sure you haven't selected a size that has details too small for your tools, or your skill, and that it does not include elements that your hand, and your eye, cannot execute. Be sure the wood you have chosen is sufficiently dense and fine-grained for the detail you plan to include, and that the grain is not so prominent that it will overpower the detail, or distort the appearance of the entire design. And, at least initially, don't make the piece so big that it is hard to handle or requires excessive waste removal before you can actually carve. Particularly in 3D carving, you may have to spend half your time getting unwanted wood out of the way before you can begin the interesting part of the work—the actual shaping of the form. I must, in all fairness, point out that the more nearly the design fits the available wood, the less waste you have to remove (and, in a sense, the less wood you waste). Also, if you plan to sell the carving, a larger carving generally commands a higher price, even though it may require less work. This thinking even affects inexperienced carvers, who will quote a lower price for a work of smaller size—and find to their chagrin that the time and effort involved are much the same.

Fig. 20.

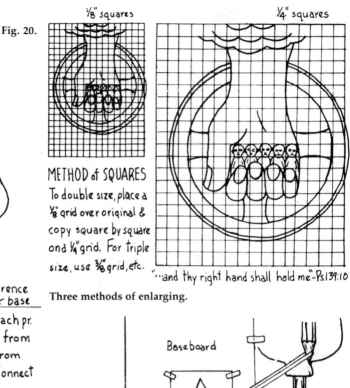

⅛" squares   ¼" squares

METHOD of SQUARES
To double size, place a ⅛" grid over original & copy square by square and ¼" grid. For triple size, use ⅜" grid, etc.

"...and thy right hand shall hold me"-Ps.139:10

Three methods of enlarging.

Fig. 21.

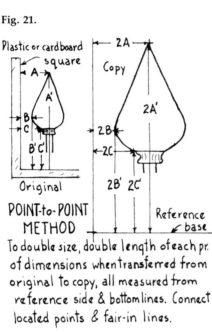

Plastic or cardboard square

2A Copy

Original   2B' 2C'

Reference base

POINT-to-POINT METHOD
To double size, double length of each pr. of dimensions when transferred from original to copy, all measured from reference side & bottom lines. Connect located points & fair-in lines.

RUBBER-BAND ENLARGING
Approximate locations & blank sizes can be obtained this way. Shown is 3X.

Baseboard

Pin   Original   Copy

Rubber band @ ink mark ⅓ of pin-pencil distance for triple size.

Fig. 22.

How to make the drawing fit the wood

VERY OFTEN, the design you want to use doesn't quite fit the wood, usually because the design is too small. It may be sensible to design the piece to fit the wood, rather than to seek out or assemble a suitable blank. If you use commercial wood, the thickness is often a controlling factor. It may be easy to get the necessary profile dimensions, but the associated thickness may necessitate the gluing of several 1- or 2-in (2.5- or 5-cm) pieces (nowadays usually ¾ or 1½ in [1.9 or 3.8 cm] as planed) to get the needed third dimension.

Another factor in selecting size is to consider whether you plan to use tools or just a knife. Whittling is most comfortable with hand-sized pieces, of course, while woodcarving is easier on larger ones, even heroic sizes, because the work need not be anchored so securely if it is large.

I must mention other factors in selecting size: What is to be done with the piece when completed? Is it destined for a particular location, or is it going to take up more houseroom and be in the way if large? What sizes of tools have you? How steady is your hand and how good your eye?

In these mechanized days, it is easy to make direct (same-size) copies on a Xerox-type machine, but the old photostat machine, which was capable of enlarging or reducing is less widely available except in

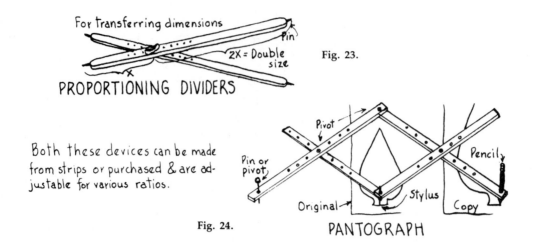

For transferring dimensions

Pin

2X = Double size

Fig. 23.

PROPORTIONING DIVIDERS

Both these devices can be made from strips or purchased & are adjustable for various ratios.

Fig. 24.

Pivot

Pin or pivot

Pencil

Original

Stylus

Copy

PANTOGRAPH

art studios, which also often have photographic enlargers. If you can take, or have taken, a negative or positive of the drawing, you can either have a print made of proper size, or put the negative in an enlarger and sketch the outlines to size, either on a sheet of paper or directly on the wood. Or you can make a rephotograph and project it onto the wood. For three-dimensional carvings, this is really all you need: a guide to saw away waste wood.

But let's say none of the above is available, and you have a two-view sketch that must be made double size. For a rough shape, the simplest method is to take a rubber or elastic band that is a couple of inches longer than the combined width of the wider sketch and the wood on which it is to be traced. (If you haven't one band that long, link several together.) Tie a pencil at one end of the band and make a small loop for a thumbtack at the other. Mark with ink a line one-half the distance from the tack to the pencil. Then tape the sketch towards the left edge of a large breadboard or other flat surface that can take a thumbtack. Put the piece of wood beside it on the right. Set the thumbtack into the baseboard at the left, so the ink mark on the band is just short of the closest line on the sketch. Now stretch the band so the ink mark aligns with a point on the sketch, and move the wood blank until the pencil point is on the corresponding point on its surface. Draw on the

block with the pencil and stretch the band as you draw to keep the ink line aligned with the lines of the sketch. (This is much more difficult to describe than it is to do.) (Fig. 22)

For triple size, the ink mark should be at one-third the distance from tack to pencil, and so on. For any enlargement, in fact, all you need is the ratio. Thus, for 1½ scale, divide the rubber-band length by 3 and put the ink mark at 2; for 2¼ scale, divide the band length by 4½ and put the ink mark at 2. This method is in fact a crude pantograph, which most of us do not have.

If higher accuracy is necessary, you can make a pantograph, or buy one. To be useful, it should be made quite accurately. I have found it easier to transfer dimensions by one of two methods.

Enlarging by squares and point-to-point

THE TRADITIONAL METHOD of enlarging is by the method of squares. Draw a grid of ⅛-in (3.2 mm) squares on transparent paper, larger than the original sketch you have. Draw a similar grid on the wood blank or on a plain sheet of paper, but make the squares as much larger as you need, that is, for double size use ¼-in (6.4 mm) squares, for triple size ⅜-in (9.6 mm) squares. Now lay the transparent grid over the sketch and copy the design on the block square by square. Save the grid, by the way; it can be used over and over—even on good silhouette photographs of a subject—and is particularly useful in laying out relief carvings, where precise outlines are necessary. (Fig. 20)

I lose my place when using that system, and I have some competence at drawing, so I use the point-to-point method. (Fig. 21) I provide a base and side line on the original, either by drawing or by taping an L-shaped cardboard or paper square on it as sketched. Then I draw a similar square pair of lines on the wood or a sheet of paper. Prominent elements of the original are located on the copy by measuring their location with relation to the two faces of the square, and transferring these dimensions, multiplied by the desired enlargement, to the board or other copy. Thus, if an ear on an animal is 3 in (7.6 cm) up from the base and 2 in (5.1 cm) in from the side, and the copy is to be 1½ times the original, the dimensions are transferred as 4½ in (11.4 cm) up and 3 in (7.6 cm) in from the side. Locate as many such key points as you consider necessary, then sketch in the enlarged outline, as a child does in following the numbered dots in the comic pages. This method I find to be accurate and faster for me—simple arithmetic is my dish.

If the subject is large or animate and you want to make a reduced sketch, a series of photographs from the four points of the compass is helpful. Or you can make or procure proportioning dividers which sculptors use. These are simply double-ended dividers which can be set so that a dimension measured at one end will be reduced or enlarged by the desired percentage at the other. (Fig. 23)

For a rough approximation of blank shape, the simplest method is to use a pantograph (Fig. 24). Pantographs are now commercially available, but are difficult to use except from flat surface to flat surface, and they are of course limited in capacity. They can be used to reduce size by interchanging stylus and pencil. The rubberband method is cheaper and simpler, but less accurate.

If the original is three-dimensional and there is no time to take photos, you must use the proportioning dividers or calipers in transferring dimensions. (They can, by the way, also be used in the point-to-point method to avoid the computation if the enlargement is some odd ratio.)

5

What Wood to Use

WHEN EARLY MAN developed his first crude cutting edges he found wood to be an amenable and plentiful material and soon discovered differences in the characteristics of the various species available. There was so much work involved in his shaping of increasingly sophisticated things—whether they were tools, idols or toys—that he *had* to learn which wood was good and which was not, depending upon the final purpose of the piece.

In rural and remote areas this is still true to an extent, although in general we buy lumber from far away for local structures and usage and although the relative importance of wood as a material has been greatly reduced. Thus, the typical modern whittler or woodcarver must in most cases use what is readily available, whether or not it is ideal for his purposes. In other words, most of us carve lumber rather than trees and are limited to woods that are commercial locally. Furthermore, even in remote areas, a perfectly suitable local wood may be discarded in favor of something that must be bought even sight unseen from a catalogue; the resulting work is, therefore, limited by the particular block bought.

One example that leaps to mind is "mahogany," a word used to describe an increasingly divergent group of imported and expensive woods. There are mahoganies from Africa, Mexico, Cuba, Central and South America, and the Philippines. I have six samples from the Philippines, all presumably mahogany, that vary from almost white to a darkish red-brown, with the heaviest twice the weight of the lightest. And none of these is lauan or lauanda, now the usual surface veneer of "mahogany" plywood, or primavera, a white wood which when stained looks like good mahogany. The best mahogany is still that from Honduras, which is fine-grained although relatively soft. Cuban mahogany is dense and varies in hardness; South American varieties tend to be grainy and splinter easily; Philippine commonly available is coarse and the poorest of the lot.

So much for mahogany, which is so familiar because of its long record of use as a furniture wood. The best wood to start with is probably basswood, known in some areas as bee tree, but similar to European linden, followed fairly closely in popularity by American white pine (which tends to split) and imported Indonesian jelutong. These tend to be soft, readily carved and sanded, and straight-grained with few knots or other areas of difficulty. Carvings made from them will have little distinction in most cases. Because of their lifeless color and lack of any distinctive grain, they need to be tinted with stains, acrylic or oil paints, although the common tendency to stain them a standard color or paint them with solid colors is unfortunate. Of the so-called white pines, ponderosa is good if you avoid the strongly colored pieces. Sugar pine (commonly called "white pine") is a bit more porous. Avoid yellow pine, which is hard, often knotty, and resinous.

Among other soft woods are poplar, which bruises easily and tends to grip tools,

Fig. 25 (right). Cedar tends to crush unless tools are very sharp, but this panel was worth the effort. The panel itself is a 1 × 5½ × 10-in (2.5 × 14 × 25.4-cm) piece of Western red cedar, from a log blasted to a dark grey in the Mount St. Helens eruption in 1981. Inlaid are three pieces of Virginia cedar, natural in color but 8,500 years old, plus or minus 500 years, according to a carbon-14 test. About the third oldest piece of wood known, the tree was found in a marl pit in Ohio several years ago.

Fig. 26 (above). Wood that is bad for the cabinetmaker may be good for the carver. This piece of spalted (partially dry-rotted) curly broadleaf maple makes a very intriguing stylized nighthawk that is 2½ × 4 × 9 in (6.4 × 10.2 × 22.9 cm).

Fig. 27 (right). Black walnut, the best American carving wood, will support a great deal of detail but tends to be dark, as this snapshot of a coat of arms I recently carved shows.

so is hard to cut smoothly; cedar (Fig. 25) which is also easy to cut but bruises and has a distinctive reddish color; willow, which has a tendency to split; cypress, which does not wear well; and alder, from the West Coast, usually carved green because the carving is easier and the wood does not check as it dries, at least in small pieces. Slightly harder are butternut and, quite recently, paulownia, which are light tan with darker grain.

Whittlers' woods

MANY WHITTLERS have always used local woods, particularly the fruit and nut woods. All are harder than those previously mentioned, tend to check and are subject to insect attack and warpage, but they will support more detail and undercutting, take a better finish and have a grain that does not interfere with carving and a color that makes painting unnecessary. Among them are pear, pecan, cherry, apple and black walnut. Cherry and black walnut (Fig. 27) are particularly good, the latter probably being the best American carving wood. It has a fine, tough grain and good color and finishes beautifully, but may turn quite dark if oiled. (This may be as much of a disadvantage as the whiteness of basswood or holly.)

Old-time whittlers used whatever they had: willow for whistles, fruit woods for small figures, ash or hickory for tool handles, and so on. Nowadays, most whittlers begin with woods such as white pine, basswood and jelutong (a recent import from Indonesia) that are fairly soft and readily available at the local lumberyard.

Local availability

THE WOODCARVER, unlike the whittler, tends to use harder woods like cherry and black walnut, even oak and maple, or imports like mahogany, which will support more detail, take a better finish, and have some grain to give them variety. All of these are much harder to cut than pine or basswood, but that is not particularly important when you use chisels.

There is also considerable variety in the woods used, because of their local availability as trees. Thus, red alder and myrtle are carved on the West Coast, ironwood and osage orange (both dense and quite hard but prone to splitting) in the Southwest, buckeye and basswood in the Northeast, walnut in the Central States, tupelo (cottonwood) and cypress among others in the South. Eastern mountaineers use holly and fruit and nut woods like pecan. South of the border, Mexican carvers work an endless variety of woods because Mexico has more varieties of wood than any other country, some 2,800.

There are many woods used for carving in the areas where they grow, like buckeye, cypress, cottonwood, poplar (gum), chestnut, willow, birch, maple, butternut and myrtle. Maple is much harder than the others, but takes a good finish and supports detail. Look out for warping and splitting with chestnut. Hickory, sycamore, beech and magnolia are hard to cut and good primarily for shallow carving. Ash is

Fig. 28. One of the distinctive African woods is vermilion or amboina. It is a brilliant dark red in color. I carved this panel, about 12 × 19 in (30.5 × 48.3 cm), in vermilion to go outside a door on a modern brown-stained house. The wood is spectacular when finished, but tends to splinter when carved to such detail as this.

stringy but can be carved quite successfully. Eastern white oak is inherently strong and will take detail, but should be carved with tools. Swamp or red oak has a very prominent grain and coarse structure: avoid it. Dogwood is very dense and hard and can stand shock without spltting, but it is difficult to carve. Holly, our whitest wood, is hard and tends to check, but it holds detail well. You may know or have heard of others; the best advice I can give is to try them. I have carved macadamia from Hawaii, kerosene, garamut and kwila from the Trobriand Islands just for tryouts.

Imported woods

AMONG THE IMPORTS, rosewood, which comes from many Latin-American coun-

Fig. 30. Bovine group for a Nativity scene was whittled from white pine and antiqued with sal-ammoniac stain. The bull is 3 in (8 cm) long. Better quality figures can be carved from pecan or holly and not tinted.

Fig. 29. This pillar from Bali was exhibited at the New York World's Fair in 1939. It is teak, with the carving of Siva on top made of blinding wood (also called blind-my-eyes in Australia because of its poisonous tendencies).

tries as well as Africa, varies widely in color from rosy red to brown; I have a Mexican piece that includes suggestions of purple and green. It is hard, but not as hard as cocobola or lignum vitae. These woods are very expensive, and should not be used for casual carvings. Most of the African woods, like beef, bubinga, zebra, thuya and the like, tend to split and are a nuisance to carve. This is true of purpleheart, greenheart (from Brazil), and vermilion (Fig. 28) as well, but these three woods have distinctive colors and therefore make fine pendants, for example. There are dozens of other woods, some with extremely elaborate "figure" (that may interfere with your carving) like harewood and satinwood, for example. Then there is pink ivory, the most

expensive wood of all, a delicate pink-white to red in color. If you can afford it—and find it—it is interesting to work. But, in the end, the choice must return to what you can get and the effect you want to create.

Many woods are now imported in lumber that will cut into carving-size blocks or panels. They tend, however, to be relatively expensive, particularly in recent years. Among them, my favorite, particularly for panels, is teak (Fig. 29), from Thailand or Burma, which will support detail, does not warp appreciably, and is impervious to water, rot and insect attack. It can be carved easily with chisels and mallet, but does often contain silica, which takes the edge off tools despite the deceptive smoothness of cutting created by the oil in the wood. This is true also of some kinds of rosewood, which (like mahogany) can come from many sources and vary widely in color and characteristics. I have pieces ranging from red to dark reddish-brown and even containing purple, green and yellow. Chinese teak is not brown, but red and harsh-grained, which is why the Chinese enamelled it black and most Americans think of teak as a shiny black wood, just as they assume that all black African carvings are ebony.

Fig. 31. Grinling Gibbons was the most famous of English carvers and the great worker in lime. His floral swags have been popular for 400 years.

Lime (Fig. 31) and boxwood, both used extensively in Europe (and boxwood in China), are not readily available in the U.S. Both are hard and good cutting wood. European linden is like our basswood. English sycamore (called harewood when cut and stained in a particular way) carves well, and is white like our holly and available in wider boards. There are also available such woods as English and Austrian oak, both more dense and finer-grained than American oaks, hence much used in religious carving. English walnut has too much "figure" for good carving usually; Italian walnut has a fine texture, close grain and cuts like English oak. Others surface occasionally, but Europe has fewer woods than we do, particularly if the 2,800 varieties growing in Mexico are included.

Many woods have been imported from Africa in recent years, mostly for veneers or specialty uses like pool cues and arrows. Others have been imported from Central and South America. All are expensive, hard to find and finance in suitably sized pieces, and tend to be more trouble than they are worth unless you are after a special color, graining or other effect. I have carved most of them in making up fish and dinosaur mobiles each with 16 or more units of a different wood, but have found they tend to split and splinter, among other things. Lacewood, satinwood and sandalwood are scarce nowadays, but can be useful. There are also such woods as zebrawood, beautiful in grain but as hard to carve as American redwood or cypress because of variation in hardness between winter and summer wood.

Popular among sculptors are such woods as ebony (Fig. 32), cocobolo, and lignum vitae, all very hard but capable of fine finishing. (The latter two are called "ironwood" locally in Mexico because they sink in water, and may also be called guayacan.) Ebony is really another general term, because the wood comes from Africa, India, Indonesia (particularly the Celebes—now Sulawesi), Ceylon (now Sri Lanka) and South and Central America. It varies in color and marking from solid black (Gabon and New Guinea) to dark brown with black striping (macassar from Sulawesi and calamander from Sri Lanka), and black with lighter striping (striped or swirled ebony from New Guinea). All these woods, as well as rosewood and mahogany, can create lung-inflammatory dust when sanded.

I have mentioned pink ivorywood from Africa which is the world's most expensive wood, something like $300 a pound at this writing. It has been described, apoc-

Fig. 32 (left). Real ebony is becoming very scarce because it is being carved up much faster than it can grow. Bali, for example, must import it from a rapidly diminishing supply in the Celebes (Sulawesi), largely because so much was used on carvings like this one, about 4 feet (1.2 m) tall.

Fig. 33 (above). These two lengths of Mexican "blanco" about 2 in (5.1 cm) in diameter, I carved in the images of the old Aztec gods. It is very much like white pine.

ryphally, I think, as the private wood of the Zulu kings; anyone else found with it was beheaded. It varies from pinkish white to dark pink, is relatively hard and tends to split, and in my opinion is more a curiosity than a useful carving wood. I have a couple of pieces and use it on occasion for jewelry.

If you have a particular interest in identifying various species, beware of such countries as Mexico. One day in Oaxaca, I visited half a dozen one-man carpenter shops within blocks of each other. In several I found exotic woods and got samples with their local names written on. Each carpenter had a different name for the same wood, and there is no publication that begins to identify them. There are good guide books in the United States, as well as the International Wood Collectors Society (current address, Drawer B, Main St., Chaumont, N.Y. 13622) that publishes a monthly *Bulletin* (retitled *World of Wood*) containing much information on available woods. Considering, however, that there are something like 7,000 species of wood in the world, identifying the odd foreign piece is almost hopeless.

Basically, the easiest way to determine what wood to use initially is to try it with the tools you intend to use. Many carvers and whittlers simply buy wood at the local yard, or even send away for blanks to round up and shape, because that's easier and less "messy" and requires no extra tools.

Finally, start with familiar and easy woods and work up to the others. The exotic woods make wonderful carvings, but take much in sweat, blood and tears. I have indicated, piece by piece, my choice of wood—or that of other carvers—throughout this book. Also, regardless of wood, avoid a blank with knots, flaws or checks if you can. Knots take the edge off tools and may fall out later. Both knots and flaws re-

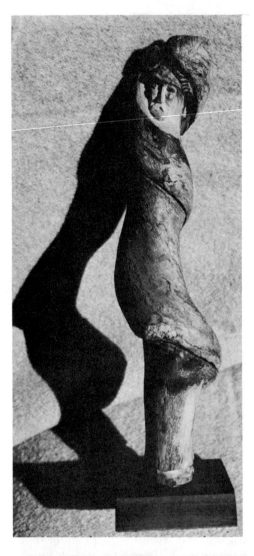

Fig. 34 (left). *Windswept,* carved in a section of branch distorted by a vine. It is about 15 in (38 cm) tall, with actual carving only around the face.

quire some skill at finishing. Checks have a disconcerting way of opening and closing with humidity changes, and filling a check to hide it may cause pressure that will crack the piece later.

"Bad" wood can be beautiful

MOST CABINETMAKERS REJECT or repair any flawed or abnormal section of wood. Wood-carvers, however, can often capitalize on flaws such as knots and dry rot, or holes, lines and other deformities caused by insects or worms, to say nothing of unusual root or driftwood shapes. Some years ago, I carved animals in a low-relief spiral around a section of apple-tree trunk, exploiting natural projections, and got a much more dramatic effect than if I'd cut them away. I have since carved sections of trunks distorted by vines or other interferences, done a "bug tree" with designs around worm holes and rotted spots, and made cups and bowls of apple burls and sculptures of roots and cypress knees. I even have one client who intentionally selected boards with knots for panels!

Study a piece with an unusual shape or some intriguing defect; the result may be much more than salvage. I have selected several examples. One is a statuette from a vine-distorted branch (Fig. 34), another a lion with mane created by insect infestation of a South American tree (Fig. 35), and the third is a toad (Fig. 36) carved in dry-rotted, curly broadleaf maple, along with two cypress knees converted into statuettes (Figs. 37 and 38).

Pieces of bough like the lion's head are sold in Latin-American markets; they are found by Indians who sometimes carve

Fig. 35 (left). Lion head carved on a scrap of Chilean or Peruvian wood from a native market. Natives say such abnormal growth is caused by insects or fungus infection.

Fig. 36 (right). Toad atop a columnar base, all of spalted curly broadleaf maple. The toad is about 2 in (5.1 cm) high, on a spectacularly patterned 3¼ × 4 x 5-in (8.3 × 10 × 13-cm) base. Eyes are glass.

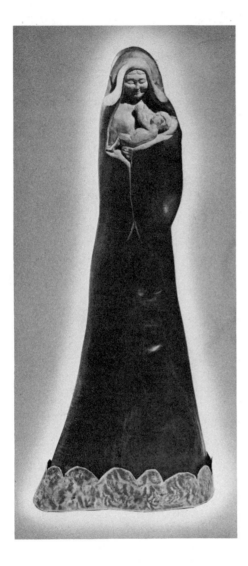

Fig. 37 (above). Madonna and Child carved in a cypress knee, about 15 in (38 cm) tall, with hammered-copper base strap. Again, the only carving is at the top. Knees have brown inner bark atop white growth wood, so contrast is marked.

Fig. 38 (right). Centaur and oread carved from a cypress knee. The figure is about 8 in (20 cm) tall.

them into Indian heads, with American Sioux headdresses from the distorted areas, and other designs, depending upon shape. In a sense, this is the same idea as that of American carvers of driftwood, diamond willow and rotted wood.

The toad in Fig. 36 was suggested by the shape of the piece I was given, and by the beauty of the wood itself. The top had a slope like a seated frog or toad, but the patterning of the wood definitely suggested a warty toad rather than a smooth frog; the greyed creamy color also supported this choice. While Americans collect frogs in many materials, and abhor toads, Orientals consider toads lucky. I have a toad carved in cryptomeria (Japanese "cedar" finished by sandblasting to make growth rings stand out), a netsuke in ivory from Japan—these were once used as thong buttons on purse strings—and a red-stone toad from China, atop a stamp with my name in Chinese characters and the symbol with which I sign carvings.

This kind of wood is often so beautiful in itself that carving detracts rather then helps. I felt this was true of the maple block used for the toad carving, so most of the surface is uncarved and serves as a pillar or base. I finished the toad with satin varnish, and the base with gloss to stress its appearance. The varnish also reinforces the areas of the wood that tend to crumble at a touch. I originally carved bulging eyes from the wood, but replaced them with small grey-pearl-finished glass pendants for more gleam. Black-enamel spots were painted on for pupils, and then the pendants set in so only oval shapes are visible. These pendants, incidentally, can be found at any notions store, and cost less by the dozen than would one set of glass eyes.

Dry-rotted wood, incidentally, is wood that has been infected by decay fungi to an extent sufficient to cause discoloration, creating in the better pieces a marbled appearance on smooth surfaces. Because deterioration of the cell structure by the fungi is progressive, condition of the wood varies from apparently sound to noticeably softened and crumbly. If the wood is dried, the decay stops; but the fungi can remain dormant for years. Thus, if the wood again achieves a moisture content of 20 percent or so, the fungi may develop again and continue the process. This dry rot cannot occur except in the presence of moisture; thus, it is really *wet* rot.

You can carve thick bark

THE ESSENTIAL HERE is a tree that produces a fairly thick bark, such as the catalpa, black cottonwood or ponderosa pine. There are also harder and denser barks, like that of the pochote in Mexico, which is dense enough to use as patterns for casting precious metals, or show a village façade in miniature. I first encountered such work many years ago in Mexico, and found the carving of ponderosa pine bark more recently there. (Figs. 39, 40)

Ponderosa is carved by the Tarahumara Indians, a primitive tribe living in the state of Chihuahua, Mexico, whose idea of sport includes running down a deer for food. Their pine carvings are crude, though they do make quite good guitars and violins! I got some of the bark and found I could make a fairly complete carving in 20 minutes or a half hour because the bark is so soft. It is laminated and quite brittle, but is more satisfactory for an exercise wood than balsa, for example, and far less expensive because it's free. Catalpa bark is similar, but pochote is dense, dark red with a greyed exterior, and is not at all brittle nor noticeably laminar when carved. Also, it tends to be in "domes" rather than strips, and has an inherent design that frames a carving.

Bark can be finished with sprayed matte or satin varnish to increase surface strength and combat the tendency to crumble. Nebraska carvers, who cut faces in the solid wood of a slab beneath catalpa bark, use a heavy and shiny multi-coat, plastic-based finish to contrast with the rough bark exterior.

Fig. 39. At left is a profile, in the middle the Pope wearing a fan-dancer headdress, as he did during part of his visit to Mexico, and at right a frontal face. All were carved in pine bark by the author in 1979, during a Mexican visit.

Fig. 40 (right). Female figure, with headdress, and triple god faces carved in ponderosa-pine bark by a Tarahumara woman, about 1979. The taller figure is 13 in (33 cm) long.

Try carving nuts, pits and gourds

VARIOUS NUTS ARE CARVED all over the world, because they provide a basic shape and a woody texture. One of the first things I learned to carve was a peach pit, but it was many years later that I realized it was also possible to carve plum and apricot pits, coconut shell and hard-shelled gourds. In recent years, I have also seen carved avocado pits (Israel), olive pits (China), nutmeg and walnut shell (Mexico), hickory nuts and butternuts (USA) and many kinds of hard seeds used for beads, particularly in the Pacific Islands.

Perhaps the most unusual carved nuts come from an area in Ecuador. They are from a palm, the tagua, which grows there and in Colombia. These nuts are slightly smaller and flatter than hen's eggs, with brown skins and hard white meat—so hard, in fact, that it is called vegetable ivory and even carves like the real thing. Designs range from pipes to chess sets and elaborate assemblies such as the skeleton in Fig. 41. The nut is not available commercially, except as carved, as nearly as I can dis- cover—a pity—but the designs can be done in holly or other dense woods.

My general experience with carving nuts, pits and gourds has shown all of them to be brittle and hard. Chips tend to break away rather than cut, and carving is a slow process that requires frequent resharpen-

Fig. 41. Tagua-nut skeleton from Ecuador is an assembly of 16 pieces, including a turned base. The scythe blade is also tagua, the handle a wood dowel. The carving, about 8 in (20 cm) tall, is made for the Day of the Dead, November 1, like the American Halloween the night before.

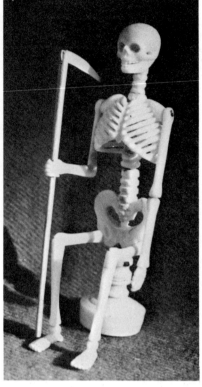

Fig. 42 (left). Peach-pit assemblies from Chile involve at least ten shapes of familiar animals and birds. Here are a rabbit and a swan, of pieces glued together and tinted.

ing of tools. But finished pieces will take a good finish and can usually be stained or painted.

The carved gourds of Peru are particularly noted for intricacy of detail in the shallow carved and painted surfaces, usually in brown and black only. The tagua nuts are often in full color, painted expertly with oils, and the heads are accurate likenesses. The 2-in (5.1-cm) long "olive" pits that formerly came from China were far more intricate, however—I found one carved as a sampan, with window shutters that actually opened and showed images behind them, all from a shell wall under ⅛

Fig. 43. Older tagua carvings tended to be unpainted, as shown by these examples. Two of the five are heads of Jesus and two are Atahualpa, last Inca emperor. The fifth, at right, is a Spaniard.

in (3.2 mm) thick! These were undoubtedly the work of ivory carvers.

Work like this is almost unknown to Americans, even tourists, because these pieces are produced in small quantities and are not generally available in tourist shops. The assembly of parts made from separate nuts or other materials is also very unusual. In Mexico, walnut and coconut-shell segments are assembled into various animals as decorative units, some of which can be opened to reveal scenes assembled from bits of paper and wood, painted. In Chile I found about ten varieties of animal shapes glued together from sections of peach pits. And pendants and buttons sawed from hickory nuts have been around for years. Start with them or with peach or nectarine pits, which are readily available. A knife is really all the equipment you need for peach-pit carving, plus a little imagination to see what the surface convolutions suggest.

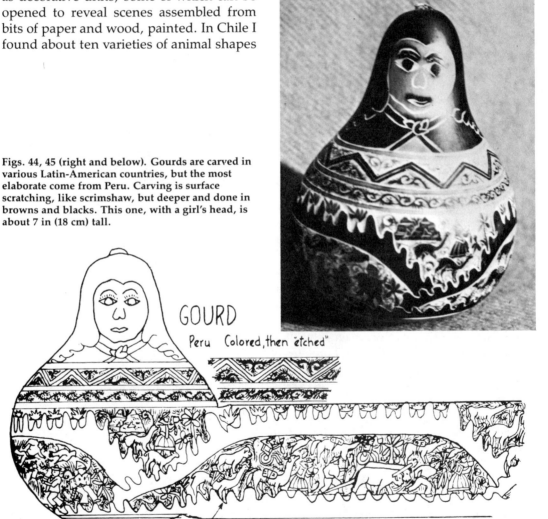

Figs. 44, 45 (right and below). Gourds are carved in various Latin-American countries, but the most elaborate come from Peru. Carving is surface scratching, like scrimshaw, but deeper and done in browns and blacks. This one, with a girl's head, is about 7 in (18 cm) tall.

GOURD

Peru Colored, then "etched"

Light-colored background filled with fern-like patterns

(More on nuts, pits and gourds in Appendix I)

6

Some Finishing Suggestions

How about surface texture?

WOODCARVERS are given to repeating the old, old saying that many carvings are ruined in the finishing. That is true, of course, because many carvers use whatever finish they have available or have used before, and their taste may be regrettably bad. Cheap carvings, particularly from under-developed countries, were frequently doused with shellac or cheap varnish, and some American carvings were (and are) finished the same way, making them shine like cheap furniture. This has encouraged purists to use no finish whatsoever, or simply oil and wax, although this combination is at times unsuitable as well, depending upon wood, exposure, humidity and occasional other factors, including insect infestation.

Some primitive carvers have felt their way into much more specialized finishes of many kinds, ranging from natural dyes to a "secret" formula used by a few carvers in Haiti and which gives a head or bust a smooth but slightly dusty surface exactly matching the complexion of some native women. What many of these carvers are actually striving for is not a finish, but a *texture* that somehow simulates or suggests the natural.

Quality wood sculptures commonly have one of two surface textures, either smooth and polished, which emphasizes the figure, color and grain of the wood; or tool marks, planes or surface patterns to emphasize the carving or the figure itself. The low-gloss finish is by far the most common,

Fig. 46. Stylized "Mother and Child" is in mahogany, about 12 in (30 cm) high, sandpapered smooth and antiqued.

perhaps because the sculptor is more adept with sandpaper and riffler files than with sharp-edged tools, or because the wood proves recalcitrant. The textured surface may also be added after the carving, simply as an allover pattern of small scallops that catch the light without having any relationship to the strokes actually used in cutting and shaping.

Occasionally, artists break these patterns

Fig. 47 (below and right). This "Deer Dancer" was surface-textured with gouge lines over a blocky silhouette. Texturing changes angle in stress areas. The only untextured areas are the antlers, rattles, and feet. The piece is 16 in (40 cm) tall.

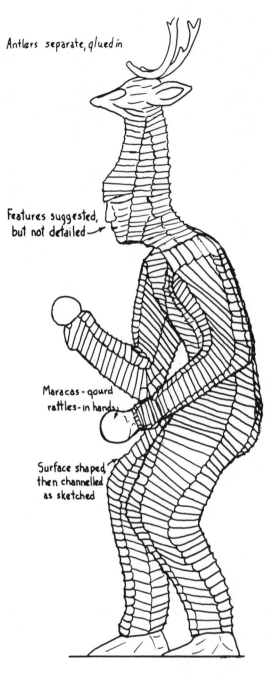

Antlers separate, glued in

Features suggested, but not detailed→

Maracas - gourd rattles - in hands

Surface shaped, then channelled as sketched

and strive for a surface that will have a dramatic look or feel or create a particular response of the figure to light, just as artists in other media apply pigments with a palette knife or leave the tool marks or fingermarks showing on a clay model. Some carvers actually develop a surface finish that eventually becomes a sort of personal trademark and others simply drift into coloring their work out of simple frustration.

The pictured figures from Mexico, Bali, New Guinea and Haiti illustrate the point. "Mars," in carving the Haitian mother and child (Fig. 46), relied upon the silhouette for strength and design, so finished his piece smooth, with many of the lines fading into the body of the piece. He did not detail the features, the digits, or the musculature. He was striving for a smooth, flowing, har-

monious shape, the result being reminiscent of many Balinese carvings.

In contrast, "Old Man of the Sea" amplified the erosion of a piece of driftwood into a pattern of fillets which simultaneously produces the effect of hair and frames the face (Fig. 48). More than half the area is thus textured, so light tends to bring out the smooth surface of the face within a greyed

Fig. 49.

Fig. 48 (left). "Old Man of the Sea" was carved in a greyed piece of driftwood. Hair and beard were textured with V-grooves blunted at the bottom to resemble fluter cuts.

Figs. 49, 50. Two versions of the Virgin of Soledad (Mexico) are alike in the overall patterns in robe and skirt although one was textured with punches, the other with knife cuts.

Fig. 50.

or softer aureole of hair and beard. Pigments have been rubbed in to add a bit of color to lips, cheeks, teeth and eyes, but their effect is only to tint the grey wood slightly.

The two Mexican Virgins of Soledad (Figs. 49 and 50) are much more primitive than the preceding two figures. They have obviously been copied from earlier models, but have been stylized and interpreted as well. Crown, face, hands and flower are modelled, but the rest of the figure is primarily silhouette. The robe surface, however, is textured to suggest the opulent embroidery of the cloth robe. In one example, the irregular pattern is painstakingly pro-

duced with stamps—one a ⅜-in (9.6-mm) circle and others a ⅜- and ⅛-in (9.6- and 3.2-mm) straight line. The wood, like pine, is soft and preserves the stamp pattern clearly. The figure, overall, is only 8½ in (21.6 cm) high. In the other figure, the pattern is incised.

The two dancers, carved in Mexico City a score of years before I acquired them, represent two of the traditional tribal dances of Mexico: one is the deer dance of Sonora (Fig. 47), the other the feather or plume dance of Oaxaca (Fig. 51). Both dancers are in animated poses, and the carver has contributed to their animation by giving them slightly blurred outlines and avoiding sharp detail. As a result, they appear to be caught in motion, particularly the plume dancer. The figures were rather carefully shaped, then the majority of each surface was textured—the deer dancer with parallel

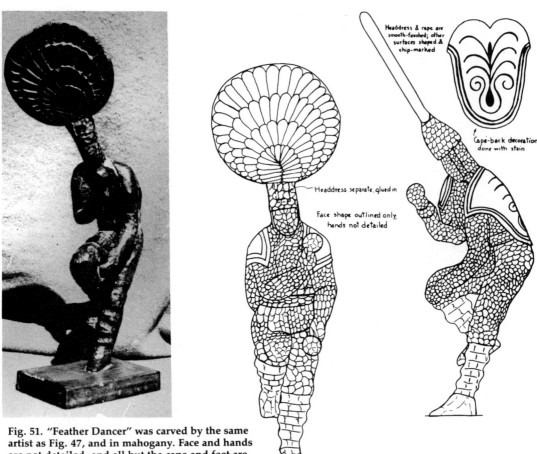

Headddress & cape are smooth-finished; other surfaces shaped & chip-marked

Cape-back decoration done with stain

Headdress separate, glued in

Face shape outlined only, hands not detailed

Fig. 51. "Feather Dancer" was carved by the same artist as Fig. 47, and in mahogany. Face and hands are not detailed, and all but the cape and feet are covered with small scallops.

channelling by a small gouge, the plume dancer with scallops produced by a larger, flatter gouge. Neither face is detailed, although the deer dancer's has a nose shape and a fortuitous placement of channels to suggest the mouth and eyes, both on the dancer and on the deer. Texturing covers most of the body surfaces of the dancers, except for the feet (which are presumably solidly supporting the figure), and a few other details. In the deer dancer, these are the ears and horns of the deer head (this is an assumption on my part because I had to replace missing parts) and the gourd rattles (maracas) in the hands. The gouge lines are not all parallel, but in some cases suggest lines of movement or of stress, as across the shoulders and the chest.

The plume dancer wears the familiar headdress, cape and apron, with the apron practically blended into the lines of the body. The cape, however, in real life ornately embroidered, is smoothed and patterned with stain. The headdress is regularly patterned with larger gouge scallops to suggest rows of feathers, but has an essentially smooth surface, while that of the real-life headdress is much rougher.

This particular carver, by the way, used a finishing technique that preserved, but partially obliterated, the lines of his carving. He apparently poured melted beeswax over the entire surface, so that it congealed and collected in all the hollows. Over the years, this clouded and collected dust, so it was necessary to scrape off larger accumulations, then alternately heat and wipe to get rid of most of it. No solvent

Figs. 52, 53. These trays suggest the variety of forms and treatments in woodenware. From Takamatsu they are sanded smooth to show the fairly prominent grain. The circular tray (left) has an iris tinted with real gold, the floral group on the square tray (right) is untinted. They are finished in clear lacquer, without stain.

available would dissolve this hard wax—as chemists who use hydrofluoric acid know, because they store it in beeswax bottles.

There are a number of other surface textures, like lining for hair, cross-hatching for roughness, and so on. They are worthy of a little thought and may give your work more real "polish" than can gloss varnish.

There are many other aspects of texturing, of course, including effects obtained by utilizing the figure or grain of the wood itself. In most cases, the carver positions his work, or modifies his design, to take advantage of surface irregularities or imperfections, like knots or color changes, or selects the piece of wood because its shape suggests the ultimate carving. In other cases, the carver must adapt his design to the shape of the available wood, so he makes a virtue of necessity.

The Japanese have long used the grain in still another way. They carve turtles, badgers, frogs, toads, goldfish and dragons in cryptomeria with alternating hard (dark) and soft (lighter) stripes in the grain, and then erode the soft wood so that the surface has a series of ridges. The same technique has been used in this country on pine, redwood and cypress to create the

effect of aging (we have done it by sand-blasting), and has recently been "discovered" by tyro carvers. Another texturing technique is pyrography, used commonly by bird carvers to simulate the veining of feathers. A pyrographic needle can make the equivalent of veiner cuts with a dark-brown surface burned on, and can be quite

Fig. 54. This textured tray with two gingko leaves is the famous red-lacquered kind from Kamakura. It can be cleaned with a damp cloth, and withstands moisture. It is one of many designs.

dramatic in suggesting feathers, fur or long hair on light-colored wood figures.

How much modelling and texturing?

IN INDIA, and in China to a lesser degree, it was customary to cover the entire surface of a woodcarving with decoration, particularly if it was a panel in relief. In Italy, the tendency was to cover as much as 80 percent of the surface, but in other countries, this might be reduced to 30 percent or less. The Maori and the Balinese also kept surfaces busy, while the Seri Indians of Tiburón carve a profile of the subject and rely on the inherent beauty of the wood and a relatively high polish to create the desired effect.

Throughout the world of carving, there have always been these variations in amount of detail in form and finish, in coloring, polishing, toning, mounting. A common present-day question is whether or not carved figures, particularly in soft woods, should be painted, and if so, to what degree. Exhibitions differentiate between painted and unpainted figures, and in decoy shows the pieces are as much paintings as they are carvings. But this was also true in Egypt and Greece, where most carvings, even in stone, were painted originally. In Indonesia, statues have been provided with seasonal or festival costumes which are changed regularly, and some of the ancients in Europe did the same thing. In many countries, careful carving of a surface was followed by lacquering in color to make the surface smooth again. Thus precedents can be found for whatever any particular carver decides to do; the weight, if anywhere, being on the side of coloring. Only in sculpture has color been banned in favor of the natural texture of the wood— and even there the surface may be textured in areas, and inconspicuous and artful tinting may be done.

Thus it is difficult to lay down rules about amount of modelling or detail, texturing and finishing. Authorities disagree at every level, as do artists and clients. It eventually

Fig. 55. This rectangular apricot tray has faint tinting of the design, and is finished in clear lacquer, without stain.

becomes a matter of what the individual likes, as it always has been, plus the dictates of fashion, local or worldwide.

Actually, the density, grain, color and other characteristics of the wood; the subject and proposed treatment; the skill of the carver and the eventual disposition of the piece must all be considered from the beginning if a happy marriage of modelling, texture and finish is to be attained. If the wood has a strong figure and dense structure, it will combat any texturing or coloring, unless the coloring is opaque.

Many people once thought teak is black, because the Chinese, in particular, lacquered it to destroy the grain, and possibly to suggest ebony. Grain may also distort modelling lines and even a silhouette. I once carved an Arab stallion head in mahogany in which the grain enhanced the arch of the neck, and shortly thereafter a madonna in pine who wore a perpetual grin because of a grain line passing through the modelled mouth. (She *had* to be tinted.)

Similarly, texturing can overpower the basic design or enhance it, depending upon how it is done. The very rough coat of a bear can be simulated either with flat planes or with veiner lines, but some of the most dramatic bears I've seen are smooth and finished with a low gloss.

The best decoys have exact feathering carved and painted and veined with a pyrographic needle, but most bird sculptures show no texture whatsoever and avoid the problems of eyes (glass inserts in decoys) and legs—usually metal in painted birds—by not showing either at all. The emphasis in one case is realism, in the other it is suggestion. Take your pick.

My tendency, as a mechanic and engineer, is to over-detail, to blur the profile and surface by excessive modelling and texturing. Other carvers I know are too dependent upon files, rasps and sandpaper, or upon single-coat gloss finishes reminiscent of cabinetmaking. Their efforts are directed towards obtaining precision—one mark of a good piece of furniture—and art, strength and individuality may be sacrificed in the process. (I am not making a case for the slapdash wood butcher, but simply warning that exactness can be overdone.)

There is little point in putting a great deal of detail into a carving that will be displayed some distance from the viewer, even though detail is easier as the piece becomes larger. There is no point in carving detail and deep modelling into wood that is too soft or too inclined to split, then have to support it. If the wood is still green or its moisture content is likely to change for any reason after completion, checking will be encouraged by cut lines, and the finish will not stop it. If a piece is likely to be handled, details and weak areas are likely to be damaged; and if the wood is light-colored, they will certainly pick up soiling. On the other hand, a table top to be covered by glass can be quite intricate, because it is likely to be inspected at close range. A carving to serve as a screen is a natural subject for openwork (piercing), and the openwork may actually help reduce the tendency to warp by equalizing humidity rapidly on the two faces.

To sum up: There are *no* rigid conventions about modelling and texturing. It appears to be more acceptable, however, to use both in moderation, particularly on small carvings. Remember always that texturing tends to subdue, rather than accentuate, a surface. Color is usually best as thin tints which are more suggestive of the color than realistic and show the wood beneath. Further, color is in most cases effective primarily on soft and colorless woods with no decided grain, or where it is necessary to overcome the effect of grain, or if the fact that it is a carving rather than a moulding or a cast form is unimportant.

The possibilities of silhouette shape and pierced carving on flat-panel design should not be neglected. Beautiful hardwoods should be permitted to be themselves unless the carved object must serve some utilitarian purpose. Finishes usually are better if a low gloss is obtained rather than a high one, and carved surfaces should not be sanded before finishing unless the risk to carved lines is justified; it should then be done with care. Finally, and perhaps most important, all of the factors of modelling, texturing and finishing should be kept in mind when the design is selected or created.

Fig. 56. By piercing and silhouetting, this toreador and bull from Ecuador looks deeper than it is.

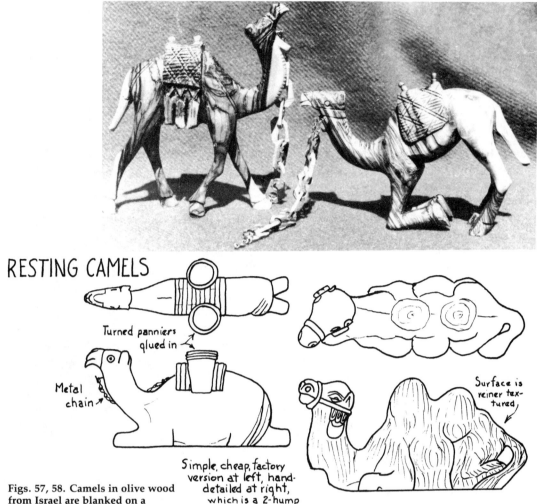

RESTING CAMELS

Turned panniers glued in

Metal chain

Simple, cheap, factory version at left, hand-detailed at right, which is a 2-hump Bactrian.

Surface is reiner textured

Figs. 57, 58. Camels in olive wood from Israel are blanked on a bandsaw and largely sanded to shape, hand carving being limited largely to head, hoof and saddle details. Even the chain links are sawed from a double-drilled block, sanded and assembled by splitting and reglueing each alternate link.

Machine-roughed carvings

MANY people have taken to power equipment for roughing, and even for finishing, what were once hand carvings, often not because of economic necessity but because we have been imbued all our working lives with the importance of time. Many amateurs who try woodcarving find it to be hard and painstaking work, so use machinery, as do many professionals, who find that hand work can be a low-priced com-modity. Also, when you start with milled lumber instead of a log or branch, there is less inspiration, less likelihood that the wood itself will suggest a design worthy of taking the time to "feel" it out. The process of waste removal becomes more mechanical because the design is fixed. The product is "sudden sculpture," often crude in details and finish.

In Oberammergau, West Germany, a traditional woodcarving town, carvers struggle against continually rising costs by profiling most duplicates of larger work, and abandoning familiar pieces which do not lend themselves to machine roughing or are too easily duplicated in plastics or moulded compositions.

In Israel, which gains a high percentage of its income from the tourist business, central "factories" rough out small figures like the camels shown here (Figs. 57, 58) then hand-finish them. They are sold in shops in the souk of Jerusalem, for example, some even equipped with the stage dressing of a lathe or other machines, a few hand tools and shavings on the floor. The proprietor may—or more likely may not—be a carver. But carvings are somewhat cheaper in the factories themselves, where I got these.

The traditional wood in Israel is olive, which is slow-growing, hard, an attractive yellow and brown, and highly figured. It is fairly common because some olive groves are being replaced by housing, but it is by no means plentiful or self-replacing, and there is very little other wood in the area. However, among the emigrés who come to Israel are artists and craftsmen from many other countries, and these are trying to continue and develop their particular skills.

There are rationalizations for machine roughing beyond the time saving. The long legs of many animals are an onerous carving chore, so production time and the danger of breakage can both be vastly reduced

Fig. 65 (below). Market woman of Bali is very graceful and has a flower-pattern texturing around the hips. Note irregular base.

Fig. 59 (above). Girl in feast costume is of ebony and wears a flower headdress. Note natural foot positions. Base is important.

by sawing out silhouette blanks. The Israeli camels are an excellent example, because not only are the silhouettes band-sawed but also the wood between the legs. Panniers, saddle components and lead chains are made separately and put on, the gross-linked wooden lead chains being ridiculously proportioned, but strongly traditional. Also, much of the forming is done on a sander or with a rasp, and the eyes are formed complete with a special cutter. Study the differences in detailing and texturing of the two resting camels to see how much can be done by machine. The simple version sells for a pittance; the elaborately detailed handmade one costs six times as much.

Fig. 61. (left) This panel has been varnished, antiqued with teak stain and waxed.

Base or no base—which?

WHETHER OR NOT a carving should have a base is superficially a matter of taste or circumstance. The human figure, like most mobile devices, tends to terminate in rather unstable bottom surfaces; if it is to stand firmly, it requires a base. Also, we have been trained to expect a base for any three-dimensional figure, just as we expect a frame for any picture. Thus the abstract sculptor finds a piece of beautiful and exotic wood upon which to mount his most recent glob, and the modern puts a pin in a block to support his assemblage of scrap iron.

To the whittler a base can be a problem, because it requires him to bore holes to separate the legs and to chew away wood across grain in order to create a surface which he must then texture in one way or another. The base will give his standing figure stability, but it often also detracts because of its size or rigid shape. On the other hand, a base provides the woodcarver with a means of holding the piece during carving. It offers him a choice between carver's screw and vise, and gives him the freedom to suggest rough or smooth ground, rocks, sea, or however he ul-

timately textures it. Of 50 small figures of people on my plate rail, 42 have bases.

I have mixed emotions about bases, as the foregoing remarks may indicate. On good carvings—meaning that they take some time, effort and skill—I tend to include a base, but it may or may not be of the same wood as the original. Thus, for example, my squash player has a separate base or can grow out of one. (Fig. 62, above)

Figs. 62, 63. Sketch (below) and photo (above) of "Squash Player," 6 in (15 cm) high over the base. Designed from frontal photo.

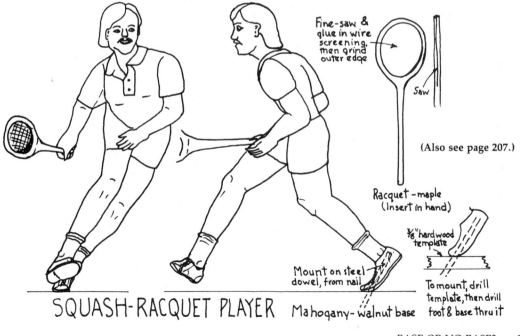

Fine-saw & glue in wire screening, then grind outer edge

Saw

(Also see page 207.)

Racquet-maple
(Insert in hand)

⅜" hardwood template

3   2

To mount, drill template, then drill foot & base thru it

Mount on steel dowel, from nail

SQUASH-RACQUET PLAYER   Mahogany-walnut base

From the owner's standpoint, the base makes life much simpler. It suggests the amount of space that must be allotted to the carving, gives evidence of one-piece construction in the cases where that is of importance, reduces the likelihood of injury to a leg, contrasts with the supporting surface, even gives a convenient place for a label and/or the carver's signature. But a massive base may check and split the carving, which of itself would adjust to humidity changes.

A base can, and should, be considered as either a help or a hindrance, depending upon the carving. If contact between figure and base is minimal, as in the squash player, an integral base is a constant nuisance during carving, but a base is essential for display, so it can be added later.

For some figures, a base of contrasting or exotic wood can enhance the value of the carving. A rosewood base, for example, suggests that what's above is worthwhile. In a figure, the grain normally should be vertical and adding a horizontal-grained base may provide a pleasing contrast. But, in general, the thick, squared-off base for a light and lithe figure is anathema; the base should also be light and thin, or very tall, not just a block. If it is integral and massive, it should be hollowed out somewhat underneath to inhibit checking and rocking.

Balinese carvers often use a triangular base which provides one corner for each foot and a third for the base of a net, or a background stump, or a larger area to support the buttocks of a seated figure and a narrow one for extended feet. An oval or a circle or a free-form shape can be as effective. The base can contribute rather than confine.

The sides of the base can help as well, if properly treated. They can suggest the terrain or carry a simple design—anything to avoid a flat and uninteresting block, unless the carving is of itself so interesting that the block will not be noticed.

Lastly, there is the matter of base size. The conventional base is the size of the original block. That is faulty. If there is a base, it should look like it can and does support the figure, but not be so obtrusive that the figure dare not move off it. A larger base may give more solidity and save wood and time if added later; but often a figure is more dramatic if an elbow or foot projects over the base (however, increasing the risk of damage when displayed).

Let the wood show

FINISHING is so much a matter of personal preference that I hesitate to make suggestions. I mention, project by project through this book, how I finish my own pieces and, when I know, how other carvers finish theirs. This, and general observation through the years, have led me to some general conclusions.

The typical cabinetmaker strives to attain a high gloss on his pieces by sanding in many steps and applying many coats of finish. So do some sculptors. But many professional woodcarvers try to achieve instead a soft glow, unless the carving is incorporated in a piece of furniture or there is some special reason for high gloss—like a carving of a supposedly wet seal.

With the rise of plastic, the tendency has been to avoid sanding to a high polish and to avoid using fillers; instead, some tool marks are left and the texture of the wood itself is preserved so the piece *looks* handmade. This is particularly true of the harder woods. For white pine and basswood, for example, the skilled carver applies thin tints of color to give variety without destroying the feeling of the wood. He does not apply a dark stain in the vain effort to make the wood look like what it is not.

My own method for soft wood without visible grain is to spray with matte or satin varnish to inhibit end-grain absorption of color. Then I apply tints lightly and wipe them down immediately so the color remains in cut areas but is removed from higher surfaces and planes, thus suggesting the color but not denying the handwork or the wood. To prevent color from soaking

Figs. 64, 65. The Scandinavian Kubbestol, or block stool, has been made for centuries. This one is more elaborate than usual, with most surfaces carved. It is ash, about 14 × 33 in (36 × 84 cm), and weighs 24 lb (11 kg). Seat is red Naugahyde® atop plywood. Back view (right) points up benefits of antiquing with dark stain, painted on interstices and lines and then rubbed away. This provides surface contrast and emphasizes the patterns, along with the shape of the log itself and darker streaks in the grain.

in and over-coloring cross-grain areas, I flat-spray varnish first. Then I use oil pigments thinned with flat varnish or drier, but acrylics can be thinned and used the same way.

I also use colors or stains to get an "antique" or darkening effect in cut areas of any carving as well as to darken backgrounds, thus making the carving appear deeper than it is. Some of these stains include wax, and thus are really single-coat finishes, but I usually use either a good furniture wax or neutral Kiwi® shoe polish to provide final finish on interior pieces. For exterior ones, there are both gloss and satin varnishes that

will weather quite well. The only problem is that they do tend to fill in the carved areas and will eventually almost obliterate the carving as well as make the surface look grey. My solution to that has been to use teak for outdoor pieces whenever possible—it can be maintained with semiannual coats of oil alone.

It is also possible to dye or stain softwood pieces; I have done both with pleasing results. I recently dyed the small birds of a mobile with cloth dyes in the absence of anything else; the colors were vivid at least. I also have a series of German sal-ammoniac-based stains called "Beiz," developed particularly for wood. These include wax, so color and polish are applied in a single operation, as with some American oil-and-wax stains. With the latter, and contrary to instructions on the can, it is usually preferable to give the piece a coat or two of flat (satin) spray varnish before staining; this prevents the stain from over-soaking in end grain and causing overemphasis there.

There are, of course, a host of special situations that require special finishing. Objects to be handled a great deal must be protected more than those which are not handled at all; this usually means varnish. Objects like bowls or ladles to be used with food should *not* be varnished. Some carvers use lacquers; I use a salad oil that will not turn rancid. Such carvings as coats of arms or basswood doors finished to resemble bronze require special finishing, such as gold leaf and antiquing.

For hardwood carvings, I prefer not to use fillers or much of the other paraphernalia and procedure of cabinetmaking—unless the carving is on a piece of furniture and must have a similar high gloss. There are two schools of thought on this, and all the variations between. Some sculptors like a high gloss on their work, so they sand and polish and fill and varnish or shellac, and rub down with steel wool just as furniture makers do. (There is now a plastic foam impregnated with grit, to replace steel wool.) The opposite school, of which I am a member, prefers texture, so uses sandpaper sparingly if at all, preferring to let tool marks show. Also, the wood is left without fillers or coloring, unless it be antiquing for depth, and finished with flat varnish and wax, oil and wax, or wax alone, depending upon wood and subject. We don't want a high polish, but a soft glow. There are now also several kinds of one-coat finishes, but they tend to create too high a gloss for me.

You can obtain good results in a natural finish on hardwoods simply by oiling and waxing. I have found processed oils such as Danish finish and tung-oil finish to be better than boiled linseed, though more expensive; they're all that's needed on teak, for example, even for constant exposure. Teak will retain its color and finish with such oiling semiannually. (Kiwi® shoe polish is the "wax finish" used in such divergent places as Bali and Sri Lanka.)

"Antiquing"

PANEL CARVINGS can often be improved by antiquing, the application of a slightly darker stain and immediate rub-off, so the darker color is retained only in crevices. This is what happens anyway as a panel ages—dirt collects in crevices and darkens them, thus giving the panel color contrast and greater apparent depth. If you plan to antique, give the panel a couple of coats of spray matte varnish first; it helps seal the pores and prevents instant absorption of the darker stain in cross-grain areas.

There are a great many ways to finish carvings, of course. Outdoor signs, and panels, usually in pine, basswood or possibly oak, should be painted in most cases, but may be "antiqued" on an instant basis by beating with chains, scorching slightly with a blowtorch or sandblasting to take off sharp edges. (Some carvers start with old boards to get authenticity; in that case the poorer the finish the more authentic. Poor finish goes with splintered ends and rotten spots—and poor carving. I've known of carvers who buried their products for a week or two to give them antiquity—or dealers who did it after them.) If an outdoor panel is not painted, it should probably be marine-varnished—which means high gloss; matte and satin finishes simply will not hold up in the weather.

Gold-leafing

OUTDOOR SIGNS, NAMEPLATES and liturgical carvings are quite common in relief carving, and may require gilding or gold-leafing of anything from lettering to the entire surface. Gilding is actually just another kind of

Fig. 66. A 150-year-old mahogany table leaf is the base for this quotation from Goethe. The leaf is 12 × 36 in (30 × 91 cm) and was handmade, so the end lobes are not exactly alike. Also the edges slope into roundness, and the whole had a fine patina. The lettering is Old English from the tomb of Richard II. Finish is matte varnish and natural shoe polish.

lacquering, and the technique is detailed on the container. Bronzing, coppering and silvering are similar. All can be applied in many tints with spray cans—with a spray-can result. I have done better with rub-on compounds, particularly for various shades of gold. These are apparently gilt in a wax, so careful application with the fingertips and rubbing in improves the finish. Paints, brush or spray, tend to pile up in crevices and show brush marks. They are not durable when exposed to the weather and somehow look synthetic. If used, they must be covered with some sort of finish, such as a polyurethane varnish.

The ultimate in such work is to apply gold leaf, which is ridiculously expensive today. Real gold leaf is about one three-hundredth as thick as a human hair! There is, of course, imitation gold leaf just as there is silver leaf, also an imitation. Imitation gold is readily available in paint and hobby stores, comes in packets containing 5.2 sq ft (.468 sq m) as 25 leaves, each 5½ in (14 cm) square. The imitation gold is thicker than the real thing, harder to pick up, handle and cover an area with, and usually comes in loose sheets separated by thin paper. Imitation gold must be protected or it will tarnish, particularly out of doors.

Real gold comes in packets of 25 leaves, each 3¼ in square (21 sq cm) totalling 284 sq in (1,832 sq cm). It is actually quite hard to find. It can range from 13½ to 23 karats in purity; real gold is 24 K but has a tendency to split when worked. Woodcarvers use 22 to 23 K gold leaf. Real gold leaf comes either in loose or transfer sheets, the latter held to the backing tissues by jeweller's rouge. The transfer gold is easier to use because it is applied just like a decal, the tissue peeled off after it is applied. It avoids a great deal of fussing with brushes and specialized transfer devices, but is somewhat less economical because parts of sheets may be lost or incorrectly applied.

If you plan to use real gold leaf, the carving should be suited to it. This means selecting a wood that is not too coarse in grain—basswood is ideal—and without undercuts or extremely complex or difficult-to-reach areas. The gold may bridge over such areas or not adhere properly. (See Appendix II for further details on gold-leafing.)

Part II

7

Small Pieces

Whittling gnomes

THESE THREE ORIENTAL GNOMES are adapted from a little figure I saw in Tokyo as a decoration in a jeweller's showcase. They are caricatures, of course, and quite simple in shape as well as adaptable to a number of poses. All can be pine or basswood, and painted. The seated and bent-over figures are each 3¼ in (8.3 cm) long, the nose-in-the-air one just under 4 in (10.2 cm) tall. The blanks are sawed out of 1-in (2.5-cm) wood, and will also serve here to amplify the instructions on handling the knife.

All the little men have stylized bulbous noses, slanted eyes and no mouths or ears. The procedure is shown in Figs. 67–73.

GROUND WATCHER
MUSICIAN→

SKY WATCHER

ORIENTAL GNOMES
White pine-painted

Fig. 67.

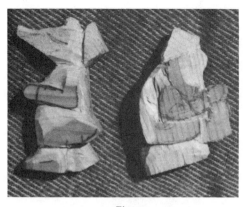

Fig. 68.

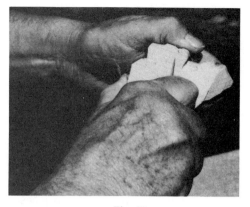

Fig. 69.

Figs. 67–73. Grains for the Oriental Gnomes run with the beards. (68) After the blanks are sawed and roughed to shape, point the hat and beard by paring cuts where possible, and thumb-push cuts otherwise. (69) Make outline or stop cuts across grain first. Draw the knife along the bottom of the arm of the seated figure, so slices can be cut from the coat up to them. (70) Some cuts are best made by pushing the knife edge, rather than paring; however, they are difficult to control. So the left

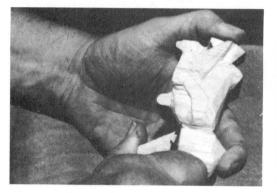

Fig. 70.

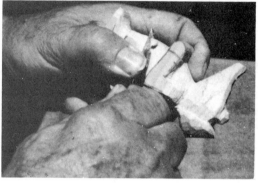

Fig. 71.

hand is used to provide thumb force behind the blade. (71) For the paring cut, wear a thumb stall to protect the ball of the thumb. (72) The stooping figure is completed, and details on the other figure have been sketched but not cut. (73) The procedure of cutting the arm free is shown on the seated figure. If outlining is done thoroughly and cleanly, the modelling of arm, umbrella and nose is rapid. Eyes are formed by cutting slits with the knife; pupils will be painted black spots.

Fig. 72.

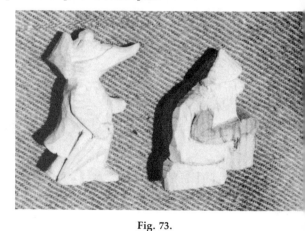

Fig. 73.

Neckerchief slides and the like

PROBABLY THE MOST POPULAR whittling project among Boy Scouts has been the neckerchief slide. The designs can also be used for pendants, pins and bolos, and many can be carved extensively or simply be painted silhouettes, depending upon the maker. The primary shape is provided by the silhouette itself, and modelling is minimal, so the designs are very practical for beginning whittlers.

I have sketched about 40 of H. M. Sutter's designs, and pictured others. They are basically silhouettes jigsawed from ¼- to ⅜-in (6.4- to 9.5-mm) pine or basswood, although they can be made of harder woods, and thicker if more modelling is desired, as on the Indian chief head or the thunderbird. Most of the designs are variants of a few basic shapes. Most versatile is the shield, which from a defensive weapon became the principal basis for heraldry. Family escutcheons or coats of arms can be carved on a shield background, but it can also be used as a blank for arrowheads, masks, and can be turned sidewise or upside down to provide a blank for animals, birds and fish. It can be rounded as a plain boss also.

The arrow is a popular slide design; it can be interpreted in a variety of ways, depending upon the skill of the individual. The hiker sole or shoe sole is similar in that the shape itself is simple. It can be whittled as a sole with a date and/or location. However, it

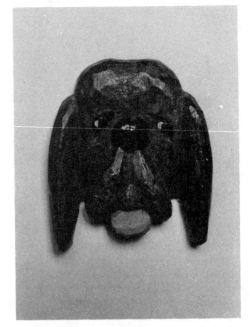

Fig. 74. Neckerchief slide. Slides can be derived from shield blanks, but can, of course, be cut out directly to shape.

NAPKIN RINGS

Giraffe   Elephant

Fig. 75. Seven napkin ring designs.

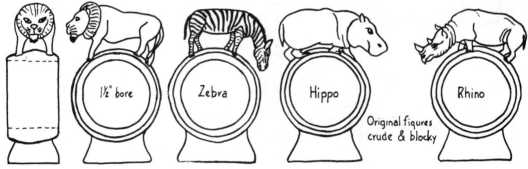

Kenya   Lion

1½" bore   Zebra   Hippo   Rhino

Original figures crude & blocky

Fig. 76. Some typical bolo patterns.

can also be carved into several quite complex shapes, like the lobster, fish and duck. The same is true of the canoe paddle, which with a little interpretation becomes a snowshoe, fiddle or tennis racket.

The owl and covered wagon are just for fun; both are somewhat more complex. The thunderbird is one of the most used and most significant of Western Indian designs, often changed in detail to suit the whim of

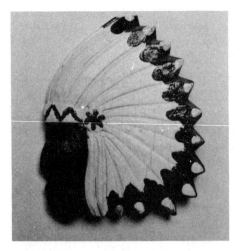

Fig. 77.

Fig. 78.

Fig. 79.

the maker. It is used on rugs, pins, baskets, beaded items, costumes and jewelry.

The square knot is the most useful knot, and so is very familiar in Scouting and elsewhere. This is a more complex carving because it involves a good deal of precise modelling. Even more complicated is the double carrick bend, a more complex knot used for joining two hawsers. Similar in difficulty are the intertwined six-point star and the crossed links.

The problem on all of these designs is to use soft wood and carve it without splitting off sections with the grain. It is very easy, for example, to accidentally split off the feathering or points of the arrow or the ends of the canoe, the head of the thunderbird, or the arms of the cross, and easier still to break out sections that are chip-carved.

If made into neckerchief slides as Mr. Sutter did it, a second piece of wood with a ¾-in (19.1-mm) hole drilled in it is simply glued edgewise on the back. It is also possible, of course, to whittle the slide in a thicker block, so the hole is integral. The same designs can be used for bolos, although in this case it is necessary to have the "finding" to fasten on the back, or to make it. To make a pin, a "finding" with a flat-backed pin can be glued on, or one made by gluing a safety pin into a slot. In any case, the piece should be brightly painted unless it is in a fine wood.

Belt buckles, plain and fancy

BELT BUCKLES ARE AN EASY, utilitarian way to display both beautiful wood and good carving. Structure and design can suit your fancy, ranging from simple line patterns to elaborate modelling, appliqués or inlays of metal or stone on both exhibited front and important back ends. You can also inset small shaped pieces, such as gears or animals, in a plastic set into a well of wood. My childhood crony John Phillip, late of Whittier, California, and Harrison Neustadt, of Sunrise, Florida, have each made dozens of buckles for gift or sale. Mr. Neustadt has even designed jigs for bending and inserting the findings into the wood without splitting. He usually makes the buckle of wood alone, while Mr. Phillip backs the wood with a metal frame to which the findings are soldered.

The basic ingredient is an interesting piece of wood cut to a blank of the desired shape—round, oval, square, rectangular, petiolate or free form. It should be ¼ to ⅜ in (6.4 to 9.5 mm) thick and a bit wider than the standard belt widths of 1, 1½ or 2 in (2.54, 4 or 5.1 cm). If buckle length is more than about 2 in (5.1 cm), the shape should be slightly curved to fit the abdomen. If the blank is circular, it can be turned and ridged or otherwise machine-shaped before carving.

John Phillip's favorite fastening is based on a clip, or combined hook, that can be stainless steel, brass or even a coat hanger or similar stiff iron wire. The bent form should be strong enough to resist midriff expansion after a heavy meal, so that anything attached need only support itself. The loop end (see Appendix I, pages 313–315) is made to fit the desired belt width, and the hook engages in the belt holes. The belt, incidentally, is usually the kind that comes with snaps for easy buckle interchange. You can also cut an undistinguished buckle off a standard belt and rivet one of these in its place because the new assembly adds a couple of inches.

Least complicated is stapling the clip to the back of the blank. You can make suitable staples by bending brads into U's after sharpening both ends. The brads should not be long enough to go through the blank and in brittle or very hard wood, or in cross-grain pieces, they should be driven into predrilled holes. A more secure design involves routing or grooving a slot of the desired shape into the wood, then glueing the clip in securely. However, Mr. Phillip usually solders the clip onto a plate of thin stainless, brass or copper of the blank shape and contour, roughens the face of the backing and glues on the wood. The backing plate should not be more than ⅟₁₆ in (1.6

Fig. 80.

Fig. 81.

Fig. 82.

Fig. 83. The owl is tinted and has inlaid eyes.

and boiled linseed oil, applied with an old sock. He says that his earliest pieces have improved with age and now have a lovely patina.

If you want to inlay metal or stone inserts in the face of the buckle, set them securely so they do not catch clothing. Mr. Phillip does it by placing the insert where he wants it, clamping it, then scratching around it with a sharp scriber. He reinforces the scribed line with a series of sharp center-punch holes, then routs the socket in his drill press with a small bit running at high speed. In this way he can shape areas that a knife would chip and break out. He drills only as deep as the insert, of course. The cavity is filled with Goodyear Pliobond® cement, enough so that the adhesive will seep out around the edges when the insert is seated. Next, he sprinkles fine-sanding dust from the wood (be sure it is the same wood) all around the edge and mixes it with the adhesive. Then he taps the insert all over with a small mallet—or hammer, if it is metal—to fill any gaps or small breakouts. He folds a small piece of waxed paper over the glued assembly to prevent sticking, on top of which is laid a block of hard wood, sawed to the same radius as the buckle top, with a gap to clear any projecting surface. He then sets three small clamps at ends and center and allows at least 48 hours drying time. When the assembly is dry, he removes block and paper, sands and fine-files the surface, then paraffin-buffs.

mm) thick or the buckle will be overweight. You can use a very thin plate and leave it sufficiently oversize to crimp it around the wood as a jeweller sets a gem into a bezel, but this is normally unnecessary because there is little stress on the facing.

Mr. Neustadt uses no backing. His findings are just the C-shaped clip and a pin, both forced by a jig into predrilled holes. The findings have grooves near the ends, so glue will hold them in place.

Finish can suit your taste. I usually use a spray coat or two of matte varnish, followed by waxing. Mr. Neustadt has been using his own mixture for 20 years on all of his craftwork, including furniture, bowls and platters. It is a 50-50 mixture of polyurethane

(More on small pieces will be found in Appendix I starting on page 313)

8

Carving Animals

Variations on a theme

THROUGHOUT HISTORY and in every field or profession, there have been two schools of thought, one stressing innovation, the other improvement. One worships creativity, newness, difference—in short, strives to produce or do something that has not been produced or done before. The other worships perfection, accuracy, intricacy—in short, strives to make a familiar thing better. One is concerned with ideas and dreams, while the other is concerned with reality.

There have been, and always will be, both kinds of craftsmen, both kinds of artists. Few of us are at the poles of this difference, but most of us lean strongly one way or the other. We have the whittler who strives to carve a longer or more complex chain, or the carver who tries to make a more lifelike or anatomically correct bird, or the sculptor who strives for a perfect copy of an ancient Greek figure. On the other hand, we have the whittler who creates new and sometimes amorphous forms of animals, the carver who refuses to duplicate his own or another's work even if he feels that it can be improved, and the sculptor who creates forms that are sometimes not even understandable from their titles. He is marching to Thoreau's different drummer, and the idea of sameness appalls him. Paradoxically, this difference may be the vital factor in making the individual famous as compared with commercially successful, a sculptor as compared with a craftsman. It is the innovator who wins prizes at art shows and exhibits, the craftsman who wins ribbons at fairs.

Famous artists have said repeatedly that there is no shortcut to art; it takes an enormous amount of practice, of trial and error. Only when the basics are mastered can the artist strike out on his own successfully.

There are many ways in which to be original, in which to vary even a familiar design; not all innovation must be total in concept. There may be newness in pose, in detail, in overall silhouette, in arrangement or contrast, in texture, even in finish, for innovation is largely the meeting of a challenge adjusted to the abilities of the individual. It

Fig. 84. Lounging jaguar 8 in (20.3 cm) long, orange with brown markings, is a compound of a shaped branch of copal with tail and legs tacked on. Head is carved from the branch, but ears are tacked on.

Note how elements support each other.

About 2' tall

CRANES & SNAKE Bali Ebony

Fig. 85.

Eyes inlaid

Ears & tail inserted

BULL Mexico Granadillo 4½" long

Fig. 86.

POLAR BEAR U.S.A. Sycamore 5" long

Fig. 87.

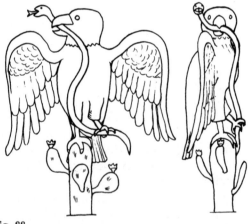

Fig. 88.

is a branching out, an effort to achieve something that is a definite step ahead *for the carver concerned*, an attempt to convert a mental picture into a physical one.

Most of us cannot hope to visualize the bird-and-flower compositions of the Balinese; our traditions and instincts do not seem to lead us in that direction. The cranes and snake pictured here (Fig. 85) are a simple example, in which the fragile bird legs are reinforced—quite frankly—with foliage, and the heads with crest and snake, without robbing a particle from the overall effect. The entire composition is fitted to the available wood but without being inhibited by it; there is no blocky and angular look. The composition flows upwards from the base in lines that are not at all reminiscent of the original block.

For contrast, study the Zapotec Indian (Mexico) effort to reproduce the national symbol: an eagle on a cactus with a snake in its mouth. (Fig. 88) The carver was not very skilled, but he achieved something which became part of a national exhibit. One worked almost entirely (except for the snake) from a single block, while the other was content to carve the bird, then mount it on a sawn assembly reminiscent of cactus. Yet both are strong and original.

The bull (Fig. 86) is in granadillo, made by a Zapotec from wood given him by a visitor from northern Mexico, and the polar bear (Fig. 87) is in sycamore chosen for the color and figure by an American carver. Each depicts its subject fairly accurately, but distinguishing characteristics of the animal and the innate coloring of the wood are emphasized. Contrast these in turn with the African animals on napkin rings (Fig. 75) which are basically true to life, but adapted for a different purpose. These animals are miniatures, relatively speaking, and the silhouette is the important element in recognition. However, the carver avoided the ungainly effect of the over-tall giraffe by eliminating the troublesome legs.

There can be much originality in a frankly comic figure that brings a smile to the observer, as in the American goat and the Japanese owl (Figs. 90, 91) with attached and rolling eyes. These, like the napkin rings, are made for sale, hence are simple in design, but they are different from run-of-the-mill objects. Another example of the same thing is the Noah's ark from Israel (Fig. 92), which, like the owl, is assembled from unit carvings. This design has the advantage that the stylized ship can be assumed to have no deck, so that the body of each animal is either within the cabin or below the bulwarks. The carvings are only the heads and necks of the animals, and they can be arranged as you wish about the composition, but the effect is unique and different. The same idea could be carried out in a fully 3-dimensional ark, with animals on both sides. The reed roof could yield to a single-piece one of textured or grooved wood, and so on, so that every ark could be an individual composition.

This suggests another idea that is relatively uncommon, that of using the same elements in a variety of arrangements, or—better still—allowing the ultimate owner to vary the composition at will, as children build with blocks. A series of building

Fig. 89. Dog is carved from a bent branch, with legs, tail and ear added. It is from Oaxaca, Mexico.

fronts against a common background, or amorphous human or animal figures that can be arranged in various ways on a base, are examples. One possibility of this sort is to provide flat elements with magnetic-tape

Fig. 90.

Owl has separate feet set on dowels

COMIC GOAT U.S.A. Pine
Joe Rothrock, after Bob Horbison

COMIC OWL Japan Cedar
Fig. 91.   Plastic inserted eyes have rolling pupils

NOAH'S ARK A. Klein, Jerusalem, Israel

Animal heads & reed roof glued in place

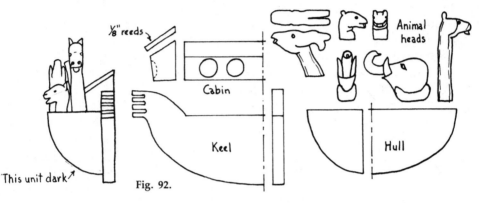

⅛" reeds

Cabin

Keel

This unit dark ↗

Animal heads

Hull

Fig. 92.

or other "tacky" backs, and set them against a cloth-covered, sheet-iron plate or a felted board (not illustrated).

There are many ways in which some individuality may be expressed. The large-sized birds are two of my own examples. (Figs. 94, 95) When I originally carved a "bug tree" I decided to crown it with a large cardinal. So I carved a fat, stubby bird from a wild-cherry log and put him atop an assemblage of more than 150 bugs—although

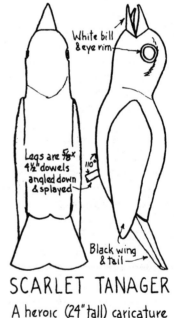

White bill & eye rim

Legs are ⅝" x 4½" dowels angled down & splayed

110°

Black wing & tail

SCARLET TANAGER

Fig. 94. A heroic (24" tall) caricature

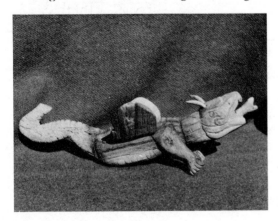

Fig. 93 (left). Fantastic dragon assembled from whittled pieces in Yucatan is about 18 in (45.7 cm) long and ingeniously put together from pieces of approximate shape.

the cardinal is a seed eater, not a bug eater. Some of my neighborhood "birders" were upset. After ten years, when the cardinal had succumbed to dry rot and the ministrations of friendly woodpeckers, I replaced him with a scarlet tanager, although I haven't seen one in my neighborhood in the more than 40 years I've lived here. My point is that you *can* cut loose and do as you like. You, after all, are the carver, the artist, and you have some license. Also, the bird need not be anatomically accurate unless it is being produced as a portrait. The cardinal was happily fat, the tanager has dowel-rod legs and no depiction of feathers. To anyone who criticizes, I can say that the tanager at least eats bugs, but I don't like him as well as his predecessor.

Another example of the same sort of thing is the angelfish (Fig. 97) I chose for a pendant and earring motif in the rare and beautiful pink ivory wood. Because the wood has so much color and figure, I elected to make the pieces across grain, despite the long trailing ends of the dorsal and ventral fins. As it turned out, the wood simply cannot support such long thin sections, and even a minor bump of the pendant against something hard, or something pressed against it, breaks off the fin ends. Thus I have drawn an alternate design, which ties the trailing edges into the tail. It is not as accurate anatomically, but it is much more durable. This wood, by the way, is extremely rare still.

Another example of a fish design will reinforce my point about the permissibility of varying a design as it occurs in nature.

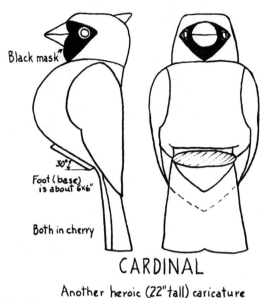

CARDINAL

Another heroic (22"tall) caricature

Fig. 95.

Take the loaves and fishes (Fig. 96). Both loaf shapes and fish shapes are generally known and accepted. But the man who laid the mosaic in Tabgha, Israel, long ago distorted the fish and showed only the ends of three loaves in a basket, to depict the whole

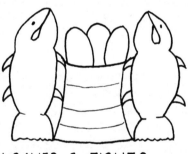

LOAVES & FISHES

Fig. 96. Modified from the mosaic at Tabgha

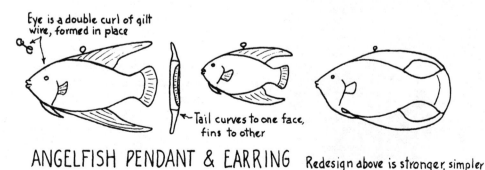

Fig. 97. ANGELFISH PENDANT & EARRING Redesign above is stronger, simpler

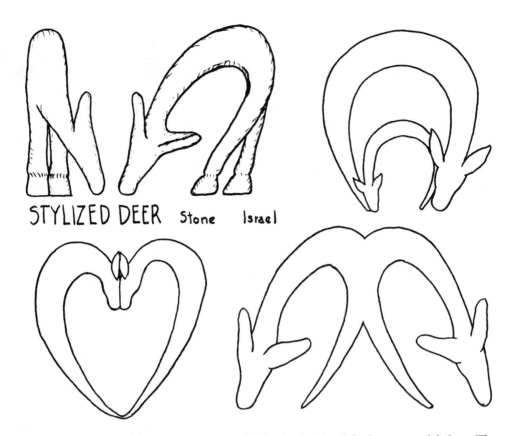

STYLIZED DEER   Stone   Israel

Fig. 98. (above). Various ways of treating a stylized deer. **Fig. 99 (below).** Granadillo stylized bird and deer, each about 10 in (25.4 cm) high from Guerrero, Mexico.

Biblical miracle of the loaves and fishes. The fish are not very realistic, although still recognizable. I have adapted the group for a barrette or pendant and modified it still further. This can be done, and, again, it is artistic license.

As a final example of variations, consider the doe and fawn (*ayelet* in Hebrew). I felt when I saw it in Israel that the legs were too heavy, and that they had probably been made that way because the material was stone. With the heavy legs, it is possible to saw such a figure completely from wood by sawing through at the nose, then gluing and filling the kerf later. However, the hooves were more nearly equine, as you can see from my copy of the original. So I modified the design to make the hooves more delicate, then went on to make eight further adaptations. All have a common ancestor, but they become less recognizable as they change. Three possibilities are shown here (Fig. 98) as my variations; you can certainly produce your own with a little thought. You will not have the same inhibitions or freedoms as I do, so your designs will inevitably be different. That is not necessarily bad. The point is that you can and should vary designs to suit your purposes or inclinations, and have no compunction about doing so. Sometimes, you'll improve the original idea in the process.

"Different" subjects, poses, textures and finishes

ANIMALS, birds and fish offer a tremendous variety of designs. There are so many species, so many shapes, sizes, surface textures, poses. The possibilities for new poses, techniques, surface textures, and finishes are far greater than they are in carving figures of people. (We are one very limited species of animal ourselves, although we tend to forget it.) What's more, the typical observer has far less intimate knowledge of animal anatomy than he does of human anatomy, so he is less inclined to be critical of minor errors, or even of the exaggerations of caricature. All in all, this is a rich field for the carver.

There are specialized books on carving decoys, eagles and birds, but they are devoted to copying the living bird (or animal) precisely; in fact there are major awards for producing a decoy that looks as much like a stuffed bird as possible. There is, however, an entire field beyond this, that of carving birds and animals which are unmistakable, but are not slavish copies of living ones. Take as a case in point the photo of four totally different treatments of the turtle (Fig. 100). In this section are other examples, together with a variety of other ideas in animal and bird carving. My hope is that they will stimulate your imagination to try still others. You can go as far as you like, into great detail, or total stylization, freeform, caricature, and unusual finishes,

with little fear of the nit-picking criticism that any carver of the human form is likely to get. We usually cannot distinguish individuals within an animal species, and in fact we do not know anatomical details. This is borne out by general animal and bird books—in which sketches often widely disagree.

I have carved many kinds and many poses of animals in recent years, some small, some large, but most of them not the familiar domestic animals nor the familiar poses. These form a mixed grouping, which includes work done at various times, for various reasons, and in a variety of woods. Most effective in terms of observer comments has been the pair of long-tailed weasels. (Fig. 101).

The stylized Pekingese (Fig. 102) and the toucan caricature (Fig. 103) were both made from the butts of timbers discarded as scrap by a nearby piano company. The weasels were a serious effort at animal portraiture, and the musculature and poses were carefully checked with available references. The Pekingese, on the other hand, exploits the texture of the surface and the great plume of tail as well as the pug nose that characterizes the breed. Because the grain is vertical—that is, across the animal's body instead of along it—fluting with a flat gouge was relatively easy and did not generate the

Fig. 100. **Four variations of the lowly turtle, ranging from caricature to serious sculpture: the upper right figure is from the Galapagos Islands, the other three are from Mexico.**

Fig. 101. Two long-tailed weasels in mahogany. The weasel on all fours twists around the standing one. The polished finish suggests the slick coat of the animal. 4 × 10 × 10 in (9 × 25 × 25 cm).

splinters that normally occur when mahogany is textured. Also, the tail has more strength than it would have with the grain lengthwise. The result is a piece that makes an excellent and durable doorstop, if nothing more.

The toucan is a composite or assemblage which resulted from buying a toucan upper mandible from a Cuna Indian in the San Blas Islands off Panama. The body was carved in scale with the mandible, which

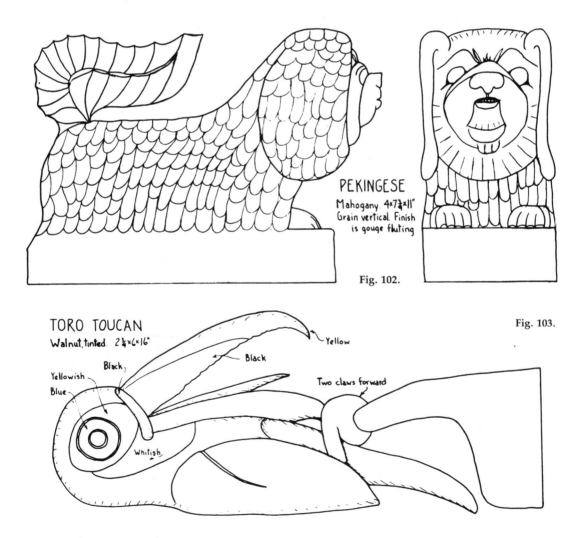

PEKINGESE
Mahogany. 4×7¾×11"
Grain vertical. Finish
is gouge fluting

Fig. 102.

TORO TOUCAN
Walnut, tinted. 2¾×6×16"

Yellow
Black
Yellowish
Blue
Whitish
Two claws forward
Black

Fig. 103.

was glued over a stub. Also, the walnut body was tinted with oils to suggest the garish colors of the bird and to carry out the tones in the actual mandible. This is a caricature, of course, as is the perplexed penguin (Fig. 104).

The bear (Fig. 105) is a reversible piece, combining a stylized animal on one side with a caricatured troll on the other, so the exposed face can match the observer's mood. The bear design is taken from a smaller Swiss original I saw in Brienz many years ago, and I designed the troll to fit the same silhouette. (This can be done with various silhouette carvings. It converts them really into double-sided free-standing panels, thus avoiding the often dull rear view of a conventional in-the-round carv-

PERPLEXED PENGUIN   Jelutong, tinted

Fig. 104.

BEAR & TROLL
Silhouette of bear is used for troll on reverse of a 4x6½x16" butternut block. (Some Scandinavians suggest that the troll legend is based on a bear seen dimly.)

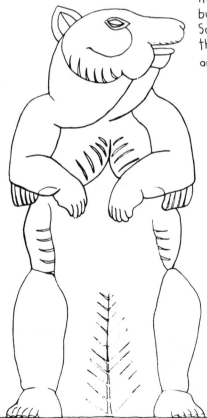

Fig. 105.

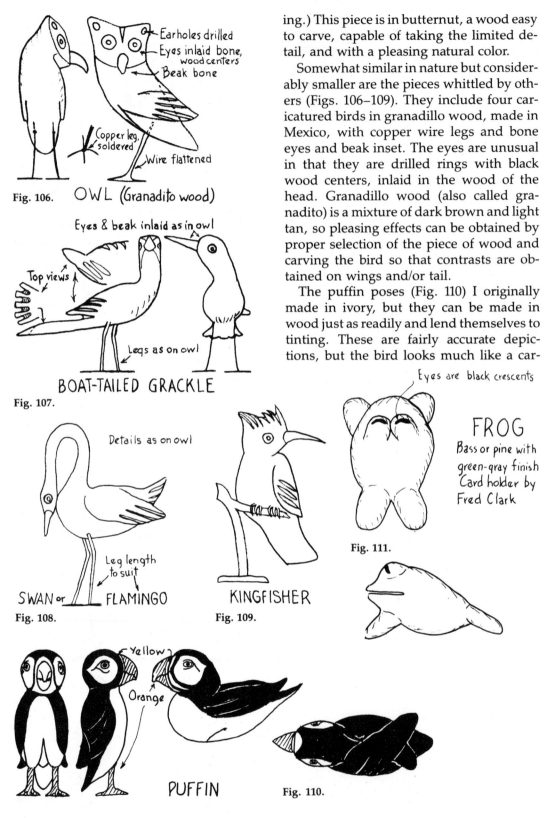

Fig. 106. OWL (Granadito wood)

Earholes drilled
Eyes inlaid bone, wood centers
Beak bone
Copper leg, soldered
Wire flattened

Eyes & beak inlaid as in owl
Top views
Legs as on owl

BOAT-TAILED GRACKLE
Fig. 107.

Details as on owl

Leg length to suit

SWAN or FLAMINGO
Fig. 108.

KINGFISHER
Fig. 109.

Eyes are black crescents

FROG
Bass or pine with green-gray finish
Card holder by Fred Clark

Fig. 111.

Yellow
Orange

PUFFIN
Fig. 110.

ing.) This piece is in butternut, a wood easy to carve, capable of taking the limited detail, and with a pleasing natural color.

Somewhat similar in nature but considerably smaller are the pieces whittled by others (Figs. 106–109). They include four caricatured birds in granadillo wood, made in Mexico, with copper wire legs and bone eyes and beak inset. The eyes are unusual in that they are drilled rings with black wood centers, inlaid in the wood of the head. Granadillo wood (also called granadito) is a mixture of dark brown and light tan, so pleasing effects can be obtained by proper selection of the piece of wood and carving the bird so that contrasts are obtained on wings and/or tail.

The puffin poses (Fig. 110) I originally made in ivory, but they can be made in wood just as readily and lend themselves to tinting. These are fairly accurate depictions, but the bird looks much like a car-

Fig. 112.

Background pierced between figures →

WOODCHUCK GROUP (for silhouettes)

icature anyway The woodchucks (Fig. 112) were a silhouette group for the top of a breadboard, but can be done as a three-dimensional group, as a flat plaque or a silhouette carving, as you wish. The frog (Fig. 111) is a place-card holder if so desired, because his sawn mouth can hold a card or a message. (Fred Clark carved it.)

All of these figures can be laid out on suitable blocks or boards and sawed out on the band saw, with details cut by coping saw. This saves enormous time in carving. The larger pieces are best done with chisels, the smaller ones with the knife. I have used a variety of finishes on my carvings in this group, each suited, in my opinion, to the particular subject. The weasels are varnished and waxed to a sheen, suggesting the smooth coat and sinuousness of the animal. The toucan is toned to contrast with the basic dark brown of the walnut. The Pekingese is textured with a gouge on all areas except the face and paw fronts. The bear is spray-varnished and antiqued with a darker stain in crevices. The frog is tinted green on top and lighter greenish-grey beneath, with oils or acrylics. The puffins are finished with oils, and the other birds left natural.

One of the most enduring of carved bird forms is the eagle, because of its association with the United States and because the bird itself is so impressive. I include three examples of eagle carvings in this group (Figs. 113–115), because they are somewhat different from the norm and might not otherwise be available.

I was also intrigued by a truly giant

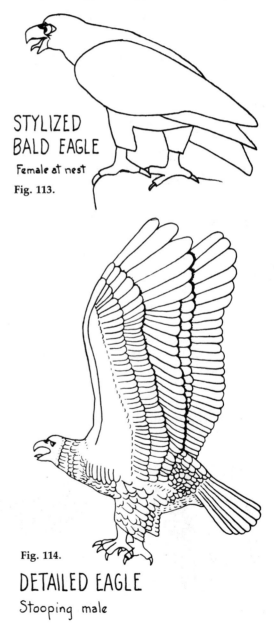

STYLIZED BALD EAGLE
Female at nest
Fig. 113.

Fig. 114.

DETAILED EAGLE
Stooping male

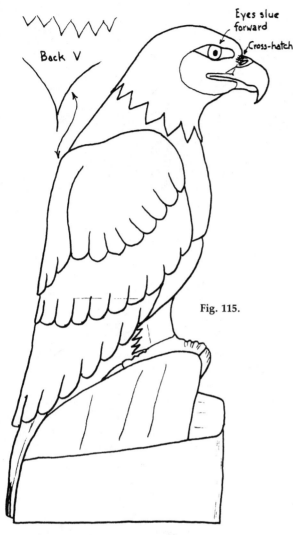

Back V

Eyes slue forward

Cross-hatch

Fig. 115.

AMERICAN (BALD) EAGLE

was designed exceptionally well. This goes also for the rearing stallion from Bali, a distorted but very dramatic pose (Fig. 117). In sharp contrast is my ramshorn snail (Fig. 119), which was an experiment in making carvings that can be placed on the floor. The weasels and the Pekingese are also "floor pieces."

At one time, not so recently it was the fashion for both sexes to wear neck chains with pendants; the more bizarre the pendant the better. Pendants are also used for chain pulls on light fixtures, curtain pulls, or just for decoration. A duck, frog and rabbit in wood are pictured (Fig. 118). Such designs can be carved from scraps of exotic woods and are interesting alternatives to standard or heroic figures. Blanks can be carried about conveniently and carved with the knife in almost any surroundings.

Feathering detailed, prominent

Legs 8 feet oversize, not textured

BIG ROOSTER
Mato Generalić (Yugoslavia) 1975 35"

Fig. 116.

rooster 35 in (88 cm) high included in the Yugoslav naive art shown in the United States in 1977 (Fig. 116). In this case, the carver overemphasized the feathering for effect, and even provided stumpy legs and feet, seemingly a characteristic of Yugoslav peasant carvings of humans. The result is quite a dramatic bird.

Other examples of stylized, and perhaps caricatured, animals include three which, as far as I am aware, are not native to the countries where the carving was made. The lion from the Philippines (Fig. 120) is probably a result of tourist interest in lions, but it

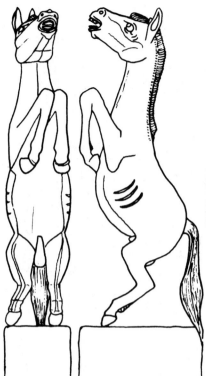

Fig. 120. Stylized lion has exaggerated musculature and mane. It is about 18 in (46 cm) long.

REARING STALLION Bali

Original 21" high, in a white hardwood

Fig. 117.

Mexico   Original onyx

CHESS KNIGHT

Fig. 120.

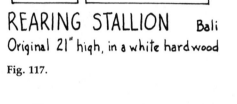

PENDANTS Soft stone or wood

Fig. 118.

Fig. 119.

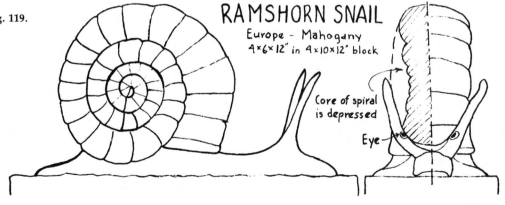

RAMSHORN SNAIL

Europe - Mahogany
4×6×12" in 4×10×12" block

Core of spiral
is depressed

Eye

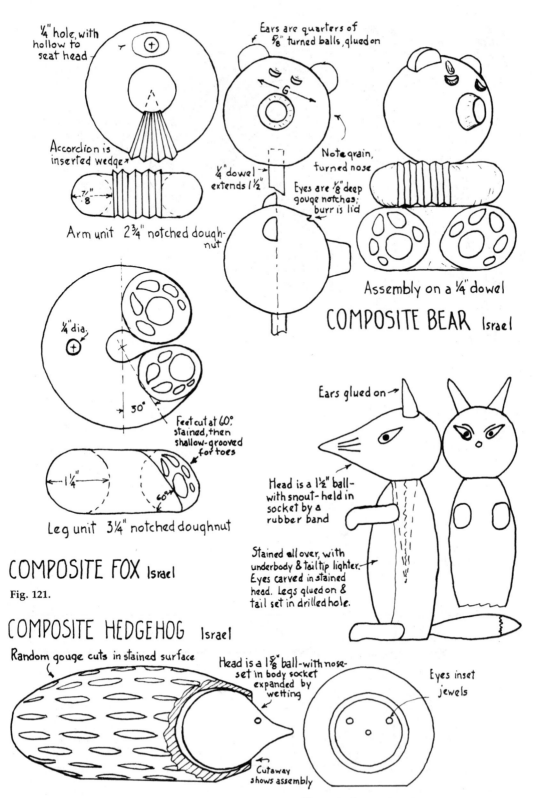

¼" hole, with hollow to seat head

Accordion is inserted wedge

Arm unit 2¾" notched dough-nut

⅞"

Ears are quarters of ⅝" turned balls, glued on

¼" dowel extends 1½"

Eyes are ⅛" deep gouge notches; burr is lid

Note grain, turned nose

Assembly on a ¼" dowel

COMPOSITE BEAR Israel

¼" dia.

30°

Feet cut at 60°, stained, then shallow-grooved for toes

1¼"

60°

Leg unit 3¼" notched doughnut

COMPOSITE FOX Israel

Fig. 121.

COMPOSITE HEDGEHOG Israel

Random gouge cuts in stained surface

Head is a 1⅝" ball-with nose-set in body socket expanded by wetting

Cutaway shows assembly

Eyes inset jewels

Ears glued on

Head is a 1½" ball-with snout- held in socket by a rubber band

Stained all over, with underbody & tail tip lighter. Eyes carved in stained head. Legs glued on & tail set in drilled hole.

Fig. 122. Composite of animals.

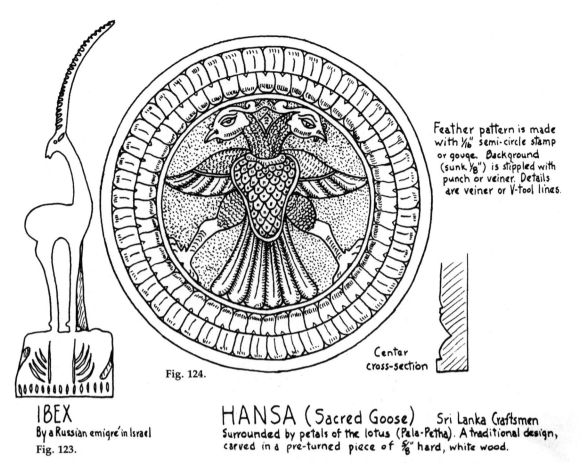

Feather pattern is made with ¹⁄₁₆" semi-circle stamp or gouge. Background (sunk ¹⁄₈") is stippled with punch or veiner. Details are veiner or V-tool lines.

Center cross-section

Fig. 124.

IBEX
By a Russian emigré in Israel
Fig. 123.

HANSA (Sacred Goose) Sri Lanka Craftsmen
Surrounded by petals of the lotus (Pala-Petha). A traditional design, carved in a pre-turned piece of ⅝" hard, white wood.

One finds pieces in Israel like the bear, hedgehog and fox made by a German immigrant and the ibex (Figs. 120–123) in cow bone, made by a Russian emigré. (The latter has produced a number of other pieces in the same material, some quite complex, but his market is limited because tourists tend to buy souvenirs rather than art. Bone is not nearly as susceptible to machine production as is wood.)

The German emigré has designed his pieces so that most of the heavy work is done on a lathe. The hansa carving (Fig. 124) from Sri Lanka (formerly Ceylon), can also be turned in a lathe, including the shallow V of the outer border and moulding circles, always difficult to hand carve. Then the background can be bosted (sunken) with a small router, leaving the carving of the two-headed bird and the leaves as the hand work. It it also possible to do some portions of the feather-texturing with a stamp that makes several of the small arcs at

a time. (This is not the way the original was made. It bears all the signs of being hand-textured.)

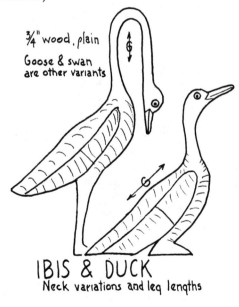

¾" wood, plain

Goose & swan are other variants

IBIS & DUCK
Neck variations and leg lengths

Fig. 125.

CAT CARD HOLDER
Stylized, stained black or mahogany
Fig. 126.

This is true of the very blocky cat card-holder (Fig. 126) which is square in cross-section and obviously sawed to shape, then sanded. Carving is minimal, because not even the features are outlined, but the silhouette, plus the slight narrowing at the nose, creates an unmistakable cat, even though its tail is the full width of the body and no modelling is done. Such a piece can be turned out by the dozen on a band saw, and be finished with a sander and staining.

Sometimes, detailed modelling is necessary to a design, as in the Celtic bird brooch (Fig. 127), where the various levels are separated by texturing and modelling, and important elements are emphasized—in this case by textural lack. Incidentally, this particular design emphasizes another point: You don't have to stick to the letter of the original design if you are changing medium. The original was a small cast-brass brooch; mine was a 6-in (15-cm) bird carved in low relief on vermilion wood, where it was the subject of view, not primarily a decoration. So I intensified some elements. Also, vermilion takes a high polish from the cutting tool, so some texturing and modelling was necessary to make the carving stand out. I could, of course, have sanded the whole thing and blurred the lines.

Contrast the Celtic bird with the animal

The ibis and the duck (Fig. 125) are interesting because of another shortcut. Body shape is the same, but various species are suggested by altering neck and leg lengths and positions. This standardization makes preparation of blanks quite simple.

Because some animals are so familiar in general outline, it is possible to conventionalize or even alter or distort that outline slightly and still produce a recognizable animal. It is, perhaps, a form of caricature.

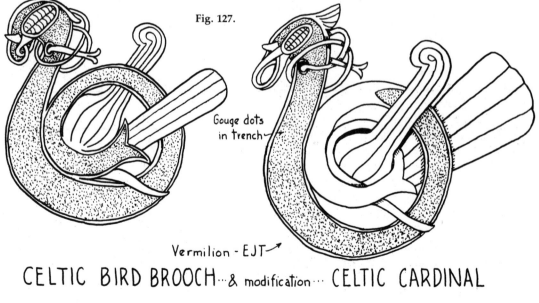

Fig. 127.

Gouge dots in trench

Vermilion - EJT

CELTIC BIRD BROOCH ··· & modification ··· CELTIC CARDINAL

Fig. 128.

ANIMAL PANELS
Shower-curtain designs in Chiapas, Mex.

panels (Fig. 128). These are obviously adapted to incising—mere carving of the outlines on a flat surface—or to shallow bosting and roughing of the background, so the elements stand out. Wavy lines under some of the animals could be incised in either case, and color could be used or the background roughened to increase the contrast. Note that the veiner, which makes these fine lines, is an essential adjunct to either knife or chisels. In fact, these designs offer so many possibilities in interpretation that I copied them from a shower curtain in Mexico—and haven't attempted to carve them as yet. The panels and the cardinal (Fig. 95), incidentally, provide an answer to that perennial question of tyro carvers, "Where can I get new ideas?"

Another example of careful use of texturing to obtain a pleasing effect is the owl from Bali (Fig. 129). It is, of course, a styl-

Veiner details

Ebony - Bali

OWL

Fig. 129.

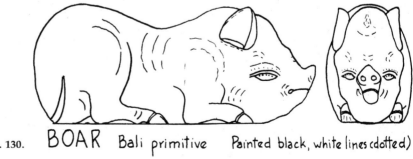

Fig. 130. BOAR Bali primitive   Painted black, white lines (dotted)

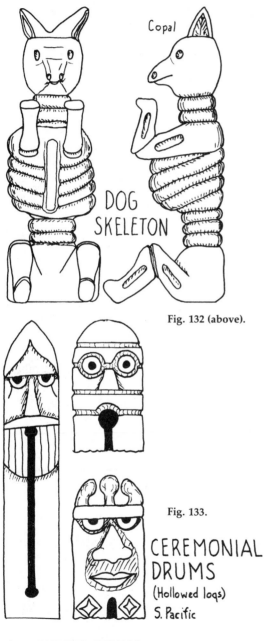

COW SKELETON
Inserted horns & tail-Copal
Fig. 131.

Copal

DOG
SKELETON

Fig. 132 (above).

Fig. 133.

CEREMONIAL
DRUMS
(Hollowed logs)
S. Pacific

ized owl, so its "feathers" are simply outlines. The "rays" around the eyes are used to add emphasis to the eyes and bill as well as to give the "ears" shape. However, a large part of the body is unmarked except for occasional pairs of veiner lines to emphasize the curvature. The boar (Fig. 130) contrasts with it in that it is much more true to life; it has wrinkles and bends and even some white lines painted on it for wrinkles, a seemingly unnecessary addition as far as I am concerned.

Modelling is obviously necessary for the cow and dog skeletons (Figs. 131, 132)—which aren't skeletons at all in reality. The ridges in spine and ribs and the slots in legs suggest a skeleton, which is belied by the complete head. These two, by the way, were made by Indians in the village of San Martín Tilcajete, Oaxaca, Mexico, who are primarily farmers and adobe makers. These Indians have become well known, however, for their carvings of similarly designed human skeletons, popular in Mexico to celebrate the Day of the Dead, November 1. Painting such figures would be rather absurd, even though they are carved in copal, a soft and very white wood.

A stylization somewhat akin to these is the armadillo, from the same town (Fig. 135). Here the carver used knife crosshatching to suggest the scaly coat of the animal, but again used no color. A very elaborate and imaginative sculpture from this town is the two-headed monkey, which is about 10 in (25 cm) high (Fig. 134). I am at a total loss to explain the symbolism, and the carver had nothing to say; he felt it was strong enough to live without explanations.

By Agostino Cruz, in copal

STYLIZED ARMADILLO
Oaxaca. Copal, with knife grooving

Fig. 135.

2-HEADED
MONKEY

Body has "scales"

Serpent

Fig. 134.

Gouge cuts

FISH - Guerrero, Mex.

Fig. 136.

Strangely, he provided scales on the monkey body with random crisscross lines, as well as on the bell of the trumpet-shaped object the monkey is holding, and drilled holes at the base of the dog head and slots in the bell of the trumpet. The result is a conversation piece, if nothing more—and one that was snapped up by a Mexico City collector.

Some carvings almost cry out for strong lines and color. Examples are the ceremonial drums from the South Pacific (Fig. 133). The carving is simple and strong, and only resembles people by coincidence. Actually, these faces represent spirits, and are highly colored in consequence.

Another example of this is the little fish from Guerrero, Mexico (Fig. 136). It is decorated with gouge cuts, but also has stylized color to suggest the trout that inspired it.

The ultimate in present-day stylizing and use of color is the bebek, or dragon duck, from Bali, a ritual object carved with a hidden compartment in its back for prayers to

GIANT DOME TORTOISE
GALAPAGOS ISLANDS, ECUADOR

Fig. 137.

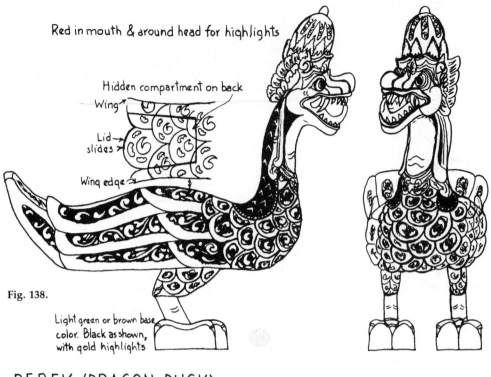

Red in mouth & around head for highlights

Hidden compartment on back

Wing

Lid slides

Wing edge

Fig. 138.

Light green or brown base color. Black as shown, with gold highlights

BEBEK (DRAGON DUCK) Bali Painted

the gods (Fig. 138). It is made in parts and carved in very great detail, then highly colored and gilded. There is no likelihood that it will not be noticed regardless of location, because the original is life-size! Designed for religious purposes, it has become a spot of color in American and other homes far from Bali, largely because it contrasts in boldness with most moderate present-day decoration. It also contrasts sharply with most modern Balinese figure carving, which relies on flowing lines for its effects.

Birds are in style

PREPARING THE BOOK, "Carving Birds in Wood" (Sterling, 1984) apparently stimulated my bird buds or heightened my dormant birdwatching, because I've since found and made a number of birds, all new to me, some species dating back a thousand years and more. Most are Mexican, but some are not, and they embody ideas read-

ily adaptable for any purposes you may have.

First, there are those odd scraps of wood, too small to be useful and too big or of too-good wood to throw away. An enterprising Indian in Michoacan evidently had some, as well as imagination and a band saw or scroll saw. The wood is a hard and dense red-colored one, unknown to me. From those scraps he made a number of amusing birds and animals, none more than 2 in tall. They sold very rapidly in a smart shop a long way from Michoacan. (Fig. 139)

I don't usually *buy* waste wood; I use it. The swan is a case in point. Ted Haag, in Tualatin, Ore., enjoys sending me odd bits of diseased or spalted (partially dry-rotted) wood with an implicit challenge that I recycle them. The latest example is the swan (Fig. 140), whose body is spalted curly broadleaf maple, and whose head and neck are my own knotty and off-color scrap of walnut growth wood. The shape of the

Fig. 139 (right). Five birds, two rabbits and a fox were obviously made from scraps of hardwood. They are Mexican tourist items, so as much as possible of the "carving" has been done with a saw, but designs are one-of-a-kind to fit the scrap and quite imaginative.

Fig. 140 (below, left). Assembled and carved from otherwise useless wood, this swan has considerable "color" from the figure of its walnut growth-wood head and neck and the feather-like coloration of the spalted curly broadleaf-maple body and tail. The spalted (partially dry-rotted) maple block has been "stabilized" by soaking in paraffin, so neck and tail pieces had to be nailed in place.

Fig. 141 (below, right). Here are the rough-sawed walnut head and neck, and the body block of maple, together with another thin section of spalted maple.

3¼ × 5 × 7-in maple intrigued me, but it was weeks before I saw the swan in it. The maple, incidentally, was so near rotted that Ted "stabilized" it by soaking it in hot paraffin, which gives it body and makes it cut easily, but utterly defies glue and finish when you make an assembly. I made one anyhow—with finishing nails supplementing the glue and such finish as I could obtain over wax, which is a finish in itself.

Mexican examples come from Apaseo el Alto, Guanajuato, where I visited a family "carving factory," Tonalá, Jalisco, which has recently produced a number of very color-

Fig. 142. Korean wedding drake (see "Carving Birds in Wood" for details). This was probably the inspiration for the swan, which has now been equipped with a double gilt tassel.

Figs. 143, 144 (below). These miniature birds are from designs in ceramic of the Acoma, New Mexico, pueblo. They are finished with black-painted lines, but could be done with carved lines. Note the reversed head of the bobwhite and the tricky eye designation.

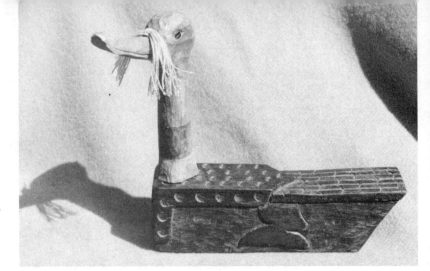

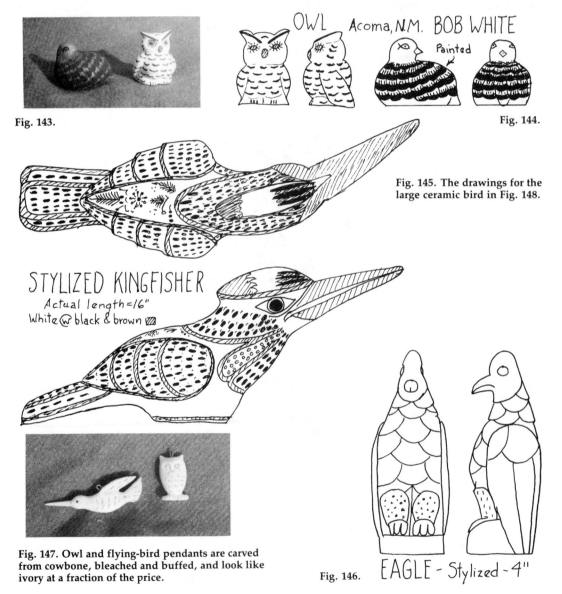

Fig. 143.

OWL   Acoma, N.M.   BOB WHITE

Painted

Fig. 144.

Fig. 145. The drawings for the large ceramic bird in Fig. 148.

STYLIZED KINGFISHER
Actual length = 16"
White w/ black & brown

Fig. 147. Owl and flying-bird pendants are carved from cowbone, bleached and buffed, and look like ivory at a fraction of the price.

Fig. 146.   EAGLE - Stylized - 4"

Fig. 148. One of a series of large (16-in-long) ceramic birds, this stylized kingfisher particularly appealed to me as a woodcarving design. Compare it with a picture of an actual kingfisher in a guide book to learn the elements of caricaturing other, more common birds.

ful stylized birds recognizable by species, and two very ancient examples in pottery that I copied in wood—the originals are in the Rockefeller Wing of the Metropolitan Museum of Art in New York City. The two, interestingly, were both ducks, indicating that the current rage for decoys has ancient ancestry. Incidentally, do not dismiss pottery as a source of carving patterns; the tiny 1½-in owl and bobwhite (Figs. 143, 144), as well as the stylized kingfisher (Figs. 145, 148), were also originally in pottery, the first two in New Mexico and the third in Mexico. These three are the only ones for which I have suggested color, although the Olmec and Colima ducks undoubtedly once had color too over their pottery.

Mexicans are adept at substituting cow bone for ivory in such pieces as the owl and bird pendants (Fig. 147). The owl pictured is 1¼ in tall, the flying bird twice that in length. Bone can be bleached and polished by buffing until it looks very much like ivory, and can be carved with similar detail.

In a visit to a "factory" in Apaseo el Alto, I uncovered three birds which are not part of the family's regular production of carousel horses of all sizes from 4 in to 4 ft tall. As nearly as I could discover, all were experimental designs, and one of a kind, practically speaking, although I did find two similar ducks, both only slightly stylized. The dove (Fig. 150) has an inflated body and small head, a stylized wing and an ex-

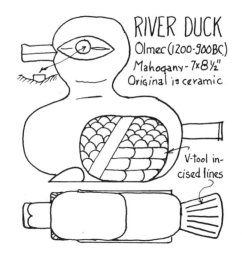

RIVER DUCK
Olmec (1200-900 BC)
Mahogany - 7x8½"
Original is ceramic

V-tool incised lines

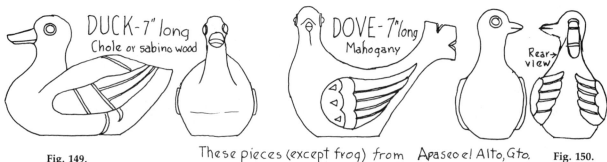

Fig. 149.

DUCK - 7" long
Chole or sabino wood

DOVE - 7" long
Mahogany

Rear view

These pieces (except frog) from Apaseo el Alto, Gto.

Fig. 150.

Fig. 151 (left). I thought this Olmeo river duck, originally a ceramic jar with a hole in the top of the head, was quite an interesting design so I copied it in available Honduras mahogany 7 in tall. The original is dated 1200 to 900 B.C.—so this is a 3,000-year-old decorative decoy.

Fig. 152. This puff-cheeked and ball-bodied duckling is from Colima and dated the second or third century A.D. Note the stub tail and the merely suggested feet, plus a bell-shaped mouth. The original was a container with a hole in the top of the head.

tended trefoil tail. The eagle (Fig. 146) has completely stylized feathering and a lengthened head which contributes to his morose or doleful look.

Also apparently from Michoacan is the road runner (Fig. 153), an obvious concession to ease of quantity manufacture from sawed planks, because his body is 5 × 13 in but only 2½ in thick. The eye is a double inlay of ebony within a lighter-colored

Fig. 153. Also a Mexican tourist item is this life-size road runner. Eyes are inlaid and decoration is a series of cuts with a circular saw on crest, wings and tail. A base replaces the normally difficult creation of feet and legs.

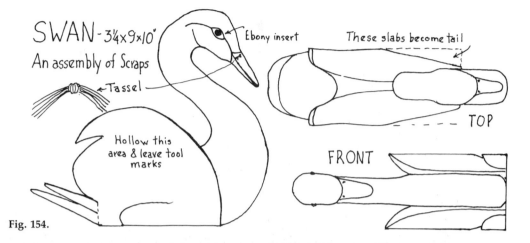

SWAN - 3¼ x 9 x 10"

An assembly of Scraps

Ebony insert

← Tassel

Hollow this area & leave tool marks

These slabs become tail

TOP

FRONT

Fig. 154.

Fig. 155. Potential "factory" designs are these three birds from Apaseo el Alto, Mexico, the dove in a local mahogany, and the other two in woods unknown to me.

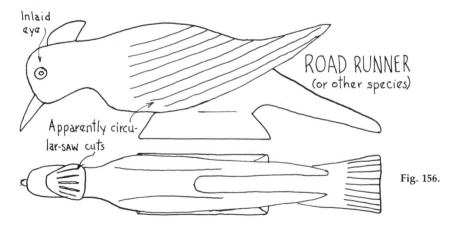

Inlaid eye

ROAD RUNNER
(or other species)

Apparently circular-saw cuts

Fig. 156.

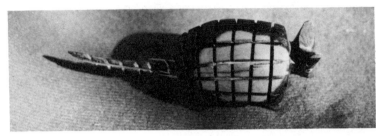

Figs. 157, 158 (left and below). Stylized armadillo from Mexico. Tail is inserted, as is typical.

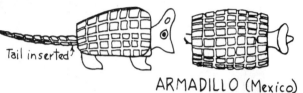

ARMADILLO (Mexico)
Granadillo

wood, and the decoration on crest, wings and tail is a series of grooves cut with a circular saw. However, he is in a good wood and well polished.

The swan (Fig. 154) is an example of serendipity: the unusual shape of the body block suggested the design. In a sense, he is also a variation of the blocky Korean wedding ducks (Fig. 142), of which I have made—and sold—more than a dozen, and can be adorned with a similar double tassel at the base of his bill—or so my wife has decided.

All of these birds are stylized to a greater or lesser degree, of course; neither the Indians nor I seem particularly interested in carving from life, although they have better opportunities than I do to study their subjects. Also, in sharp contrast to their tendency to paint animal carvings, the painted bird is a rarity except for cheap miniature decoys produced for the American market.

Caricaturing and stylizing animals

THE BASIC RULE OF CARICATURE, as opposed to crudity, is that the designer emphasizes—subtly—true characteristics and peculiarities of a particular subject. It is much the same with stylizing; you formalize and simplify the distinguishing characteristics without destroying the overall semblance of the original. Stylizing, however, stresses general shape and form at the expense of detail, while caricature highlights notable features of a given subject and, thus *adds* detail. In either case, you must be familiar with the subject. Lengthening the long neck of a giraffe is not enough; the head and stance must be a giraffe's as well. A pig's snout and tail must be accompanied by the

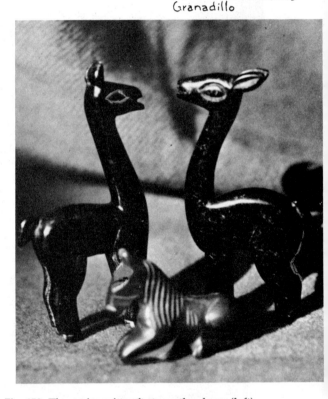

Fig. 159. Three pieces in soft stone, the alpaca (left) and llama in soapstone—from Chile—and the pony in red feldspar (Brazil). All three are polished; none has rough or hard edges.

stocky body and some suggestion of a difference in attitude from that of a giraffe.

The figures shown here come from many places and are done in many different ways. Some are from Latin America, where life is still comparatively simple, where the

Fig. 160. Monolithic and stylized, this life-size duck was in a shop in Java. The body is fine-lined all over, with a few ruffled wing and tail feathers projecting. Eyes are carved, not glass, and the entire bird is tinted in soft colors.

Fig. 161. Heraldic lion by Domingo Fernandez Rimachi, self-taught Indian carver of Cuzco, Peru. Wood is cedar, and the piece is about 18 in (46 cm) tall, a decorative boss. Note that the mane is elaborately detailed although stylized, and that six front-leg claws are shown instead of eight.

carver is still quite familiar with nature and unaffected by the artificiality and sophistication that warps our sense of humor. Some are meticulously detailed, such as the wood armadillo in Figs. 158, 159 (compared with Fig. 135), while others, like the alpaca in Fig. 160, are virtually stripped of it. The heraldic lion from Peru (Fig. 161) still retains a great deal of realism, though the shapes have been simplified and formalized. By comparison, T. E. Haag's *Cat and the Fiddle* and *Adder and Eve* (Figs. 164, 165) retain only the barest suggestion of the original subject—but it is there nevertheless.

Fig. 162. Owl from Guerrero is in strongly grained granadillo, and has inserted beak and double-insert eyes that characterize pieces from this area. "Ears" have drilled holes and the claws are delineated, though feathers are not even suggested.

The owl and cat caricatures in Figs. 162, 163 have painted-on comic features. The other animals in Fig. 166, all from Argentina, also have painted eyes and pupils—black for a male, red for a female—and a silhouette effect enhanced by using a thicker block for the body. The cat even has

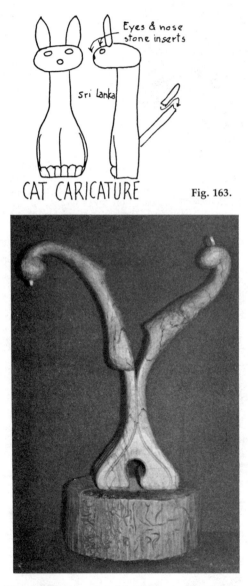

CAT CARICATURE   **Fig. 163.**

the suggestion of a smile—a smile, but not a horse laugh. Remember: Something must be left to the observer's imagination, something that will repay his observation by stirring an emotion (usually humor). The stirring should not be done with a club, as is so often the case.

Bull and fawn (Figs. 167 and 168), from Spain, show excellent stylizing. The bull breathes power, the fawn airiness. Both rely on simple sawn silhouettes to convey their characteristics; the bull is thick, with horns ready, while the fawn is carved thin and leaping. Very little shaping has been done on the fawn, and none on the bull. And both abandon rigid reliance on wood. You'll notice that the fawn's tail is a bit of rough cord, frayed, and that the bull has inserted silver-strip horns and tail. Now compare these to the penguin in Fig. 169, which uses sharp contrast for its effectiveness. The simple form is painted to simulate the

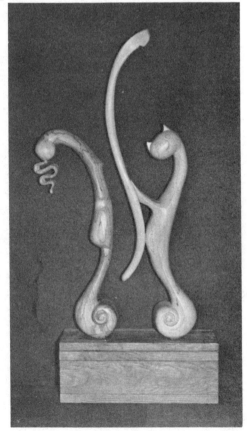

Fig. 165 (above and right). "Adder and Eve" and "Cat and the Fiddle," by T. E. Haag, Tualatin, Oregon. Though extremely stylized, subjects are still identifiable because basic elements such as bosom and bottom, fiddle-string ends and ears are emphasized.

Fig. 166. Three Argentinian animal caricatures have the same painted-in eyes, the cat's with blue lids! They are assembled sawed pieces, but could readily be modelled.

Fig. 167 (above). Stylized bull from Spain is in a dark, grainy wood. It is 6½ in (17 cm) overall, with inserted silver horns and flat tail. There is no detailing.

Fig. 168 (left). Spanish fawn is in olive wood, so grain is very prominent. It is quite stylized, but very whimsical, having a bit of cord for a tail and prominent downcast eyes.

Figs. 169 (above, left to right). Penguin by Ted Haag is a simple form, with no detailing except the black painting to simulate the darker feathering. It is 4 in (10 cm) high.

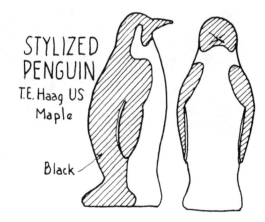

STYLIZED PENGUIN
T.E. Haag US
Maple

Black

Fig. 170. This spreadwing bird in ironwood has only a suggestion of feathering and a streamlined body.

darker feathers; again, there is no detailing, not even an eye.

The Seri-Indian-carved birds and fish in ironwood (Figs. 170, 171) are unusual and compelling because they are readily identifiable. The shapes are realistic, but only a minimum of detail is included so that form and the beauty of the polished wood become most important.

What is considered over-detailing in one country is often the essence of stylizing in another. Americans think 30 to 50 percent of a surface is enough carving, the Italians go to 80 percent or thereabouts, and the East Indians go to 100 percent. Consider the Japanese temple carvings in Figs. 172, 173. They are 200 years old and include fanciful

as well as real animals. They are very definitely stylized, particularly in the fantastic waves and ground growth, but also include much more detail than anyone would use nowadays, even the Japanese. It is hard to avoid over-detailing—take it from an ex-engineer!

With a little experience and effort, you can do your own stylized carvings and have fun at them. The primary requirement is to study your subject to find out what is different or dominant about it, and then to combine those elements in a pleasing design—with smooth, long curves and lines. The little variations are eliminated, and geometric shapes can then be substituted.

Fig. 171. A 12-in (30-cm) Sailfish in ironwood emphasizes the dorsal fin, which shows ribbing.

Figs. 172, 173 (above and below). Extremely elaborate stylizing is evident in these two sections of temple carving in Honso, Akita, Japan. Done about 200 years ago, it includes dragons in stylized waves and a tortoise amid mushrooms and reeds, all originally tinted. Photographs are by Donald P. Berger, an American teaching in Tokyo.

Why not a cat?

CATS ARE a neglected carving subject, for some reason. Pasht, the cat-headed goddess holding a sistrum, was familiar in ancient Egypt and the cat was also a frequent element in sculpture there. But, although cats are quite familiar pets in the United States, one rarely sees a carving of one. I know of only one carver who frequently carves kittens, Hope Brown of Brasstown, N.C., and she does a very good job of it. In years of travel to foreign countries, I recall seeing only a few cat carvings, one or two in Mexico, a caricature in Sri Lanka, and a stylized-cat cardholder in Israel.

The infrequent cat carvings in foreign countries are understandable; in many countries cats are scarce as well. In Haiti, as a gruesome example, my landlady had two cats which she kept caged; earlier ones had disappeared by way of poor and meat-starved neighbors. Here there are many cats, cat shows and even cat-owners' magazines, but few cat carvings, possibly because most cat lovers are women and most carvers are men. Probably more important

Fig. 174 (left). This cat with hanging tail was carved by a skilled Mexican for sale in a West Coast art shop. The shaping and tinting were exceptional. Horsehair was used for whiskers.

Fig. 175 (above). Sitting cats from the Southern Highlands. The one on the right is a better-proportioned, more-natural pose. Both are in cherry, whittled and sanded.

Fig. 177 (below). This 6-in kitten in walnut was an early effort of mine—at least 40 years ago. It is just passable.

PERCHING SIAMESE Mexico

Horse hairs

Stands here

Fig. 179.

3 SILHOUETTES

Fig. 178. This kitten face provides a good indication of the triangular head shape and relatively low eye location.

Fig. 180. This caricature was turned out in quantity some years back in Sri Lanka (Ceylon). The tail and ears were carved separately and inserted, as were moonstone eyes and nose, although the cat is only about 2 in tall. Also see Fig. 163.

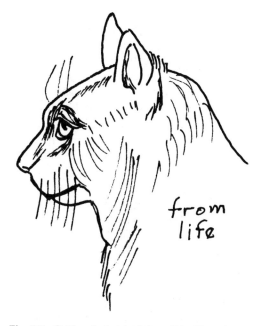

from life

Fig. 181. Cat head sketched from life. Note the blunt face, low and forward-faced eyes, perky ears, receding lower jaw. The mature cat has feeler hairs in its eyebrows as well as around the mouth. Hair direction is also suggested here, in case you are carving a head large enough for such detail.

is the fact that a cat is very difficult to carve well, although this argument breaks down in the face of the number of carvings of other members of the cat tribe: lions, leopards, jaguars, tigers, mountain lions. All offer the same basic problems in carving, so why the big cats in greater profusion? This is understandable in countries where lions are almost worshipped, as in Africa, or jaguars, as in parts of Mexico.

The fact is that if you can carve a good cat, you can carve any of the others. The lion has a larger nose, a bigger head, and heavier forelegs than any of the others. The leopard has a longer nose, as does the puma. Our domestic cat carries its tail high when prowling; all the other cats carry theirs low—but these are minor differences in shape, just as are the male lion's mane and the leopard's spots.

The cat's hind legs appear to be longer than the forelegs and are much heavier in musculature. The fur is usually thick enough to hide and round the skeletal shape, yet fine enough that it cannot be suggested successfully except in very large carvings. On any small carving it is best to consider the cat's shape as a series of curves and its fur is best depicted by a smooth, even glossy, surface. Body lines at best are indistinct, and there is danger that they will be overemphasized as most carvers overemphasize the wrinkles on a human face.

The cat head is quite round in back, but from the front it has a distinctly triangular shape, with the point of the chin and the ears forming the angles. The ears are quite pert usually, but are *not* pointed at the tips; they are actually delicately rounded. Also, the front of the jaw is quite narrow, although the face itself is very blunt when viewed from the side. Study the sketch of a cat head (Fig. 181) and the frontal view of the kitten-pin silhouette (Fig. 179). Note that the eyes are not high on the head and around to the side as they are in rabbits and deer—those animals have to expect attack from the sides, rear and even above. A cat does not, so its eyes are almost centered on

KITTENS Buckeye Hope Brown

Fig. 182. Hope Brown's curled-up kittens from the Campbell Folk School are sketched here for comparison with the Siamese cat head in Fig. 178, the Siamese in Fig. 174, and the sleeper in Fig. 177.

carver of one cat pictured did, and he added another fillip: he projected the tail below the foot line, so his cat can be displayed only by being placed on the edge of a shelf—which makes it look very natural (Fig. 174). The Mexicans also use horsehair on their jaguar heads, plus horse teeth on larger mask sizes. The result is considerable realism. My suggestion is that you study a cat when opportunity offers; note the differences in the way a cat and a dog sit, stand, lie down. Study the head shape— and go to it!

Dogs and horses are popular

MANY PEOPLE WHO HAVE PETS or favorite animals are interested in having likenesses, not of the breed or species, but of their particular animal, particularly if that favorite is getting old. And animals are as individual as humans when you study them; each varies a little from the norm, and the owner or admirer is very conscious of those variations.

I remember two of my early attempts at likenesses of animals almost 50 years ago. One was an Arabian mare, the other a bulldog, and I pictured them in my first book, *Whittling and Woodcarving* (Dover), in 1936. In each case the owner provided profile pictures or the equivalent, but I learned that it requires several photographs, and preferably a chance to study the animal, if you are going to get a likeness that will satisfy the proud admirer. What's more, an animal anatomy book will provide you with some basic understanding of skeleton and musculature that photographs often obscure because of the lighting or the animal's pelt.

I have reproduced these early likenesses here. "Honey Girl" (Fig. 183) was in mahogany and mounted on walnut. Note how the grain helped show the swell of the neck. "Bill" (Fig. 184) was also in mahogany and similarly mounted. Both had leather additions, the harness finished with silver buckle and snaffle, and the collar a section of an actual dog collar with brass nameplate and chain. I think the leather harness

the skull (as human eyes are) from the front, and they also face front and are only about an eye-width apart.

The final problem in depicting a cat are those long whiskers. I have tried to suggest them by incised lines on the upper lip (Fig. 178), but this is a subterfuge at best. The Mexicans have done better. They actually drill small holes in the upper lip and insert individual horsehairs. They can also thus suggest the feeler hairs projecting from a cat's eyebrows. That's what the skilled

Fig. 183. I carved this mahogany-on-walnut portrait of Honey Girl, a prize-winning Arab mare, almost 50 years ago. Harness is cut from thin leather and fittings are silver.

Fig. 184. Bill was an aging bulldog. I carved him from mahogany and, again, used a walnut base for mounting. Collar is a section of a real one chained to the brass plaque with a screweye. The head is about 3 in (8 cm) tall.

Fig. 185.

Fig. 186.

MAMSELLE - Female long-haired St. Bernard — Basswood

Figs. 185–187. Mamselle, a female St. Bernard, was carved in basswood and painted with oils. Some knife lines were left and some paint rubbed thin to retain the idea of wood. Fig. 185 shows one of a series of photos I took to try to get the lifted foot and tail the owner wanted. Dog was carved integrally with base, which was then appliquéd on a rosewood base block.

added something, but the dog collar was a bit overpowering, and I'm fairly certain that if either carving is still extant, the leather trim has rotted away. No trim, or a carved harness or collar from the solid, would have been better. Both were, however, finished with low gloss, of which I'm proud.

In this section are additional examples of dogs, which are the most popular subjects. The female St. Bernard (Figs. 185–187) is in the round, and desk-size, 6 in (15 cm) long, finished with oils, while the setter panel (Figs. 188, 189) is natural-finish except for the darkened or antiqued background. The

Figs. 188, 189. Walnut panel of Ludi, a seven-year-old Irish Setter, is ¾ × 11 × 12 in (1.9 × 28 × 30 cm) overall. It was carved by Hugh Minton, Jr., of Aiken, South Carolina. Much of the carving and all of the texturing was done with palm tools; background was then antiqued with walnut stain to make the head stand out.

Fig. 188.

Fig. 189.

setter was carved by a student who previously had used the knife almost exclusively, while this carving was done mostly with palm gouges.

Although a St. Bernard and a schnauzer (Figs. 190–196) should be relatively alike in difficulty, hence in time to carve, I found the schnauzer twice as difficult. One factor was size, another the wood, and hence the texture and finish. I had photographs of both dogs, and each pattern had to be a composite of elements in several photographs. But the schnauzer, cowed by the camera, never did strike the basic "show" pose of the breed that his mistress wanted; I had to adapt that from a magazine picture of another dog. Also, he had normal ears, not lopped ones, and he carried both ears and tail down because of his concern over the photography. I decided on myrtle wood because of its grey-white color, very much like that of the dog, instead of painted white pine or basswood, so that added complications. As completed, the carving required only a slight tinting around the jowls to get the characteristic head coloration and likeness, and is much more realistic and natural than the St. Bernard portrait.

Figs. 190–193. Rarely will one photograph depict exactly the personality and peculiarities of a particular animal. The one above shows body shape and proper ear pose. Myrtle wood gave coloration quite close to the dog's, while touching up nose tip with black, eyes with brown and eyebrows and face hair with gray (below) created a recognizable and individual portrait. White pigment was also tipped on feathery hairs of lower legs.

Fig. 191.

Fig. 192.

Fig. 193.

Getting a likeness

IN ANY LIKENESS of a pet, you must be conscious not only of the visual distinctions to your untrained eye, but also to the real or imagined distinctions that the owner sees, particularly those he or she considers important. Thus a schnauzer is supposed to have a hollow under his belly that accentuates his chest curvature, coloration around the muzzle, a definite goatee line around the mouth, a forward and alert pitch of the ears, a straight back and multiple-curved hind-leg line, etc.

These elements are essential to a likeness because the client sees his animal ideally. You, as a stranger, will rarely see all these things together, and are even less likely to capture them in photographs. Also, photos

Figs. 194–196. Here is another recognizable study of the dog, this one a caricature rather than a likeness. Eyes, eyebrows and nose are emphasized; face hair is only suggested. Because this is low relief rather than in-the-round, some contours must be accentuated and others played down as seen in the next two stages of carving. Note knot in center of forehead and check running down nose from it. Both were filled with glue and sawdust, then sanded and tinted to match adjacent wood.

Fig. 195.

Fig. 196.

are two-dimensional; you have a third dimension to recreate, usually by trial and error. In this case, the block was half of the original 7-in-diameter (17.5-cm) tree trunk, so I had to guess at the proper thickness to saw the blank.

The schnauzer has a more complex head shape than the St. Bernard, and the difference in wood is also a delaying factor. But the major expenditure of extra time was in the meticulous texturing of the dog's pelt, which was done with small veiner and

fluter and took almost a day and a half. The eyes, set deeply behind shaggy brows, and the feathery character of the lower legs, also took extra time to achieve.

I mention all these things to draw the contrast between a likeness and a simple depiction. It is reinforced by the low-relief head of the same dog I carved from the remainder of the slab of myrtle—about 6 × 6 × 1 in (15 × 15 × 2.5 cm) at its thickest (Fig. 196). This head was laid out by eye alone (no laborious squares or point-to-point), sawed to a rough silhouette, and shaped with a ½-in (12.7-mm) flat gouge while held to the bench with a carver's screw. The rough shape of the head was achieved in about an hour, and the head was finished with smaller gouges and a V-tool in a few hours more, or less than a fourth of the time required for the scaled likeness.

Perhaps to anyone except the owner, the head is as dramatic and interesting as the full dog, even though its proportions are not exact. The left eye, for example, is set too deeply, texturing is rough and only suggestive, and the mouth and nose are not detailed. These examples emphasize the differences between a quick study and a portrait.

Fig. 200. The Bonkura horse is made in various materials and sizes in northern India; it is a stylization of an old time warrior's horse or a trader's horse, according to different stories.

Fig. 197.

PRANCING HORSE
Cherry –Jack Hall

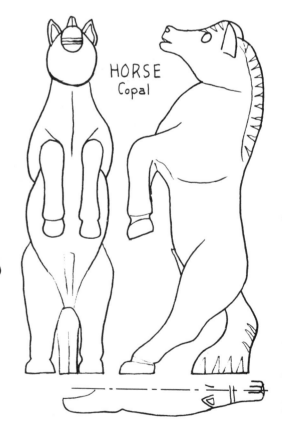

HORSE
Copal

Figs. 198, 199. A horse in cherry by the skilled Jack Hall and one by a Mexican Indian. Note contrasts in proportions. (See Fig. 204)
(Circus horses can be found in Appendix I.)

Fig. 201. Two running horses by Eric Zimmerman in curly buckeye wood.

Fig. 202. Mexican caricature, 4 in (10 cm) and Chinese horse 2 in (5 cm).

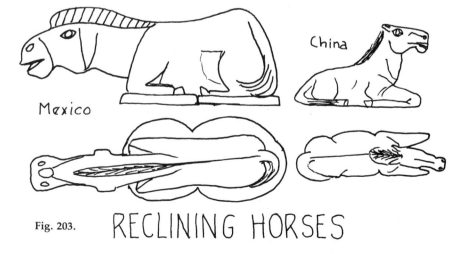

Mexico

China

Fig. 203.   RECLINING HORSES

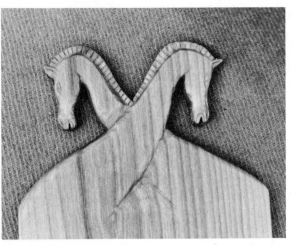

Fig. 204. Cherry prancing horse sketched in Fig. 198, an original by the late Jack Hall.

Fig. 205. Small size breadboard in cherry with stylized horse motif. By the author.

Fig. 206. Commemorative relief panel in walnut, based—in part—on an old silhouette.

A dinosaur mobile

MOBILES can be interesting whittling projects for a number of reasons. They are flexible in number of elements, size and composition. Elements may be alike or different, and need not all be of one wood. A mobile can offer an opportunity to work, compare and display a variety of woods. Further, the number of elements is up to you. I chose dinosaurs as an unlikely subject, because they varied so in shape and size and because relatively little is known about them.

Wood can be selected for color and figure, because dinosaur colors are not known anyway. I also disregarded relative time and size of species, so they are not in scale and species may have lived millennia apart.

SABRE-TOOTH TIGER

EARLY TAPIR (?)

Egg-laying dinosaur

PROTOCERATOPS & EGG

3/8" dowel

STEGOSAURUS

TRACHODON

TRICERATOPS

DIPLODOCUS
(Largest - 50 tons)

PTERANODON

ERYOPS

Main whiffletree - 1 req'd, 9" long
(Music wire retains natural curve from coil)

UNITS FOR A DINOSAUR MOBILE (Above)

NEANDERTHAL MAN

TYRANNOSAURUS

3" whiffletree - 2 req'd

2" whiffletree 2 req'd

4" whiffletree - 2 req'd

Fig. 207.

GLYPTODONT

Some of the figures were carved in the round, but some were flattened to catch vagrant breezes and because only thin scraps were available.

I used vermilion for the stegosaurus, jelutong for the man, rosewood for the pteranodon, mansonia for the sabre-tooth tiger, and an unknown wood from a Vietnamese crate for the trachodon. This was to test these woods in comparison with the teak of the triceratops, the maple dowel that gives a starting shape for the egg, and purpleheart for the big diplodocus, largest of the dinosaurs.

UNITS FOR ADDITIONAL ARMS

These designs are adapted from sketches in "National Geographic" magazine for August, 1978, which show more details

STRUTHIOMIMUS 80,000,000 yrs.

PLATEOSAURUS 225,000,000 yrs.

Flat-gouge scallops

Spurs

ANKYLOSAURUS 135,000,000 yrs.

TARBOSAURUS 135,000,000 yrs.

195,000,000 yrs.

MEGALOSAURUS

65,000,000 yrs.

CORYTHOSAURUS

IGUANODON 135,000,000 yrs.

STRUTHIOMIMUS (Running alternate)

ANATOSAURUS 65,000,000 yrs.

ARCHEOPTERYX 140,000,000 yrs.
(Oldest known bird)

Fig. 208.

Purpleheart, by the way, is extremely hard—somewhat like ebony, but not as brittle—and has occasional checks and faults. These secrete a black dust which must be cleaned out before gluing or filling. The wood itself is an ordinary brown, but lengthy exposure to the sun turns it lavender. Heating it in the oven can turn it anything from lavender to a dark purple, with thinner sections darkening first. Mansonia, by contrast, is a tannish-brown wood that splits and splinters easily, somewhat like some mahoganies, but it finishes very well.

Figures were finished without sanding, because the small planes left by the knife will reflect light. Figures were sprayed with Krylon® matte varnish to keep them clean, but finish, at least of harder woods, can simply be wax if you prefer. To suspend them, I drilled small holes at the center of gravity and glued in eyes bent from straight pins. The proper point for suspension can easily be determined by a little trial and error with a pin. Monofilament nylon makes a good suspension thread, but must be double-knotted and glued to keep the knots tight. Initial length of the nylon should be about a foot, to allow for later adjustment.

At this point, you must decide whether you prefer a wide mobile or a long one, and cut whiffletrees (balance beams) to suit. I wanted one that was longer than its width, so my top whiffletree was 10 in (25 cm) long, eye to eye. Piano wire makes good whiffletrees, because it comes off the coil with a good natural curve and because it is polished; this tends to delay corrosion. It is also, of course, much stiffer than other wire of similar diameter. I used No. 18 wire (0.041-in [1 mm] diameter) for the long whiffletree and No. 10 (0.024 in [0.6mm]) for the smaller ones, but any similar sizes will do. The wire may have to be sawed, then should be filed smooth on the ends and bent with gooseneck pliers. Eyes should be small and closed tight, or you will be plagued with nylon threads slipping out during adjustment and assembly.

Begin assembly from the bottom. The general principle is to pair off two elements of approximately equal weight, one tall and one wide, and differing in color if possible. The wide one must clear the support thread for the tall one, or be hung below it. Leave the threads long and double-knot or slip-knot them at the whiffletree, because single knots will promptly loosen and come free. Considering that the whiffletrees are relatively heavy compared with the figures, they will actually make balance easier. This is important, because even the usual postal scale will not read accurately enough to get exact weights of the elements and it is preferable to have the whiffletree hang almost horizontal to keep the threads it supports at maximum distance apart. Knot a thread over the center of the whiffletree and move it until the elements below it balance, then glue it in place.

Assemble the second short whiffletree in the same way. If your mobile is to be wide, you'll tend to balance two elements against two. If it is to be long, you'll tend to balance two elements against a single one on the medium-length whiffletrees. Other whiffletree assemblies are made just as the first one was. A particularly heavy element may have to hang alone, or be balanced by a light element hung from the center of a smaller whiffletree supporting two others. I did this with the man, the pteranodon, and the diplodocus. This also serves to fill in otherwise open areas of the mobile and make it look busier in motion.

Hang the rough-assembled mobile from a ceiling hook or a projecting arm. I use a dowel stuck under books on a bookshelf at shoulder level, a convenient height, and check elements for interference, as well as the general "look" of the mobile. Usually, interference can be corrected by raising or lowering one of the two elements that collide. You may want to shorten all suspensions to make the mobile more compact. This is a matter of taste, location and strength of likely breezes—the longer the threads, the more likely they are to tangle if the wind is fresh. My mobile is about 14 in

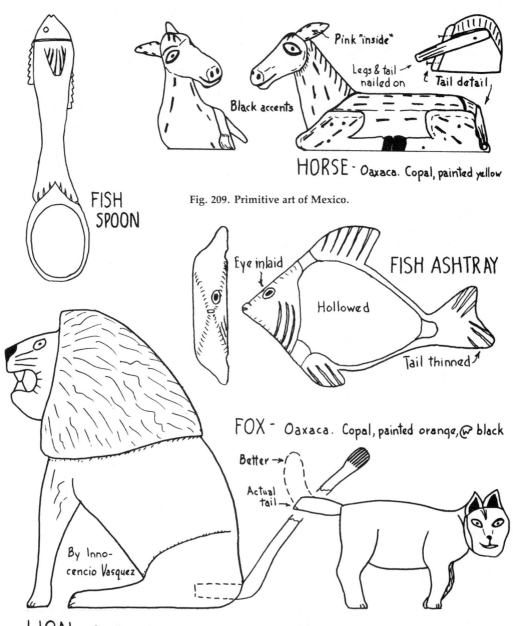

FISH SPOON

HORSE - Oaxaca. Copal, painted yellow

Pink "inside"

Legs & tail nailed on

Tail detail

Black accents

Fig. 209. Primitive art of Mexico.

Eye inlaid

FISH ASHTRAY

Hollowed

Tail thinned

FOX - Oaxaca. Copal, painted orange, @ black

Better →

Actual tail →

By Inno-cencio Vasquez

LION - Oaxaca. Copal. Painted yellow, with black lines

(35 cm) wide by 2 ft (61 cm) deep. You may even have to change the length of a whiffletree, particularly if you have many elements in the mobile. When everything is adjusted, glue the knots and spray the assembly with varnish to inhibit rusting of whiffletrees. Also trim off loose ends of the nylon threads.

After about a year, I felt that I wanted additional elements in my mobile. Just about that time, there was an extensive story in the *National Geographic* about recent dinosaur discoveries. So I added two more arms to the mobile (one long whiffletree) to accommodate an additional nine elements. These were in additional woods: ankylosaurus in Virginia cedar 8,000 years old, iguanodon in maple, plateosaurus in red-

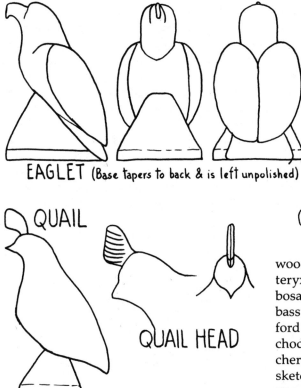

EAGLET (Base tapers to back & is left unpolished)

OWL   Base left rough

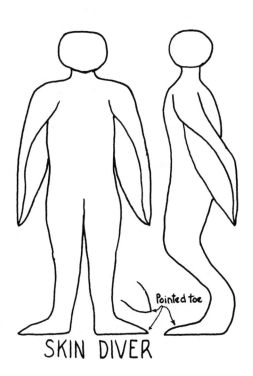

QUAIL

QUAIL HEAD

Fig. 210. Primitive art of Mexico.

Pointed toe

SKIN DIVER

wood, megalosaurus in shedua, archaeopteryx in pecan, anatosaurus in walnut, tarbosaurus in chinkapin, corythosaurus in basswood, and struthiomimus in Port Orford cedar. (In the original group, trachodon was in pine, tyrannosaurus in cherry and protoceratops in oak.) I have sketched a running struthiomimus in case you want a long and narrow element, but his legs can be a real problem to carve unless you select a hard and largely nonsplitting wood for the figure. Assembly of this group is similar to the preceding one, except that in these figures I used tiny silver eyebolts instead of bent pins.

(8" high)

PELICAN (Base left rough)

Fig. 211. Primitive art of Mexico.

Struthiomimus, by the way, apparently lived off eggs laid by other dinosaurs, so what he is clutching is such an egg, which was simply a long oval.

Mobiles can be quite simple. To make a "hostess present" in Mexico, I found a ¼ × 1 × 15-in (0.63 × 2.5 × 38-cm) slat of pine on the street, and whittled five birds from it, entirely freehand and of no particular species. They were suspended from white sewing thread through holes drilled with a knifeblade tip. The whiffletrees were thin copper wire from a nearby electric-motor repair shop. Birds and their suspending threads were dyed in bright colors—red, blue, green, brown and gold—in the dye vats at a weaving plant across the street.

Animals of South America

FOLK CARVINGS in wood tend to result from a happy pairing of forests and skill; either alone is not enough. Thus, in all of South America, there is little folk carving except in the Andes Mountains of western Bolivia, southern Ecuador, and northern Peru (which was also southern Ecuador until Peru won it, as south Tyrol was once part of Austria). Carvings from this high terrain, regardless of country of origin, are well-formed and smoothly finished; they are not primitive but are obviously made by skilled carvers to familiar patterns attractive to tourists. Subject matter is wide-ranging,

from Indian portraits through religious figures to animals, particularly the llama. Both in-the-round and relief work are done, and mahogany is the preferred material. The exact duplication of design and availability in several sizes suggests profiler roughing for quantity production, but sellers insist this is not true.

Shown here are typical animal designs. Surprisingly, there are no birds. Included are a typical pair of primitive carvings—an anteater and an armadillo—from the Amazon basin in Peru. Drawings of three ancient house posts—over 1,000 years old—from Ica and Paracas, Peru, offer very sharp contrast to the more refined modern pieces.

The llama is the traditional beast of burden, and the source of wool for cloth and meat for food. There are three species, the llama, the alpaca, and the guanaco. Another familiar figure is, of course, the bull.

All of these designs appear to be the products of woodcarving tools, except possibly the Amazon animals and the bull, and they show gouge marks. The Amazon ani-

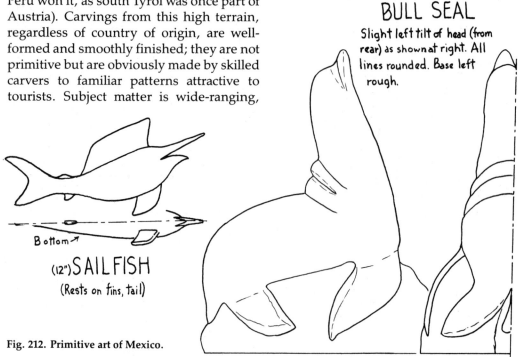

BULL SEAL
Slight left tilt of head (from rear) as shown at right. All lines rounded. Base left rough.

Bottom ↗
(12")SAILFISH
(Rests on fins, tail)

Fig. 212. Primitive art of Mexico.

Fig. 213. Two llamas flank an alpaca. The figure at the left is from Bolivia, the other two from Peru. Woods and facial details are the principal differences. The llama on the left is carved with the base integral, and its legs are foreshortened. Detail is avoided on all three.

mals are painted, then carved, so the natural color of the wood is recovered—a technique that I have seen previously in Fiji and among Australian Bushmen. It is, of course, now in use in the United States and elsewhere for routing name signs in laminated or "sandwich" plastics. It offers ideas for carvers as well.

(Also see Fig. 159.)

Fig. 214. South American designs.

LLAMA Ecuador
INDIAN & LLAMA HEADS Peru (Plaque)

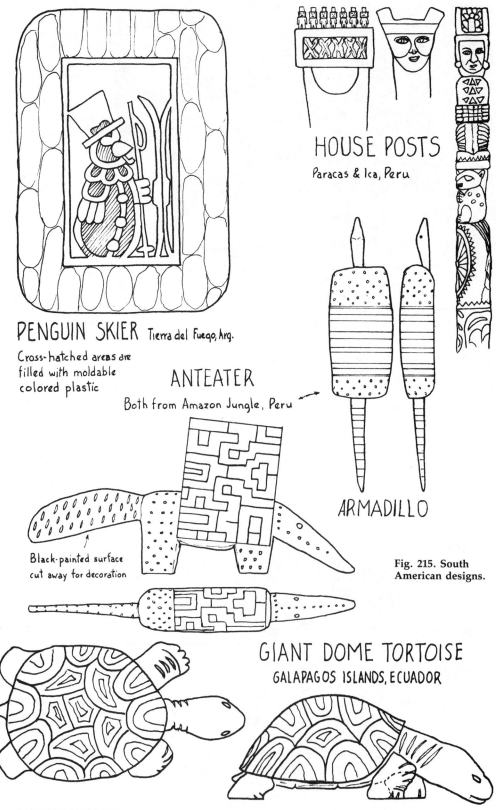

PENGUIN SKIER Tierra del Fuego, Arg.

Cross-hatched areas are filled with moldable colored plastic

HOUSE POSTS
Paracas & Ica, Peru

ANTEATER
Both from Amazon Jungle, Peru

ARMADILLO

Black-painted surface cut away for decoration

Fig. 215. South American designs.

GIANT DOME TORTOISE
GALAPAGOS ISLANDS, ECUADOR

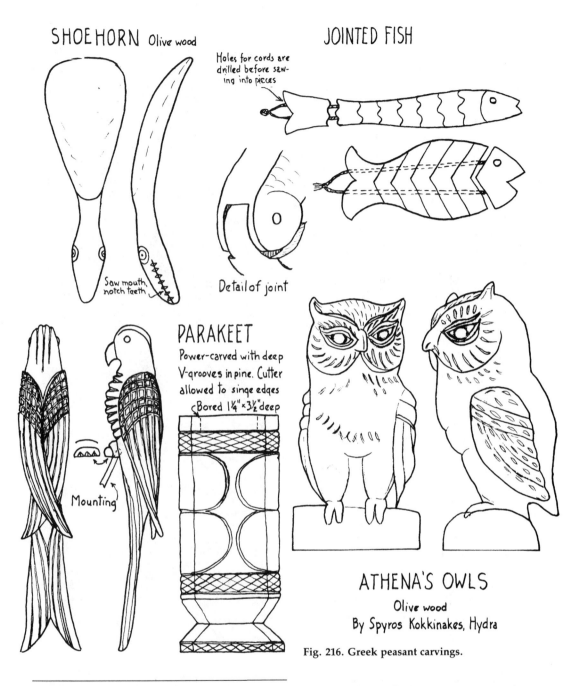

SHOEHORN Olive wood

Saw mouth,
notch teeth

JOINTED FISH

Holes for cords are
drilled before saw-
ing into pieces

Detail of joint

PARAKEET
Power-carved with deep
V-grooves in pine. Cutter
allowed to singe edges
Bored 1¼"×3½" deep

Mounting

ATHENA'S OWLS
Olive wood
By Spyros Kokkinakes, Hydra

Fig. 216. Greek peasant carvings.

Greek peasant carvings

WITH ITS CONSIDERABLE TRADITION in sculpture, one would assume that woodcarving would be common in modern Greece as well. Actually, even carving in stone is uncommon, and practically all of that is copied from classical models. The explanation that Greeks give is that wood is scarce, but in Israel, where the same statement is even truer, there is a great deal of carving. The practical answer is probably that the Israelis have built the craft, while the Greeks have lost it.

The jointed fish suggests a number of possibilities for other designs, although it does involve the problem of small-diameter drilling for almost its total length, and small-diameter drills are also correspondingly short. The holes can be drilled by brazing a shank on the drill bit, or by drilling to available depth, then cutting off sections until the bottoms of the holes are reached, making certain that drill "pits" are left in the stub to provide guides for the next drilling step. Assembly cords are glued into the heads. The principle can of course be applied to articulate snakes, lizards, and some birds.

The parakeet is a quite modern design, and much of the work can be done with power tools if desired. The shape is relatively simple, and the decoration entirely V-grooves, stained or singed by a rotary power cutter for an "antique" effect. A piece like this can be quite crude and still be effective.

The owl designs, made in olive wood on the island of Hydra, are unusually good, in my opinion. Owls were sacred to the goddess Athena, so owl motifs appear in a variety of Greek products, from pottery to wearing apparel, but these are free-standing figures. One of the virtues of the design is that the carver avoided excruciating detail—every feather is *not* delineated; the lines suggest only general areas and directions.

Carve your own trout

A FRIEND ASKED ME to do a leaping trout for his fishing club. We agreed on walnut, partly because I had an air-dried log 7 in (17.5 cm) in diameter and relatively free of checks. I would use a largely vertical pose.

So far, so good. But what about the water? Anyone who has ever caught a trout knows that when he leaps there is more spray than water around him, and any woodcarver knows that spray and clouds are the most difficult elements to portray in carved wood. This time I couldn't evade the problem by mounting the fish, because we both wanted an action pose.

The best answer was to stylize the water in one way or another. The Japanese have

Figs. 217, 218 (top). First rough out portion of the fish above splash level with a carpenter's saw, allowing added thickness for twist in upper body. Portions near base are split out and shaped with a 1-in (2.5-cm) gouge and flat chisel. Upper body is then rough-shaped with 1¼-in (3.2-cm) carpenter's gouge and 1½-in (3.8-cm) low-sweep spade gouge, with block held by carver's screw on a bench edge. Rough outlines of fins are put in with fluter and ¼-and ½-in (6.3- and 12.7-mm) deep gouges. Note early shaping of wave and tail areas.

Fig. 219. Templates of stiff cardboard guide in body shaping and in positioning of elements.

Fig. 220. Tail elements are now shaped and fins defined and fluted. A double row of wavelets in an irregular pattern was developed, with minor undercutting. One-fourth- and ⅝-in (6.3- and 16-cm) low-sweep gouges, veiner, V-tool and several medium-sweep gouges of various widths were used to attain variety in wavelet shape.

done this for some hundreds of years in their temple carvings. They depict water as a sinuous, stylized wave, with small and elaborate curls along its upper surface to suggest spray.

In my carving, the fish had to appear practically free of the water and yet be supported by it, so I designed him as if he'd just delivered a mighty tailslap to the surface to free himself of the snagged hook.

The carving is shown in the step-by-step photographs (Figs. 217–221).

Butterfly mobiles and ornaments

BUTTERFLIES have long been a staple of decorative design (several are on stamps), but they are uncommon in woodcarving, probably because they are so fragile and so wasteful of wood if sculpted from a single piece. However, they do provide an unusual opportunity to display attractive

Fig. 221 (right). Wavelets rise higher in back, since a trout hitting the surface would cause such a pattern. White growth wood in back was carefully retained to suggest spray. Right ventral fin did not project sufficiently and was replaced by a separate fin.

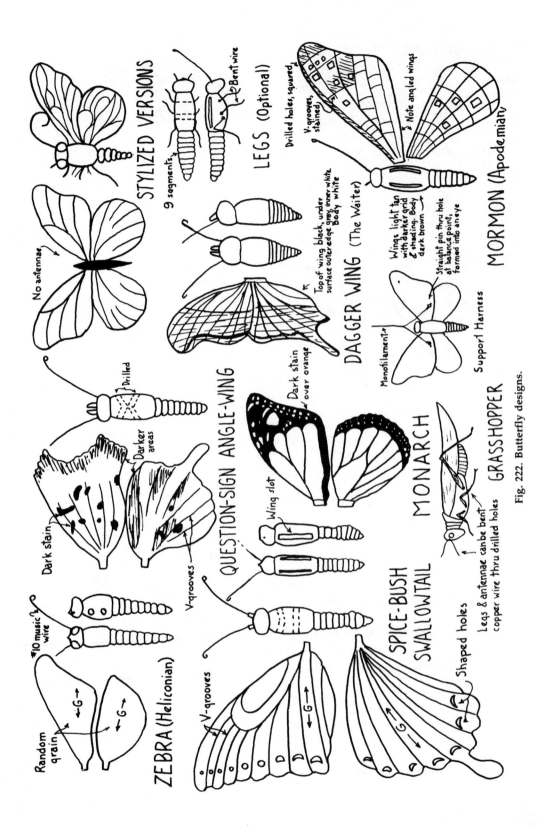

STYLIZED VERSIONS

9 segments

Bent wire

LEGS (Optional)

No antennae

Drilled holes, squared

V-grooves, stained

Note angled wings

MORMON (Apodemian)

Top of wing black, under surface outer edge gray, inner white. Body white

DAGGER WING (The Waiter)

Wings light tan with darker grid & shading. Body dark brown

Straight pin thru hole at balance point, formed into an eye

Monofilament

Support Harness

Drilled

Darker areas

Dark stain over orange

Wing slot

MONARCH

QUESTION-SIGN ANGLE-WING

Dark stain

Random grain

#10 music wire

ZEBRA (Heliconian)

V-grooves

G →

G →

SPICE-BUSH SWALLOWTAIL

Shaped holes

Legs & antennae can be bent copper wire thru drilled holes

GRASSHOPPER

G →

G →

V-grooves

Fig. 222. Butterfly designs.

wood grain or figure, exotic colors, and growth-wood and saw-cut variations because of the large and relatively flat wing areas.

Among the attractive woodcarvings you can make are single-butterfly curtain or drape decorations and three-unit mobiles. Other uses which suggest themselves are adhesive- or magnetic-backed units, pins, pendants, or desk ornaments, because these designs can be almost any size.

I began with two fairly large swallowtails (Fig. 223) in purpleheart, principally because I wanted to experiment with variations in tone and wing position. My wood was ¼-in (25 mm) finished, so I could get four wings from each blank, because wing thickness is less than ⅛ in (3 mm). In this species, the wings are visibly distinct from the body, so I arranged grain to permit whittling ⅛-in (3-mm) pegs at wing termini to fit into corresponding holes in the separate body. Also, this species has some white near the outer edges of the wings, so I drilled holes of suitable sizes, then shaped them with a long-pointed penknife blade. Wings were thinned along the edges to make them appear thinner and more delicate than they really are. The latter proved easier by rotary sanding than by carving because purpleheart is hard and resistant to shaving. Veins in wings were made with parallel knife cuts.

The color in the wood can be brought out by heating, and it is possible to control the depth of color in several ways. Wings placed in a small electric toaster oven will darken along edges and openings and in thinner sections first. Other zonal effects can be obtained by careful heating with a propane torch, but this is tricky because the surface burns easily. Oven heating can also be used—again carefully.

A butterfly's body is extremely complex in actuality, but it can be simplified into three major parts, the head, thorax and abdomen, the abdomen normally being about the length of the other two put together. On the head, the principal visible

Fig. 223. The "look" of a butterfly can be changed considerably by adjusting the angle at which wings are set into the body. Note wing veining and shaped wing-edge holes. The higher the wing angle, however, the more difficult is the balancing.

features are the antennae, which can be simulated with piano wire, often left with the natural curve of the coil, and with the outer end formed into a small loop. They may project from small clubs at the base, or simply from the head itself. The thorax carries all the organs of locomotion, including six legs and the four wings. It is actually segmented into three parts, but these are not visible unless the insect is dissected. The abdomen has nine segments and can be simulated as a cone, although it varies in exact shape from species to species. Also, the body itself can be small or large with relation to the wings. (If you want to be a purist, there are butterfly guides available.) But normally, bodies as drawn here are better than observers will expect. Wings can be separate pieces, or in most species can be combined because of the slight overlap. The upper wing laps over the lower midway of their length.

The principal aim is to display the varieties of wood anyway, so the wings are the crucial elements. I have tried to provide here the major variations in shape and size, and a variety of the possibilities in handling them. The monarch is such a distinctive and well-known butterfly that I made mine of pine and dark-stained the pattern over a lighter-colored background. In the case of multiple stains, it is advisable to give the wood a coat or two of flat (matte or satin) varnish before the stains are applied, to reduce the tendency of the stain to soak in and run. The same is true if you decide to paint butterflies in their approximate natural colors. Over varnish, color where you don't want it can be removed by wiping or scratching.

Because the wings are heavy compared with the body, you may have problems with any support for hanging. Balancing the insect fore and aft is difficult unless the wings are mounted relatively flat. The bent-pin method sketched is neat if you can find a precise center of balance and put the pins well out on the wings; otherwise it is easier to make a 4-point suspension, with a hole in each wing, so the insect can be posed at the desired angle front and back as well as side to side. Whiffletrees (balance beams) for the mobile are made of No. 18 or No. 20 piano wire for the longer one, No. 10 for the shorter. Each whiffletree need be only long enough to clear half the width of the butterfly to be suspended at the higher level. If monofilament nylon is used for suspension, it is advisable to double-knot and glue when balance is achieved; nylon will loosen and slip if you don't.

All parts for these butterflies were made by hand, but wings can be band- or jigsawed, of course, and ⅛-in (3-mm) wing thickness obtained by planing or sanding. The best tool for shaping holes and veining I found to be a knife with hook blade. It is stiff enough to work any wood and is readily interchangeable with a standard blade for normal knife cutting.

If butterflies are to be used singly, you may want to add legs. These can simply be copper wire put through straight holes in the thorax. If the butterfly is to stand, glue the legs in position and splay them out to support it. If it is to hang on a curtain or drape, sharpen the two forward leg tips so they will penetrate the material, and bend them into tiny hooks. You will find that many variations are possible in wing position and angle of suspension, as well as in

color, particularly if exotic woods are used. It is possible also to make butterflies simply of two wings glued together at an angle—with no body at all. The wings can be thin slices of burl or other figured areas, and backed with a pin. However you make them, butterflies are very pleasing.

Making a design your own

YEARS AGO, I WAS FASCINATED by the study of gravestone rubbings that showed how a skilled itinerant stone carver had gone from town to town westward from New England. His designs and techniques were readily recognizable from those of both his contemporaries and his imitators. The same thing is true of familiar woodcarving designs; they may be "standard" but, unless they are turned out on a duplicator, there will be slight but identifiable variations piece to piece. This is true whether it is all the work of one carver or that of several in turn. I have seen copies of my designs that are better than my originals because the carver has more skill or took more pains. I have also seen copies that are so painstaking that they have somehow lost verve and fire. Making a given design over and over should obviously lead to improvement, but sometimes it leads only to change because the individual is not capable of further improvement or becomes bored with the repetition.

To illustrate facets of this question, I have selected two groups of designs (Figs. 224 and 225), one with Indian variations on a bird profile, the other showing variations in the design of an American eagle for the top or splat of a wooden clock-case.

The bird designs are symbolic, and don't to my knowledge attempt to depict any particular species. They are shown in a 1916 book, *Evolution of the Bird in Decorative Art*, by Kenneth M. Chapman; all are suitable for incising, inlaying, or similar applications. They show how far stylizing can stray from the near-exact reproduction of the decoy-carver.

The second group of sketches depicts research by Sheldon Hoch of White Plains. New York. He has carved mahogany copies of these eagles from his own or others' pho-tographs of the originals. These were shown in the *Bulletin* of the National Association of Watch & Clock Collectors (Feb., '81, pp. 20–9) in which Mr. Hoch explained his project of "Hunting for Birds and Beasts in Connecticut Shelf Clocks." They are all from the American Empire period, running through Andrew Jackson's presidency (1829–37). Most clocks of that period had wooden Terry-type movements and hand-carved cases with splats depicting eagles, acanthus leaves, pineapples, paws and varied birds and beasts. Such clocks were turned out by the hundreds by a number of makers using duplicating machinery for the works, and sold for about $8. You can imagine how much the carver got for a splat; it behooved him to cut corners and work fast. None ever took time to sign his name.

First designs of this period were apparently baskets of fruit and horns of plenty (cornucopias), which were on short-case clocks. Eagles came later, usually on long-case clocks, and were more prevalent on eight-day wood-movement and 30-hour long-pendulum clocks. Each maker had his own design, almost a trademark, probably made by one or two carvers. One or two

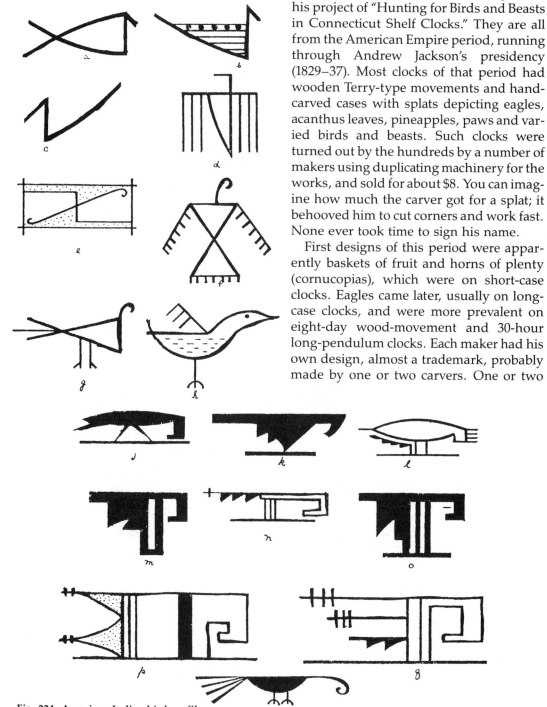

Fig. 224. American Indian bird profiles.

Chauncey Ives 30-hr long case. Rare

Riley Whiting   Note differences

Ely Terry & Son 8-day.   S.B. Terry

Silas Hoadley 30-hr. Note shield

Hopkins & Alfred   Rare

G & E Bartholomew 30-hr long-pendulum

Marsh-Gilbert 8-day.

Rare

Universal Eagle - many 30-hr clocks

Putnam Bailey - One of a kind?

Fig. 225. American eagles.

makers had more than one design, and some occasionally had unique ones. As wood-movement clocks lost out to brass-movement ones, some makers went to increasingly unique, often one-of-a-kind casings with splats to match, featuring coats of arms, stylized birds and beasts or what-have-you (sometimes to order).

There are relatively few left-facing eagles. (I seem to recall that left-facing was thought to be unpatriotic by some purists.) Right-facing ones are essentially alike, suggesting a common ancestor or source design. In fact, some of the carving conventions, for feathers to name one, are repeated. Some designs have crests, others do not.

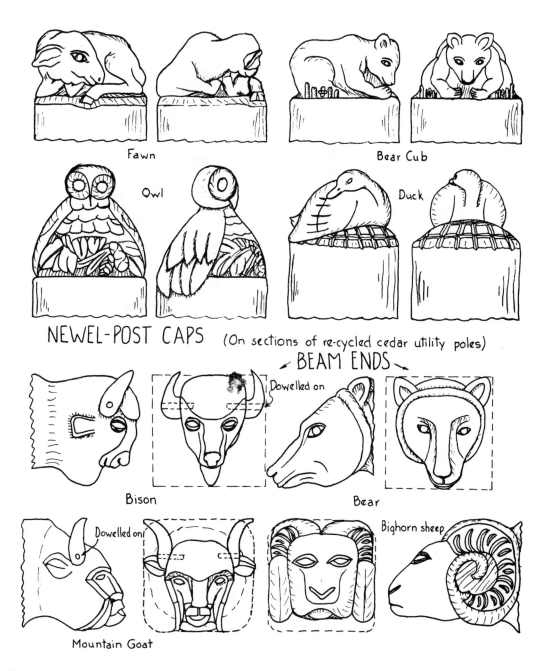

NEWEL-POST CAPS (On sections of re-cycled cedar utility poles)

Fawn

Bear Cub

Owl

Duck

~ BEAM ENDS ~

Dowelled on

Bison

Bear

Dowelled on

Mountain Goat

Bighorn sheep

Fig. 227. These unusual and powerful woodcarvings include panels in pioneer and Indian motifs, newel posts (recycled cedar utility poles) with animal-motif caps and beam-ends with animal heads. These are true folk art, made by tyros of Timberline Lodge, Mt. Hood, Oregon. All motifs are readily adaptable to smaller carvings. Such work calls for bold and deep cutting, with very limited detail.

Fig. 228. The tail and hockey stick on this beaver award plaque are inserted in holes in the body, which in turn is mounted on brass skates set into the 6 × 12-in (15 × 30-cm) base. Body is not in the round, but flattened on the sides to reduce bulk and fit available wood. Lower body is textured and tail cross-hatched. Stocking cap pompon, edge of cap and pullover sweater are tinted with oils.

How to suit a client's needs

MENTION has been made of the infinite variety of designs that can be based upon a particular animal or bird. Here's a case in point. It has to do with an unlikely animal—the beaver. My experience with it derives from the fact that a particular client has sons who are members of a hockey club having the unusual name of Beaver Dam. She has had need at one time or another for Christmas tree decorations, pendants and awards with some tie-in to the group. On occasion, she has given me carte blanche to provide what is necessary. Here are some of my designs, which may suggest ideas if you have a similar need. Many other designs are possible, of course, their form and function depending upon the animal and the need.

The beaver is not a particularly prepossessing animal, but he is appealing in that he goes his own way and lives a somewhat distinctive life. He is also rather easy to caricature because of his distinctive tail and bulky shape.

The first request I had was for awards for two volunteer hockey coaches—and they had to be produced in 24 hours! My solu-

tion was a silhouette panel of the "business end" or head of a hockey stick (Fig. 229A), about actual size—7 in (18 cm) wide. Upon it was carved a beaver and the suggestion of a dam, as well as the name of the man and the season. It was in ¾-in (19-mm) mahogany, natural finish, and was made so it could be a wall plaque, or a stand-up or lie-flat desk ornament.

The next request was for Christmas tree decorations. I made a number, including a series of miniature skates of various eras, miniature shoe skates and typical skaters; but of most interest here were a hockey goalie (C), a player (D), and two other beavers. These were 3 or 4 in (7 or 10 cm) tall, the teak beavers textured with a veiner and finished in natural color, the hockey players tinted to suggest the colors of the club.

A further request, a year later but also for short-term delivery, was for a somewhat more ornate award, this time for a single volunteer coach who had led the team to the championship and also conducted them on an 8-day, hockey-playing visit to Finland. The championship was to be mentioned prominently, the Finnish visit some-

Fig. 229.

what less so, because some members of the team had been unable to make the trip. My solution was a larger beaver in mahogany, mounted on brass skates of the latest hockey style, on a Mexican mahogany base. Base dimensions were 6 × 12 in (15 × 30 cm), and the beaver was about 10 in (25 cm) tall, with separate tail inserted. The beaver was carved with cap and turtleneck sweater. On one upper arm was a miniature Finnish flag. Flag and cap were lightly tinted with oils in appropriate colors. On the base was incised the single word "Champions" and the date. The base edge was carved with a random pattern suggesting the logs of a dam.

9

Why Not Carve Flowers?

THE ANSWER TO THAT QUESTION is that, sooner or later, everybody does. Foliage and fanciful figures—especially gods and heroes—were popular subjects for ancient carvers. The Egyptians, for example, were partial to the lotus and to creatures—like the Sphinx—that combined the attributes of various species; the Greeks favored the acanthus and their gods; Europeans carved the oak, the grape, folk heroes like William Tell or Charlemagne, the griffin, and the dragon; China and Japan carved unicorns, dragons, vines, and water lilies; the Norsemen doted on strange animals and gods; the Germans and Dutch were masters of high-relief forest scenes.

The situation hasn't changed much. American carvers try Paul Bunyan, Babe Ruth, Abraham Lincoln, or the current president, and carvers in Bali, Japan, China, Africa and other faraway places still incorporate foliage, gods and heroes, as well as fanciful creatures into their work. One reason is that foliage, with fabulous figures interspersed, is an interesting and infinitely variable way of decorating a surface or tying together elements of an in-the-round composition, or even for providing such utilitarian service as supporting otherwise fragile parts of a figure. Another reason is that foliage and fable are part of the basic fabric of our past; both are pastoral and rural in feeling, rather than sophisticated and urban.

In this section, I have tried to assemble examples of a wide variety of floral and fabulous subjects, while consciously avoiding the trite and familiar examples available

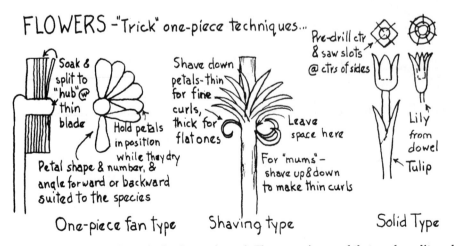

Fig. 230. Simple flowers made from single pieces of wood. These require wood that can be split or shaved.

Violet	Daisy	Chrysanthemum	Tulip

Fig. 231

elsewhere. They offer fascinating possibilities, among them the pragmatic one that exact portraiture—either of foliage or of mythical heroes—is not required because we don't observe foliage that closely, and authentic portraits of the ancient gods and heroes do not exist. Even a tyro can achieve creditable results.

Many of the pieces shown here are my own originals, sometimes adapted from traditional sources, and sometimes, of necessity, entirely imaginary. For typical designs I have provided step-by-step photographs, with hints for the solution of knotty problems. For most, there are front and side patterns; suggestions for your own designs, for finishing, for wood, tool selection, and for size, are all included as well. The tedious research has been done, leaving the way open for pleasant, fascinating and rewarding carving.

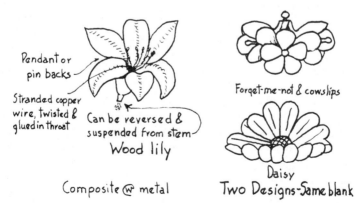

Fig. 232. Pendants carved from colorful hardwoods. The lily is in vermilion, the other two from the same blank of purpleheart.

Special tools?

FLORAL AND FOLIAGE ELEMENTS traditionally have been the basis of much formal woodcarving design. Because foliage has so many concave and similarly formed surfaces, specialized woodcarving tools were developed long ago. Simple flowers and fruits can be shaped in the round or in high relief with the knife alone, of course, but such forms as oak, grape and acanthus leaves, bunches of grapes, vines, and complex flowers take shape much faster with chisels.

For most work, a blade length of 1½ in (4 cm) or less is advisable; longer blades tend to bend, catch near the heel, and are difficult to control when you cut with the tip. The wider the blade, the straighter and more stable your cuts, but the greater the difficulty in cutting concave areas and in tight places. If you are delighted by heavy chips and big cuts, you'll break the narrow blades. I should warn you that you should *cut out* chips, not try to wedge them out— that's likely to break both wood and knife.

It is, of course, possible to make your own special knives as many whittlers do. They're usually special-purpose to get into particular spots and for the repetitive carving of a particular shape. Such knives are made from slivers of safety-razor blades bound into dowel handles, reground straight razors, or other pieces of good and tempered steel. The principal cautions here are to grind very slowly to avoid burning the cutting edge, and to bind the blade securely into the handle. A blade that wobbles or tends to snap closed is likely to cut you rather than the wood.

A Band-Aid® or tape on the middle joint of your index finger will be helpful; it prevents blisters if you haven't built up a callus there. When you whittle, you must keep your mind on what you're doing; you can't watch TV or converse. Many whittlers have remarked that they only cut themselves when demonstrating or teaching, because they talk when they should be intent on carving. Learn to be careful with the knife.

As would be expected, we have mechanized woodcarving as far as possible. Circular saws and band saws help shape blanks; routers cut away backgrounds; coping saws, power drills and sanders are also used. Carvers of totem poles and wooden Indians and other heroic figures have adopted the chain saw—with a great gain in speed of cutting but a great potential for making the user deaf and driving his or her neighbors insane. Carvers of small objects and/or very hard materials use hand grinders or flexible-shaft machines with shaped cutters, and claim extraordinary results with them. Some have even adopted dental drills. My experience is that they are hard to control, chew rather than cut the wood, and throw dust and chips over a considerable area, so the user needs safety glasses. I have even met a few carvers who use pneumatic or electric hammers with fitted chisels. Like the profiler and duplicator, such equipment is primarily commercial. It may save time and effort in some instances, but hand finishing is usually required anyway if the surfaces are to have any quality.

You don't need nearly as many tools as you or a tool salesman may think.

Simple flowers

GRINLING GIBBONS, the Englishman, was noted for his swags of flowers and leaves in high relief, and many a carver before his time and since has used flower motifs, particularly the rose and the acanthus leaf. Most of these were used in essentially formal carving, and usually were carved in rather high relief. However, many whittlers have also made flowers, some of them as one-piece "tricks"—variations of the puff of curled shavings or the fan. In recent years, the flower produced by multiple shavings has been particularly popular as a demonstration and low-priced commodity at woodcarving shows.

To make a curled-petal flower, the only requirements are wood that shaves well with the grain (like white pine or basswood), a sharp knife, and a good eye.

Figs. 233, 234. Exercise #1, "the eternal knot," requires cutting across grain and top rounding. (See pages 131,132.)

You may prefer to soak the wood in advance, so that the shaving will not split ahead of the knife. All you do is whittle the stick roughly circular, then make thin shavings around and around it until you have the desired number of petals. The individual petal normally should be started on the side rather than the end of the stick so that the petal end is round, and the cuts should be ended at a fixed point set by the first row cut around.

Such a flower can be carved double, or "mum" shape, by running shavings from both directions, but you must take care that the cuts from above and below are kept ¼ in (6.4 mm) or so apart so petals are not split off. It is also possible to carve miniature Christmas trees in this fashion by making a series of collars of shavings, each one with progressively shorter shavings. (That's the way we Boy Scouts also made "fuzz sticks" to act as core tinder when we started a fire.)

Once the flower is formed, it can be trimmed to a special shape with scissors, if desired; then the core on the top is cut off and the stub shaped into a dome like a daisy eye, and the bottom is thinned into a fairly thick stem. It is also possible to cut

several longer and heavier chips along the stem to suggest leaves. The flower can be colored by spraying or dipping it in dye or vegetable coloring.

Flowers can also be made by sawing or cutting a cross-grained blank in soft wood, particularly white pine, and whittling a petal shape both sides of center, then soaking the blank and splitting out a series of thin petals (as shown in Figs. 230–232). The petals can be spread and held in a regular fan pattern, or, with a little more difficulty, alternated in direction. If they are held in position until the wood dries, they will stay that way, or they can be held more securely by interlacing them with a colored thread near the outer edge.

If the blank is for a flower like a daisy, which has the bloom at right angles to the stem, the stem itself must be carved across grain or added later, either of which is a nuisance. However, if the flower is formed parallel to the main stem, as in the violet (Fig. 231), the stem itself can easily be carved later. Again, the petals can be shaped by knife or scissors and the flower head tinted as desired.

Flowers like the tulip can be carved from

Figs. 235, 236. Exercise #2, a diaper pattern, allows for individual variation.

the solid blank by drilling a core hole in the end of a stick (of any wood) so that the flat sides are fairly thin, then sawing down in the middle of the flat sides almost to the base of the core hole. Each corner can then be whittled into a petal with a projecting point (Fig. 230), and the leaves and stem carved below the bulbous head.

Somewhat more elaborate and difficult is the carving of flowers for pendants and pulls. These can be in the round, of course, or they can be in low relief like those shown (Fig. 232)—either single flowers or groups depending upon the shape desired. I've usually made such flowers in brilliantly colored woods like vermilion, purpleheart, or

Figs. 237, 238. Exercise #3, a stylized tulip, requires a more careful cutting of lines.

Figs. 239, 240. Exercise #4, a floral pattern, requires bosting or grounding out.

in a white wood like holly. Flowers are challenging enough so that they deserve a good wood, although they can be made in softer woods if they are to be painted. It's fun to suit the pattern to the available scrap, as I did in the case of the purpleheart carvings (Fig. 232); the blank was over ½ in (12.7 mm) thick, so I could really make two different pendants from the same basic blank.

How to start carving with flowers

H. M. (MACK) SUTTER, of Portland, Oregon, has taught panel carving as well as whittling for more than 40 years, and has developed what is proving to be a highly successful and rapid method of learning.

The first lesson, surprisingly, is not particularly easy; it requires a great many dif-

Figs. 241, 242. Exercise #5, a stylized lily, incorporates more intricate detail.

Figs. 243, 244. Exercise #6, the dogwood, involves texturing and long, fragile stems.

ferent types of cuts. It is called the *Eternal Knot*, and the student must work in all directions, so that he or she learns about grain immediately.

His designs are carved in basswood ¾ × 7 × 8½ inches (1.9 × 17.5 × 21 cm) with a beginner's set of short chisels and no mallet. Tools include a firmer, a V-tool, and 3 or 4 small gauges plus a knife.

It is quite possible for a deft beginner to teach himself by this method; it is actually the way I learned—except that I had no book for reference until several years later. The virtue of this method is that the individual is immediately challenged and never bored by repetition and tedious detail.

The second panel is the ancient diaper or allover pattern, for which Mr. Sutter provides only a basic outline. Each individual can work out his or her own detail design; Mack says that no students have ever made exactly the same design. These designs are

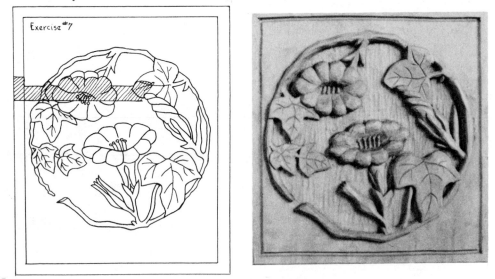

Figs. 245, 246. Exercise #7 is a flower group combining previous problems and veining.

Figs. 247, 248. Exercise #8 is a traditional pattern of the kind used for door panels.

large and open, so they are basically not difficult to carve in soft wood and can be done with hand pressure alone. Also, the opportunity to vary the design in the second project provides the individual with the opportunity to adjust the intricacy to his own natural ability; he can make something as simple as mounded diamonds or as complex as the pattern in Fig. 250. Neither design requires the setting-in or backgrounding that takes added competence, yet either can be shown with pride when completed.

Mack figures that the basic course should consist of about ten 2-hour lessons. However, when a student has tools he can continue carving between lessons, of course, so more material is required. Thus Exercise No. 3, the tulip pattern, is expected to be completed as well. (Figs. 236 and 238 are adapted from designs in "The Book of Wood Carving," by Charles Marshall Sayers, recently reprinted by Dover Publications, Inc., New York. Exercise No. 8 is adapted from Sayers' Design No. 8. They are reproduced here by special permission.)

Fig. 249 (left). Two artifical roses on a store-bought birthday cake inspired me to copy them on a panel (Fig. 250, right). It is, appropriately, of rosewood, about 1 × 6 × 12 in (2.5 × 15 × 30 cm). Elements were drawn on it, then the background was routed ½ in (12.7 mm) deep and the units were modelled. Background was scalloped with a flat gouge.

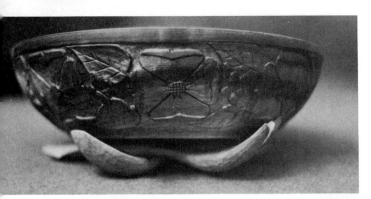

Figs. 251, 253. The dogwood pattern used on this salad bowl and the napkin rings were copied from the actual flower and leaf of the dogwood. The pieces are in myrtle, which has strong color variations. The bowl was finished with a gloss varnish outside, vegetable oil inside; the rings were gloss-varnished.

DOGWOOD MOTIF on a salad bowl

The intermediate series of lessons begins with Exercise No. 4, the flower group, and this is the only required panel, because to learn setting-in and bosting, or grounding (cutting away the background), takes some time. However, those who complete No. 4 may go on to projects of their own or select from No. 5 the lily, No. 6 the dogwood, No. 7 a circular flower group, and No. 8 a regular design involving precise curves. Again, the middle of No. 8 can be any of many patterns.

Advanced classes usually undertake individual projects that require specific advice and instruction, or may broaden out into general carving.

Variety in florals

FLOWERS AND FOLIAGE are a traditional part of, or decoration on, many other works: plaques, coats of arms, doors, frames, nameplates, boxes, bowls, vases, even handles, chairs and seats. They have been carved as decorations on robes, dresses and

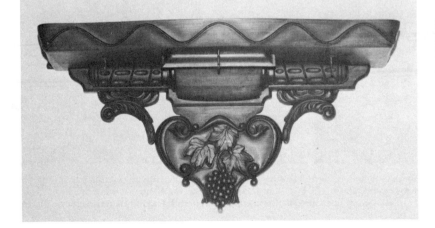

Fig. 254. T. E. Haag, of Tualatin, Oregon, carved this grape design into a cherry-wood shelf.

Fig. 255. Decorative plaques often incorporate foliage (as do coats of arms). This walnut plate was made by Gunther Goetz, of Denton, Texas.

Fig. 255. Decorative plaques often incorporate foliage (as do coats of arms). This walnut plate was made by Gunther Goetz, of Denton, Texas.

hats of 3D figures. All this is undoubtedly because foliage is so adaptable to space requirements and can be made into a non-obtrusive background. It can also convey a concept, such as the oak leaf or acorn for strength, wheat or corn for life, the lily or rose for many religious concepts. Flowers and foliage also have been stylized, as in the Tudor or Luther rose, the acanthus, and the papyrus. Vines have been combined with other motifs to produce openwork screens for all sorts of purposes.

Because they tend to be fragile when carved, flowers and foliage are usually carved in relief rather than in the round. In recent years, much of it has been done in low relief to avoid problems of undercutting and fragility, because foliage is often an integral part of the decoration of utilitarian objects. It is particularly adaptable to filling and closing a circle or other geometric shape, without elaborate and mathematical pre-layout. Thus a design can be carved on the circumference of a bowl, plate, and gourd, with no worry about whether or not the design will "meet itself coming back"; an extra leaf or twist in a stem or vine will compensate. Further, the usual design can itself be expanded or contracted slightly as you go by making flowers a bit wider or narrower, adding leaves and the like. A geometric or other exact pattern will be difficult to accommodate to the changing curvatures of a bowl or vase, but a floral design can simply be pulled in or expanded a little to compensate for changing contours. In fact, the possibilities and variations are so great that I shall try to cover the ground by illustrated examples rather than verbal description.

Floral polyglot panels

SOME YEARS AGO, I CARVED a number of polyglot panels in teak, grouping animals in one, birds in another, "bugs" in still an-

Fig. 256. Polyglot panel of English sycamore depicts 62 flowers and five birds selected for familiarity and distinctive silhouette (see Fig. 257).

Identification: Flower and Bird Panel

Flowers
1. Blue vervain
2. Wild sunflower
3. Columbine, or 4-o'clock
4. Frangipani
5. Queen Anne's lace
6. Jack-in-the-Pulpit
7. Oxeye Daisy
8. Heliconia
9. Purple coneflower
10. Common plantain
11. Trumpet creeper
12. Shooting star, or American cowslip
13. Jewelweed
14. Morning glory
15. Tulip
16. Day lily
17. Purple virgin's-bower (clematis)
18. Evening primrose
19. Dandelion
20. Dayflower
21. Lousewort
22. Oswego tea, or bee balm
23. American lotus (a water lily)
24. Black-eyed susan
25. Angel's-trumpet (small tree)
26. Lily-of-the-valley
27. Wood anemone
28. Atamasco lily
29. Iris
30. Painted trillium
31. Flowering dogwood
32. Skunk cabbage
33. Clover
34. Wild rose
35. Lady-slipper (yellow)
36. Forget-me-not
37. Thistle
38. Nightshade
39. Water arum
40. Bluebell
41. Fringed gentian
42. Bottle gentian
43. Buttercup
44. Rose mallow
45. Anthurium
46. Coral trumpet (floweret)
47. White violet
48. Bluet or innocence
49. Bird-of-paradise
50. Marsh marigold
51. Pitcher plant
52. Hibiscus
53. Daffodil
54. Indian pipe
55. Plantain (water reed)
56. Water lily
57. Indian pink
58. Wild ginger
59. Cow or yellow pond-lily
60. Wild geranium
61. Cattail
62. Moss pink

Birds
A. Ruby-throated hummingbird
B. House wren
C. Cardinal
D. Robin
E. Saw-whet owl

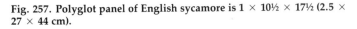

Fig. 257. Polyglot panel of English sycamore is 1 × 10½ × 17½ (2.5 × 27 × 44 cm).

other, and so on. These all evolved from my so-called "bug tree," which was a polyglot group of insects, worms and spiders carved in heroic size on the 12-ft (3.6-m) trunk of an apple tree they had conspired to kill. Units were placed where they fitted and as whim dictated, without regard to relative scale or viewing aspect. This *stele*, or column, was in reality a carved panel wrapped around a tree.

This panel (Fig. 257) is a lineal descendant—a commission for one panel featuring flowers and birds. I had available a plank 12 in (30 cm) wide, of English sycamore (harewood) which is very white and dense, with a crossfire figure in fiddle pattern, enough to give the wood interest without being obtrusive. It is amenable to both chisel and knife, does not split or crumble, and will support a great deal of detail. (It is customarily a veneer, used as an alternate to American holly, and as the client was English, the wood was a happy choice.)

Panel width was about 10½ in (26 cm), so I selected a length of 17½ in (44 cm—the

"Golden Mean" calls for a width 60 percent of height), which, with a reasonable self-border all around, left a 9 × 16-in (23 × 40-cm) working area. The panel thickness was 1 in (2.5 cm). I decided on a background depth of only ⅛ in (3.2 mm), with limited modelling of elements. Birds and flowers drawn from field guides were laid out directly on the wood. I tried to select birds and flowers that are familiar and have distinctive silhouettes, and I altered scale to make the subject fit the space. Layout and carving were done simultaneously from one corner. Slight overlaps are advisable to avoid gaps and the stringy look of straight stems, of course, and care must be taken not to "carve oneself into a corner." As my panel worked out, it included 62 flowers and five birds.

Because the carving was relatively shallow and the wood so white, I darkened the background with a light-tan, German, sal-ammoniac stain to make the elements stand out. This was preceded by a spray coat of matte varnish to avoid overabsorption of stain in cross-grain areas. The carved sur-

Fig. 258.

Fig. 259.

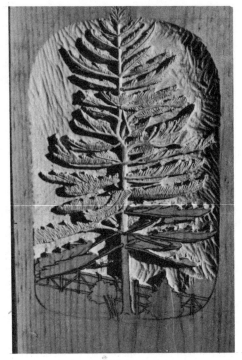

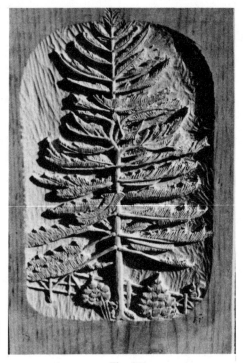

Fig. 260.   Fig. 261.

face was also coated with the same stain, but in small areas at a time, so the stain could be wiped off again at once, leaving high spots almost white, with darker lines.

You probably won't want to make an exactly similar panel. The designs are flexible, so you can make another arrangement or use them individually.

Portrait of a pine

TREES, CLOUDS AND SPLASHING WATER can be the nemesis of a woodcarver because all have feathery, ill-defined edges, and a carving tends to make them look rigid and blocky. Therefore, it was with some trepidation that I undertook this panel portrait of a particular pine tree. It was planted almost 40 years ago by the client's son, and both have since grown taller and older, although the pine had suffered from the breaking of an upper fork that had stripped branches down one side; hence it was somewhat misshapen. The finished panel was to be accompanied by some very spe-

cial verses written by the client about the tree and the growing child, so it had to be personal and whimsical in feeling.

Obviously, it was impractical to depict every needle, or even every little branch. As in making a portrait of a person, it was advisable to idealize, *not* caricature, the subject a little. Thus it was helpful to fill out a few scrawny branches and to remove interferences around the tree or in the background, as well as to picture it from the side that is usually seen. It was also essential to retain the identifiable shape of the trunk and larger branches as well as major elements of the surrounding terrain. Yet one can justifiably add a little animal life or slightly move a bush or the like in the interest of a better composition—that's "artistic license."

I began by taking a series of photographs of the tree to get the overall shape and the effect of perspective on the eye of the viewer from the usual viewing point as well as from others. These turned out to be less helpful than I had anticipated, because a picture taken against the sky—even on a snowy and relatively dark day—loses considerable detail because of the contrast. I could, however, determine general shape and composition and lay the tree out on a 2 × 12 × 19-in (5 × 30 × 47.5-cm) Oregon-pine panel, then go to the site and sketch in added detail. I made no preliminary sketch because there was no need for that kind of a record or guide, and I used pine because it was relatively soft and because it was the same material as the subject. The step-by-step pictures tell the rest of the story (Figs. 258–261).

Of the seven pictures taken, one photo was helpful to attain general shape, including the masses of needles and the slight curve of the trunk as well as the disfigurement where the fork had broken years ago. However, the needle masses obscured the actual branch positions. The brush around the tree base and a neighbor's shed beyond the fence, as well as the trees in the background, were left out of the final composition primarily as confusing factors, although the fence and an adjacent bush and small hemlock were included. (Fig. 261)

(Fig. 258) The tree was drawn directly on the block by the point-to-point method. Fortunately, the carving was to be exactly three times the size of the key photo, so transfer of dimensions was relatively easy, although detailed. Some branches could be placed by eye, others modified slightly in the interest of better composition. It is also important to remember that extremely small openings between branches and elsewhere should be avoided when possible because of the difficulty in carving them. The fence is cross-grain and difficult, but unavoidable. The sketch was modified by direct observation of the tree, then blocking outlines were inked in.

(Fig. 259) Setting-in and grounding-out are extremely tedious and painstaking in this case, but essential to retain the character of

the tree. Setting-in must be done carefully to avoid breaking of narrow cross-grain sections. One way to reduce this likelihood is to set in the second side of a narrow section by driving in the chisel at an angle *away* from the opposite side, then later correcting the cut to vertical. Also, depth must be severely limited in such cuts, at least initially. (As you get deeper, the danger of breakout is reduced.) I selected a ground depth of ½ in (12.7 mm) as most practical. For setting in, I lined in with a veiner, and set in with a ¼-in (6.3-mm) firmer, ¹⁄₁₆-in (1.6-mm) flat gouge (No. 3), ¼-in (6.3-mm) medium gouge (No. 5), plus knife and hook knife. Grounding required the same tools, plus a ⅜-in (9.6-mm) deep gouge (No. 7).

(Fig. 260) Grounding could be left quite rough and cleaned up as modelling proceeded. To suggest the needle structure, I used parallel cuts with the veiner, or vees with the knife, depending upon the size of the area. Each branch was first modelled to a general shape, and the branch itself suggested by cutting a vee on each side of it, usually with the knife to avoid breakouts. A V-tool might have been used, but it would have caused trouble because of narrow sections and cross-grain cuts. Even the veiner caused some trouble, although it was razor-sharp. As carving progressed, I modified the original sketch here and there to suggest branches on the face that had been stripped. Also note that the branches are quite visible at the top of the tree but are obscured lower down because of the point of view of an observer. Needles are not continuous lines in one direction; they vary across a branch to suggest multiplicity. The lines are also carried down the set-in sides to the ground, to break the solid look of the edge as much as possible.

(Fig. 261) A bird to scale on a tree of this size would be almost invisible, and a bird flying in the sky would be both a nuisance and somewhat trite, so I carved a slightly oversized bird alighting on an upper left-hand branch. As carving progressed, I also added a squirrel sitting on the fence and a raccoon peering around the base, although the raccoon is essentially a night animal, at least in my suburban area.

As carving was completed, it was necessary to reduce the prominence of some branches and leaf structures, and to emphasize others, as well as to clean up the ground after set-in sides were textured. I also elected to leave tool marks on the background in a somewhat haphazard pattern, although they were principally vertical to reduce tearing of edges. These were cut with the deep gouge as far as possible. Light sanding was done in some areas, particularly on branches and on rough portions of the background. Then the entire panel was given two coats of spray matte varnish, "antiqued" with teak stain, and waxed.

10

Carving Fabulous Creatures

The unicorn for ladies

THE UNICORN HAS ALWAYS been popular, especially with females, probably because of the well-known legend which claims that when it meets a virgin, it will put its head in her lap and become tame and powerless. It has also become associated with power, purity, spiritual force and divine creativity. It is depicted in the famous French tapestry, the Virgin and the Unicorn, as well as in others.

The unicorn (or *monoceros*) is an excellent example of how myths are born. The ancestors of the Vikings had the boats and the nerve to hunt in northern waters far from land, and they encountered narwhal herds. They carried the tusks home, and some tusks found their way into central Europe through trade. But the Norsemen either didn't tell the origin of the tusks, or

created the legend. Gradually, a complete myth was built up about the animal and the horn, and it became a popular medieval symbol. The story grew that the horn came from a creature described as essentially a horse with antelope legs and cloven hooves, a tail like a lion, and a goatee, plus a very luxuriant mane. The horn was of varied length, but twisted upon itself (as is that of the narwhal), and was considered to have magical powers in medicine and aphrodisiacs. Royal jewelry, sceptres, even thrones, were fashioned from it, and pieces were ground into a very marketable powder to be added to potions.

The unicorn was depicted in various works of art, including tapestries, and was incorporated in the British royal coat of arms. Popular playing cards depicted a wild man, or hairy man of the forest, riding

Extend horn 50%

UNICORN
Port Orford Cedar 8" o.a.long

Fig. 262.

Fig. 263.

Fig. 264.

a unicorn, thus combining two legends. The myth was brought to America and carried over into our folk art and tales as late as the last century—and is used in popular designs even today.

Like the legend of the biblical flood, unicorns also appear in the literature of other cultures. A unicorn-like animal, more leonine but with a single horn and its ruff forming an aureole around its head, occurs in Chinese folklore, notably the Chi-Lin. It was supposed to appear only at the birth of a great sage.

When I was commissioned to carve a

Fig. 265.

small unicorn, my client and I agreed upon a *couchant* pose (lying down with the head raised). Preferably, the figure was to be carved in a light-colored wood, with the head turned back rather than an action pose (see Fig. 262). I selected Port Orford cedar, partly because I had a block of it that measured 3½ × 6 × 10½ in (9 × 15 × 26.5 cm) and was relatively free of visible knots. I planned on a separate and contrasting horn and a luxuriant mane. The front legs would be side by side, and the animal would appear to be resting on a ledge. This would permit a base that could be clamped during carving. So much for sketches and planning! As it turned out, the block tapered from 3¾ in (9.5 cm) to 3½ in (9 cm), from one end to the other, and was short of the height needed for the head.

Carving the unicorn—step by step

(Fig. 263) The sketch was transferred to the block and the block was rough-sawed to silhouette. The slab that was cut away from the back was glued at the head to increase the height there to 7½ in (19 cm). Wood was chiselled away behind the head and the

back and tail areas, then the rounded-mane shape was scroll-sawed. It immediately became obvious that the centerline of the mane had to be a spiral to meet the back at the foreshoulders, and that the animal had to lie on its far side if the forelegs were to be side by side. If the body was to be relatively vertical, the forequarters had to be twisted forward, or the legs—at least the right foreleg—had to extend towards the front rather than being brought to the left.

(Fig. 264) It seemed advisable to shape the head first and to resolve the body pose thereafter, because the nose had to be at the front of the block to allow sufficient depth for the rest of the figure. Therefore, the head was rough-formed with a ¾-in (19-mm) flat gouge, the neck curve worked out, and the front line of the shoulders established. The head was sawed to approximate thickness and taper, so ear positions could be established as well. It turned out that a knot ran exactly through the center of the goatee, so this was left attached to the body wood of the shoulder as long as possible to support it.

Fig. 266.

(Fig. 265) About this time, it became apparent that the head pose was complex, so it was worked out in detail, including the mane, neck garland, throat, and ear and horn locations. Reference to horse photographs gave head details but no example of a head turned back. I remembered two sets of Chinese horses I had, each with one horse with its head reversed. Neither turned out to be particularly helpful, because the Chinese had simply swivelled the head 180°, and in the case of the ivory head, the carver had depicted the mane running straight down so it ended between the forelegs! Also, I wanted to avoid a prosaic, flat base, and to suggest instead a sylvan ledge. I had already tilted the sketch on the block to make the base thicker at the front of the animal.

(Fig. 266) A reasonable spiral for the centerline of the mane was drawn, and a technique for the mane worked out—primarily large curls at both sides of the centerline and in an irregular pattern. Also, the body was to lie vertical, with the right foreshoulder somewhat advanced, as it would be naturally, and the right leg, even though

tucked under the chest, would of necessity not cross as far as I had originally drawn it. The new position was easy to estimate by using the dimensions of the visible left foreleg as a guide.

Fig. 267.

(Figs. 267 and 268) Once these decisions were made, blocking out of the rest of the figure was relatively easy. The tail was carved, and the legs defined. The base was rounded to make the hooves stand out, and textured with a flat gouge. The neck decoration, instead of being a simulation of a decorated leather collar, was made to resemble woven miniature flowers, with a heart hanging over the breastbone. For the horn, an available scrap of walrus tusk was ground into a spiral shape, then sanded and scraped to a dull sheen. Fortunately, the ivory had a slight curve, which helps the effect. The entire piece was sprayed with three coats of matte varnish, then the neck garland and areas of the belly and under the legs were tinted slightly darker, and, finally, the whole piece was waxed.

Fig. 268.

Fig. 269. The finished unicorn.

Fig. 270. Chinese dragon with elaborate tendrils about head, multi-frond tail and tongue, partial scaling on back and foot tops. This is a good relief pattern.

be with three toes forward and one in back like a chicken or with four toes forward like a cat, although in both cases the toes should be long. The back ridge can be nonexistent—in which case your dragon may look more like a dinosaur; it can be a simple sine curve or a notched ridge (like my winged dragon in Figs. 273, 274); or it can have a wave pattern as the long dinosaur's back ridge does (Fig. 272). Such decisions you must make because they are a function of what use you plan to make of the beast and how much time and skill you have. I have even seen dragons with back ridges consisting of spaced spikes carved from the solid! (If I undertook that one, I would carve the spikes separately and set them in drilled holes; they would be stronger and better, and so would my nerves.)

Here are five variations of the dragon theme, illustrating the preceding points. A classical Chinese dragon design is modified for relief carving on a walnut box top. Note the tendrils around the head and the multiple-forked tail. I also reduced the labor considerably by showing scales only along the back. This, too, makes the design less complex, as is the second (Fig. 271).

Carving a dragon

DRAGONS, LIKE UNICORNS, are a perennial favorite, but can be quite difficult to carve, depending upon their complexity. The legendary dragon, particularly the Chinese variety, has all sorts of excrescences around the head. It may have wavy tendrils around the mouth and/or ears, a spiky backbone line, hair or whatever on the backs of its legs, and some sort of addition to, or multiple forking of its tail. Because dragons are largely imaginary (except for the Komodo dragon), you can simplify the design somewhat to make it less fragile to carve, but in any case I would suggest a harder wood to repay the effort involved as well as to provide greater strength in thin sections. If you must have tendrils and elaborate poses, I would suggest carving your dragon as a relief panel; the background will then provide some support for fragile elements both during and after carving.

It is also possible to vary the backbone pattern and the foot pattern. Our general concept of a dragon is a lizardlike animal, so it would have clawed feet that can either

Fig. 271 (right). Derived from a clay figure in an ancient Chinese tomb recently opened, this stylized dragon is very simple in design and a good project for the whittler or carver with moderate skill or time. The only detailing is in the head. A good size is 6 × 6 in (15.2 × 15.2 cm), from a 2-in (5.1-cm) blank. This carving is by Hugh C. Minton.

Fig. 272. Completed sinuous elongated dragon. It makes an excellent over-door decoration, and the texturing gives a realistic scale effect at that distance.

Longest of the dragons is a 27-in (68.6-cm) snakelike pose in walnut (Fig. 272), with undulating body and loop-the-loop tail. He has no scales, but scales are suggested by the texturing, which is done by scalloping the body surface with a flat gouge. The effect is almost as good as scales, and takes less than half the time.

The final and most elaborate of my dragons is a winged variety (Figs. 273, 274) with looped tail and folded wings so he would fit the piece of walnut I had available. I have, incidentally, frequently compressed the third dimension of subjects to stay within the limitations of commercially available wood. The two latter in-the-round dragons, for example, are carved in 2¾-in (7-cm)

wood—because that is what I had. Given thicker wood, the wings could be extended more, but would be fragile.

If I were to make this particular carving again, I would make the back ridge like that on the elongated dragon; its slightly greater elaboration would go well there. This dragon, 16 in (40.6 cm) long, took 33½ hours, of which 15 were spent carving scales (including the difficult areas under the body and in the tail loop), as compared with 21 hours spent for the elongated dragon, of which only 5 hours were scaling.

Whether or not your dragon has scales is a decision you will have to make based on the amount of effort you want to put into the carving. The answer, of course, lies in

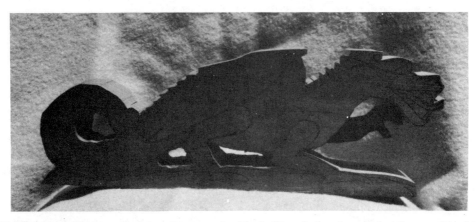

Fig. 273. The winged dragon requires a more complex blank. It can be bandsawed, but then must be drilled and shaped under the belly and the tail and inside the curve of the tail. Some of the complexity could be avoided by eliminating the integral base. It is walnut, 3 × 5 × 16 in (7.6 × 12.7 × 40.6 cm) long. If thicker wood were available, the wings could be spread more widely.

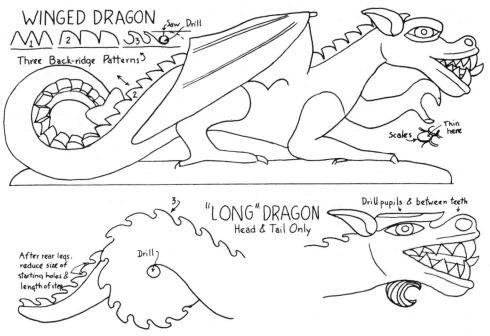

Fig. 274.

the areas difficult of access. It would be far easier to scale the long dragon despite his double-whirled tail. The winged dragon has an integral base, so it is difficult to reach his chest and belly, as well as the inner curve of his looped tail. The difficulty is, as always, that texturing must be done over all *visible* areas, and the eye can see where no tool will go.

The scale pattern of itself is simple. I create the rounded-end scales with half-round gouges of three sizes, ³⁄₁₆, ⁵⁄₁₆ and ³⁄₈ in (4.8, 7.9 and 9.5 mm), so scale size can be graduated down towards the tail and underbelly and on the upper legs. (Large fluters, which have a U-shaped cross section, would make longer scales faster, but I have none sufficiently large.) If the gouges are set in so the ends of one meet the tops of the two below it, the gouge itself completes the setting-in, but the scales will be very close and inflexible in pattern, so going around curves and the like will be complicated.

I prefer to make the scales slightly longer, so the loops of one row stand away from the loops of the preceding one. This will often require use of a small V-tool to extend the ends of each scale until they meet the preceding loops. Once the stop cuts are made, the scales are shaped individually by shaving off the inner end of each, so the rounded ends of scales in the preceding row apparently stand above it. I do this with a ⅛-in (3.2-mm) firmer so I can work around the loop, except where I cannot reach with it and I must use a knife. The knife and V-tool may be necessary to rough-shape scale outlines in such areas as the inner part of the top of the tail loop. (If the figure is carved without an integral base, there is more clearance for tools, but the piece is harder to hold while shaping and there is constant danger of breaking off legs.)

One problem with making a patterned texture, such as scales, is that extra scales must be added on the outside of a curve, if the added spacing between rows is excessive. This can be done easily by forking the scale pattern at the sides. This is easier to do than it is to describe. Another problem is presented by the necessity of bringing the scale pattern up to an edge, such as the

Fig. 275. The selection of tools for carving the scaled, winged dragon includes a special knife, ¼- and ½-in (6.4- and 12.7-mm) firmers, gouges ranging from ¾ in (19.1 mm) flat to ¼-in fluter and long-bent half-round (to get scale pattern in otherwise inaccessible places) and V-tool. The longer dragon, because it is not scaled, goes much faster and requires fewer tools.

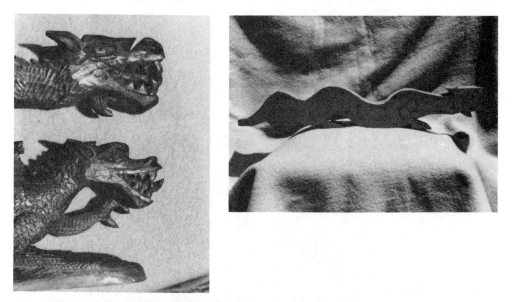

Fig. 276 (left). A comparison of heads and skin textures of the major dragons. Both are in walnut, the winged one somewhat more detailed in head and body. Fig. 277 (right). Both larger dragons were made from pieces of walnut plank about 2¾ in (7 cm) thick, so bandsawing of the blank made sense and saved time. The only complicated parts of the long dragon are the head and looped tail.

ridged back; every other line of scales will require a half scale there. This can be handled by using a shorter gouge of the same radius if one is available, or by simulating the half curve with a V-tool—which is often easier and quicker.

The third problem is with grain on such surfaces as the looped tail; one must be constantly aware of the grain direction to avoid splitting off a scale during shaping of the base. The fourth problem is that any gouge tends to break out the wood inside

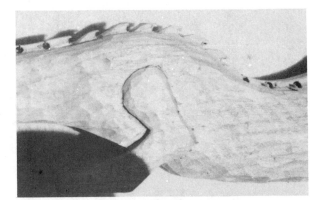

Fig. 278. Spines on the long-dragon backbone are wavy, produced by drilling spaced small holes across the ridge and sawing in to them, then cutting away one side in a long curve.

Fig. 279 (left). The mouth is formed by drilling between the teeth with a tongue visible between. The tongue could be extended at the front. Fig. 280 (right). The double loop of the tail can be confusing. I made it as simple as possible by showing the loops parallel on top and making the entire crossings underneath. The ridge is also carried down onto the tail-tip wedge ultimately.

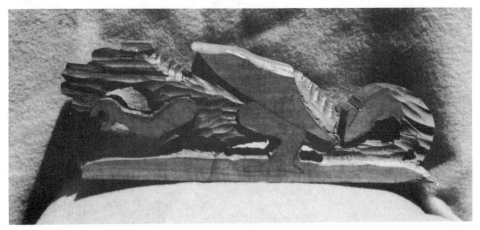

Fig. 281. A large gouge is the fastest way to clear off excess wood around head and tail, and will be useful as well in removing the wood on the far side of the upraised left foreleg. Don't forget the curvature of the tail!

Fig. 282. Sawing is an alternative to gouging away wood around head and tail, and will be useful as well in removing the wood on the far side of the upraised left foreleg. Once again, don't forget the curvature of the tail!

Fig. 283. Graduated scaling done with three sizes of gouge covers the body, tail and upper legs. (This took two days!) Lower legs and toes are covered with cross-hatching rather than scales; it goes quite well with the more exact design elsewhere. Claws are delineated and long. Difficult areas to scale are the inside of the tail loop, under the belly and bottom of the tail, and the inside of the raised foreleg; they are visible but hard to reach with tools. Note that the wings are treated to look leathery, like bat wings.

during setting-in, particularly if the set-in is across grain. The problem is accentuated by driving in the gouge at a backward angle, or even by driving it in straight. It is easier to bullnose the gouge-cutting edge slightly (so the ends of the arc are slightly behind the center), then drive it in at a slight for-ward angle (with the handle ahead of the cutting edge). This relieves the stress on the entrapped wood.

When scales are cut, there may be tiny splinters here and there. Cut them off as you go, and clean up the job; they will be hard to find later.

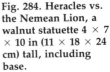

Fig. 284. Heracles vs. the Nemean Lion, a walnut statuette 4 × 7 × 10 in (11 × 18 × 24 cm) tall, including base.

Assembling a statuette

MOST COMPLEX of the classical statuettes I've made, the confrontation between Odysseus (Ulysses) and Polyphemus, a Cyclops, illustrates several additional points in design and carving. It is not one piece, but an assembly of several. The two small figures are individual carvings (Figs. 287, 288), as is the spear in the hand of one of them. The giant figure is built up as well, the arms giving the necessary shoulder width while saving wood thickness by almost half, reducing carving time and cost, and making it possible to alter arm position in final assembly. Even the base is in two sections of 1-in (2.5-cm) walnut, one across grain of the other to combat any tendency to warp, utilizing wood that had a bevelled edge—the natural surface of the trunk from which the plan was cut. Incidentally, the added base-piece made it possible to pose the spear thrower more accurately and dominantly.

Assembling a carving has a number of advantages: It permits last-minute adjust-

ments, such as the proper contact between the giant's foot and Odysseus, makes full carving of the small figures relatively easy, permits insertion of the soldier's arm in the giant's hand so that he appears to be squirming, and the like. In a solid carving, all of these decisions must be made in the original design and wood must be allowed for them thereafter. Also, sawing and carving are complex because of obstructions and grain problems. If the carving is commissioned, carving in parts saves time and wood—and the client's money. Overall effect is not harmed, and only the careful observer will note that the work is not a single unit.

The original Greek myth had it that Odysseus and his men were captured on their way home from Troy by Polyphemus, chief of the Cyclops, the one-eyed giants. Polyphemus imprisoned the Greeks in his cave. In any case of man versus giant, the ostensible hero is dwarfed. To counter this to some degree at least, I gave Odysseus a breastplate and greaves which were slightly

Fig. 285. Upper-body major lines have to be defined so arm positions can be established. Clearances between limbs are quite close.

Fig. 286. Joined figures are tested on base. They will be pinned and glued to base at point of contact.

whitened (pigment rubbed in and wiped off), the only "color" on the carving, so that the observer's eye would be attracted to the smaller figure.

The Cyclops is about to push Odysseus over with a contemptuous kick. This adds action, difficult in such carvings because of the diminutive size. Figures in a composition should not just pose; rather, they should be under stress, suggesting that some action is taking place, or about to take place. The carving should, in effect, tell a story. Initially, the angle of Odysseus' spear was not exactly correct (if the Cyclops' one eye is the target) and I didn't want solid contact between the figures (which would throw off Odysseus' cast), so poses could be adjusted during assembly.

Note that the Cyclops' feet are in line with each other and with the center of his body. This is important. When a man stands on one foot, his body shifts sidewise to center over the support, and even the upraised foot will tend to center as a result. Note also that Odysseus' left arm is not

extended straight forward but slightly to the right; this again is natural. Also, his left foot is forward to balance his throwing arm and give maximum force to the throw.

Polyphemus' single eye can be a problem. It is centered in the brow, but does it protrude or is it recessed as ours are? What happens to the facial areas occupied by our eyes? What of the point where eye and nose meet? Obviously, the eye is not shaped, but symmetrical, and normal eye sockets must not even be suggested although the cheek shape must be retained. I decided to bulge the eye and use what would normally be eyebrows to provide an underemphasis, leaving a flat area below them that rounded up into the cheek; the nose is normal, as is the hairline, when this is done.

There are no particular problems in carving these figures. The two small ones, which are only about 3 in (7.5 cm) high, are easy, except for Odysseus' strained backward position. The other figure can be carved with his arms in any desired position because the arm will be cut through at

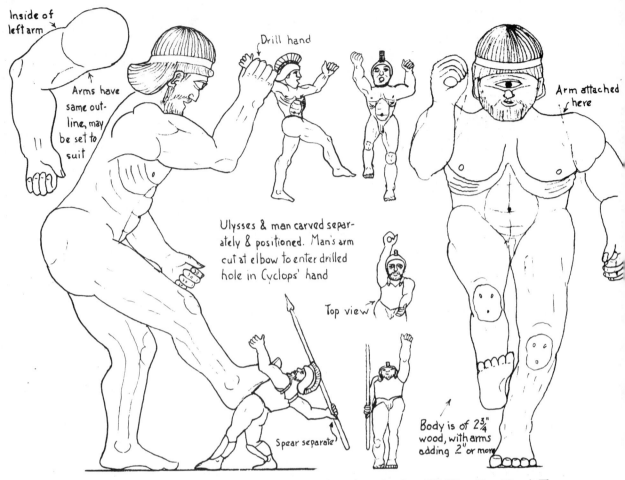

Inside of left arm

Arms have same outline, may be set to suit

Drill hand

Ulysses & man carved separately & positioned. Man's arm cut at elbow to enter drilled hole in Cyclops' hand

Top view

Spear separate

Arm attached here

Body is of 2¾" wood, with arms adding 2" or more

Fig. 287. Ulysses fighting Polyphemus is a statuette in walnut about 6 × 8 × 10½ (15 × 20 × 27 cm). The giant's arms, the two smaller figures and the base are separate pieces which have to be assembled.

the elbow anyway to allow his upper arm to go in one side of the hole in the giant's hand while his forearm goes in the other. It is obvious that Odysseus' feet should be flat on the bottom to provide secure mounting. I increase security of such mounts by inserting a steel pin made from a finishing nail in each, and the same for the giant. These supplement gluing. A pin could also be used between Odysseus' chest and the giant's toe, but a spot of glue is probably enough.

Because the arms are made separately, they can be set wide at the elbows to make Polyphemus appear very brawny and wide. This is done by sloping the shoulder

pads on the arms and on the body as well. Both sets of shoulder pads should, by the way, be cut too large initially and not cut to size until the arms are applied, so the pectoral and deltoid muscles can be faired in as they should be. I made the arms alike in silhouette, so they could be sawed together from the scrap triangle behind the head of the Cyclops, then cut into two half-thickness sections. (Allow extra wood around the hands also, because the right fist must be larger than the left to allow for gripping the Greek soldier.) And don't forget that the arms are a pair—a right and a left—and carve them accordingly.

After the arms and body are rough-shaped, cut through the arm of the Greek soldier and insert the parts, then try the giant's arms in various positions. (Note that I drew them in one position and placed them slightly differently—Figs. 287 and 288.) Check the bevels on the shoulder pads to be sure they are flat and mate properly, remembering that there are natural clefts at the inner edge of the pectoral and deltoid muscles which can mask the joining line. The shoulders for a burly person should be about three head-widths, so the space from head to bevel on the body and bevel to outer edge of the shoulder should each be about half a head. This can, of course, be adjusted after assembly, but it is preferable to get them approximately right beforehand.

When you are satisfied with the arm poses, make sure that you've done what carving you can in the tight area under the arms, then glue and pin the arms in place. Be certain that the arms are neither too high nor too low on the body, and that the right arm is slightly higher than the left, because the arm is raised, bulging the pectoral and deltoid muscles on that side. Final forming of the arms and shoulders can then be done (be sure to have a good anatomy text at hand).

Fig. 288. The planned base was a section of 1-in (25.4-mm) walnut with one edge tapered as it came from the tree. It seemed better to place Ulysses on a slight rise, both to reduce foot contact with Cyclops and to aim spear, so a cross-grain block was added.

On a composition such as this one, I find that a combination of carving with chisels for the heavy cuts and whittling the details is fastest and easiest. Small gouges and veiners are, of course, essential in putting in hair, shaping eyes and ears and the like.

11

Portraying Buildings

BUILDINGS, EITHER HOMES or historic structures, have a special appeal for most of us. What's more, they can be depicted relatively easily in a panel carving—if one starts with the right view. If you have a photograph or a detailed sketch of the building façade, that can serve for a low-relief pattern. What's more, a photograph usually incorporates the necessary perspective so that difficult and tedious task is avoided. The photo or sketch can be enlarged to the desired size by photostat or point-to-point drawing to get the basic outline, which is what you need to start.

With a head-on view, perspective problems are minimized and outlines are usually square. If the building is set in bare surroundings, you want to add a tree or two, some shrubbery, etc., and to strip it of such unsightly excrescences as TV antennae, telephone and electric lines, and even such difficult elements as porch railings, if they contribute little to the design. All such elements are difficult to carve. Greenery is not easy either, but it can be conventionalized or stylized.

To carve a structure in perspective is somewhat more difficult, of course, because lines that otherwise would be horizontal, angle to vanishing points at either side of center—and the vanishing points may be out far enough that drawing some of the lines will be difficult, let alone carving them so they look right. I have in this instance, however, undertaken such a plaque as a step-by-step project, to illustrate the method. A carving like this will provide excellent practice in two directions—one of carving in perspective, the other in achieving surface textures that appear realistic.

The house I chose is set on a slight eminence well back from the road. I took several photographs of it and selected one taken from the left-hand front corner. Because the house is set high, the camera lens was at the level of the house basement or below it, so all perspective is above center; the ground line is practically horizontal, while the roof lines are in high perspective. Note how the windows in the end gable are sloped, while first-floor windows are almost level with the base.

The house originally had a fireplace in every room, so it has five chimneys, three of which are visible. The walls are laid up roughly in courses, odd sections of stone being set in to maintain the lines. (Actually, relatively flat stone surfaces are achieved on interior and exterior courses, with rubble filling between them.) The big trees in the foreground at each side are maples, while the shrubbery is mostly evergreens, two trimmed vertical yews flanking the front door. Chimneys are brick.

Tools are indicated step by step—at least the ones I used. The wood was Oregon sugar pine, $2 \times 12 \times 18$ in ($5 \times 30 \times 46$ cm). I decided to make the drawing directly on the wood, and enlarged the photograph by the point-to-point method, including window and door locations. I had no later use for the drawing, so I did not make it on paper first; you may prefer to have a drawing of exact size for reference. It is conve-

Fig. 289. Historic Broadstairs in Ghent, New York, is 250 years old with walls of Yonkers traprock nearly 2 ft (.61 m) thick. This photo, with a close-up, provided the basic pattern and detail of rear shed and far-side porch. Flanking trees were stylized and modified to obscure less of the building; they soften the house ends and amplify the illusion of perspective. Base planting was modified slightly for clarity. Front-step railing was eliminated; if added, railing could be formed of music wire set into drilled holes.

nient, by the way, to enlarge from the photograph in direct ratio. I had a 3 × 5-in (7.5 × 12.5-cm) print and enlarged it exactly three times. I left framing branches on both sides, stylizing them to soften the edges of the carving.

Step-by-step carving of a house "portrait"

(Fig. 291) The sketch should be strengthened on the outer outlines to guide in the grounding-out. The depth of carving is somewhat arbitrary. I decided in this instance to lower the background 1 in (2.5 cm) and to self-frame the carving. Setting in the lines is not too vital because any crushing of the upper fibres will be cut away anyhow, including the edges of the foliage swags. (Foliage swags are stylized from those in the photo to reduce the obscuring of the house and to permit convenient carving of the background.) Only major outlines are

Fig. 290. This plaque portrait of the historic house is 2 × 12 × 19-in (5 × 30 × 48-cm) Oregon sugar pine. Background is lowered 1 in (2.5 cm), while house ends are ½ in (12.7 mm) below the surface at left and almost ¾ in (19.5 mm) at right. Finish is matte varnish followed by antiquing with teak oil stain.

Fig. 291.

necessary at this juncture. To permit the house corner itself to be at the surface, small blocks were glued on at the eave and for the corner bush at the base. These simplify carving and give a desirable projection to the near point of the finished piece. Bost-

ing was done with ⅛-, ¼-, and 1-in (3.2-, 6.3-, and 25.4-mm) flat gouges, ¼-in (6.3-mm) round gouge and ⅛-, ¼-, and ½-in (3.2-, 6.3-, and 12.7-mm) firmers. Depth was checked with a machinist's 6-in (15-cm) scale with a slider that could be set to 1 in (2.5 cm). Any pin with a 1-in (2.5-cm) mark on it will do, but the scale is convenient.

(Fig. 292) A photo flattens perspective, so if relief is to be unusually high, the sketch must be modified from the photo, depending upon the depth of relief. (If the house were in the round, all dimensions would be true to scale instead of foreshortened; this would be nearly true of very high relief as well.) When carving the sloping side and front, the dimensions of windows and other details must be carried in from the surface *vertically*, so I carved around each to get the desired slope to the wall—about ½ in/8 in (1.3/20 cm), or ¹⁄₁₆ in/1 in (1.6 mm/25.4 mm). If the depth at the edges were to be increased to several times that, the widths of windows and other details would have to be increased from those in the photograph to gain a realistic effect. Some care must be used in setting-in to maintain vertical sides. To maintain a constant slope on the end wall, begin by carving the desired slope on the portion of the wall between first- and

Fig. 292.

Fig. 293.

second-floor windows, which is unob-structed, then work outward from this base. Tools must be kept very sharp, and can be the same as those for grounding-out, plus a knife for tight corners.

(Fig. 293) Once the general wall surface is carved, window surfaces can be cut back to the same slope. Remember to allow wood for the projecting sill and capital on each window, as well as for the eaves of the house itself. Eaves can be shaped and chim-neys cut back to shape, then scored to sug-gest bricks. (I actually carved vees with a knife to outline bricks, which is perhaps excessive detail.) A V-tool can be used for some of this, but it is likely to tear wood across grain unless it is unusually sharp at the tip. Window mullions are not projec-tions, but V-grooves. You can show sash outlines, but such detail is unnecessary.

Fig. 294.

Fig. 295.

(Fig. 294) The front is roughed in the same manner as the end wall was. It is more complex than the side, particularly at the outer end, where contouring is deep and windows are small and close together. Also, the central pillar of the front door and the decorative windows over it make it impossible to get a continuous surface except at the eave. Immediately cut down the level of the windows at far right for tool clearance, unless you have short-bent tools. Allow extra width at a major projection like the front door to get later slope and mouldings depicted on it, as well as a small porch and simulated steps in front. (I abandoned the stair rail as unnecessary and not particularly attractive.) I worked out varying textures for the nearby trees and for the bushes, actually carving stylized maple leaves on the tree areas and using gouged surfaces with enhancing lines on the bushes, all done with fluter and veiner. The flared capitals on the windows can be carved originally.

(Fig. 295) Note the difference in the widths of the left and right windows caused by perspective, also the difference in the heights of the yews flanking the porch, which in actuality are alike in size and position. In this case, the photograph is the best guide for perspective. Once wall and window slopes are attained, details can be carved, including various capitals on columns and mouldings. The far-right window has been antiqued; compare the effect. Note dentate moulding under the eaves and over the door. Texturing of the yew is done with a V-tool, cutting out small chips. Maple leaves are an approximation of 5-lobed leaves, much larger than scale. The wall is textured, as are the porch steps and other elements. The carving was not sanded. It was given two coats of spray matte varnish to seal end-grain areas and avoid stain buildup there. Then a teak oil stain was painted over the surface and immediately wiped off with a cloth, so it is retained largely in depressions. Final surfacing was to polish with neutral shoe polish.

Doors and entrances

DOORS HAVE ALWAYS BEEN SYMBOLIC as well as functional: they bar the world or invite it to enter, but in either case they are the focus of the building and, as result, have received special attention from architects, builders, and owners. Carved doors, usually highly individualized, are familiar, particularly on public buildings—flat surfaces invite decoration.

Both foliage and fanciful beasts have been common motifs in design, alone or mixed with geometric patterns, scenic panels, busts or other significant elements for highlights. The doors pictured here are only a sampling of what can be done, but they range from the blocky carving of stylized animals in Fiji (Fig. 296) through a very appropriate grape pattern in Peru (Fig. 298), to the many variations possible in Moorish distortion of the Arab alphabet to obtain a scroll pattern of a holy phrase (Fig. 299).

Fig. 296 (above).

Figs. 297, 298. The double doors of a winery in Pisco, Peru, are also an advertisement for its product. They show the juice of the grape entering the characteristically shaped aging jars.

Fig. 298 (right).

Fig. 299. Traditional leaf patterns are combined with Arabic letters on a Moorish carved door in Toledo, Spain.

12

Carving Models

I SUPPOSE every boy at heart is a model builder, as is every grown craftsman. Almost every whittler is a model builder in a sense, for what is an in-the-round figure, a decoy, a windmill? All are models. And a model builder must be a whittler as well, because the knife is the most versatile of tools and wood the most versatile of materials, be it only for patterns for metals or plastics. Of course, any model store these days has a variety of kits with plastic and metal parts for model ships, planes, boats, autos—whatever will appeal to the person without the skill or the desire to make his own from scratch. Somebody, however, whittled the originals.

The secret of good model making is accuracy and attention to detail. You *must* get a likeness, even though it is mechanical or geometric. Two other points that I must mention about models are that they tax your ingenuity and that you will be able to use up not only many otherwise too-small wood scraps, but also some of those odd bits of metal and other materials that you've been saving for so long. I find myself using little bits of ivory, brass, bronze, aluminum; for instance, I used a found wedding ring for a crown, a tiny silver cross in a steeple, an odd-shaped bit of metal for the central figure in a fountain, and so on. Models provide an excuse to paw through all sorts of out-of-the-way stores, and they provide a great opportunity to show off your ingenuity. And it's something to talk about—modestly, of course—when the model is displayed.

Model boats and panels

INEVITABLY, SOME CARVINGS, particularly models, almost demand components of other materials. This project is such a case, a proposed gift for the owner of a 28-ft (8.5-m) cruiser. It could have been a scale model, an in-the-round carving, a panel, or almost anything else. The model would not just be a woodcarver's job; it would have too many metal fittings and a fibreglass hull. An in-the-round carving would be, in effect, a model devoid of some of the fittings, and likely to be somewhat static as well. My solution was a panel of the boat at high speed, coming almost head-on, so practically none of the deck fittings and similar hardware are visible. However, this introduces the problems of bow waves and wake, which for such a boat are mostly foam, and of a distorted perspective.

When the project was first discussed, I saw the boat and took a number of photographs, both of it and of an oil painting which included it. All were static to me. However, we did find a catalogue that provided deck cross sections and a 2 × 2½-in (5 × 6.4-cm) color photograph that suggested the present pose. I enlarged the silhouette by the point-to-point method to fit a piece of butternut I had, assuming that, when the time came, I'd be able to solve the problem of the waves, and that either music wire (tempered steel) or silver wire would form the visible portions of the rails. Whether or not the windscreen would be plastic like the original was also a moot question.

Fig. 300. Photo taken for details, note the many fittings, which would clutter up a woodcarving. Only the horns (whittled maple dowel, silvered) and rails are included in the carving. (Photo courtesy Bertram Yacht Company, Miami, FLorida.)

The accompanying step-by-step pictures (Figs. 302–307) show my solutions, some of them compromises. I tried the waves in various forms and techniques, and ultimately simply stylized them. I added a front block to make the boat project still more from the background, and I decided upon music wire rather than silver because of its greater stiffness and resistance to casual mistreatment. Teak or walnut would have been a better wood, particularly for the figures—except their color would probably have been too dark. Pine or basswood would have been too soft, at least in my opinion. There is no tinting or color.

Step-by-step carving of the cruiser

(Fig. 302) A point-to-point sketch was made of a 2 × 2½-in (5 × 6.5-cm) catalogue picture to provide this pattern; pictures I could take were of necessity only details. The panel is butternut, 1¾ × 12 × 18 in (4.5 ×

30 × 46 cm), with a bit of the scrap glued on to extend the top of the hull where it bulges, thus effectively increasing the panel depth to 2¼ in (5.7 cm).

(Fig. 303) An hour's roughing with ¼- and ½-in (6.3- and 12.7-mm) firmers and a 1-in (2.5-cm) flat spade gouge, produced this blank. Background was lowered 1¼ in (3 cm) on a tentative basis, and left with gouge marks plainly visible. Fortunately, grain was largely parallel with the surface, so only in one or two spots (upper left, for example) was it necessary to change the direction of the cut.

(Fig. 304) Experimental cutting was done to create some sort of wave form, because the spray actually resulting from the passage of a cruiser at speed is impossible to convert to solid lines. Original form was a deckled irregular surface (left), but this looks more and more like a mushroom or a sponge

Fig. 301. Bertram 28-ft (8.5-m) cruiser before a storm, a 1¾ × 12 × 18-in (4 × 30 × 46-cm) medium-relief plaque in butternut with music-wire rails. Finish is varnish, spray matte or satin, with Kiwi® shoe polish (neutral on hull and people, brown on background and sea).

Fig. 302.

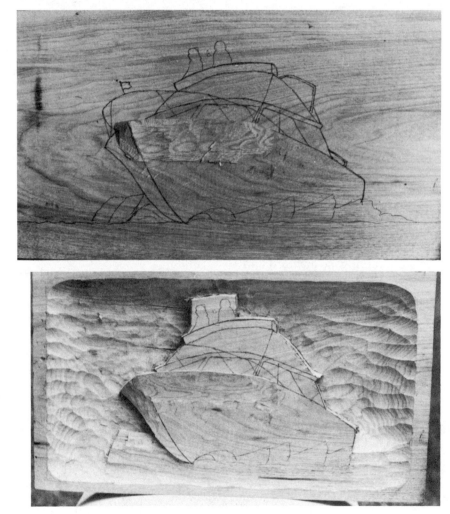

Fig. 303.

Fig. 304.

now. Tools are ⅛- and ¼-in (3.2- and 6.3-mm) gouges and a veiner.

(Fig. 305) The later wave form on the right is a simple series of loops suggesting the solid part of the waves created, with little effort to simulate spray. The hull shape was also refined and the decision made to retain the glued-on portion, at least for the time being.

(Fig. 306) Getting the proper slope and angle to the superstructure is an exercise in forced perspective. This is *not* an in-the-round carving, so the third dimension must be foreshortened. In this case, the superstructure cannot be carried all the way back to the background at the left (as viewed) because this would not allow enough wood for the female figure, and the forward slope of the front of the boat must be faked as well. This can be done by eye, using the right front (as viewed) of the superstructure as the high point. It was finished with firmer and flat gouge.

(Fig. 307) How close the left-hand edge of the superstructure can come to the background depends upon the female figure on that side. I carved her practically against the background and with her right hand resting on the windscreen (which determines its location and slope exactly), then sloped other surfaces in accordance. She is in partial profile, which adds complications, particularly in carving the face so close to the background, but the male is full-faced, which makes only the ears a problem. Figures were done with knives.

A power cruiser is extensively decorated with chrome-plated gadgetry: vents, funnels, chocks, mooring lights, rails and stairways all over the place. In this "pose," most of the deck appurtenances are fortunately not visible, but the rails are, and in forced perspective at that. With an action picture (Fig. 300) as a guide, the railings could be distorted to suit. I began with the simple ones at the stern, and left the main rail until last. Almost all of the metal work here is #18 music wire (0.041 in [1 mm] diameter), which is stiff and difficult to cut, but will stay in position once it has been placed. The burgee is copper mounted on a straight pin, which in turn is bent around the rail and glued with "magic" glue, as are the joints of the supports. To reduce bulk, the wire is flattened before being formed into the loops on the supports.

The background was too light and patterned, and the block glued on the front

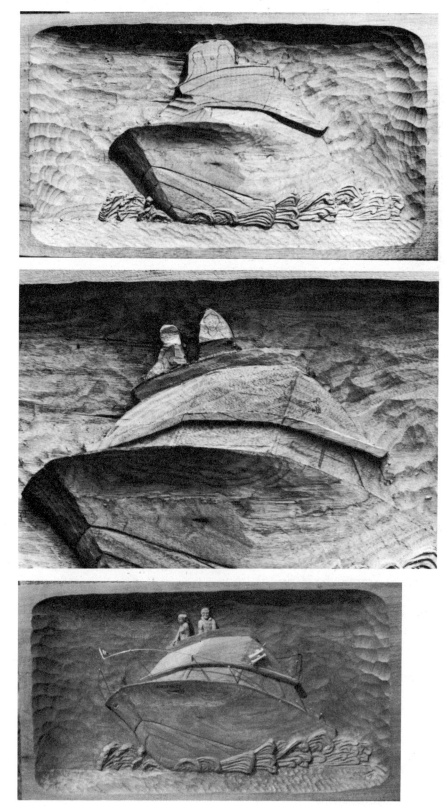

Fig. 305.

Fig. 306.

Fig. 307.

Fig. 308. Iceboat (with red-and-white Manhasset Yacht Club burgee) and Dyer Dink® 10, a sailing dinghy. The iceboat, tallest of the models, has aluminum runners and is sloop-rigged (has two sails). They are of sen wood.

Designs for the 22 yacht-club burgees, or identifying flags, were taken from a piece of fabric, but are also available in yachting books. They were sawed from ¼-in (6.4-mm) plywood, varnished, then painted with oils in the three American-flag colors of red, white and blue (or two of these three). To give them a little flair, each has a stub mast of gilded ¼-in (6.4-mm) dowel nailed to its inner edge.

Of the ship models, one, about 4 in (10 cm) long, was carved as a double-sided low-relief silhouette in mahogany; the others are assemblies with separately carved hulls, masts and spars of split bamboo from a discarded window shade. Sails are of exotic veneer woods carrying identifying symbols made with oil paints, while rudders and centerboards—or dagger boards—were whittled from birch tongue-depressors and inserted in whittled mahogany hulls. Tillers were whittled from toothpicks. Tallest of the boat models is about 7 in (18 cm). Most elaborate is the Mako 17-ft (5.2-m) outboard in Fig. 309, with a plastic windscreen, a music-wire rail, seats cut from dowels set on brads and a whittled outboard engine with a rotating aluminum prop. It is about 4 in (10 cm) long.

All burgees and boats in Figs. 308–310 have miniature screw eyes at balance points, while the sailing models are suspended from wire hangers through holes in the tops of the sails, as near balance point as possible, so that they will hang in sailing position. Sailboats were sprayed with matte varnish after assembly to protect them in the event of moisture or mishap.

was visible, so I "antiqued" some areas with teak stain, and accented the background darkness with brown Kiwi® shoe polish, using neutral Kiwi on the rest. This provides the low gloss I prefer. If the dark polish is applied and then wiped off before it dries, it will create darker edges and lines to generate the "antique" effect. The twin horns are whittled from dowel rod and silvered. The only other decorations are the twin white chevrons on the burgee, which otherwise is a natural copper color. (The club burgee is dark red and white anyway, so copper is close, and is less artificial against the background brown.)

Model boats and burgees as Christmas-tree decorations

A PROFESSIONAL MAY BE ASKED to carve some rather unusual things—which sometimes involve more painting, modelmaking or cabinetmaking than actual carving. These Christmas-tree decorations, for a family very much concerned with sailing, are a case in point. They are really individual mobiles, and offer ideas for other carvers who want to do something different.

Fig. 309. Mako 17 (left), Blue Jay (lerado sails), Laser International (jungle aspen sail) and Cape Dory 14 (commonly used for frostbite sailing in the winter, with striped sail—which is tinted veneer).

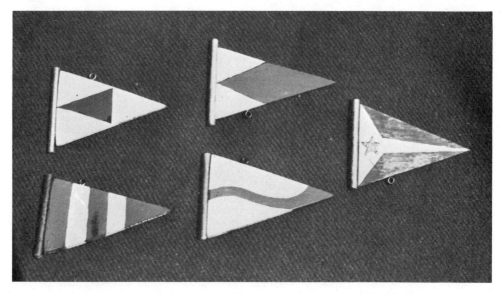

Fig. 310. Burgees are uniform in size, 2¾ × 4 in (7 × 10 cm), with ¼-in (6.4-mm) gilded dowels for stub masts, but differ widely in coloration—as would be expected. They are more painted than carved. Colors are red, white and blue pigments mixed with gloss marine varnish, two coats for opacity. Identification names were lettered on the lower edges.

Fig. 311. Before World War II, I photographed this model of the 1746 shop of "Thos. Shaw, Cabinet Maker & Turner." It was complete with working lathe (belt-driven), stain-mixing and painting area. tools, fireplace and products.

Figs. 312, 313. Miniature toilet and wash basin for the bathroom of a dollhouse, which I made to standard 1:12 scale and painted white. Toilet seat and cover are hinged.

Fig. 314. Fireplace of the shop model in Fig. 311.

Fig. 315. Miniature furniture in the same model shop.

(More on models and miniatures in Appendix I).

13

Carving Faces and Heads

THE HUMAN FIGURE is probably what we know most intimately and think we know best. Other things around us—animals, flowers, man-made and other inanimate objects—impinge upon us and we know them after a fashion. We give them human attributes and describe human attributes with them interchangeably. Other elements—heat, cold, rain, distance, mountains, water, fire, etc.—affect our well-being, so we interpret or represent them in various ways, but basically we relate everything else to ourselves. This is particularly true of primitive artists.

It follows that the most interesting subject for a whittler or a woodcarver is the human figure. Many of the carvings pictured in this book are primitive, but they are basic as well. They show much more graphically than words the many approaches and attempted solutions to the problem we know best, yet never solve—ourselves. This author tries to provide answers, both by supplying basic proportions and techniques, as well as by showing how woodcarvers all over the world have solved the problem, or have tried to solve it.

We who have always had trouble carving the human form can take heart from the knowledge that we are not alone. A few of us, gifted with a second sight, are able to carve the human form or face with little difficulty. For the rest, it is a slow and painful process. But that is no reason to abandon the effort; the way to make a good human body, or a good human face, is to make one after another until they approach what our inner eye sees.

First: likeness

THE FIRST STEP IN ACHIEVING A LIKENESS is to attain a general similarity. You must be able to carve a pig before you attempt to carve a particular one. For centuries primitive carvers have carved the familiar objects around them, and the more gifted or trained among them have gone on to carve the personality of particular individuals—portraits. This is a fundamental urge all carvers have: to carve a recognizable likeness.

This is not easy. It involves careful study of the individual to see how that individual differs from the norm, particularly in the face and head. It is relatively easy to duplicate bulging muscles, a flat or bald head, a crippled limb, but harder to emphasize the smaller, and more important, variations. If you fail, you have a caricature at best, but more likely a cartoon.

The layman is most critical of an attempt to carve a human, because he is best schooled in the differences between individual people. But it is just as important, if you are carving an animate or inanimate subject, to be able to see how that individual subject varies from what the observer expects, and to stress those variations enough so that you have a likeness. Regrettably, a great many carvings of such subjects are inaccurate, and hence lose what I might term a sympathetic treatment. You can put a trunk on a post and call it an elephant, or add a forked tongue to a grub and call it a snake, and perhaps get away with it. But the keen observer sees the difference and rates your carving accordingly.

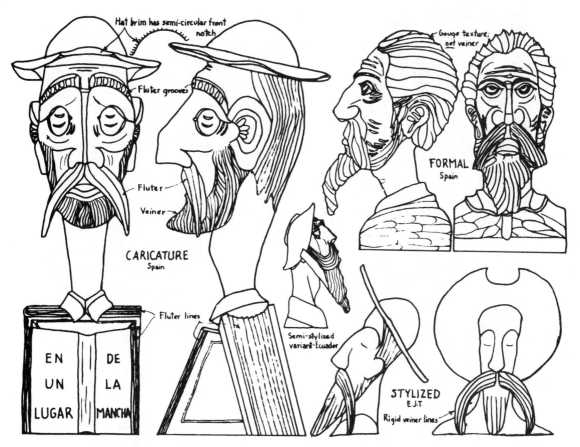

Labels on figure: Hat brim has semi-circular front notch; Fluter grooves; Fluter; Veiner; CARICATURE Spain; EN UN LUGAR; DE LA MANCHA; Fluter lines; Semi-stylized variant-Ecuador; Gouge texture; not veiner; FORMAL Spain; STYLIZED E.J.T.; Rigid veiner lines

Fig. 316. Four versions of a popular subject, Don Quixote. Compare the simplification, streamlining, and lack of detail of the stylized version (lower right) with the detail of the others, which also put more stress on texturing.

How to carve a face—and head

"HOW DO I CARVE A FACE?" is probably the most common question asked by woodcarvers intent upon improving their work. Unlike some other operations in the art, there is no simple answer here. This question leads to a question in reply: "What kind of a face do you want to carve?"

We all use the face as the most important recognition feature among humans. We establish race, mood, background, experience, state of health among strangers and identity among friends. We worry about the "face we present to the world." We know a great deal about the face, which we normally look at first and longest when we meet someone, so we set a higher standard for its proper reproduction. A carved fig-ure can be misproportioned, awkwardly posed, or otherwise distorted and we are not particularly conscious of it, but we are immediately conscious of any error in a face, however small. What's more, we have memorized an endless number of stereotypes for races, for nationalities, for ages, and particularly for specific individuals. We have a catalogue of images for historical figures based largely upon the face—for Jesus, Washington, Churchill, Lincoln, Jefferson, Napoleon, Franklin, and an endless number of other people—all from some particular portrait or traditional description.

The individual may, in point of fact, have differed markedly from the accepted facial image, but both his face (and his age!) are

Fig. 317 (left). Contemporary Spanish caricature of Don Quixote (left), with somewhat stylized eyes and nose. Formal head (Fig. 318, above) of the same subject is rough-finished and tinted, and also from Spain. Hair and beard variations are suggested by gouge cuts rather than the fine veiner lining of the first piece.

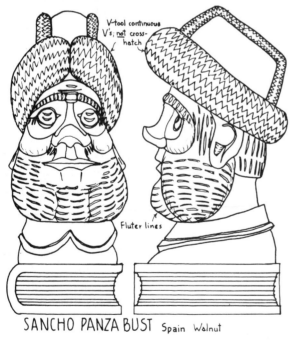

V-tool continuous V's; not cross-hatch

Fluter lines

SANCHO PANZA BUST Spain Walnut

Figs. 319, 320. This head of Sancho Panza is a companion-piece to the Don Quixote caricature (Fig. 317), and contrasts sharply with it in that it is stubby where Don Quixote is attenuated. Similarities in eye treatment identify them as products of the same sculptor.

now fixed by convention. You can vary his body structure and even his clothing with some impunity and few are likely to notice, but change the face even slightly and even your friends will dismiss the carving as faulty.

There is, for most of us, a long and painful process before the achievement of good faces. No formula will help us beyond the initial stages. One can memorize facial proportions and a series of steps in carving and still not produce memorable faces for a very long time. This may be, in fact, one area in which there is no alternative for apprenticeship; that is, for long and painful practice. You must carve a thousand faces, as Michelangelo said, to carve one *good* face.

Initially, it is important to understand your goal and the steps towards it. What kind of face do you want to carve? Is it to be grotesque, caricature, formal face, or portrait? (see Fig. 316) Is it to be in the round or in low relief? If you are shooting at formal faces or portraits, endless carving of caricatures, for example, will be of little help. And once you abandon the profile depiction to carve faces at various angles, low-relief carving can be most difficult of all, because actual proportion must be replaced by a simulation of proportion in the third dimension. The smooth, well-rounded cheek may actually become almost angular in cross section, and eyes and mouth are no longer uniform. The Egyptians, for example, spent centuries learning how to carve a relief head other than in profile.

The head is an egg

THE HEAD IS roughly like an egg set on its point on the neck which is half a head long in front for a male, thinner and longer for a female. The neck is like a tree growing out of the shoulders and leaning forward, so that the head is set forward, more so in the female than in the male. The face—forgetting for the moment any receding hairline—is the length of the hand and about two-thirds as wide as it is high. A most important fact is that the eyes are almost centered vertically—a very common mistake is to place them too high. Each eye is a fifth to a quarter of the width of the head, and they are normally about an eye-width apart. The tip of the nose is about halfway from the center line of the eye to the chin, and the mouth center one-third of the distance from nose tip to chin. Mouth width is 1½ to 2 times eye width, lip thickness (at center) a fifth of the distance from nose to chin. The ears are roughly as long as the nose and aligned with it front to back. They are just behind the center of the skull.

The most common mistake in face carving is to have the cheeks too far forward. The angle formed by nose tip and cheekbone is roughly 90° and the nose projects from the egg shape of the head when viewed in profile. The chin also projects from the same viewpoint, but not as much—only the classic witch has chin and nose tip aligned vertically, and even vertical alignment of brow and chin is rare (and makes for a very pugnacious face).

All of these ratios are averages, of course; any face varies from them. That's what makes us individuals. The face is not symmetrical, even if it looks that way; the small differences from side to side account for the abnormal look of a mirror image. Also, hairdos, beards, jowls and fleshiness tend to obliterate the egg shape, so the basic proportions are merely takeoff points for carving. (The Spanish caricature carver capitalized on this by making Don Quixote's face much longer than an egg shape and making Sancho Panza's almost pear-shaped—see Figs. 317, 319 and 320.)

To me, there are two vital elements in making an in-the-round head in repose. One is the eye size, shape and positioning; the other the profile, which includes brow, mouth and chin. The profile is particularly important in portraiture because it establishes the basic structure of the face to a considerable degree. (Typical profiles belonging to certain races or even tribes are being obliterated by intermarriage, particularly in the United States, so that children today often show decidedly mixed profiles. In countries where there has been a considerable period of such inter-marriage, Mexico and Latin America for example, many mestizos are a mixture of Spanish or other European blood and one or more Indian tribes, and their precise origins are almost impossible to establish visually.)

The basic face, whatever its eyes and profile, is distorted by expression. Surprise shoots the eyebrows up, anger pulls them together and down, joy widens the mouth and lifts its outer ends, thus partially closing the lower eyelids, while pique and despair draw mouth corners down (tending to narrow the mouth). The face is also affected by age: vast networks of wrinkles, crow's-feet at eye corners, deep lines around the mouth, hollowing of cheeks, bulging of the nose, possibly greater prominence of the chin from loss of teeth, sagging jowls. It is also affected by corpulence—the fat face is wider in the jowls and has few wrinkles. These are refinements of face carving, but are essential if the face is to be representative and alive, rather than static and frozen. Try a single head, starting with the nose at one corner of a squared stick. This automatically leaves wood for the ears and gives a reasonable slope to the cheeks, an idea which the Mayans used on cornice ends a thousand years ago.

Carve a step-by-step head

START WITH A SQUARED BLOCK. Mark off from one corner, both ways, a line down from the top 1½ times the width of the block; i.e., if the block is 1 in (25.4 mm) square, put the line 1½ in (38.1 mm) down from the top. This is the chin line (Step I, top left, in Fig. 323). Halve the distance from this line to the top and put in the eye line. Now, a third of the way down from nose to chin, put in the mouth line. (Some authorities make this two-fifths of the way; the difference is not too vital.) Now cut in perpendicularly across the corner at the chin and nose lines, and notch out wood

from below so that you create a new sloping flat about a fourth the width of a side.

Notch the corner at the eye line (Step II), cutting from both above and below. Also mark notch-outs for the ears, the bottom one in line with the bottom of the nose, the upper *above* the eye by an eye width. (It is convenient at this point to draw in a "reference eye" on the eye line, about a third of the block width in length and shaped like the oval of the complete eye, not just of the "open" part between the lids: Step II in sketch.)

Begin to round up the head on top, notching over the ears to make this easier, and splitting off the wood above the eye notch to flatten the brow (Step III). Also notch below the ears and rough-form the neck. Draw in eyebrow lines on the brow as arcs meeting at the center of the eye notch and rising to 1½ eye widths over the eye line at each side.

Mark in a nose triangle with its apex in line with the *top* of the eyebrow arcs (so there is some width of nose at the eye line). Cut V-notches along the nose line to meet perpendicular notches cut in along the eyebrow line (also Step III). Mark in the mouth line again, and extend the lines on each side of the nose to the lower edge of the jaw. Cut a small notch to denote the mouth-center line, then cut away the sharp point of the chin and round the chin and mouth area to notches extending down from the nose.

Now begin to rough-shape the eye (Step IV), remembering that the eyeballs and lids are about an eye width apart and that each eye is about a fifth of the finished width of the head. Making these shapes involves deepening the grooves between eye and nose, and carving grooves between brow and eye, and eye and cheek.

This completes rough-forming, and you're ready for the shaping of Step V. Form the eyeball more accurately and slope the line below the brow. (Here we're carving an inset eye. Many people have eyes with folds or laps in this area, but let's leave that for a later head.) Rough-form the nostrils and fair off the cheeks next to them. Draw in a hairline to suit your fancy, then the ears and nose, and carve the shapes. Remember that there is a bulge along the brow line, particularly in males, so slope back from just above the eyebrow line to the hairline.

Now you're ready for Step VI, finishing. Final-shape the ears and put in whatever convolutions you wish. Do the same for the nose and nostrils, as well as for the lips and chin. Normally the lower lip is shorter and fuller than the upper, and there is a definite groove between lower lip and chin—the chin is a fat oval bump, actually. Open the eyes by drawing in lid lines and hollowing out—*very* carefully—between them. Drill pupil holes and suggest the outline of the corneas by shallow V-notching. These latter steps determine the personality of the face, so they must be done carefully. Suggestions and ideas for carving the features are given in this chapter, including sketches. Study them! And good luck.

Carving the eyes—fine points

THE EYES are normally just above the median line of the head, but setting them at the median line is fairly accurate. There is an eye width between normal eyes, two eye widths between the pupil centers. There is one open-eye width between the eye and eyebrow, and the eyebrow is highest and widest over the outer third of the eye. Eyes may be larger, or smaller, open wider or less, be wide apart or close. The forehead ends in the outer rim of the orbital (brow) circle.

All of these factors must be considered in laying out and carving eyes. Some other factors are sketched. These include: The upper lid normally covers the upper edge of the cornea; the lower lid is at its lower rim or below. (When the eye looks down, the upper lid lowers with it; the lower lid does not. When the eye looks up, the space between the lids is increased and usually the eyebrow is lifted as well.) The upper lid extends over or outside the lower at the outer

Fig. 321. Step-by-step carving of a head.

edge, and the lower outer corner of the upper lid extends below the center of the globe of the eye.

The *canthus major*, the eye muscle next to the nose, must be shown if eye shape is to be right. So must the bulge of the cornea and the bulge of the upper lid over it. Eye-cavity position and shape are very important; whether eyes bulge or are recessed, whether the line where brow meets nose is above or below the eye center, and the exact shape of the folds below the upper eye-brow, all are important if a likeness is to be obtained.

Most of the motion in the eyelids is made by the upper lid. In fact, a closed eye looks as if the upper lid had come down to cover the eyeball, an effect accentuated by the upper lashes, which cover the lower. Lowering the upper lid therefore creates a brooding or sleepy look; raising it can suggest, successively, attention, or alarm and fright. In this last emotion, the cornea may practically disappear upwards.

A wink is not just a closed eye, unless the winker is an expert. The normal person winks by pulling up the cheek muscle below, so the whole side of the face, including the mouth, is pulled up. The crease between cheek and eye is intensified and the lower lid pushed up. Wrinkles radiate from the eye corners.

I begin an eye by shaping the oval of the eyeball, taking care to make it large enough to include the lids and allowing for any bulge between eye and brow or anything abnormal—like a puff—beneath it. The eyes may actually slope upwards or down-wards slightly at their outer corners, and they may be slightly above or slightly below the normal eye line. (For rough purposes, the eye line is the center of the skull; actually, for most of us the eyes are just a bit above that, the skull center line running along the center of the lower lid.) Once the eyeball is shaped, be sure the eyeballs are roughly parallel with each other, because the eyeballs are basically in line from the side. The brow and the cheek slope back, so

the eyeball is nearer the surface of the face at the outer edges.

Now lay out the lines for the upper and lower lids. The upper lid is normally up above center a bit more than the lower lid is below it, and the *canthus major* muscle at the inner edge points slightly downwards towards the nose; this is actually a slight extension of the eye oval. Cut along the eyelid lines and bost or ground out wood between them, retaining the curvature of the ball (which isn't a ball but a long oval, as we see it). If you want to be accurate, carve the cornea as a slightly raised circle extending slightly under the upper lid. It is a circular shallow dome about a third of the width of the visible eye.

The upper lid has a slight hump over it. Also, the upper lid extends just beyond the lower at the outer edge. In small figures the pupil can be just a hole drilled (again *very* carefully to avoid splitting off wood above and below) deep enough to appear black in normal light. Final shaping of the lids is the last operation, with perhaps a slight accenting of the cornea edge by V-grooving.

There are many simpler ways to make eyes, beginning with the rough V-notch and painted dot of quick caricatures. I have sketched a number of conventions (Figs. 321, 322); suit yourself, depending upon figure size and your abilities. If you really want to be meticulous, don't drill the pupil but carve it out, leaving a tiny regular or arcuate triangle at the top to simulate the "glint."

Carving the nose and profile

WHEN STATUES, ancient or modern, are damaged, it is always the nose that bears the brunt of it. The same can be said for prizefighters and caricatures. The nose is often considered to be a major factor in determining race and disposition. Nose shape is inherited, so we have Roman noses, Semitic noses, retroussé noses . . . you name it. Actually, much of the lore about noses is untrue. They have certain

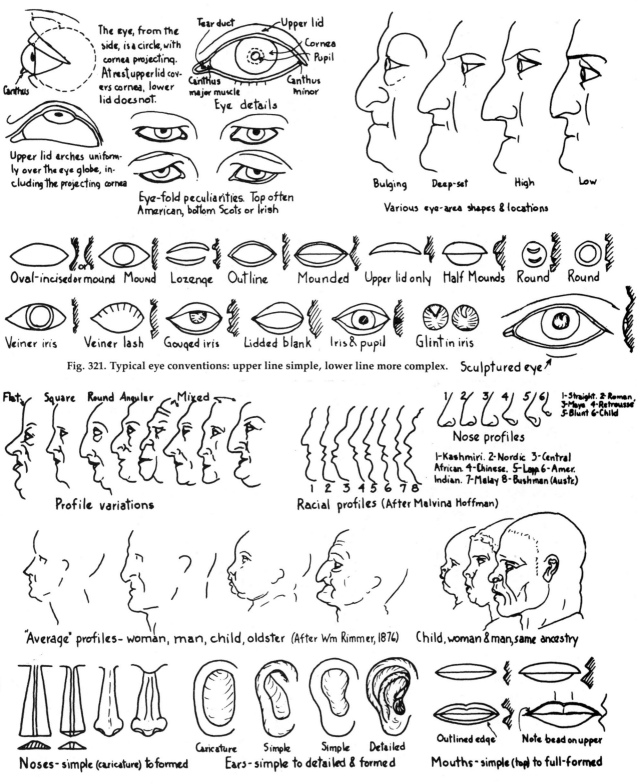

The eye, from the side, is a circle, with cornea projecting. At rest upper lid covers cornea, lower lid does not.

Canthus

Tear duct — Upper lid
Cornea
Pupil
Canthus major muscle
Canthus minor

Eye details

Upper lid arches uniformly over the eye globe, including the projecting cornea.

Eye-fold peculiarities. Top often American, bottom Scots or Irish

Bulging   Deep-set   High   Low

Various eye-area shapes & locations

Oval-incised or mound   Mound   Lozenge   Outline   Mounded   Upper lid only   Half Mounds   Round   Round

Veiner iris   Veiner lash   Gouged iris   Lidded blank   Iris & pupil   Glint in iris   Sculptured eye

Fig. 321. Typical eye conventions: upper line simple, lower line more complex.

Flat   Square   Round   Angular   Mixed

Profile variations

1-Straight. 2-Roman. 3-Maya 4-Retroussé 5-Blunt 6-Child

Nose profiles

1-Kashmiri. 2-Nordic 3-Central African. 4-Chinese. 5-Lapp 6-Amer. Indian. 7-Malay 8-Bushman (Austr.)

Racial profiles (After Malvina Hoffman)

"Average" profiles- woman, man, child, oldster (After Wm Rimmer, 1876)

Child, woman & man, same ancestry

Noses- simple (caricature) to formed

Caricature   Simple   Simple   Detailed

Ears- simple to detailed & formed

Outlined edge   Note bead on upper

Mouths- simple (top) to full-formed

Fig. 322. Profiles and facial variations.

Fig. 324. This street orchestra was commonly produced in the Tyrol of Austria about 50 years ago. The figures are tinted and stand about 6 in (15 cm) high.

physical shapes, but to translate that into disposition and the like is folly.

Be that as it may, the nose is a key element in carving a face, and the shape it is given can be vital. Actually, the nose, forehead and chin are interrelated, and are based on the shape and structure of the skull. If the skull is rounded in front, the nose tends to be wide and flat, the forehead receding, and the mouth and chin profile both receding and longer than the norm. If the skull is squared off, the forehead and chin tend to line up in profile and we get the classic relationship of eyes at mid-head, with nose tip halfway down to the chin, and mouth centerline one-third to two-fifths of the distance from nose to chin.

The effect of all this is to make the nose very important in portraiture—more so than perhaps it deserves to be. But it is a very visible feature, particularly in profile, so all the details must be right, including the ridge line and overall height, as well as the spread of the nostrils, their shape and inclination, the meeting of nose and brow, its projection from the face, and so on. Miss the nose and you miss the portrait, and no mistake. As a matter of fact, make the nose genteel and you have a poor caricature, so the rules work both ways.

Nose width is primarily a frontal element, but it does influence nose shape and projection. A wide nose is usually flat, tilting the nostrils and making the flesh outside them appear wider than from the front. A retroussé nose makes the nostril openings more visible from the front and raises the nose tip above its base, making the septum more prominent. Also, there is considerable variation in how the nose joins the brow. In some individuals, the brows meet in a V over the nose; in some there is a transverse wrinkle at the joining; in others, the nose actually runs up above the brow line or joins it without the declivity that most of us have.

The swell of puffy eyes, the shape of the lips and chin and the cheek profile are all much more visible in the silhouette than in the frontal view. So are many of the more subtle distinctions of race, sex and age. If the correct profile is achieved in a carving, much of the frontal forming of lips, chin and nose is simplified. Thus it pays to study the various profiles in which I have tried to show the variations, and perhaps have overemphasized them slightly (Fig. 322).

The nose itself can be a simple tapered wedge in quick studies, but can be very detailed in faces expressing a particular emotion, or in a portrait. Even more important, however, in portraiture or emotion is

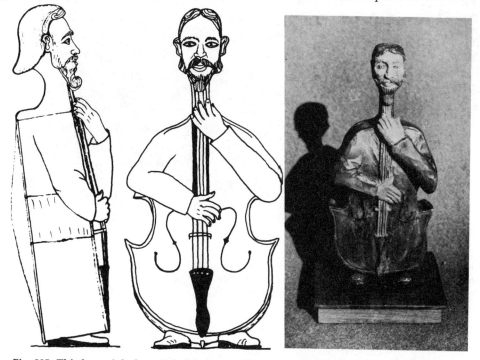

Fig. 325. This bass viol player is in jelutong and is a caricature of a friend. Personalizing inanimate objects is a common form of a caricature and can be quite challenging.

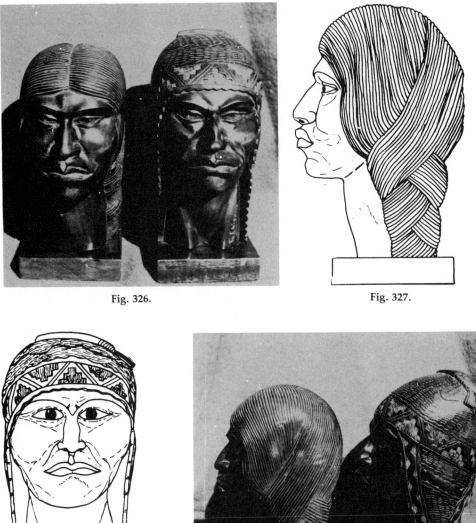

Fig. 326.

Fig. 327.

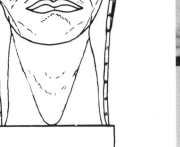

Fig. 328.

Fig. 329.

Figs. 326–329. These male and female heads of Bolivian Indians offer interesting contrasts despite having the same basic look. Note the wider eyebrows and thicker lips of the woman, and the prominent Adam's apple and stronger neck of the male, for example.

the mouth, which actually is the biggest single element in expression. It is changed in shape to express an emotion, and the rest of the face must accommodate itself. Also, we have come to associate full lips with sensuousness, thin lips with severity, restraint, even parsimony.

The mucous portions of a full mouth may occupy as much as two-fifths of the total distance from nose base to chin, particularly in female faces. The female is customarily carved with thicker lips than the male, perhaps because we have become accustomed to artificial widening if the lips are too thin. (Paradoxically, the brutish male face also has thicker, more protruding lips.) The hearty laugh is supposed to show teeth—which adds a carving problem.

There are an endless number of details about carving the mouth, including the amount of cupid's bow in the upper lip, the comparative "pouting" fullness of the lower lip, the groove from upper-lip center to septum, whether or not to carve a bead along the top of the upper lip. (It is very rare in nature, but even the Egyptians knew it enhanced the face of Queen Nefertiti.) I always seem to have trouble with the subtle curves at the end of the mouth, and between it and the chin, because a slight change alters the expression so much.

Shaping the ears and jaws

THE EARS, once the amount of projection has been established, are basically also a matter of the silhouette. Many carvers give them a fairly standardized shape, with a few token gouge lines to suggest the convolutions inside. I have drawn, and usually carve, a somewhat more exact shape, because it is quite visible in the full head. Also, the jaw line comes up to meet the middle of the ear lobe. It can be quite prominent in a square-jawed male, almost indistinguishable in a soft-faced female, and shape varies widely with individuals. But it does establish the beginning of the neck, and the position of the Adam's apple in male necks with prominent ones. It also

establishes the thinning of the head bulge behind the ears, which in turn has to do with the shaping of the back of the head. It must always be kept in mind, even when you carve a bushy-haired and bearded head.

Carving portrait faces

TO MAKE A PORTRAIT—or a caricature—of an individual, you must identify and catalogue the features that are unusual or abnormal, even if only slightly so. This is relatively easy with some individuals— witness the distinctive hair styles and moustaches of Hitler and Charlie Chaplin, the big ears of Clark Gable, the craggy face and mole of Lincoln, the square jaw and mouth of Washington (caused, I am told, by poorly fitted false teeth made of wood), the bushy hair and youthful face of Kennedy, the toothy grin of Carter, the specially shaped and prominent noses of Durante, Nixon, and Hope. Only when a face is near the norm—as in the case of Gerald Ford—is there a problem.

The men I mentioned above are public figures and have been cartooned so often that the eccentricities of their faces are well known. The cartoonist and the caricaturist accentuate these eccentricities, of course, but often so does the portraitist, although his accentuation is more subtle. Indeed, the line between portrait and caricature may be very hazy—one may be produced when the other is intended. I have a life-size portrait of myself in oil that my wife has never hung because the artist crossed that hazy line into caricature—at least in her opinion.

Some of us seem to have been born with the ability to distinguish and depict subtle differences in countenances. This is true of most portrait artists; the rest of us can approach portraiture only with much effort, time and difficulty. Also, the portrait artist seems to get some of the personality, the inner feelings, of his subject into his rendering. It may be a special position of the head, a quirk of an eyebrow or the lips, a "look" around the eyes. This is especially

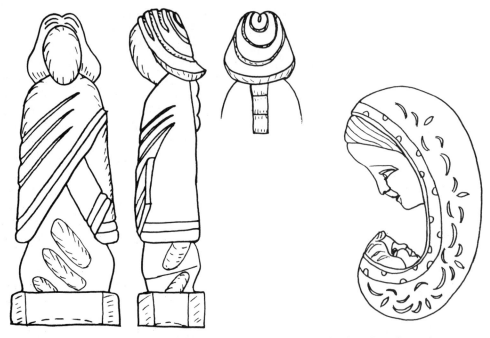

Figs. 330, 331. The faceless, highly stylized girl (left) is, surprisingly, from Ecuador, as is "Madonna and Child," a simple treatment that is carved both left- and right-handed to be mounted in pairs.

difficult to accomplish in wood because the material is solid and opaque, while flesh may vary subtly in tint or tone, even, occasionally, in translucence. Also, it is difficult in sculpture to reproduce the eye, to distinguish between pupil and iris, as well as to show the paleness of the eyeball around the iris, and the color and density of the eyelashes.

Another difficulty is to express the fleeting expression caused by muscle movement and the interrelationship of muscle, bone and skin. This is particularly hard when the subject is a child or a fleshy adult, because of the absence of the lines and wrinkles that personalize a mature face. In my own limited efforts at portraiture these elements have caused extreme difficulty, so it is with complete bewilderment that I watch portraitists capture a likeness. They have an inner "eye" which I do not, apparently, possess. I have had some success in working from photographs, which "freeze" an expression, particularly when they include strong light and shadow. (The usual

frontal flash photos are almost useless because they flatten shadows.)

Portraitists have told me that they look for and record, either mentally or by quick sketches, the slight abnormalities we've been talking about, and then exaggerate them slightly in producing the portrait. It can be a lengthy process of trial and error, which is difficult when the base material is wood. Even the meticulous transfer of physical dimensions may not work, particularly if the wood has grain or imperfections, or is difficult to carve. This suggests walnut or mahogany, or teak if you can get it, all of which have enough inherent color to create an initial disadvantage. Maple and holly are better for color, but much more difficult to work. Pine or basswood are scarcely worth the time for anything but a quick caricature supported by tinting. And texturing—the development of tiny flat planes or an overall roughened surface, which delights the sculptor in clay and gives his work a personal touch—is doubly difficult in wood because such effects are usually obtained by appliquéing more base material upon an already well-sculptured likeness, and the woodcarver can't put material back that he has already cut away. All in all, if you attempt portraiture, I wish you luck. You'll need that, as well as skill and patience—both for yourself and your subject—because a fairly sure way of losing any likeness you may have achieved is to fiddle with it in the absence of the subject.

Carving caricatures

CARICATURES have undoubtedly brought pleasure and enjoyment to more people than formal carvings, whether it be to the carver or to the recipient. Until very recently, caricature has not been recognized as an art form because it violates a great many of the principles of formal art. Now it is an acknowledged folk art. Items can be made rapidly, thus sell at popular prices for the most part, and the quality does not have to meet some traditional standard. While we tend to think of caricature and whittling as knife products, caricaturists in Europe are much more likely to use chisels—because they have learned to carve that way. And American caricaturists with considerable experience supplement the knife with small gouges, like the veiner and the fluter,

because they're so much faster and more convenient in producing concavities and fine lines.

Not all so-called caricatures *are* caricatures, of course; some are simply crude and some result from mistakes; some are simple and some quite sophisticated; some are original, while many are copies of traditional patterns. The line between realism and caricature is ill defined and caricature is often an unintended result. The carver is seeking to achieve more than a frozen, sticklike figure, or to suggest an emotion or idea that goes beyond physical characteristics. He must do this by providing expression, or by exaggerating a pose or physical characteristic, which is what an artist does when he achieves a portrait that is somewhat beyond a photograph of the subject. Overexaggeration makes a likeness into a caricature, but where the line between them is, no one can say exactly.

Caricature and "Western-style" carvings come closest to having a standard formula—most use a series of notches and surfaces to suggest facial contours. The competent caricaturist tends to develop his own style, often based upon his own countenance, and tends to repeat the head in the same position and with the same expres-

Fig. 332. Caricature of Don Quixote is not a direct copy of Spanish versions. This one is from Ecuador and has a flow and unity that many caricatures often lack.

GAUCHO & GAUCHO BUST Argentine

GAUCHO & PONY Argentine

Gauchos stained black & antiqued

Hat separate.

COWBOY Peru 150 yrs old Originally painted

HUASO (Cowboy) Chile

Primitive... carved by a huaso

Fig. 333. South American versions of cowboys: "gaucho" in Argentina, "huaso" in Chile. They are unpretentious and powerful, and often primitive in design.

sion until it becomes a stereotype. Further, a great many such faces are not caricatures as much as three-dimensional cartoons or, more properly, grotesques—they rely for their humor upon a gross distortion of one facial feature, usually the nose. Such a face can be carved rapidly, with little practice, and its deficiencies in detail are compensated for by judicious touching up with paint or ink. To the serious carver, such a face eventually becomes trite. He seeks expression, likeness, normalcy, and comes to realize, as a sculptor friend remarked, "Caricature is a cop-out." But it doesn't have to be.

It is possible to personalize an object in order to create a character from a particular calling or to suggest a personal characteristic. Thus, an identifiable caricatured human face can be put on the body of an animal or drawn within the outlines of an object such as a kettle, a pot, a bottle, or whatever. One example of this kind of caricature is the bass-fiddle player I carved in jelutong (Fig. 325). In point of fact, the possibilities in caricature are almost endless and there is little reason to repeat the same one, unless it is done simply for commercial reasons.

South American heads

IN SOUTH AMERICA, as on other continents, there are concentrations of woodcarvers. The largest, at present, is in a contiguous three-country area: southern Ecuador, northern Peru (which not too long ago was southern Ecuador), and western Bolivia. This is a high-altitude, wooded region. Carvings, regardless of the country of origin, are generally similar in type and subject, well formed and well rounded, smoothly finished (in contrast, for example, with those of Argentina, which tend to be angular, rougher in finish and stained a fairly uniform black). These are not primitive carvings—they are obviously made by skilled carvers to familiar patterns and are designed for sale to tourists.

Ecuador is by far the most prolific producer of these carvings, with a wide range of both three-dimensional figures and panels, as well as a wide range of subject matter, from religious figures to animals, particularly the llama. Mahogany seems to be the preferred wood. There is evidence of a kind of mass production: the same figure will be available in several sizes, with larger sizes showing more detail. Exact duplication of form and detail suggests profiler roughing, although sellers insist this is not so.

Peruvian carvings are less regular and include a number of individual pieces made by Amazon Indians and other remote tribes. There is less of the Spanish and church influence in the work there, and still less in Bolivia, where favorite subjects appear to be the Indians themselves, although the technique and finish suggest considerable training and direction atop inherent skill. The Argentine figures, on the other hand, lean heavily to gauchos and horses, but each figure differs in pose and other details from its fellows. In Chile, there is relatively little woodcarving, probably because much of the country is treeless or nearly so. The emphasis appears to be on the carving of other materials, except on Easter Island, which is Chilean only by agreement and treaty.

Most interesting of the carvings shown here, at least to me, are the Bolivian Indian busts (Fig. 326). They have similarly "fierce" faces, but they are precise in facial detail, and I have tried to point out in my sketches some of the elements that distinguish the feminine head and face from the masculine one. They are superficially alike, but the subtle differences between the sexes are quite clear upon close inspection. How many times have you carved a face that somehow was of the wrong sex? (The cop-out is of course to put on a moustache or beard, or to rely upon the difference in hairdo to distinguish between them, but that's not sure-fire either.)

Fig. 334. Stylized gypsy seer was carved almost entirely with ¾-in (19-mm) No. 6 gouge and finished with wax only. A later commission (foreground) included a 1¾-in (4.4 cm) crystal ball.

Carving for a crystal ball

PERIODICALLY, I FIND IT INTERESTING to make a composite carving, combining wood with some other object or material to provide a striking contrast. Thus, I have used a gold wedding ring to make a king's crown, an actual fishing fly caught in a trout's jaw, real chain or cord and so on. The idea is merely a variation of the familiar inlaying with shell, metal or other woods for contrast. In this particular example, however, my intention was to provide some form of display mounting for a 4-in (10-cm) crystal ball I have owned for over 40 years.

The original thought was merely to carve a pedestal covered with cabalistic symbols, primarily a pillar with the ball at the top. It seemed more interesting, however, to carve a gypsy woman with the ball, so that the crystal-gazing concept would be emphasized. The objective was to feature the ball and allow it to catch the maximum amount of light. Any frontal panel seemed to enclose it too much, as did any composition in which the hands of the figure hovered over it. My ultimate choice was a side view with the ball cupped in the gypsy's hands, the entire figure of the gypsy thus becoming a silhouette and a support for the ball (Fig. 334). This effect was accentuated by the decision not to detail the figure and, further, to cover it with a scalloped texture produced with a relatively flat ¾-in (19-mm) gouge. I had a block of well-seasoned maple 4¼ × 16½ × 16½ in (11 × 42 × 42 cm).

The final decision was simply drawn on the block and sawed out on a band saw.

14

Carving the Human Figure

Carving a famous nude

CERTAINLY one of the best-known nudes in the world is the Little Mermaid who sits forlornly on a boulder in the harbor of Copenhagen, Denmark. I had seen a great many pictures of her, but when I decided to carve a miniature, all I could find immediately was a color photo I had taken years before. I projected that to a 6-in (15-cm) height and copied it for my basic pattern, deciding to develop the figure as I carved. I guessed that a 6-in (15-cm) figure would be a bit under 4 in (10 cm) through, even posed at the angle of my available photograph, and I had a piece of mahogany 4 × 10 × 10 in (10 × 25 × 25 cm), slightly checked on the top, and therefore discarded by a nearby piano maker. By the time I had the figure roughed out, I had also found an additional photograph (Fig. 336) through the Danish Information Service in New York. They helped but were frontal views, so the Mermaid's back had to be largely improvised.

The procedure outlined by the step-by-step photographs previously can, however, be applied to any copy from a photograph or painting, and most will be far less exacting. As you will note, my version is a bit more plump and buxom than Edvard Eriksen's original (see Fig. 335) and makes her look a little older. The original mermaid, according to the story by Hans Christian Andersen, was a 16-year-old who fell in love at first sight with an earthly prince when she made her first trip to the surface

of the sea. She saved his life in a shipwreck, but had to leave him on shore, where another girl found him and revived him. Although the mermaid sacrificed her tongue, her 300-year life, and her tail to become an earthling, the prince eventually married the other girl, and the mermaid became a mere spirit of the air.

The story I read has her changing directly from tail to legs and feet, but the sculptor shows her with attenuated feet and fins up and down shin and calf, so I made her the same way. You may recall, also, that some years back vandals beheaded her. The Danish government found the original plaster model and replaced the head, complete with downcast mouth and sad eyes—but no tears. Mermaids cannot cry.

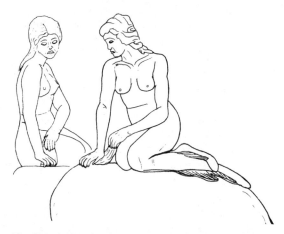

Fig. 335. A sketch of the famous bronze by Edvard Eriksen.

Fig. 336. The Little Mermaid, made by Danish sculptor Edvard Eriksen, is the symbolic statue of Copenhagen. She sits on her stone at the entrance to Copenhagen Harbor. (Photo copyright Royal Danish Ministry for Foreign Affairs.)

(Fig. 337) Lay out the silhouette on a planed side, using a template or carbon paper, and reinforce the lines with a soft-tip pen. If possible, lay out the back as well. If you have a band saw, you can now saw out the shape. I used a carpenter's crosscut saw and ripsaw, sawing straight lines to salvage the wood at upper corners. A coping saw can be used, but it is extremely slow and somewhat inaccurate on a 4-in (10-cm) thickness. Shorter cuts can be made about

the head; then the profile is roughed to shape with a 1-in (25-mm) flat gouge or equivalent. Roughing should be about ⅛ in (3.2 mm) outside guidelines at crucial points. The parallel-faced base can be clamped in a vise for this.

(Fig. 338) A double template will prove helpful in the next few steps. The interior template or pattern will provide the base line of the figure itself and makes early

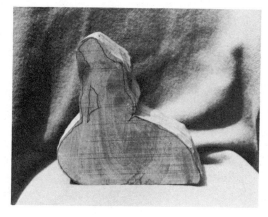

Fig. 337.

checking easy. The outer template is of little use until final-shaping of the silhouette. Plastic, cardboard, or paper can be used; I used notepaper in this instance because these templates have short-term functions.

(Fig. 339) Bring the silhouette fairly accurately to shape. The safe way to do this is to draw lines across with a square at critical points, and to then cut guidelines with a deep ¼-in (6.3-mm) gouge or a fluter. Check these guidelines with the square to be sure that they are square with the outer faces and of uniform depth across the block; they generally tend to be high in the middle. (I have left one or two gouge lines to show what I mean.) Now, with the 1-in (25.4-mm) gouge, fair the surfaces to just outside the guidelines, using the channels and the square to check for accuracy. *Do not* detail the face or fingertip silhouettes; leave wood there in case you need it later. Be as

accurate as you can because the next steps will destroy your outline of the figure as well as much of the flat faces, which are reference surfaces.

(Fig. 340) The side view (if one is available) could now be copied on the blank and the side silhouette sawed out. But I had only a front view and didn't trust my side sketches implicitly, particularly because the mermaid is at an angle to the faces of the boulder (as was my original photo and the silhouette). Therefore, I started with her left leg almost parallel to the boulder front face, and cut back the front of the block at an angle which would place her toe ¼ in (6 mm) in from the block edge, and her left knee about ¾ in (19 mm).

(Fig. 341) Lay out the knee positions and cut back the face of the block to expose the right knee. You will need V-tool, ¼-in (6-mm) and ⅛-in (3-mm) firmers; the 1-in (2.5-cm) gouge is too big. Now begin to form the legs, shaping the lower legs and allowing wood for the fins. (Unlike the usual mermaid, she does not have a tail; instead, her feet are overlong and she has fins extending from the shinbone, back of the calf, and the heel.) Locating and shaping the feet and knees will provide the approximate location of the buttocks, and shaping the leg gives the point of contact of left elbow and thigh.

Fig. 338 (left).

Fig. 339 (right).

Fig. 340.

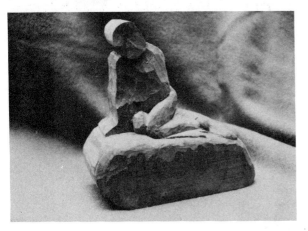

Fig. 341.

Fig. 342.

When this is approximated, the arm can be laid out and roughed. Corners of the boulder have been rounded in front merely for convenience and comfort in handling.

(Fig. 342) Set in the outline of the left arm and cut away wood above and below, sloping the shoulder back at the same time. Remember not to cut out wood high on the chest; you must leave wood for the left breast, which projects forward of the arm. Also, the right knee is in back of the left, and the line of the knee fronts will establish the line of the shoulders and buttocks fairly accurately, because her torso is not twisted. To locate a given point on the blank, place the template accurately over such surface as you can, and stick a straight pin through the desired spot into the wood. In cutting the arm, leave a little extra wood where possible for shaping. It is easy to cut away wood, but difficult to put it back.

(Fig. 343) Establish the lines of the breast bottoms and the cutout between right arm and body. Shape the breasts and cut away between them and the left arm. Also bring the right shoulder back so that it is behind the left one, a little less than parallel to the knee fronts. Begin the cutout between right arm and body. This must be done very carefully, or you'll be short of wood for the right or left arm.

(Fig. 344) Begin to cut the stomach well back, particularly on the right side. The mermaid is not sitting erect, but is slumped over in grief, which accounts for the slightly forward hunch of the shoulders and the exceptional hollowing of the stomach. It will also account later for a rounding of the middle of the back. It may be of assistance at this point to rough out the shape of the hollow between right arm and body and to begin to define the face as a reference. Note that I have merely indicated the nose, which makes quick relocation of the template possible. Once the line of the nose is established (front to back), the back of the head can be cut away to the shoulder in preparation for locating the neck. Also cut away wood above the breasts and prepare to locate the right hand by cutting back at the wrist. In this pose, the mermaid is not resting on her right hand—the heel of the hand is actually slightly raised so that her weight is essentially on her right buttock (which will be lower than the left because she is sitting on her feet, which extend to the left).

(Fig. 345) By sighting from the side, locate the rough line of the back and begin to remove wood there. Don't go too far initially: remember that the curved back and the weight on the right buttock will cause it to bulge slightly. However, the buttocks should be in line with the knees. Also, if you haven't done so previously, shape the legs and feet, allowing for the fins, and round off the boulder behind them to the general shape. Don't chamfer it yet, because we are still in doubt about the precise position of the right buttock. The same goes for the back of the head, because that depends upon where the front of the head ultimately will be. Also, begin to shape the left arm and to hole through just above the elbow, which will establish the line (depth in from the front) of that side of the stomach.

(Fig. 346) Now it is time to establish the lines of the back and the right arm. Begin by creating the hollow on the left side behind the elbow, then round the back, remembering that her back is a curve from top to bottom because her pose is one of utter dejection. Also, work in from the right side around and behind the hand so that you can establish that buttocks line. Lay out the rough banjo-shape of the back, and round the buttocks and waist to agree with the left side. I found at this point that I had estimated the top of the back of the rock almost ¼ in (6 mm) too high, because the right buttock was obviously too shallow and was not enough below the left to make the pose

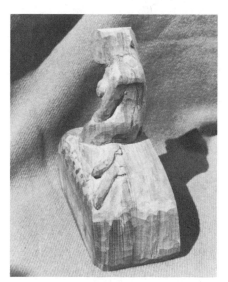

Fig. 343.

Fig. 344.

Fig. 345.

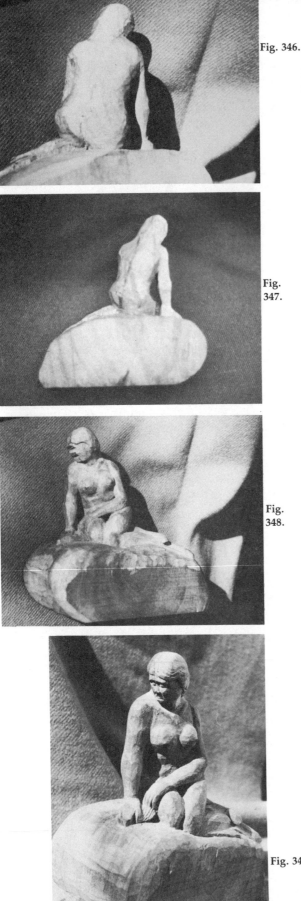

Fig. 346.

Fig. 347.

Fig. 348.

Fig. 349.

natural. When the top was lowered, the left foot gained needed thickness as well.

(Fig. 347) With the general shape of the back worked out, draw in the line of the spine. Basically, it is a curve from the base to the waist, then bends to rise almost straight up. Also round the back of the right shoulder and continue to shape the back and right buttock, working carefully on the latter so that it is in line (with respect to both height and position) with the right knee. It will help, at this point, to remove the wood behind the left arm, down to the level of the thigh. The right thigh, by the way, is almost horizontal on top, front to back, rather than rising as the left one does. It is also sensible, at this point, to hollow out between the thighs under the left arm, a tricky job that requires small tools like fluter, veiner, and a small firmer or flat gouge, preferably $\frac{1}{16}$ in (1.6 mm), or a long-tipped knife blade. The left wrist is actually free of the right thigh, but I would not cut it loose yet.

(Fig. 348) Now shape the right arm, particularly at the shoulder, to establish the line of the upper chest and breasts. This will, in turn, provide the base of the neck and the general location of the head, which is turned to the right so that the line of the nose is about midway between right nipple and right shoulder. You can also begin to rough out the head, rounding it on top and establishing the general hairline, so the face can be positioned below it. You will probably find, as I did, that the upper back should be thinned and rounded more, and that the breasts are too large and too far forward. Also, there must be a crease across the stomach because of her stooped position.

(Fig. 349) Shape the cloth below her left hand and the hand itself. The hand should hang, half-closed, from the wrist, with the cloth caught between thumb and first finger and trailing from the fingertips. Cut a deep vee beneath the wrist to lift the hand from the right knee. (This can be sawed through with a thin blade, but will be stronger if left solid in back.) Shape the face, chin, and neck and carve the face, remembering that her mouth should curve down at the corners to show dejection. Be sure the line of the right shoulder is low enough as it joins the hairline so a bit of the neck shows on the right. You will probably have to thin the neck. I did all of this work with knives, one of which had a concave edge.

(Fig. 350) Finish the right hand and lift it from the rock by undercutting. The heel of the hand should be up almost ¼ in (6 mm) so the fingertips can turn down and in. To reduce the blocky effect of the base, round the front corners, put in a notch on the front, and lower the right rear top of the rock. To get a coarse, open texture such as a rock would have, I sanded it with a rotary sander to fair in knife cuts at the same time, then finished with fairly coarse paper near the figure. The figure itself is not sanded, so that the small planes left by the knife will catch the light. This also increases the contrast between girl and rock.

A final word: Once the figure is finished, set it aside for a day, then look at it again, *closely*. You will find a number of fine

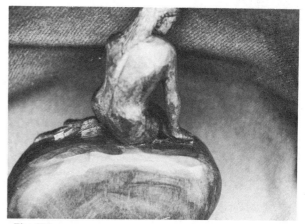

Fig. 350.

changes to make. I spent two hours, for example, thinning down and shaping the right arm and shoulder, another two hours removing fine burrs and other imperfections elsewhere. The figure was finished with spray matte (satin) varnish and clear shoe polish. I made a number of changes thereafter, and found that I could mask them completely by rubbing in a bit of polyester varnish in the shaved spots, wiping it off, then applying new coats of shoe polish over the area.

Fig. 351. The completed carving, finished in wax. Tool marks were left to emphasize the fact that she is wood, and the boulder base has been reduced in thickness to suit the wood available.

Fig. 352. This immense carving of Paul Bunyan, at Bangor, Maine, is 31 ft (9 m) tall. Peavey and ax heads are steel; base is built up of native stone. Paul Bunyan is the legendary lumberjack. Stories have it that Paul weighed 50 lbs (22.5 kg) at birth, and soon outgrew houses and had to sleep out-of-doors. Another legend claims that rocking his cradle caused the high tides on Penobscot Bay, and that the Maine lakes are in the footprints of Paul and Babe, the blue ox. (Maine Department of Commerce and Industry photo.)

Human proportions

THE TYPICAL WHITTLED HUMAN FIGURE turned out in the United States today is a male, often fairly mature and fully clothed, usually in ill-fitting garments at that. He has three wrinkles at each elbow and knee, a sagging seat, and a smirk. A major part of the reason for this is that most whittlers haven't taken the time to learn the proportions of the human figure, and it is difficult, anyhow, to work as the sculptor in clay does: making the figure in proper proportion, developing the musculature, then applying clothing or draperies. Such a procedure is difficult when one is working from the outside in. Nevertheless, any whittler or woodcarver who is familiar with proportion will turn out a better figure, as a sculptor must.

There are certain basic proportions for the figure, some of them dating back to Greece and Rome, including: an arm span equal to the height, the foot the same length as the head, and the face the same length as the hand. We also have developed a basic guide of measuring the body in "heads": the average male is 7½ heads tall, 2 heads wide just below the shoulders, 1½ heads wide at the hips, with arms 3 heads long below the armpit, and fingertips to elbow equalling 2 heads. The average female is somewhat shorter, with narrower shoulders and a broader, shallower pelvis,

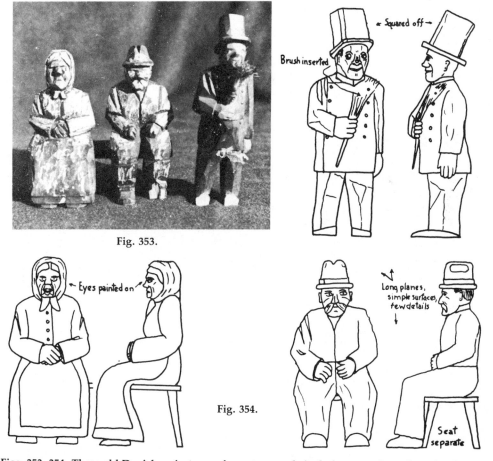

Fig. 353.

Fig. 354.

Figs. 353, 354. Three old Danish caricatures of country people include a seated couple and a chimmey sweep. Such figures were formerly carved by farmers as a wintertime occupation, and were usually colored with dull tints.

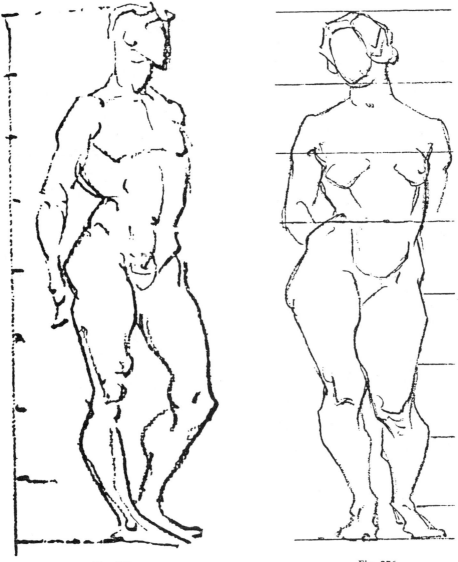

Fig. 355.   Fig. 356.

Figs. 355, 356. Michelangelo made his males 8 heads high, but his females 7½ heads tall.
(From "Bridgman's Complete Guide to Drawing from Life.")

hence wider hips. The narrower shoulders combine with shorter and straighter collarbones to make the neck longer and more graceful, but put more slope in the shoulders. Also, the female neck tends to have a greater forward angle, so there is a greater tendency to look round-shouldered, particularly in older women. The female has a shorter upper arm, hence a higher elbow location and shorter overall arm length.

The male body averages 2¾ heads for the neck and trunk (½ head for the neck, or less), and 3¾ heads for the legs and feet. The feet are a head long and half a head wide. From the ground to the crotch is roughly half the height, as is the distance from the pit of the throat to the tip of the outstretched middle finger. Upper and lower legs are equal in length. The distances from the sole to the top of the

Figs. 357, 358. Companion mahogany busts from the Philippines each about 8½ in (21 cm tall), show how the female curves are gentler than the male from shoulder to nipple.

kneecap, from the kneecap to the point of the *iliac* (farthest forward part of the thigh bone), and from the pit of the throat to the lower line of the *rectus abdominus* (front abdominal muscle) are equal. Roughly speaking, the body can be divided into three parts: neck to hips, hips to knee, and knee to sole. The distance from the sole to just below the knee is a quarter of the height, and the distance from top of head to pit of throat multiplied by 5½ is the total height. In the male figure, the elbow is at the top of the hipbone and the fingertips are halfway between crotch and knee. The female torso is proportionally as long as the male, but the breastbone is shorter, so the abdomen is deeper and the legs are likely to be shorter. However, in females the leg length varies so greatly that it is difficult to estimate the standing height of a woman who is sitting or kneeling.

Proportions of the figure vary widely with age, of course. At birth the center of the figure is above the navel; at two years the navel is the center; but at three the center of the figure is the top of the hipbone. It moves down steadily as the child matures, until it is level with the pubic bone in an adult male and slightly above it in the female (because of her shorter leg length). The child of one to two years is about 4 heads high, at three years is 5 heads high and at six years, 5½ heads. The child of three is about half the adult height, of ten, about three-quarters adult height. The gain in height is about one head between ages 1 and 4, 4 and 9, and 9 and 14—and remember that the head is growing larger as well. The small child's head is almost round; it lengthens in proportion as the skull enlarges. Lack of knowledge of these relationships is the reason so many primitives carve a good Madonna but a very mature Child.

While only the stoop is commonly recognized, both male and female figures change with age and posture. The female figure tends to become broader and thicker through the abdomen and hips as a result of childbearing. Both sexes tend to develop a

Fig. 359 (left). This modern Balinese nude is surprisingly stumpy. Note the oversized head. Fig. 360 (above). Another modern Balinese nude, again with a head that is out of proportion with the body. It is, however, more graceful than the nude on the left.

"pot" as well as the stoop, with advancing age. Women become noticeably round-shouldered as a result of added flesh between the shoulders. Compression of cartilage between the spine segments and between joints reduces overall height, and loss of muscle tone causes general sagging. The early-adult balance of the forward projection of the chest with the rearward projection of the buttocks is lost, allowing the chest to be less prominent and the buttocks more so.

Scandinavian carvers have for many years produced angular, blocky figures that are very well done. (Fig. 353) They are almost formulaic: three creases at elbow and knee, saggy breeches, wrinkled coats, slightly battered hats. Tyrolean carvers produce rounded, chubby figures. African carvers produced lampoons of the white men and women who bought them; these tended to attenuation, as do modern Haitian ones. Most of them show the subject with a smile or a grin, in many cases self-deprecating because of the smiler's dilapidated condition. We have developed a style similar to the Scandinavian in our so-called "Western," "mountain," or "Ozark" caricatures. The subjects are cowboys and Indians, tramps or workmen, but the stump or over-thin figure, the ill-fitting clothes and the V-notch wrinkles are characteristic. Better figures have strong planes, light or no tinting, and some emotion expressed in faces which are generated with relatively few cuts.

Torsos

In terms of planes, the male torso is a rough trapezoid from the line of the shoulders to the nipples, almost at right angles to the sides of the body. The abdominal plane extends downwards from the nipples as a rough triangle sloping inward to the navel, where it meets a plane rising from the crotch to the navel. In back, the line of the shoulders forms the base of a triangle that extends downwards and inward to the waist, where it meets a wider trapezoidal plane rising from the buttocks. The front planes tend to have a convex curve, the back ones a slightly concave one, which is divided centrally by the groove denoting the backbone.

The female figure is basically similar in structure, except that the plane of the shoulder extends farther outward to the nipples and meets the planes of the side in a gentler curve. (Figs. 355 and 356) The frontal planes are divided by the groove of the breastbone. Note that the breasts are set at an outward angle to the front of the torso because of the curvature of the breastbone and rib cage. In the female, also, the upper-back plane slopes outward more to the lower line of the shoulders, then inward to the waist, giving greater curvature to the backbone and a greater stoop to the shoulders. While the male neck is short and thick and rises firmly from the square shoulders, the female neck is longer, more slender and more graceful, and rises at a greater forward angle. Thus, in both sexes, the line of neck to head is not vertical, but slopes forward. Also, the neck is not simply a cylinder. It tapers like a tree growing from the shoulders, more so in the male than in the female because of his normally greater shoulder-muscle development and heavier neck muscles. In addition, the male has the Adam's apple at the top. The female figure also commonly has a considerably greater outward slope to the planes of the lower back, caused by the thicker thighs and more rounded abdomen, which creates a larger diameter at the buttocks and proportionally wider hips.

Greek and Roman artists glorified the male nude, but European artists since that time have preferred the female and considered it the ultimate in artistic achievement. Instincts aside, I find the female torso

largely a series of harmonious curves, while the muscular male torso is much more difficult to carve. A slight change in pose alters muscle location and size, and smoothing the muscle curves tends to make a male torso look effeminate. The female torso is affected by change of position also, but the surface effects are not nearly so evident.

These comments, of course, are intended to apply to formal and properly proportioned, as well as somewhat idealized, youthful figures; older people are rarely depicted in the nude anyway.

Artists tell me that it is not possible to sculpt the human figure without a live model and some training in anatomy, but this is not necessarily true. It is possible to create creditable nudes without formal training, although working with models is a distinct help in locating muscle positions and the like. (One difficulty is that many models are nowhere near ideal in their proportions.)

Nudes made as panels are quite difficult because the third dimension must be flattened, and there is the ever present possibility that the figure will look flat as a consequence. Meticulous care must be taken to produce continuous curves on surfaces. Also, the method of mounting is very important, unless the figure is a silhouette.

Musculature is vital in a male figure

WHEN JUPITER AND HIS BROTHERS ROSE UP against their father, Saturn, and overthrew him, the Titans, a race of giants, were on the wrong side. Therefore, Atlas, a Titan leader who surpassed all men in bulk, was condemned to support the heavens on his shoulders forevermore, or so goes the Greek myth. But Atlas also grew fabulous golden apples, so Hercules took over the support job on one occasion while Atlas picked him some apples, and on another, Perseus came for some. When Atlas refused him, Perseus showed him the Gorgon head, which he was still carrying,

Fig. 361. Sir Walter Raleigh is in cypress and stands 24 ft (7 m) tall, including the 5-ft (2-m) welded-steel base. Arms are pegged and glued in place, and entire figure is coated with transparent plastic-base coatings. It is now on Roanoke Island, North Carolina. (Photo by J. Foster Scott, Dare City Tourist Bureau.)

and Atlas turned to stone, becoming the present Mount Atlas in Greece.

I found this nude male to be much more difficult than the female ones. After all, if a female has enough softly rounded curves and is overlarge of bust and buttocks, that is acceptable, but a male must show muscles, particularly a male in the strained position of Atlas, and muscle bulges change radically with each change of pose. It is advisable to have at hand some standard text on anatomy or any reliable source in which muscles are delineated. The familiar statue of Atlas in Naples shows him as a somewhat streamlined figure, not at all bulky, and with no strain evident in muscles or face. If he is to embody the myth properly, he must be modified.

I chose walnut for the wood, partly because of its color and partly because I wanted tool marks to show, at least to a degree. They emphasize the strength and

roughness of the man. I carved the figure progressively, from the top down, as the photographs illustrate (Figs. 363–372), to minimize the risk of breakage. Also, carving the head and arms to form helps in proportioning the lower torso and legs later. The blank can, however, be band-sawed completely, because the wood between the legs provides the necessary early strength.

A major job with this piece is the forming of the sphere, because small inaccuracies in its roundness will be painfully evident later. Therefore, an accurate template of the desired size should be made—and used frequently. Also, frequent checks should be made to ensure that the sphere, head, and arms are in proper relationship. One tendency will be to make Atlas have an overlong neck, for example, or to give him shoulders that are too wide. Both are caused by doing too much body-shaping before the finished size of the sphere is attained, so that when the sphere is ultimately rounded, the body will no longer be in the required pressure contact. Beware if you plan to have relief elements on the sphere itself, because they may distort its shape so much that it looks grotesque. I chose the safe way and did the sphere decoration with a V-tool and knife as a final carving operation. I showed a series of constellations, each with stars indicated with silver wire. I held the figure on my knees, both to do the incising and to make the holes for the silver-wire inlay.

In any carving of this sort, it is advisable to stop periodically, as any good sculptor does, for an overall inspection. For example, on one carving I discovered I was carefully carving a six-fingered hand. Your eye will pick up such errors if you give it the

Fig. 362. Atlas is in walnut, roughly 4 × 4 × 10 in (10 × 10 × 25 cm) including base. Familiar constellations are incised on the spherical firmament, with 150 stars picked out by silver wire inserts in three diameters to correspond roughly with star magnitude.

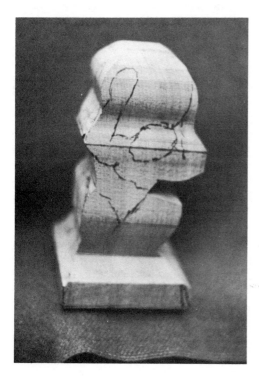

chance. Beware of concentrating too long on one little area.

When this figure was completed, I felt that the base surface should suggest a rocky area, so several parts of the surface were layered like shale. Also, the original base seemed to be too thin for the subject—size had been dictated by the wood available. Thus, another section of walnut was added to increase overall height from 8 to 10 in (20 to 25 cm).

The blank was held in a wood vise for the heavier shaping, most of it done with ½-in (12.7-mm) flat gouge and firmer, and with a light mallet. Details of face and musculature were done with smaller chisels and finally

Fig. 363 (left). Because the figure is small, the blank can be sawed on a bandsaw. Sawed-off pieces are replaced temporarily to avoid destroying sawing guides. If necessary, they can be held in place with glue or with toothpicks in holes drilled in waste wood.

Fig. 364. Relationship of head, neck, arms and hands is crucial, so begin final shaping with them. Avoid making the neck too long and shoulders too thick.

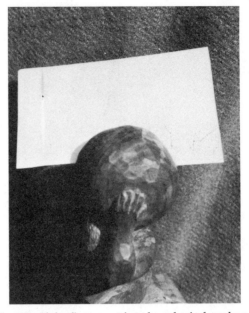

Fig. 365. If the firmament is to be spherical, make a cardboard template of the desired size and use it frequently. One side of the template should be cut away at an angle from the end of the arc to provide clearance for checking near shoulders and head.

Fig. 366 (below). With head, shoulders and arms shaped, the torso can now be defined. Legs are not separated, however, until all heavy cutting is done; nor are feet detailed. This avoids danger of splitting near base from stress at the top.

Fig. 367 (below). Back and front of figure must obviously be worked together to be sure the torso is in proportion. Here again, templates may make frequent replacement of cutaway lines unnecessary.

Fig. 368. The legs can now be separated and shaped. Base is lowered to reveal feet and permit shaping of ankles. If sex organs are to be shown, leave wood for them.

Fig. 370 (below). When contouring is complete, musculature can be put in as well as final details of face and extremities. Base has been slabbed and figure given a preliminary varnish coat to check light effects.

Fig. 369. Shaping of shoulder and buttock muscle bulges is important in achieving general body contours. Points of elbows and knees are formed and wrist and ankle bones located.

Fig. 371 (below). Musculature is as important in back as in front. Note difference in buttock heights, and stress lines in thigh muscles. Detail of base slabbing is also evident.

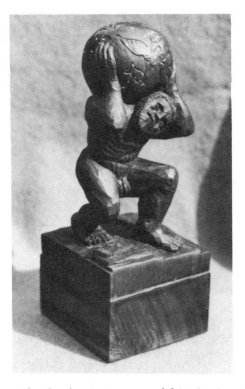

Fig. 372. Right-side view shows heavy thighs, legs and shoulders. The hands are not particularly stressed; they are merely balancing a load pressing down on shoulders and body. Star holes were drilled and plugs of silver wire driven in, glued, then filed smooth. About 150 stars are shown, in three wire diameters.

with a knife. A statuette of this size is small enough to be held in the hand for finishing, and can be turned readily for comparative viewing during the course of the carving, so it presents relatively few problems, except for those involved with depicting stress in muscles and face.

Action figures

MANY SCULPTURES are undistinguished and stiff, and so formal as to be almost unnatural. Even higher percentages of whit-

tled pieces are similarly stiff and are misproportioned as well, so they are more caricature than statuette. Often the whittler has had no training in human proportion, had no suitable model available, was limited by a particular block shape, or was timid about cutting elements free. These may be excuses of the sculptor as well; the old Greeks often carved action figures with arms, feet or legs supported by unnatural columns, bushes, or just lumps of material.

There are subjects which can readily be spoiled if any of the preceding things are done—or mis-done. Sports figures are an excellent case in point, because the best poses involve an instantaneous freeze of a moment of supreme stress. The game of squash offers a good example because the players are constantly in motion, and at about twice the speed of tennis. The player is frequently only slightly in contact with the playing surface, and his arms and legs are spread. Also, the racket represents a difficult sculptural element. (The finished figure can be seen on page 53, Fig. 63.)

Thus, it was with some misgivings that I undertook a commission of and for a squash player, to be executed in mahogany. I had available an action snapshot that was

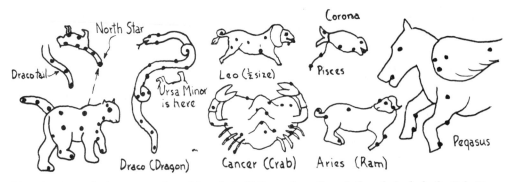

Fig. 373. Constellations were selected largely to fit the surface, though they do include the Pole Star and immediately surrounding figures in proper relationship.

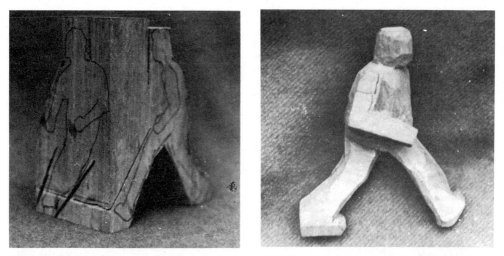

Fig. 374. Rough blanking (left) was done with a straight saw and chisels. Because the figure was small and easy to hold, whittling was the simplest method of fabrication.

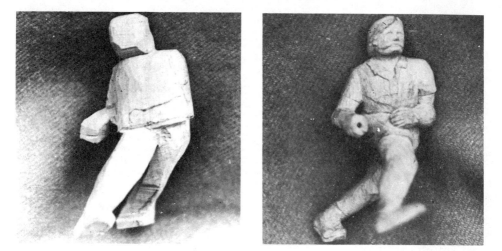

Figs. 375, 376. Rough blocking locates shoulders, hips, and limb position. Face, shoulders, feet, and hands are detailed, the right hand being shaped after the hole for the racket is drilled (right).

taken from dead front, which of itself is rather difficult to find. (Squash courts have side walls, so most photos are taken from above, foreshortening the figure.) Because the player was obviously in contact with the floor only on the ball of one foot, with his body tilted well to the side in a turn, it seemed inadvisable to make figure and base integral. By making the base separate, I could gain both strength and contrast with the figure itself. Also, the racket projects so

far across grain that it would be too fragile to withstand ordinary dusting. Thus, this figure is held to its base with a steel pin running up through the ankle at an angle designed to provide maximum support, and the racket was separately made and inserted.

A major problem was to provide a matching side view, because the legs are spread much wider than the frontal view suggests, and the elbow positions are not obvious

Fig. 377. Statuette is 4 × 7 × 10½ in. (10 × 18 × 27 cm) in walnut, over a rosewood base, and was executed from photographs of all four sides enlarged to carving size and converted to patterns. Photos of the original bronze statue, 10 ft (3 cm) high, that resides outside the United Nations building in New York City, provided a major guide to musculature.

either, nor is the twist in the back which makes the right shoulder appear narrower than the left in the front view. (This will not be a problem for those who elect to duplicate this figure; I mention it for those who elect to depict some other sportsman in some other pose.)

Because there was no base, the entire silhouette could be sawed out to avoid a great deal of roughing. By the same token, the figure was difficult to hold in any conventional way while cutting was done, and I found it necessary to whittle much of it. Also, I made the figure somewhat heavier in build than the drawing, because the client, a squash player, is sturdy, in contrast to the thin and willowy Pakistanis who are the champions in this sport. It was obviously

Fig. 378. Action poses give life and movement to figures and carry them out of the stiff and mediocre "portrait" pose. Sports pages are full of photographs that can be converted into such carvings. Carve the figure in low relief, letting the background support the fragile elements like outstretched arms and legs. (Right) Here is Peggy Fleming performing a back spiral—cut across grain. Checks were prevented from spreading by a vertically grained ¾-in (19.5-mm) backboard that also sets the plaque out from the wall. The 7-in (18-cm) circle on 1 × 9½ × 11¾-in (2.5 × 24 × 30-cm) Oregon pine suggests a spotlight.

(More Action Figures will be found in Appendix I)

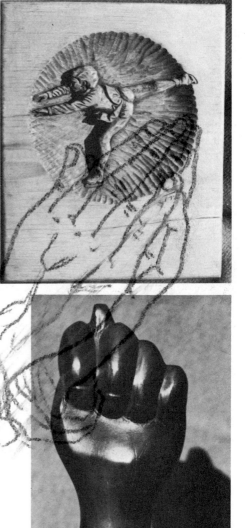

necessary to work carefully on the feet and arms because of the grain, and to be constantly aware of having wood available for the shirt and collar.

The racket is difficult, no matter how it is made. I elected to make it of some other wood than mahogany, to increase the strength. I used maple, stained to approximate the color of the mahogany. The stringing could have been done in several ways. The all-wood method is to thin the area within the rim, then to groove it with a veiner so that the string pattern is inverted. (Only a Balinese would attempt actual carving of the strings.) Another method would be to form the racket and drill its rim for stringing with monofilament nylon or fine copper wire. However, I hit upon the idea of sawing the hollowed rim lengthwise with a fine-bladed jeweller's saw, then inserting a piece of aluminum fly-screen and gluing the assembly. After the glue set, the edge of the screen was ground away to leave an edge that looks very much like that of a strung racket.

Fig. 379 (right). Figa, a fist with the thumb thrust between the second and third fingers, is a good luck symbol in Brazil, usually worn as a pendant. This one is 10 in (25 cm) tall, thrust upward, and emerges from the hat of a typical farmer. The hand has no creases.

Figs. 380, 381. Better known than any subject in the Western World, except for the Nativity, is Albrecht Durer's famous "Praying Hands." This sketch and maple carved panel is by Martin Lohs of Cincinnati.

Hands

BETTER KNOWN THAN ANY SUBJECT in the Western World, except the Nativity, is Albrecht Dürer's (1471–1528) famous "Praying Hands." The hands have been copied commercially in drawings, sketches, and paintings in various media; as plastic, plaster, china, wood composition, and wood panels or wall decorations—perhaps even in brass and cast iron at various times. But, paradoxically, Dürer himself never incorporated them in any of his famous woodcuts! The *Betende Hande* was only a sketch.

Hands are extremely difficult to carve well, and this 475-year-old design will provide excellent practice. Martin Lohs, Cincinnati, who made the copy-sketch and panel pictured (Figs. 380, 381), says of them:

"Hands are one part of the anatomy which must be brought to life as you work them, otherwise they will look like a pair of gloves. Take a careful look at your own hands while you carve this pattern. Note the difference in thickness in the fingers between the joints . . . try to get the wrinkles at the joints as you see them in your own hands." Mr. Lohs has carved this subject numerous times, improvising a different background each time (Dürer's sketch had no background). The hands can, of course, be carved without a background; these are practically in-the-round, anyway. They were carved in maple, but can be carved just as readily in pine or basswood. The work was stained to add character and shading.

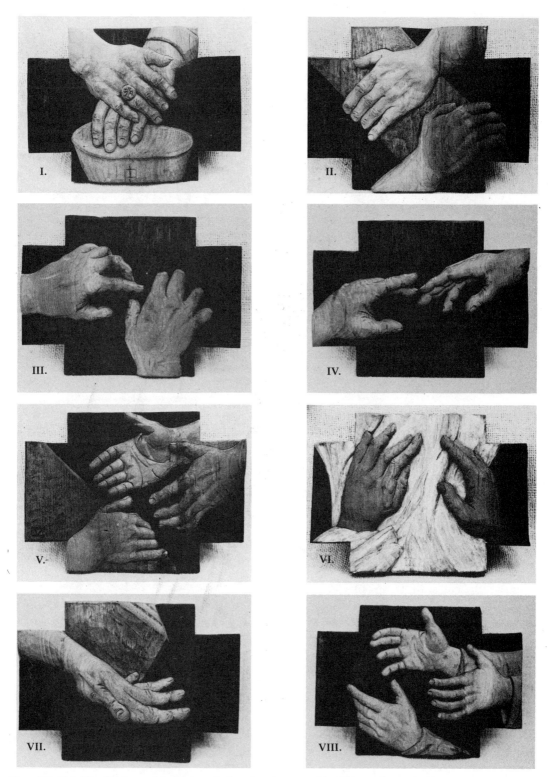

Figs. 382–389. The Stations of the Cross, designed and executed by Eleanor Bruegel of Broomall, Pennsylvania, at the suggestion of Mons. Richard J. Simons, pastor of St. Anastasia Church, Newtown Square, Pa.

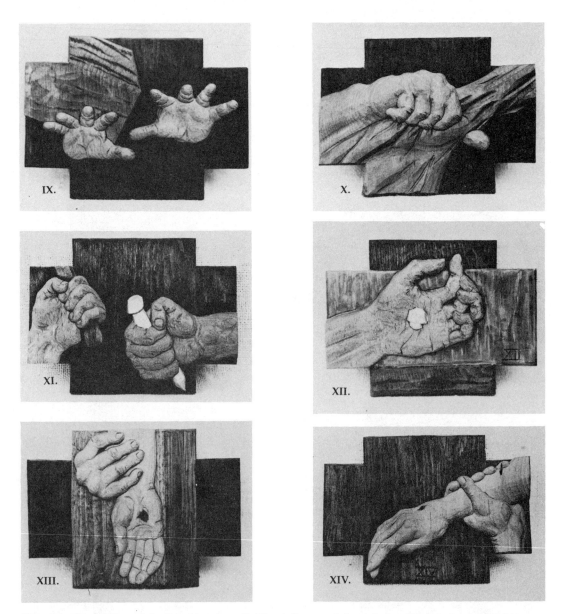

Figs. 390–395. Stations of the Cross (continued). The stations are I. Jesus before Pilate, who washes his hands. II. Jesus takes up the Cross. III. Jesus falls for the first time. IV. Jesus meets His Mother. V. Jesus helped by Simon of Cyrene. VI. Veronica wipes Jesus' face. VII. Jesus falls a second time. VIII. Jesus meets the women of Jerusalem. IX. Jesus falls a third time. X. Jesus stripped of His garments. XI. Jesus nailed to the Cross. XII. Jesus dies on the Cross. XIII. Jesus taken down from the Cross. XIV. Jesus laid in the tomb.

Humans stylized

STYLIZING THE HUMAN FIGURE CAN TAKE MANY FORMS beyond the shift from realism to some single or "accepted" treatment that the word may seem to suggest. Thus a stylized figure can become symbolic, near-abstract or so formalized that the connection with the human figure is almost indiscernible. Compare the three figures by T. E. Haag, for example. The low-relief panel of the running girl (Fig. 397) is almost realistic, except for omission of detail in face and feet, while the standing figure (Fig. 398) is recognizable only by the lines of hair and buttocks in a general human outline. Fig. 396 has a human face and general, blocky human shape, but otherwise is a geometric design.

My effort here is to point out that stylizing is not a rigid thing, but a broad spectrum of possibilities. The only requirement is that the changes from realism be based on a style or form that attracts the eye. Simple distortion of a figure is *not* stylizing; there must be a discernible plan or reason, or the work itself will simply be crude.

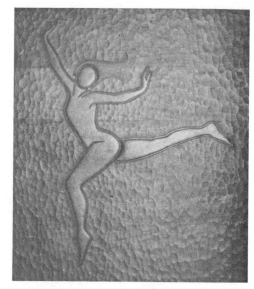

Fig. 397.

Fig. 398.

Figs. 396–398. These three stylizations by T. E. Haag show a wide range of stylization. The figure of the girl (above) merely omits details in face, feet and musculature, and possibly extends the legs to attain flow. The pedestal figure (right), on the other hand, suggests the curves of the human body and uses the hairline and buttocks as part of the design, but is otherwise barely recognizable. The third figure has a human face and shape that suggests a blocky male, but is otherwise composed largely of geometric designs.

Fig. 396.

Fig. 399.

Children can be angels

RUTH HAWKINS IS A VERY MODEST, unassuming mountain carver who sells her work through the Campbell Folk School at Brasstown, North Carolina. Many other carvers do the same thing, but most of them follow patterns provided by the school; she follows her own, which are unique both in design and technique. All of her designs are children or child angels. All are whittled (she uses only a knife) from holly ⅛ to 3⁄16 in (3.2 to 4.7 mm) thick. And all are low relief, meticulously detailed in contrast to the usual Campbell in-the-round figures. They are in theory Christmas-tree silhouette ornaments, but are usually snapped up by collectors for year-round display.

Her work has been widely copied by others—including me—but the copies, as usual, lose a little of the piquancy and dash of the original. Ruth is not concerned about copies; as one admirer asserts, "If she knew you were copying one of her figures, she'd probably offer to help."

I have attempted to sketch about half of her designs, and have pictured some that I copied as well as two of her originals. When I finish this, I'm going to try again (I just haven't quite gotten the faces right, to say nothing of the hair and hands). And I hope someday to get my hands on one design that is totally unique—a satanic little imp in mahogany or some other dark wood, which I suspect Ruth carved once when her own kids were belying her images of them!

Fig. 400.

Fig. 401 (above). Eight copies of Ruth Hawkins' figures by the author, whittled from ⅛-in (3.2-mm) holly and finished by waxing. Surfaces are thinned and contoured behind faces, hands and so on to avoid a "thick" look. Fig. 400 (opposite page). Ruth Hawkins carved the light and winsome figures at upper right and lower left; I carved the comparatively crude copy at upper left, a student the one at lower right.

15

Portraits

PORTRAITS are probably the most exacting task for a carver, particularly self-portraits, because we don't see ourselves as "others see us," to quote Robert Burns. The expression we get, even if taken from a photograph, may not be the one that our friends see most often, and our view of ourselves is always a mirror image, hence reversed.

The self-portrait pictured here (Figs. 405, 406) is particularly interesting to me because it is the first attempt at a likeness of a person by the carver, Hugh C. Minton, Jr., of Aiken, South Carolina. It is in buckeye (somewhat like basswood in reaction to tools) and is a miniature, the blank being only 3 × 3 × 5 in (7.5 × 7.5 × 12.5 cm). Height of the head from chin to top is only 3 in (7.5 cm). It was done with only knives and palm tools. No sandpaper was used before finishing with Deft®. The self-portrait was made from same-size photographic prints as a pattern, as shown (Figs. 402–404), and no templates or preliminary clay modelling were used. It is a better likeness than the photographs suggest.

In achieving such a likeness, the first step is to get the general silhouette, working from the side and front views. Then the head is rounded and modelling is begun by shaping around the nose, then the mouth and eyes. A great deal of attention must be paid to the exact shape of the nose and how it joins the rest of the face. Mr. Minton got the bridge of the nose a bit too thin and the angle between cheek and nose is too acute. Also, the nostrils are a bit small, top to

bottom—all three are defects that cannot be corrected. His modelling around the mouth and chin is very good, and the slight conventionalizing of the ears is also good. I would have softened the eyelids and bulges below the eyes with wrinkle lines and drilled shallow holes to suggest pupil and iris.

When the face form is generally correct, the lining and texturing can be done. Note that Mr. Minton has achieved a facial texture that is smooth, yet still shows tool lines, a very suitable treatment. The wrinkles from the nostrils are also well handled, but the crow's-feet near the eyes are too wide, hence too prominent. This is

Fig. 402.

Figs. 405, 406. The finished self-portrait, undeniably a wood carving. Eye treatment would be enhanced by delineating pupils and iris and softening the upper-lid line, but facial contours in general capture the subject's personality and make the bust easily recognizable.

Fig. 403.

Fig. 404.

Figs. 402–404. Three photos of the subject—both sides and dead front. Photos need to be enlarged or reduced to the exact size of the planned carving to provide precise guidance. Note hairline, crow's feet at eye corners, Adam's apple, deep lines at sides of nose and mouth and deep-sunken eyes—all distinctive featural elements.

most important, because overemphasized wrinkles convert a portrait into a caricature if one isn't careful. In addition, many carvers make the mistake of cutting away the eyebrows and the usual bulge beneath them. Mr. Minton has handled them and the center of the brow very well, not lacing the forehead with worry lines as so many carvers do. The hairline is suggested but not emphasized; I would have softened it still more by texturing along the edges. I would also have textured the eyebrows slightly, so the treatment of moustache, eyebrows and hair would be similar.

The flow of the neck into the base is quite smooth, and the base itself is relieved in front, then chamfered geometrically, thus contrasting with the rounded contours of the head.

The self-made man

A WOODCARVING OF A CARVER is quite rare. I recall only two among the thousands of designs I've seen. This is surprising, because the carver can be his own model and the material is a natural. Thus, I decided to make *Self-Made Man* from a section of 6-in (15.2-cm) walnut log and to follow the methods used by such eminent painters as Maxfield Parrish, Norman Rockwell and Andy Warhol: I took photographs from three sides to provide patterns. Further, I decided to add a fillip: I'd have me carving myself, with some of the log remaining to show the source.

The first step is to take the photographs. When the pose is selected, the photographer should focus on a level with the *center* of the subject and squarely to one side; this reduces distortion. Pictures from the front and other side should be taken at the *same* focus. Then the negatives or transparencies can be projected on paper at the desired size, and the pattern traced. (It is also possible to make photographic enlargements or reductions to the desired size, but there is usually a little distortion that makes tracing and adjustment of the various views necessary anyway.)

Because of perspective and possible shifts in pose, such as a slight lowering or raising of the mallet, the patterns should be aligned, compared and adjusted before being traced on the wood.

If you are starting with a squared-up block, the views may be transferred with carbon paper; but if you start, as I did, with a log, it is necessary first to produce squared surfaces at the top and on three sides, at least (for the area of the carving only), so that the pattern can be traced. It is also advisable to square up the base at this point, so it can be used as a starting point for vertical measurement; the top will promptly be cut up. Squaring up will also reveal checks and flaws that may interfere with the carving. Small cracks can be reinforced immediately with thinned glue (like Elmer's®, half and half with water), so they won't cause breaks during roughing out. Also, as you rough, any cracks revealed should be glued and/or filled before they cause trouble.

As usual, carving should begin at the top, with the base used for holding the piece. (On this particular log, the spongy growth-wood made clamping in a woodworking vise quite simple and flexible.) Waste wood can be cut away around the head and the mallet of the figure with a crosscut saw and flat chisel, then the back and far side are shaped.

This work can be expedited by copying the drawing on heavy paper or cardboard and cutting out templates for front and side; I actually made my original sketches on heavy stock (Figs. 409, 410) and, using these as templates, roughed the silhouettes with a coping saw. Mr. Minton (see above) did not; he sculptured from the block with only the tools. In the latter case, it is important to check dimensions frequently with a scale or calipers, and to stand off and look the head over from all angles regularly as you progress.

Cut out the upper portion of the front, between the arm and head, and shape the head and the mallet for reference points for

Fig. 407.

Fig. 408.

Fig. 409.

Fig. 410.

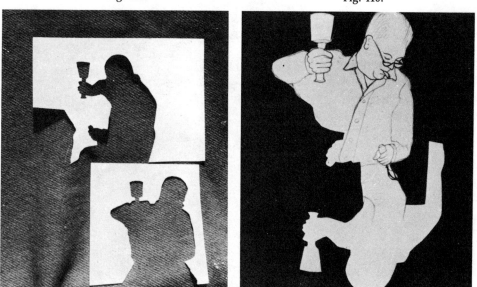

Figs. 407, 408. Two of the three photos taken 90° apart that were the basis for the pattern. The photo without sleeves was to show forearm musculature. The finished pattern is also the source of front and side working patterns. The templates (Figs. 409, 410) can be cut from light but sturdy cardboard or plastic.

Fig. 411.

Fig. 412.

Fig. 413.

Fig. 414.

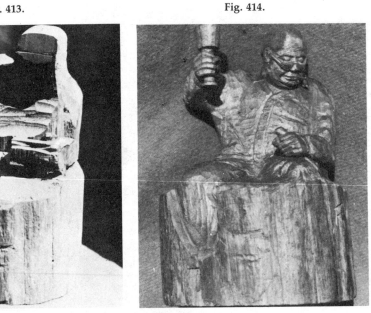

Figs. 411–414. First cuts are made at the top with hand saw and heavy chisels to clear the head and right arm; then the open area under the arm is roughed out. Removal of the waste wood between the arms is the next step, followed by a rough-shaping of the figure. The finished work is shown below right.

the rest of the carving. The body and arms can then be shaped. In carving the arms, be certain you retain proper lengths and proportions for the forearm and upper arm; obviously the carving will be more lifelike if the two arms match in actual length and the fists are the same size. Legs can also be rough-shaped at this point, and final decisions made about how much of the carver's body is to project from the log.

At this point, I got my nerve up to try the difficult portions of the carving—the right hand and the head, really the face—because if these two are not well done, the rest of the carving won't matter.

The left hand is less important, but should be done next. This hand grips the chisel, which must be straight when viewed from its side, so it is essential to position the chisel on the leg and in the hand before the hand is finally shaped, otherwise you may have insufficient finger thickness on one side or the other. Also, it is difficult to produce a believable chip at the chisel end, particularly if the chisel is cutting at a slant into the grain, as it is in this pose. Further, the head must be tilted so that the eyes are watching, or appear to be watching, the cutting edge of the chisel—so chisel shape and position are quite important. (I found it necessary to vary a bit from my sketch at this point; you may, as well.)

Remember that, as you carve, you must leave wood for such things as the collar on the shirt, the eyeglasses and the hair, unless you plan to add them later. Shape the shirt and legs, using the photographs to locate the wrinkles in their proper places.

Finish the face, carving the glasses in place and the hair (such as it is). The glasses, if you wear them, can be made separately from wire and installed; this makes carving of the face easier, but does add an element that is foreign and may cause dusting troubles later. If your figure is to include a cigar, the mouth and left cheek must be slightly distorted for it. The cigar should be made separately and inserted in a drilled hole; otherwise it is across grain and will cause both carving and maintenance difficulties.

I chose to experiment with a different method of depicting hair, because mine is cut quite short and the usual veiner lines would suggest greater length. I put a thin layer of Elmer's glue in the major hair areas and sifted walnut sawdust on top of it until no more would stick. Then I added glue and more dust where needed. It worked out quite realistically, taking a slightly darker tone when finished!

A friend who, like several observers, missed the fact that the carver is carving himself, suggested the extension of the right leg. This was a happy thought, because it not only suggests that the figure is emerging from the log but also breaks the rigid line of the log edge. This edge can show chisel marks all around if you prefer; I showed them in front only, where he is obviously working, leaving the back of the figure quite rough in shape. (After all, how would he reach his back with the tools?)

Finish was several coats of spray matte varnish (satin) followed by two coats of wax. I had originally intended to remove the growth wood as a final operation, but decided to leave it, complete with nicks and wormholes, to strengthen the impression of a figure emerging from a log. As you probably know, the lighter growth-wood darkens when varnish is applied, so it is not disconcertingly light in the piece.

16

Why Not Carve a Mask?

A MAN'S FACE IS much more than his fortune; it is the best visible clue to who and what he is, and the focus of every other man's (and woman's) eye. Thus, it is not all surprising that we ascribe certain characteristics to certain faces, identify famous or infamous personages by real or fancied facial characterics, or imagine specific faces for our particular idols and gods.

African masks that come from a broad band across the center of the continent are perhaps the best known in the United States, as a result of tourist and decorator purchases. These include the most elaborate abstract ones, but strikingly unusual masks of a similar type are also carved in Haiti. Perhaps the finest and truest-to-life masks were the more than 100 designs of the Japanese Noh masks. Because of our mixed heritage, most Americans now think of masks only as something associated with children and Halloween.

All sorts of materials have been used for masks but wood was and is the "old reliable." It is strong, relatively permanent, light and stable, takes detail and finishes well, and is not abrasive on the face if well finished inside. The usual woods are straight-grained and relatively soft, like our white pine and basswood, and even balsa and ash.

It is strange that so few American carvers have made masks, because they provide excellent training in face carving, particularly caricature. Furthermore, if they are not copies, they require the carver to study features and expressions, so he can depict such emotions as rage, fear, disdain, happiness, and devotion. Slight errors usually don't matter on a mask; they may even help. Proportions are usually not exact; the real challenge is to cut loose from diffident scraping into bold, strong cuts and lines, so shadows can do their work. Further, most masks cover only the front of the face, so there is no problem with locating ears, shaping the head, or even depicting hair. The primitive wearer uses his own ears or covers the head and ears with a cloth or other drape, headdress, or wig.

Eyes, on the other hand, are often very detailed on masks—reflecting my initial remarks about how other people always watch the face (and particularly the eyes) as a clue to what we are thinking. The mask wearer may see through slits or holes in the mask eyes or, if the shape is different, through slits cut in convenient areas. Because a mask tends to be slightly larger than the face to allow for wall thickness, holes or slits in the irises of the mask eyes will be misplaced, so actual viewing slits may be cut in the crease beneath the lower lid or, more commonly, in the crease between eyebrow and eye. Also, nostrils are pierced to make breathing within the mask a bit easier. In the case of grotesques or animal masks, placing sight holes may be extremely difficult.

Because a mask is often a caricature, sides do not have to balance; eyes and cheeks can be higher or lower, the mouth can be twisted—things that would not be done in a formal portrait. Also, because a great many

masks are painted, slight miscuts or flaws can be corrected with gesso, plastic wood, or whatever. The primary need is to make bold, slashing cuts, even if they are slightly wrong, rather than to spend an eternity nibbling away to copy precisely some formal original. The masks shown here were selected largely with that idea in mind.

Whether or not a mask is to be worn, it should be hollowed out. This not only permits piercing of the eyes, nose and mouth, but is also makes the mask much lighter and less prone to checking and warping. The hollowing is best done after rough-carving of the features; the mass of wood inside provides a convenient means of anchoring the mask during roughing, and the rough outside shaping later provides a convenient guide for obtaining fairly uniform wall thickness. Hollowing is done with fairly large gouges, working alternately from top and bottom with the grain. It is advisable to hollow inside the nose, even if the mask is not to be worn, and to follow the cheek and brow contours to a degree.

Generally speaking, mask-making is a gouge or adze job, not a knife job, the adze having a gouge-shaped blade for the

Figs. 415, 416 (top left and above). Two versions of a demon mask, from Mexico. Mask top left has articulated jaw, while the one above is about 18 in (46 cm) high and extends down over wearer's chest. Both have viewing slits between eye bulge and brow.

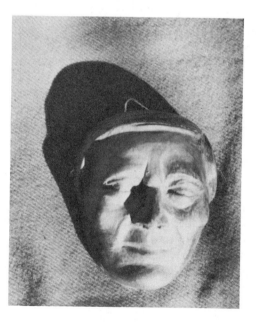

Fig. 417 (right). Some masks are realistic. This one is the face of Benito Juarez, a hero to all Mexicans. It was made near Oaxaca and is neither painted nor tinted. It is of balsa!

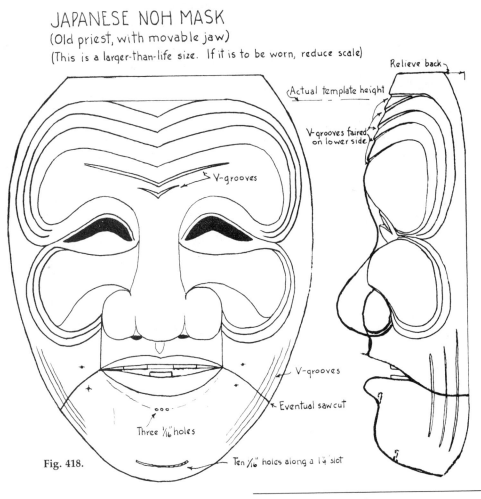

JAPANESE NOH MASK
(Old priest, with movable jaw)

(This is a larger-than-life size. If it is to be worn, reduce scale)

Relieve back

(Actual template height)

V-grooves faired on lower side

V-grooves

V-grooves

Eventual sawcut

Three 1/16" holes

Ten 1/16" holes along a 1 1/4" slot

Fig. 418.

roughing work in particular. Lines of the face, beard, tattoo marks, and hollowed areas are difficult with just the knife. Grain normally runs with the line of the nose, and complex elements which project very far, such as horns, a pointed nose or chin, or ears on animal masks, are carved separately and added, for both economy in wood and strength.

If wood equivalent to a half-log is not available, the blank can be built up in laminated layers. This also reduces wood cost and hollowing labor. Laminations cause no problems in a mask which is to be painted anyway. With modern 2-in (5-cm) planks, a simple way to gain thickness is to glue on a rough-formed nose blank, as well as brows and a chin tip if it suits the design.

Noh masks—yes!

THE JAPANESE ARE REPUTEDLY the most accomplished makers of masks in the world, and the Noh mask is considered their finest. Thus, when I learned that a book had been published on how to make a half-dozen different types of Noh mask, I sent to Japan for a copy. This particular mask of an old priest (Fig. 419) intrigued me most in the book, so I decided to make it.

Step-by-step photographs and diagrams were plentiful in the book, and the basic dimensions were provided. The text was, of course, in Japanese, and it turned out that the dimensions given were neither in English nor metric, but in some sort of ratio. As I went along, I also found that two different masks had been used for the pho-

Fig. 419. Old priest, a wearable Japanese Noh mask in myrtle, with movable lower jaw.

tographs, and they differed slightly in wrinkles and decoration. I discovered then that Confucius' remark about one picture being worth a thousand words is not literally true; there were times, in fact, when I'd have settled for the reverse.

This particular mask is normally made of a soft wood and finished with a glossy coat of off-white enamel, with tinting around the mouth and cheeks. I decided instead to make mine of myrtle and leave the natural finish. I also wanted it to fit me. I had half of an 8½-in (21-cm) log, which was thus 4¼ in (11 cm) at the center. Rough measurements of my face indicated that I needed a width of 7¾ in (19.7 cm) and a depth of 3¾ in (9.5 cm), allowing for ½-in (12.7-mm) walls. I decided to leave the additional width and depth and simply hollow the mask a bit deeper. The log half was also a bit longer than the original, but one does not waste myrtle, so I added to the forehead.

None of these enlargements caused trouble, but I did find that when I got to the hollowing, I could have decreased the width by 1¼ in (3 cm), even for my wide face, with other dimensions correspondingly smaller. Therefore, I've put no dimensions on my sketches; you can fit your own face—remembering that you'll probably

Figs. 420 (left) and 421 (right). Japanese masks illustrate the craftsmanship of that country's mask makers. Here are an old man and a demon, Obechima (right). Note that they extend back to the ears. (Masks on this page courtesy Metropolitan Museum of Art, New York City.)

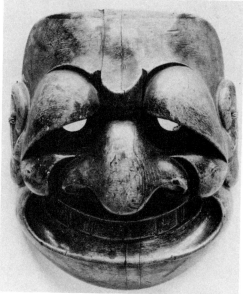

overestimate as I did. If you photostat the outside dimensions to ¾ in (19 mm) or 1 in (25 mm) wider than the width of your face at the cheekbone level, you should come out all right. All templates and sketches must be in proportion to the basic half-outline you use first. (See Fig. 424 below.)

Step-by-step carving

LAY OUT A VERTICAL CENTERLINE on both front and back of the piece. Lay out the basic mask shape on the flat back, using the template on both sides of the centerline. Fig. 422 shows the layout, and how you can saw off the corners with a straight saw to

Fig. 422.

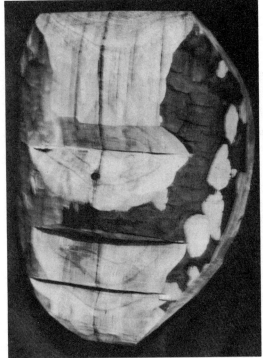

Fig. 423.

Fig. 424.

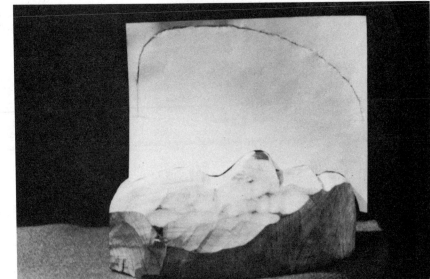

Fig. 425.

Fig. 426.

Fig. 427.

shorten the heavy chisel work. When contour is achieved, cut off the outer edges of the front of the piece, if you started with a block, so you have a rough half-log shape. Then lay out the cross lines for the low spots *below* the brow, the nose and the lips, and begin to cut away the wood until you have achieved *almost* the desired depth (Fig. 423). Shape the face profile until the profile template fits along the centerline, then re-establish the basic vertical centerline (Fig. 424).

Begin to hollow around the eyes and nose, leaving the eyeball and cheek at their original level (Fig. 425). Note that the nose template goes across at the nostril line, and that the wood is *not* cut away above the nostrils nor at the outer edges. However, the wood *is* cut away at the outer edges beyond the lip template, which is almost an extended half-circle. It is also cut away outside the chin template. As you cut, refer to the photograph showing the templates in place (Fig. 426). At this point you can round

off the sides of the mouth and chin and locate the mouth template and draw around it (Fig. 427).

At this stage, I decided to rough-hollow the interior, using straight and short-bent

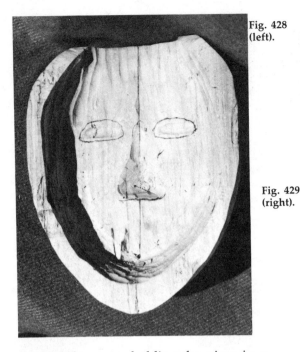

Fig. 428 (left).

Fig. 429 (right).

gouges. If you are holding the piece in a vise, be sure to leave plenty of wood at the outer edges to avoid breaking the side walls of the mask. You can also locate the eye and nostril positions and cut deeper at those points to simplify the next steps and make drilling and sawing easier (Fig. 428).

Now return to the face of the mask and achieve a rough face shape by defining the nostrils and shaping the eyeballs and cheeks. When this is completed, lay out the lines of the face and the eye slots according to the face pattern (Fig. 418). The decorative lines around the face are essentially V-slots, but they may be finished in various ways, according to what I could make out of the Japanese book. They may be V-slots with the sides faired so the areas between have a convex shape; they may simply be V-grooves with sharp edges; or one side of the V-groove may be eased or faired so they become the equivalent of teeth on a ratchet.

This is what I did, starting at the center of the brow and on the lower edge of the groove (which becomes the upper edge at the sides of the eyes). Where the grooves meet at the sides of the eyes is roughly equivalent to switches in an old-fashioned

Fig. 430.

railroad yard; study the full-face sketch carefully before you work on this area. The two short wrinkles at the center of the brow, by the way, are better as simple V-grooves, deep at the center and fading away to nothing as they move outward (Fig. 430).

Fig. 431.

It is also possible, at this point, to cut the lower jaw free. This is done with a scroll saw, and the cut is at right angles to the plane of the mask. Note that the cut enters at the points of the mouth outline, but passes above center to provide a fuller lower lip. This can be seen clearly in the side view of the mask (Fig. 431). Note also in this view how the cheeks and brows are faired into the lines, the chin shape, and the three decorative V-grooves on each side of the jaw.

Now complete the shaping of the nostrils, cheeks, and eyes. Drill and saw out the eye slots and make any adjustments necessary at the back to thin the wood behind eyes and nostril holes. Note that there is a fine groove on the upper eyelid that suggests lashes, and a shallow groove over each eye near the bridge of the nose to accentuate the Oriental eye. (This is not sketched, to reduce complexity.) The eyeball shape is also strongly accented by grooves at top and bottom that flow into the wrinkle rings at the sides.

It is also possible now to shape the lips and teeth, the latter from the wood behind the lips (Fig. 432). For some reason, the priest has a single, centered lower tooth,

Fig. 432.

which no human ever has, flanked by two upper teeth, all quite wide. These are shown clearly on the back and bottom photos of the sequence (Figs. 433, 434). The holes for the jaw ties and side fastening may also be drilled at this point.

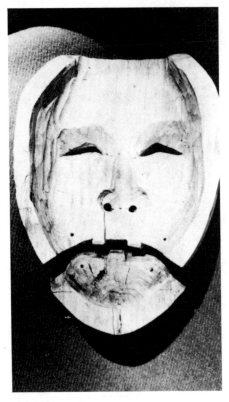

Fig. 433.

Essential work on the mask is now complete, but it will need some cleaning up and shaping, as well as decoration. The moustache is painted on—vertical stripes of black—but the beard is real. Three small holes are drilled about ⅜ in (9.6 mm) deep at the center base of the lower lip, and ten in line below the point of the chin, to take the beard hairs. The latter are set in a groove about ⅟₁₆ in (1.6 mm) deep, which makes alignment easier and will conceal peg ends later.

Horsehair is a good beard material; I used white hair from an old violin bow. Heavy thread or nylon filament could also be used, but I found 15 strands of horsehair per hole just about right. Suit length to your own fancy; I liked it about 9 in (22.5 cm) long, with ragged lower ends (Fig. 419). If you wet the ends of the horsehairs with a plastic cement, they will cling together and enter the hole quite easily. There they are anchored and spread with a driven-in plug

behind them. This can be made from a toothpick or splinter of pine.

The rosettes at each side of the forehead are about 1½ in (4 cm) in diameter. They are made from fibres of coarse cord or light rope, sisal or hemp, sewn into a disc and trimmed to shape. The disc should be quite thick, so it bunches, and is simply tacked in place. Coarse cord (I used a handmade Mexican 3-strand cord) for the ties, and to hold the jaws together, seems correct and looks good. (If you hang the mask, tack the support cords in place near the top, or the mask may hang out at the top.)

Before these finishing steps, you may want to round the mask at top and bottom in back; it fits the face of the wearer better that way and looks less rigid when hung. Also, pressure on the back lower edge of the chin forces the mouth closed. You will also want to clean up the inside of the mask and thin it down so it fits your face comfortably. I finished simply with oil and wax, but the proper Noh mask has a wax-like surface produced by filler and several coats of a thick paint-like enamel. Color is slightly off-white all over, with a faint tinge of red around the lips.

Fig. 434.

17

Relief Carving

FOR OVER FIFTY YEARS, I have been fascinated by the infinite possibilities of relief carving, ranging from geometric patterns on to portraits and full-fledged scenes. A relief carving need not be a flat, rectangular panel; it can be a silhouette with or without pierced elements that allow light or the background to show through in parts. It can be wrapped around a non-planar shape such as a cylinder, a ball, a log or even a shape as irregular as a wooden shoe. It can incorporate inlays, utilize the grain or "figure" of the wood, suggest a texture, be a simple study of a small subject or a complex treatment of an involved one. It is almost as flexible as in-the-round carving, since the third dimension can suit the wood and the subject, with the added advantage of letting you hold elements together, provide a scene or background and protect the piece against undue wear or damage. It can be traditional or modern, realistic or abstract, even "inside-out" as an intaglio or a mould. And it can be painted or stained, but usually does not need to be, thus retaining the natural warmth of the wood. In short, relief carving can tell almost any story you want it to, from a mere feeling to the setting of an entire scene, or even several scenes one within the other.

Some of the sections of this book have contained relief carvings, but none have yet been devoted expressly to relief itself. Here, then, is a wide variety of relief-carved projects, graded for difficulty and not repeated elsewhere. They include my own work and that of selected carvers around the world, to show the tremendous range and possibilities in this form. Also included are the basics of wood, tools, sharpening and finishing, as well as patterns and hints piece by piece.

What wood is best?

GENERALLY SPEAKING, THE GAMUT OF WOODS has been used in relief carving, sometimes because a wood was readily available or easily carved, sometimes because it was the right color, texture, pattern, had some significance or even rarity. Panels in churches have usually been carved in local woods such as walnut, pine, basswood, maple, butternut, cherry and apple in the United States; oak, lime, linden, apple and deal (fir or pine) in Europe; and in Egypt, sycamore and cedar. Panels carved for furniture have varied with fashion. Cherry wasn't used until 1675, mahogany didn't appear in Europe in any quantity until 1720, and teak came into use much more recently.

In the United States, the familiar woods for relief carving are black walnut, mahogany, cherry and other fruit woods; for signs or painted outdoor units, basswood and white pine are the usual choices. I have carved all of these, as well as teak, butternut, maple, pear, pecan, ash, vermilion, purpleheart, ebony and others. But for practical purposes, including available sizes and ease of working, I prefer pine, basswood, cherry, walnut and teak. Use walnut, mahogany, cherry and teak for relief work not to be painted. For exterior work, teak is superior because it does not rot or warp, and is not prone to insect attack.

Many of the exotic woods suitable for veneering are hard to carve because they split, have irregular grain or create other problems. The typical relief carving is a panel. Thus, wood should be straight-grained, so backgrounding and modelling can both be done well, without too much "figure," grain or knots, which compete with the carving, and without too much tendency to warp, splinter and split. It should also be dense enough to support detail, and preferably hard enough not to be worn away by cleaning and polishing through the years.

The color of a particular wood will sometimes suggest its use. If you plan to carve in a wood with which you have no experience, try a sample before getting started on the general project. Depending upon your experience with a wood, you may want to simplify the proposed design, or alter the arrangement to put a knot or flaw in an unimportant spot.

For any larger panels these days, it is usually necessary to assemble the panel from milled boards. On darker woods without conspicuous grain—walnut, mahogany, teak—the joining lines can be made to disappear almost entirely. They must, however, have smooth-planed edges for good joints, and should preferably be dowelled, glued and clamped to assure tightness. The wood should also be relatively thick; ½- and 1-in (13- and 25.4-mm) panels of pine, walnut and mahogany tend to warp and move with the weather regardless of finish. If you anticipate or encounter appreciable warpage, brace the back of the panel with screwed-on battens across grain, or with angle irons or aluminum angles. I have used the latter in a number of instances, even to assemble a walnut mailbox of ½-in (13-mm) wood, carved on surfaces and edges. It has held for ten years, completely exposed (with marine-varnish finish). I have also seen thick relief carvings a hundred or more years old in which the center of the back was hollowed appreciably to counteract warpage, just as old-time in-the-round figures were split and hollowed out to avoid checking.

Thin tools/speed setting-in

THIN-BLADED TOOLS are better and more convenient to use on small panels. They make setting-in, particularly around curves, quicker and easier by reducing the wedging action—hence the crushing and splitting of fibres—and the number of steps. And, small tools are less clumsy for intricate work. Such tools work just as well as heavier chisels for grounding out, but are not as safe for digging or prying—which we shouldn't do anyway. Nor will they stand mallet pounding as well as the heavier chisels, though they can be used with a soft- or plastic-faced mallet. They are lighter, cheaper and less fatiguing to hold, particularly when compared to some American tools, which are much too thick in smaller sizes.

H. M. Sutter has recently found a commercial company willing to make his style of tool, so beginner sets are now available. Each consists of six tools: a firmer ¼ in (6.4 mm) wide, and gouges of ¹⁄₁₆-, ⅛-, ³⁄₁₆-, ¼- and ⁵⁄₁₆-in (1.6-, 3.2-, 5-, 6.4- and 8-mm) width, all No. 7 sweep. The second set has No. 7 ⅜- to ⅝-in (9.5- to 16-mm) gouges and a ⅝-in (16-mm) firmer.

He rounds off the heel on each gouge and increases the length of the bevel on the firmer to make true thin blades, which allow for deeper cuts without crushing. He also reports that such tools have made a considerable difference in the quality of the work done by his students, as well as the complexity they can handle. The pine-cone design was a real challenge, even for an advanced student, but can now be done with relative ease. The same is true for the more difficult orchid design. Large curves are cut with an all-purpose knife or with larger chisels if they are available. Students have also found that this kind of tool is

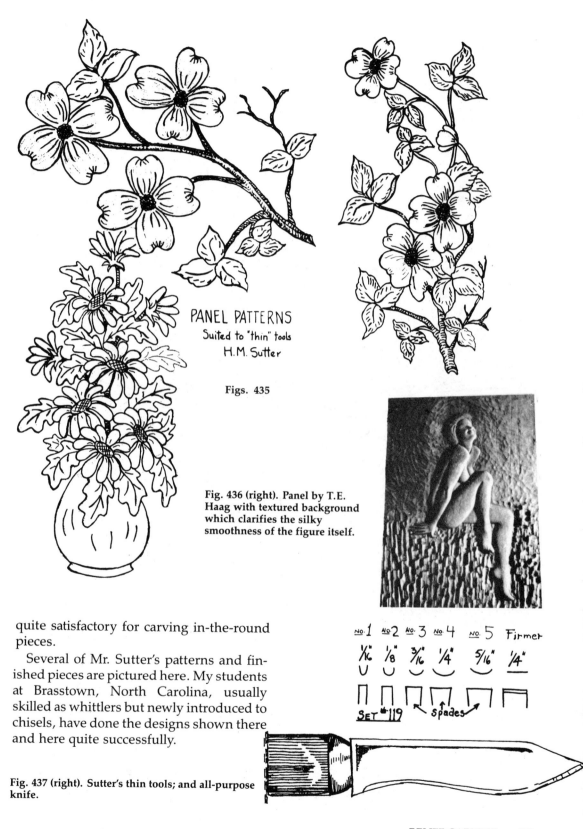

PANEL PATTERNS
Suited to "thin" tools
H.M. Sutter

Figs. 435

Fig. 436 (right). Panel by T.E. Haag with textured background which clarifies the silky smoothness of the figure itself.

quite satisfactory for carving in-the-round pieces.

Several of Mr. Sutter's patterns and finished pieces are pictured here. My students at Brasstown, North Carolina, usually skilled as whittlers but newly introduced to chisels, have done the designs shown there and here quite successfully.

Fig. 437 (right). Sutter's thin tools; and all-purpose knife.

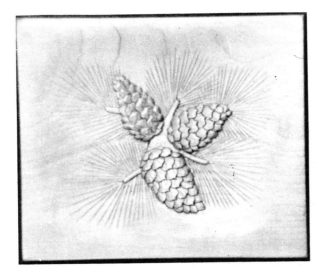

Figs. 438, 439 (left and below). Three pine cones are a good subject for thin-blade tools because of the overlapping seeds. Such designs should be trenched, with trenching sloping up to the surface all around, so needles can be cut into the surface with a V-tool. A groove can replace a raised rib here with no loss of realism.

Figs. 440, 441 (above and left). This simple head can be raised above a background, trenched or silhouetted. Modelling is shallow but precise; thus, the project is more difficult than it appears to be. This is a good exercise in using the V-tool.

Fig. 442. Head of a carousel horse is difficult to carve accurately in relief because of its twist. Although the eye is correctly positioned for in-the-round carving, it appears high and too far forward here.

Figs. 443, 444 (above and right). The rose is a complex project requiring fairly deep grounding, perhaps ½ in (13 mm) or more, to get petals well shaped. Note random-cut gouge background.

Figs. 445, 446 (below and right). Most difficult of the group is this double orchid, which requires as much as ¾ in (19 mm) of grounding to achieve the various levels and get the crenellations in the petals.

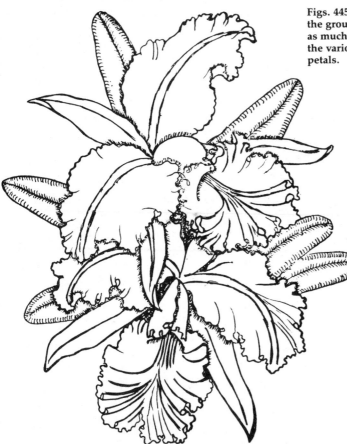

Fig. 447. For this polyglot pencil designs selected from a textbook were sketched on the wood to form a compact group. When the depth of the board was covered at one end, grounding-out was begun, followed by modelling of individual designs. Note that overlaps are left undecided until actual modelling is done, and that carving is not completely laid out and then completely grounded, as the texts instruct. It's more fun this way!

Carve a polyglot panel

AN OVERALL PANEL normally involves elaborate tracery of foliage or a grouping to tie the elements together. A polyglot panel, however, requires nothing but step-by-step carving of single subjects; the only problems are with making the elements approach or overlay each other. It does not require lengthy planning, sketching and designing, because the design develops as you carve. (I design or draw only one set of subjects ahead of my carving.) You can trace or otherwise copy all the elements without change of scale, providing there are enough potential subjects in the theme you select. And your selection of subjects and theme will also determine the level of difficulty you encounter. Further, this kind of carving provides a great deal of training in grounding out, shaping forms, and in texturing. The results are often unique.

In my first polyglot, I was immediately faced with legs and antennae in profusion. Fortunately, scale was large. This fruit and vegetable panel (Fig. 447) is an easier way to start. The individual designs are familiar to all of us, with many distinctive shapes. You can avoid difficult forms or texturing, such

as lettuce heads and parsley, if you prefer, and pictures or the objects themselves are readily available. There are at least again as many fruits and vegetables as the 63 I used—such familiar ones as lemon, orange, honeydew melon, parsnip and celery are not included.

Here, the client selected panel wood and shape. She liked the growth-wood color contrast and the sloping bevelled edge that resulted from the natural shape of the tree. Wood is black walnut, $1 \times 7\frac{3}{4} \times 16\frac{5}{8}$ in ($2.54 \times 20 \times 42$ cm) which is not particularly inclined to split, able to support considerable detail, and finishes well.

My source for almost all of the 63 designs was a handbook of fruits and vegetables from the local library. I altered scale in some cases because a watermelon and peppers create rather sharp size contrasts, and I used sliced sections in others because the whole fruit or vegetable would repeat a shape and be monotonous. A peach, a plum, and an apricot are basically alike except for color—and color is not available in a panel like this unless you use a light wood and tint it. Also, the interior of some fruits

Fig. 448. Black walnut, 1 × 7¾ × 16⅝ in (2.54 × 20 × 42 cm), was cut across the tree so there is growth wood along both edges. It was selected as the basis for this polyglot fruit-and-vegetable panel, which depicts 63 varieties. The rounded contour of the tree perimeter was originally planned to be left in its inner-bark, dark-brown condition. However, condiments were drawn there and whittled out with a penknife, through the bark into the growth wood beneath, into a sort of reversed scrimshaw.

is much more interesting than the exterior from a design standpoint.

It is unnecessary to lower the background more than about ⅛ in (3.2 mm) in a small panel of this type. You don't have to undercut, either. There can be a border or frame if you wish, the entire panel can be trenched, or the edges cut away. I trenched at the sides because of the squared edges, and cut the border away at the top. Initially, I had planned to leave pristine the irregular top edge created by the natural curvature of the tree, but I ultimately put condiments there—parsley, pepper, dill and cinnamon—and carved them in intaglio to leave the dark grooved surface and add to the contrast with the rest of the panel.

One virtue of this sort of design is that you can make such alterations as they occur to you. It is not even necessary to balance the two sides of the panel unless you wish to do so. I created a rough balance by putting the head lettuce on one side and the cauliflower on the other, and balancing the long diagonal line of the sugar beet at one top corner with that of the asparagus at the other. The fairly large and complex bunch of grapes was placed near the center to dominate the composition.

All through the panel, I overlapped drawings of subjects, and then decided which was to appear above the other when I was carving. In most instances, this decision is surprisingly easy because one subject has the overlap portion near the surface, while the other will curve away. The principal problem is to keep the background areas small and irregularly shaped, and to select subjects of contrasting shape and texture to go side by side. With a whole guide to pick from, that task is easy.

Tools required can be few and simple. I used a hook or pull knife, a V-tool, two veiners (one very small), ⅛-in (3.2-mm) firmer, ⅛- and ¼-in (3.2- and 6.4-mm) flat gouges, and a ¼-in (6.4-mm) half-round gouge. Larger half-round or semi-half-round gouges could be used to form rounded shapes like those of currants, grapes and cranberries, but I shaped them with a hook knife and left them slightly irregular. (A pro would use the gouge of proper size and shape to speed the work.) Practically all of the setting-in was done with the ⅛-in (3.2-mm) firmer, and grounding with the same tool in two steps: one roughing, one finishing. A light mallet controlled depth of setting-in and roughing, while smoothing the ground was done by hand. When setting in, allow at least ¼ in (6.4 mm) of solid wood in a filament such as a root, or to slope the tool away. If a section is to be narrower than that, it should be roughed wider, then shaved in finishing, particularly across grain. Very small and delicate filaments such as stems are best cut with the knife. Then, splitting and shattering of thin filaments won't be too much of a problem. Background need not be entirely smooth, but corners should be cleaned out as you go, so the finished work is crisp.

Texturing is largely a matter of V-tool and veiner work, either as lines or scallops. Heavy shaping can be done with the chisels, fine shaping with the knife. I found that a pocketknife—my favorite tool—was unnecessary. Except for veining, designs on the bevelled edge were carved in intaglio entirely with the knife. The peppercorn shapes were "drilled" by rotating a ⅛-in (3.2-mm) half-round gouge. It is important in such work to avoid destroying the edge of the carving, which removes the patina—or in this case, the dark veined surface.

Finish was two coats of sprayed matte varnish to seal the surface, followed by a coat of special walnut color Minwax®, brushed in and wiped off the surfaces in the dark areas, and carefully painted into the background and lines in the light areas to avoid darkening them. This "antiquing"

Fig. 449. Small oak picture frame from Italy shows florid and deep-relief formal style of the past century. It combines several motifs and is made to appear even heavier with black stain.

makes the carving appear deeper and sets off the designs. Sandpaper was *not* used, except for a worn piece of very-fine grade rubbed over the top surfaces before varnishing to add a little gloss.

Fig. 450. Detail from a massive door in the Cathedral of Seville exemplifies high-relief style of former centuries. Note that female figures and floral swags between them are practically in-the-round.

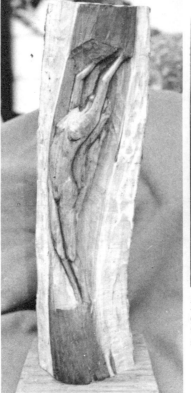

NUDE
Apple 16" on 24" pc.
Medium to high
relief

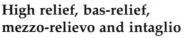

High relief, bas-relief, mezzo-relievo and intaglio

RELIEF CARVING was classified by the Italians: High relief or *alto-relievo* carries projection from the background to half or more of the natural thickness of the subject. Some parts may be undercut or completely free of the background. In low relief, *basso-relievo* or *bas-relief*, the projection is slight and no parts are undercut or detached. Less commonly defined are half relief (*mezzo-relievo*) and the very flat relief of medals and coins called *stiacciato*. Hollow relief, also called *cavo-relievo, intaglio-relevato*, coelanglyphic sculpture or simply trench carving, is that in which the background is not cut away; the figure or object being carved is outlined by a deep groove but has no elements higher than the background. This technique is effective for coats of arms, monograms, initials, lettering and other carving on a flat surface, particularly if it may be

Figs. 451, 452 (above and right). Nereid (water fairy) follows the curvature of the log. Effect is similar to that of appliquéing a figure on a contrasting background, except that the carving is integral and less contrived in appearance. Color contrast between heart and growth wood creates a cameo effect. (See page 241).

Fig. 453. Another piece by T. E. Haag of Tualatin, Oregon, in which a textured background clarifies the silky smoothness of the figure itself.

Figs. 454–456 (above and below). Araucano and Araucana (male and female) busts in mahogany-like rauli wood are modern high-relief silhouettes carved in Chile, where woodcarving is infrequent (possibly because of wood scarcity). Heads and chests are correct in the third dimension, while back halves of bodies are flattened. Each is about 6 in (15 cm) tall.

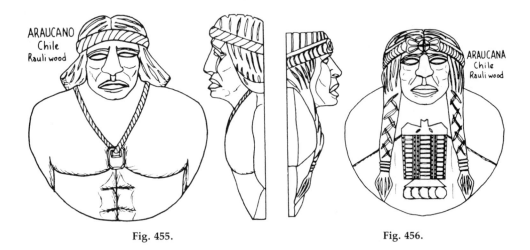

ARAUCANO
Chile
Rauli wood

ARAUCANA
Chile
Rauli wood

Fig. 455.

Fig. 456.

damaged by bumping or abrasion. This is not to be confused with intaglio, which is most easily described as reversed relief.

In intaglio carving, the design is hollowed out so that material pressed or poured into it comes out as an image in relief. The most familiar objects in intaglio are cookie and butter moulds. When a pattern is pressed into sand to create a mould for metal, the mould itself is an intaglio. This is not a cameo, which is normally limited to a head or bust carved in multilayered stone or shell so that the carving is in one color, the background in another. However,

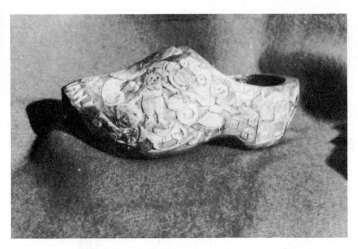

Fig. 457. Relief carving need not be on a planar surface. This is a willow-wood shoe from the Netherlands that I carved in polyglot fashion. Motifs pictured are familiar children's toys.

a head or bust carved through a surface layer of one color into a differing color beneath, so that not only color change but reversal of the depths is attained, is an intaglio and a cameo.

A figure becomes in the round only when the third dimension is correct. A dog or horse carved in silhouette but flattened in body thickness is still relief carving, as is pierced carving, regardless of whether it contains in-the-round elements. The same is true of high relief, which often contains foreground figures cut free of the background; they may be in the round themselves but are still part of a relief carving.

I have done relief carving on trees, bowls, napkin rings and even on wooden shoes. These are, in a sense, three-dimensional, as is a mobile made up of relief silhouettes. It is possible to have two relief carvings on opposite sides of the same silhouetted piece of wood, with either the same or different subjects. It is also possible to inlay relief carvings, particularly very shallowly

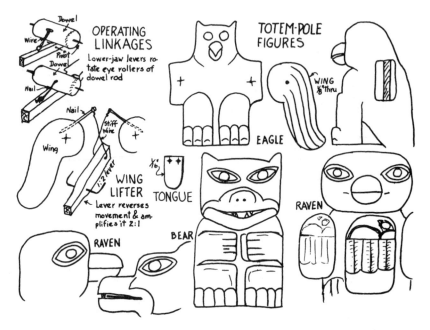

Fig. 458. Northwest Coast Indians are skilled at relief carving on totem poles.

Figs. 459, 460. Articulated totem pole 17 in (43.2 cm) high and "sleeps" normally (left), but eagle's wings can lift and all eyes and mouths open when a back lever is moved (right). The miniature pole is basswood, a quarter of a log, painted with oils.

carved ones, with metal, stone, plastic or shell, or with other woods. Some peoples particularly skilled at relief carving, like the New Zealand Maori and American Northwest Coast Indians, inlay many of their carvings with shell as a matter of custom. So do some furniture makers, particularly in France.

Figs. 461, 462. Making a small totem pole. Step 1 (below left). Block out the eagle with a saw. The core of the log is towards the front, thus providing a natural shape for beaks. Step 2 (below right). Eagle is blocked out with wing stubs instead of wings. Raven shape has been drawn below it—the eagle will stand on the raven's head.

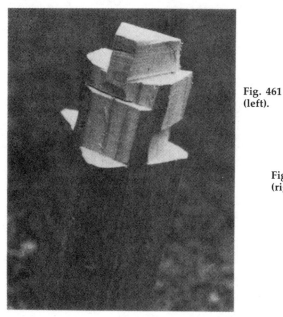

Fig. 461
(left).

Fig. 462
(right).

Fig. 463. Step 3. Raven and bear are largely shaped, eyes have been located and raven wings defined. This is done with chisels and mallet—it's faster. Fig. 464 (right). Step 4. Eye holes are drilled in, claws and mouths defined, and shaping mostly done.

Fig. 463.

Fig. 464.

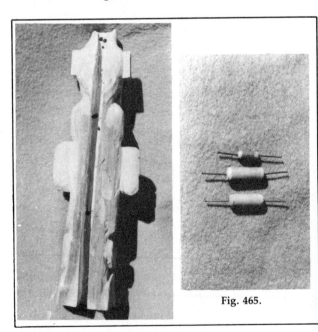

Fig. 465.

Fig. 466.

Fig. 465. Step 5 (above left). A deep slot sawed and chiselled out in the back will accommodate the levers and operating bars as well as make it possible to hollow heads for the eye rollers shown with it here. Fig. 466. Step 6 (right). Lower jaws are cut away and slots cut through to meet the ones in back. Also, slots are cut through the extended shoulders of the eagle so the wings can be fitted in.

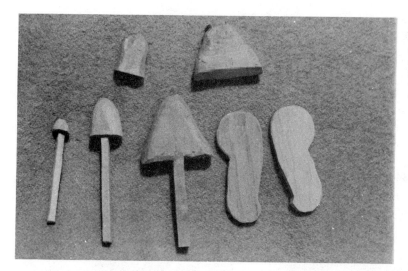

Fig. 467. Step 7. At top are the cutaway sections of lower jaw which serve as patterns for their replacements (below) which have levers. Note wing shape.

Fig. 468. Step 8. Eye roller and jaw elements are fitted individually, with brads used as axles. Also, thin sections of wood are formed into tongues held loosely in the mouth roofs by tacks, so they will drop when the mouths open.

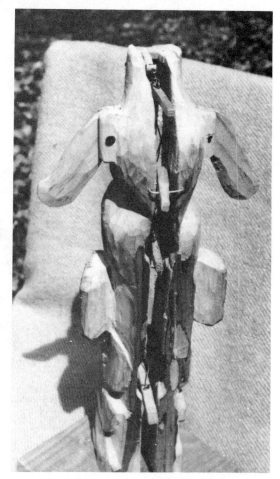

Fig. 469. Step 9. Now a vertical bar is set in place to tie the operating mechanism together. Levers may be pinned or wired to it—see Fig. 458.

Fig. 470. Step 10. Work with the motion to free it up and get maximum stroke, so eyes roll and mouths open as far as possible. When all are operating freely, saw off the axle brads (in a vise) and insert them securely flush with the surface. Mount the assembly on a stabilizing base—and you are ready for painting.

Fig. 471. Standard totem pole is a series of in-the-round animals one atop another—like this one in a Vancouver, British Columbia, Park. Some, however, may be high relief with no back carving (note that this one is backed by a pine tree).

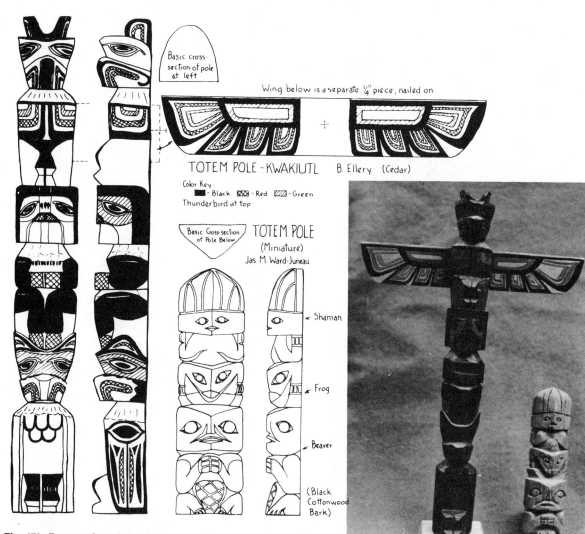

Basic cross-section of pole at left

Wing below is a separate ¼" piece, nailed on

TOTEM POLE - KWAKIUTL   B. Ellery (Cedar)

Color Key:
■ - Black ▨ - Red ▨ - Green
Thunderbird at top

Basic Cross-section of Pole Below

TOTEM POLE
(Miniature)
Jas. M. Ward-Juneau

← Shaman

← Frog

← Beaver

(Black Cottonwood Bark)

Fig. 472. Patterns for miniature totem poles pictures in Fig. 473 (right). Miniature totem poles such as these are primarily tourist items, through they may be faithful copies. The left one is about 12 in (30 cm) tall and painted, and shows two birds sandwiching a human figure. Totem pole at right is about 6 in (15 cm) tall and unpainted. A shaman is atop a frog atop a beaver; it is particularly interesting because it is carved in black cottonwood bark rather than the usual cedar.

Fig. 473.

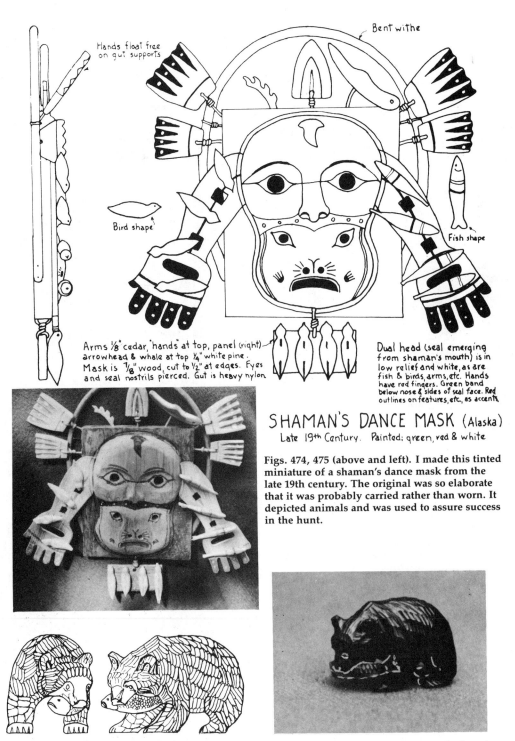

Hands float free on gut supports

Bent withe

Bird shape

Fish shape

Arms ⅛" cedar, "hands" at top, panel (right) arrowhead & whale at top ¼" white pine. Mask is ⅛" wood, cut to ½" at edges. Eyes and seal nostrils pierced. Gut is heavy nylon.

Dual head (seal emerging from shaman's mouth) is in low relief and white, as are fish & birds, arms, etc. Hands have red fingers. Green band below nose & sides of seal face. Red outlines on features, etc, as accents.

SHAMAN'S DANCE MASK (Alaska)
Late 19th Century. Painted: green, red & white

Figs. 474, 475 (above and left). I made this tinted miniature of a shaman's dance mask from the late 19th century. The original was so elaborate that it was probably carried rather than worn. It depicted animals and was used to assure success in the hunt.

Figs. 476, 477. A traditional Northwest Indian carving is this black bear with a salmon in its mouth. Now imported from Japan, bears like this are made there by Ainu carvers for less than they could be made in Alaska. Design can be either in-the-round or relief.

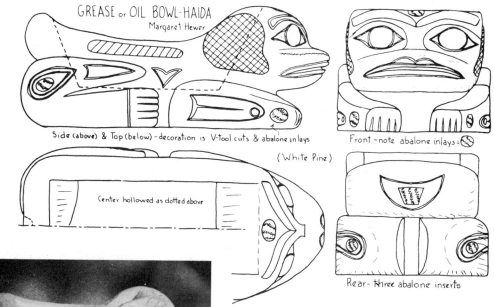

GREASE or OIL BOWL-HAIDA
Margaret Hewer

Side (above) & Top (below) - decoration is V-tool cuts & abalone inlays

Front - note abalone inlays ⊙

(White Pine)

Center hollowed as dotted above

Rear - three abalone inserts

Fig. 479.

Figs. 478, 479 (above and left). The Haida were noted for carvings with abalone inserts. This modern one, by an Indian woman, is about a foot (30 cm) long and is an oil or grease bowl—in which a wick burning in whale oil provides a house with light and some heat.

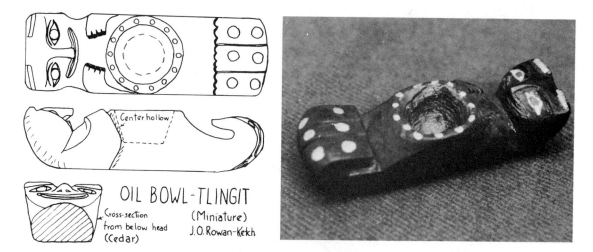

Center hollow

OIL BOWL-TLINGIT
Cross-section from below head (Cedar)
(Miniature)
J. O. Rowan-Kekh

Figs. 480, 481 (above and right). This miniature of a Tlingit oil bowl was made by J. O. Rowan of Ketchikan, Alaska. It is a sea otter on its back, with paint spots replacing the shell inserts used on full-sized carvings. Stylizing makes it practically a shaped panel.

WASGO or MONSTER

Can be panel or in-the-round figure

Fig. 482.

Most modern relief carving is low relief and made in relatively small pieces exhibited at or near eye level. Low-relief carving, however, is particularly susceptible to light intensity and direction, so such work as a pediment high above eye level or a boat counter well below may require special correction. Also, the third dimension in any relief carving is not simply a flattened version of the actual or in-the-round dimension—it often must incorporate a difference in shape. A rounded surface may have to be carved somewhat angular to produce an edge that creates a difference in light reflection. A given line may have to be shorter or longer than a matching one on the opposite side of center, since elements that would normally be at different depths must be at about the same depth. Thus, differentials must be optical.

Effects must be created by texturing, by making a simple groove different on either side, by flattening or even gouging a surface and even by tinting and "antiquing" (my own word for darkening deeper lines and areas). Tinting or painting on relief carvings, however, is not done nearly as often as it is on the in-the-round figures, possibly because the latter are often the adult equivalent of toys while relief carvings are more nearly decoration.

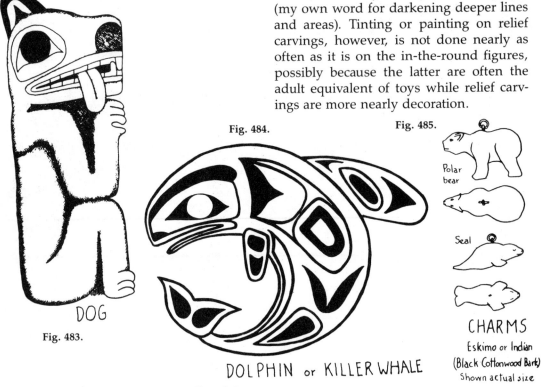

Fig. 484.

Fig. 485.

Polar bear

Seal

CHARMS

Eskimo or Indian

(Black Cottonwood Bark)

Shown actual size

DOG

Fig. 483.

DOLPHIN or KILLER WHALE

Figs. 482–485. Indian and Eskimo motifs and charms.

Fig. 486. Moorish carved panel from door in Toledo, Spain.

Economy may result from mounting a carved or uncarved silhouette against a contrasting background that may be glass, plastic or textile rather than wood.

Geometric patterns, bust portraits and floral groups are essentially in one plane, so perspective is not a problem; nor is composition, except in the case of the floral group. It is relatively easy to carve any of these in relief. But too many neophytes promptly decide to make a scene or multi-ple group. And therein often lies basic trouble, because creating an artistic composition or scene requires at least a little knowledge of art.

Elements should not all be in the same pose, or of the same size; elements should not touch, but should either be clearly separate or overlap; a line or shape in a frontal element should not be immediately next to a similar line or shape in the background.

Eliminate extraneous details as scale is

Fig. 487. Alonso Berruguete's life-size head of John the Baptist projects from this walnut panel in the Cathedral of Toledo.

reduced. Look around you and you'll see that at a relatively short distance the nails in a fence and the veins in leaves disappear. At greater distance, the fence palings or rails begin to blur and the leaves themselves merge into a green tree silhouette. At a little distance, cats don't have whiskers, birds don't have feathers and men have no lines in their faces. If you put such details in, you create a sort of cartoon or caricature rather than a picture.

It is also unnecessary to show every

Fig. 488. A surprising coincidence: The figure at left is from Haiti, that at right from Costa Rica. Both are two-sided reliefs, and only the heads are in-the-round.

Fig. 489. Mahogany panel from Ecuador is 11½ in (29 cm) tall, ¾ in (19 mm) thick. Fig. 490. The stylized head from Ecuador (below) is turned 90°, so hair is both frame and support.

branch of a tree, every number on a license plate or house, every pane in a window or every shingle on a roof, particularly if it is back a bit in the composition. You don't have to fill every part of the picture with objects. In nature there are open skies, clear fields and smooth water—you'll find the hard way that adding waves, individual leaves and clouds is very difficult in wood-carving. *Suggest* a telephone or power line; don't try to carve the wires unless you need them to support a flock of birds. Leave out elements of the background that are unessential to the story you're trying to tell or to identification of the scene.

Your eye does the same thing—you don't notice detail unless you study a scene very closely. A painter can grey or blur such elements, suggest them with a blob of color. But you cannot to the same degree, so it is often better to leave them out entirely. Even on a head portrait, it is not necessary to carve away the background all the way to the edge or to some rigid mechanical shape;

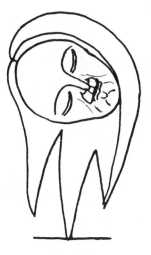

Fig. 490.

Fig. 492. Russian bowl is lacquer-finished, then decorated in relief with gouge cuts through to the base wood.

Fig. 491 (above). This "mask" from Easter Island is actually a flat panel for wall hanging. It illustrates the strength of stylized modern surfaces and shapes, incorporating pierced carving and simple V-groove texturing. It is about 14 in (36 cm) tall.

the panel itself provides that. Framing, too, is often unnecessary, as an unframed carving can suggest that a scene goes beyond the limits of the wood.

You must learn about vanishing points and how to achieve the effect of distance on a flat surface just as a painter must. If you don't, your people and buildings will look like postage stamps poorly stuck against a background, and a continuous line of anything—road, people, train, cars, flying birds—will look very wrong. Things in nature are not rigid and unchanging unless they're dead. There is always some variation between like objects, animate or inanimate. There is also perspective that affects size and shape; for example, an animal standing at an angle to you will appear to lose size at the farthest portion of its body.

Fig. 493 (left). Attenuated silhouette figures such as these from Israel are actually relief carvings—third dimension is negligible.

Fig. 494. This seems like in-the-round carving but is actually medium relief on the surface of a log. By Bogosav Zivkovic, now in a gallery in Svetozarevo, Yugoslavia.

It is very easy to design a panel so that an object in the background looks too large compared to one nearer your eye, to attempt to put an essentially tall object in a wide frame or to have a free-form object in a rigid panel (or vice versa).

There is such a thing as deliberate distortion for emphasis, but it is a weak defense for a beginner. You've got to learn first how to do it right, something many "modern artists" have never learned.

One good way to incorporate perspective and composition into a carving is to take various photographs of the subject or scene and have a jury of friends pick the best one. Then you can project the negative and trace the parts you want or have an enlargement made to your intended size (if it is within reason) to serve as both a pattern and a guide. All in all, I find the polyglot panel (see Fig. 448) much easier to plan and carve, because even scale is abandoned.

Depth of grounding

WHEN LAYING OUT A PANEL, use pencil rather than pen unless the wood is dark and you are sure all lines will be cut away. I have had cleanup problems with soft-tip pen lines, particularly in color on light woods where the ink may penetrate and stain. On most panels, it is not necessary to sink the background very deeply. I have one in ebony in which the background is so shallow that it is really distinguished only by its surface pattern. Depth of grounding (cutting down the background) is, of course, a matter of choice. The deeper you go, the more modelling you can do (and the more like in-the-round carving it is); but you will also encounter proportionately more undercutting and lateral-view problems. It is easier, and much faster, to learn something about perspective and panel carving before you attempt a piece like *The Last Supper* for your church and find, when you've finished, that the minister or priest decides it will hang best in some dimly lit alcove.

On small panels, I often do not sink the background more than ⅛ in (3.2 mm); on larger pieces I may ground to a depth of ½ in (13 mm) or more. Several factors will

Fig. 495.

Fig. 496. Medium relief on the surface of a log. This seems like in-the-round carving. Carved by Bogosav Zivkovic, it is now in a gallery in Yugoslavia.

determine a practical grounding depth—namely, how many elements are overlapping, how much detail is involved and how much modelling is necessary. If there are several planes of depth, it is best to ground a little deeper in most cases (at least until you learn how to make one object appear in front of another). Also, there is the matter of panel thickness; if it is relatively thin, say 1 in (2.54 cm) or less, it is inadvisable to ground deeply. If extensive modelling is to be done on a bust, for example, or on some other fairly complex figure, it may be advisable to ground as deeply as 1 in (2.54 cm). Also, when you ground, the difference in top and bottom surface areas may cause the panel to warp slightly during carving.

Grounding is done this way: First, outline the area to be lowered with a V-tool or veiner. This cuts surface fibres and reduces the likelihood of splintering at the surface. Then drive in suitable gouges and firmers vertically along the notch to limit the cut area. I usually use small ones, such as ⅛ and ¼ in (3.2 and 6.4 mm) wide.

If grounding is shallow, the setting-in or vertical cutting can be done in a single step, but usually it is best to take it in several steps to avoid crushing and breakage from the tool heel's wedging action. It is possible to set in ¹⁄₁₆ to ⅛ in (1.6 to 3.2 mm) per step, depending upon wood density, hardness, tendency to split and width of sections between set-in areas (a little experimenting is advisable here).

After the line is set in, cut down the area to be grounded with a flat gouge along the cut lines, then set in deeper—and so on. Final depth can be measured with a pin gauge, a mark on a rule or scale or the like, but I find that in most cases my eye is accurate enough. This is true particularly when the background is to be textured or antiqued, in which case slight variations in depth from grounded area to grounded area are unimportant. It is also possible, if areas are relatively large and simple in outline, to rout the wood out. This assures a fairly uniform depth but may create burned lines, gouged spots and the like, as is usual with power carving.

On grounding work, I almost always use a light mallet with the chisels. It gives me better control of the tool and is less likely to cause breakouts and running of the tool into splits. Avoid wedging out chips; this causes breakouts too. Also, when grounding on two sides of a section I am extremely careful when the width of that section is ⅜ in (9.5 mm) or less on woods such as teak and walnut. I ground out on one side as described above, but on the other I lean the tool when setting-in so that its edge cuts into the area to be grounded and away from the narrow section. The wood remaining will then be thicker at the bottom than at the top and require a follow-up operation to make the edge vertical, but this is better than glueing back a split-out section.

I find, from years of performing this operation, that larger tools can do more damage than the time they save. Large gouges, for example, will tend to break out the wood inside the sweep, which is just too bad if you are outlining a convex arc. Also, the flat gouge is a much better roughing tool than the firmer, which tends to catch at the corners and gouge additional, deeper lines. (A remedy for this problem is to grind off the corners of the firmer slightly, making what is called a bullnose tool.) When the ground is fairly level, a firmer can be used for final smoothing—if you really want it smooth. In this cleanup operation, you may also find dog-leg tools very helpful for getting into tight spots. I find that in really tight corners my penknife is still my safest tool.

Hints about procedure

AFTER YOU USE A MALLET for a while, you will develop a rhythm of, say, two or three light taps per cut. But watch out—the same strength of blow will drive the chisel in deeper with the grain than across it. You'll find it best to ground out large areas first and then go back to do the smaller and

Fig. 497. "Justice," an heroic 10-ft (3-m) figure, was carved of pine over a century ago to top a courthouse tower, and now is in the Shelburne (Vt.) Museum.

intricate areas with more care. You should also set in across grain first, so any tendency to split as you set in along the grain will be halted by a previously cut line.

I find that I may work progressively, doing some grounding and then some modelling and even final carving, in rotation. This relieves the boredom of setting in for days before you can get at the interesting part. I also start at the bottom of a carving in most cases. Then my hands and arms rub in some patina and, if it's a warm day, they don't erase as-yet-uncarved lines. I find, too, that I can then feel rough spots

Fig. 498. All carvings are not traditional. Here are modern treatments of a praying girl in ebony ½ × 4½ × 15 in (1.3 × 10 × 38 cm) each. They were carved in Sri Lanka, and have a minimum of modelling and decoration—quite unusual there.

or ball cutter in a rotary tool. I find darkening the background preferable because it also makes the grounding appear deeper and accents the lines of the carving. On porous woods, such a treatment should be preceded by a couple of coats of matte varnish to seal the surface and reduce contrast between end-grain and cross-grain areas. Stain should be brushed in carefully, wiped off after a short interval, and should not be a great deal darker than the surface color. On woods like apple, I use mahogany; on teak I use walnut and on walnut I use walnut stain with a little black added. (Don't use black as a background unless you intend to be startling, because black is "dead" unless it has a shine.)

When you model the surface of a design, it is actually a repetition of grounding and should be done in much the same way, with stop cuts to prevent splitting off of surface wood. The basic difference is that the modelling will probably not be more than a third as deep as the background, unless the background is very shallow. Do *not* begin by chamfering all edges the way a whittler does a dog blank. You may want to keep some edges sharp and hard so they stand out and up. Rounding an edge in relief carving tends to obliterate or subordinate it— and you want scales, feathers or hairlines and the like to be visible. Small features like an eye or a brow line can on occasion be inverted as grooves instead of raised surfaces. And errors can sometimes be corrected simply by carving the erroneous area a little deeper and increasing the depth of the adjacent area until there is no sharp break. However, any really deep correction will be visible in most lighting.

Most ancient Greek statues had the eyes painted in, so the eye itself was rounded as it is in nature, and the figure appears to be blind. My remedy for this is to drill a small-diameter hole for the iris, which blocks out light and looks appropriately black. I mention this here because it is a kind of texturing you will find necessary if panels are to be convincing. A flat surface reflects light,

and clean them up early, thus saving final cleanup time.

Finish or texture of the background varies with subject, relative areas of background, flat surfaces in the subject, depth of grounding and the like. Large areas of background should probably be subordinated in some way, either by texturing them to break up—rather than reflect—light rays or by antiquing them with stain.

In the Far East, the tendency is to texture all backgrounds with small stamps; simple ones can be produced by filing lines across the flattened end of a spike. The pattern should be small, so it does not mash major fibres and cause splintering of the ground. Another device is to break up the background by shallow veiner or V-tool lines in either a regular or random pattern.

An easier but less positive method is to produce a pattern of small depressions with a relatively flat spoon gouge or a dental burr even without sanding and reflective finishes. This is true particularly in hard woods if you cut with sharp tools rather than dull ones or rasps, rotary grinding burrs or other primarily abrasive wood removers. To reduce glare and highlights where you don't want them, you must texture the area. This can be done exactly as you would on the background—with a pattern or random cutting of shallow veiner or V-tool lines, or by stamping with very small and overall patterns. Any of these textures breaks up impinging light rays and reduces reflections.

A few more pointers: If your tool slips or something else goes wrong, repair the spot at once before you lose the chip or magnify the error. Use a good grade of glue with the cutout chip, with another whittled to proper shape (be sure it's also proper in grain and color) or even with mixed glue and sawdust as a filler. Then work somewhere else for a while, admittedly a hard thing to do. I use Elmer's Glue-all® for most carvings but find a plastic cement better for outside work. Also, Elmer's works fine for appliquéing pieces of wood or building up a blank and, in such cases, can be cut 50–50 with water. It then penetrates deeper, dries faster and saves glue by covering more surface more easily. In any case, sand or cut away any glue spillage because it is likely to affect the finish later on.

Fig. 499. Krishna and Raddha (Hindu god and consort) are depicted here in fret-sawed bamboo. Parts are carefully cut and glued to a backing, and some are even broken at proper points to flatten the natural curve of the stem and heighten the three-dimensional effect. Figures are about 12 in (30 cm) tall; from Sri Lanka.

Fig. 500. A panel like this delights Sri Lankans—and me. It is 6½ × 12 in (17 × 30 cm) and combines a bullock and an elephant, face to face to a greater degree than expected because they share a face and an eye.

Fig. 501. Moonstone is familiar as the base step to Buddhist temples, and depicts the seven steps to Nirvana. In stone, it is usually a half-circle. This one, in wood, is a complete circle 14 in (36 cm) in diameter, but shows only five steps—it lacks a ring of sacred geese and another floral ring. Carving is excellent and crisp, particularly on the animals.

and the other faired out onto the adjacent surface will make the edge behind the vertical wall appear to be higher than the adjacent surfaces. Cheeks can be given the appearance of being behind a nose by making the nostril lines sharply vertical and the nose outline above them more vertical than the curves of the cheeks. The same thing applies to brow and ear lines, beard lines and hairlines on faces, as well as to scenes.

One panel I saw recently included three houses, each looking as if it had been pasted atop a crudely shaped mound. The problem was that the carver had a vertical V-cut along the bottom of the house so that it projected from, rather than rested on, the ground. The perspective was also wrong. These things must be learned through experimentation; you can't carve a good *Last Supper* on the first try.

Far-Eastern reliefs

INDIA, SRI LANKA, Kashmir, Nepal and Tibet all have a tradition of woodcarving that spans centuries. What survives from the old days is very competent and ornate, and is usually religious in tone. The mod-

If you want particular thickness only in some areas, buy wood in a thickness necessary for the panel and glue scraps on top in the areas that must be thicker. I've done this for a coat-of-arms on a panel, the bulge of a hull and for a special element on the front corner of a house. The same technique can be used to take care of a rotted, discolored or worm-eaten area. Just cut out the rot or knot and replace it with a selected piece of the same wood carefully fitted to the hole. It may prove better to have an irregular shape than a regular one, since masking such a line is often easier. Be sure any large filled area has the same color and grain (or figure) as the wood around it. And don't sand the area until you're done, if then—imbedded grains of sand can play havoc with the edge of a woodcarving tool.

It is also important to experiment with V-cuts or others when defining the edge of something. A V-cut that makes an accurate vee with the surface will simply be a defining line, but a V-cut with one side vertical

Fig. 502. Teak box about 4 × 6 in (10 × 15 cm) is probably from Sri Lanka; it has the familiar elephant motif on the lid and even more familiar lotus and floral designs on its sides. Backgrounds, typical of East Indian work, are stippled all over—probably with a punch—and figures are stylized to a considerable degree. (See Fig. 503.)

ern work is turned out largely in "factories" for the tourist trade, and the carvers are *not* hobbyists nor artists, but craftsmen earning a living. In most instances, there is one artist-designer and several carvers, often in shops with practically none of the amenities such as power saws, grinders or even electric power and light. The factory is primarily a place to work and a sales outlet. Tools, too, are limited in number; many are homemade strictly for the particular work a carver does. There may be an antique vise or two, and nothing but the floor for a bench, but there are also helpers to do preparation, sanding, finishing, polishing and other onerous chores.

In contrast to the United States, where a high percentage of carving is in-the-round and small enough to be held in the hand for whittling, many of the carvings made in this area are in relief. This ranges from very shallow, to quite-high-relief copies of old work (particularly in India, where some copies are claimed to be antique fragments). What's more, the variety is marked;

carvings may be framed or unframed, geometric shapes, free forms or silhouettes, non-planar or pierced work, in a bewildering variety of woods. Carving is of good quality, as are designs, and although it may also have pieces from other factories for sale, a particular factory is likely to be specialized.

In Sri Lanka, panels are carved in the Kandy area, ebony 3-D figures in Galle, masks of *nux vomica* in one particular south-coast village, and so on. I could have traded a pocketknife in any factory for a really good carving; one carving school up a dirt road outside Sigiryia, Sri Lanka, had a cheap set of six American tools kept carefully in its original cardboard box. This school had no power, so used gas-pressure lamps at night for its 15 or so apprentices, who were schoolboys aged 12 to 20, who went to school in the morning and then came to apprentice in afternoons and evenings for eight long years. They should be good!

Edge of front
Edge of top panel
Elements are modelled

Hinged joint

Note that flower has 7 petals

Background stippled with punch or veiner

Lotus-petal bands on top rim

Fig. 503.

EAST INDIAN MOTIFS on a teak box

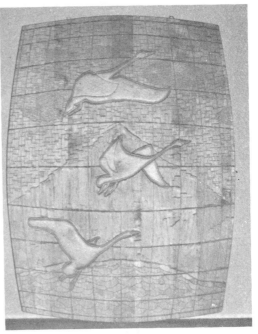

Figs. 504, 505 (above and right). Two bird panels by T. E. Haag illustrate the wide range of scenic depiction possible in low relief. (Above): A detailed duck against a textured background. (Right): Three stylized flying swans against a patterned background. One is framed, the other has unusual outlining with latitude and longitude lines, bowed and spaced to give the flat panel a global effect.

Fig. 506. This Nepalese scene is in sisso, an antiqued light wood, and depicts village and city with adjacent countryside. Dominant is a stupa (temple) with "paper" prayer streamers from its peak, surrounded by typical multi-storey brick and stucco buildings. Stylized rural area in foreground and at left includes rice paddies. Size is ⅞ × 6½ × 11 in (2.2 × 17 × 28 cm).

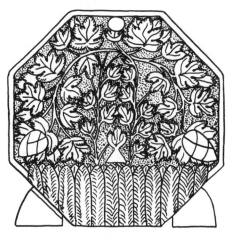

Fig. 507.

Figs. 507–509 (above, right and below). From far-off Tibet comes this octagonal triple folding tray in walnut. The 7-in (18-cm) sides fold down (below) to reveal carved-tray inner surfaces, plus a tilting tray in the middle. Motifs are floral.

Fig. 508.

Fig. 509.

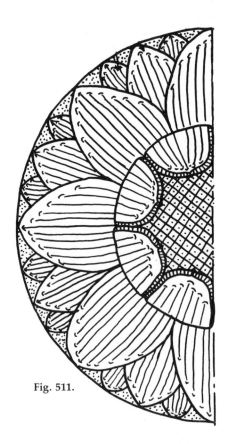

Fig. 511.

Fig. 510. A carver works on a mask—of nux vomica (a wood like balsa, with poisonous berries used in medicines) in a factory in Sri Lanka, while his partner tests the edge on his chisel. Carvers are pieceworkers, with nothing beyond a circular saw, flat table and bench, and a tool or two apiece.

Figs. 511, 512 (right and above). The lotus has deep religious significance to Hindus and Buddhists alike, and is a frequent design motif. Here is an 8-in (20-cm) disk from Sri Lanka that features this design.

Fig. 512.

Fig. 513 (left). Head-size mask, depicting the fire demon featured in Kandy dances in Sri Lanka. A mask such as this takes about a week to complete, including carving and elaborate enamelling. Side projections are removable and plugged into the semi-cylinder face.

Figs. 514, 515 (right and below). Another delight to Sri Lankans is this variation of the Chinese puzzle box, with elephant and lotus-blossom border on its cover. It looks like a 6 × 9-in (15 × 2-cm) light-colored book, but then backbone is pushed down and back, allowing central panel to slide to the side, revealing the ¾-in (19-mm) "secret compartment."

Fig. 514.

BOX COVER
"Secret" panel in mahogany book-shaped puzzle. Sri Lanka

Fig. 515.

Animals in relief

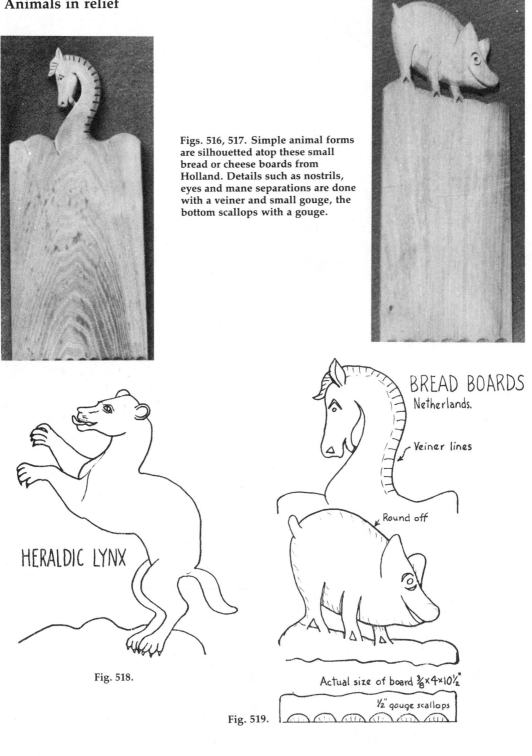

Figs. 516, 517. Simple animal forms are silhouetted atop these small bread or cheese boards from Holland. Details such as nostrils, eyes and mane separations are done with a veiner and small gouge, the bottom scallops with a gouge.

HERALDIC LYNX

Fig. 518.

BREAD BOARDS
Netherlands.

Veiner lines

Round off

Actual size of board ⅜x4x10½"

½" gouge scallops

Fig. 519.

Fig. 520.

Fig. 521.

Figs. 520–522. These three figures from a kubbstol (block stool) were made by the author from an ash log. It is an example of extreme foreshortening, because background depth is only ¼ in (6 mm), while the subjects are 10 in (25 cm) or more tall. It is essential to create the visual effect of depth to separate the warriors from their horses and saddles. Designs of this sort require a great deal of cut and try. Staining the lines and background helps to create depth.

Fig. 522.

Door panels

Fig. 523. Flower panel is 1-in (2.54-cm) teak, tree panel comprises two glued pieces 1¼ in (3.2 cm) thick, and fish panel is ¾ × 9⅜ in (1.9 × 24 cm) wide.

Fig. 524. All three of these panels are ¾-in (19-mm) teak 9⅜ in (24 cm) wide. Insect panel is most complex of the group because of antennae and legs.

From clouds to sheep—
step-by-step

THIS PANEL in pine is relatively simple to carve compared to the door panels and will help you learn to handle firmers and gouges. The design is modified from a poster and provides a smile as well as a carving. My blank was 2 × 12 × 14½ in (5.1 × 30.5 × 36.8 cm) and I laid out the composition directly on it. Now follow the carving, step by step.

Fig. 525. Step 1. Lay out the design to suit the available wood. I showed single sheep in various poses, some groups, and added a lamb or two as an afterthought. They are posed on a hillside, with clouds floating down so low that three are actually below the horizon; they repeat the general shape of sheep immediately below them. The original layout was in pencil; I tried not to overload the composition, and to vary poses. Shallow low-relief carving of the sheep has here been started as a test.

Fig. 526. Step 2. It may be advisable to alter poses of individual animals to improve the balance. In this closeup of the lower right-hand corner are two such changes, one lowering the head of the ewe at left towards the lying-down lamb, and the other to attain a more compact grouping at center, leaving a larger area of open grass. Legs must be sloped back towards the feet so they apparently are behind an irregular pattern of grass spears. Units have been outlined with soft-tip pen.

Fig. 527. Step 3. I decided to leave a border and slope in from it to the ground and sky. My testing indicated that a depth of only ⅛ in (3.2 mm) for the grass area was enough to set out the sheep, permitting the easy solution of setting the hill fold at left back an additional ⅛ in (3.2 mm) and making total depth of the grounding at the top ⅜ in (9.5 mm). This was worth the time of setup for routing, as was the ¼ in (6.4 mm). Note that routing is only approximate around the nebulous cloud shape, which is best determined as it is carved. Shapes are important only to avoid crowding and to suggest the transition to sheep at the bottom.

Fig. 528. Step 4. The remainder of the meadow is grounded out and left with vertically gouged scallop marks to suggest a grassy field. Clouds are carved in swooping billows, with very little undercutting. Individual sheep are modelled slightly, and pelt textured with irregular gouge scallops to suggest a fairly short coat of wool and avoid flatness which would reflect light. The grass is a tint of green, of course, darker in the distance, sky a light blue, and the sheep white with black eyes and slight antiquing with grey to bring out modelling. The general effect, however, is attained by not overdetailing the sheep.

Fig. 529. Clouds become sheep in this pine panel, 2 × 12 × 14½ in (5.1 × 30.5 × 36.8 cm), painted with oils.

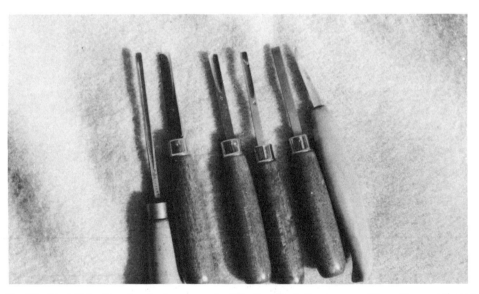

Fig. 530. Tool Note: Very few tools are required for the cloud-sheep composition. Here are those I used (except for the router): left to right are a ¼-in (6.4-mm) V-tool; ½-in (12.7-mm) wide gouge, ½-in (12.7-mm) radius; ½-in (12.7-mm)-wide gouge; ⅜-in (9.5-mm) radius; ½-in (12.7-mm)-wide gouge; ¼-in (6.4-mm) radius; ⅜-in (9.5-mm)-wide gouge, and a whittling knife. The knife took care of details around the head, like the eyes and mouth, and was useful in general modelling. Even the clouds were left unsanded. Colors were oil pigments in varnish, and the finished job was given a spray coat of satin varnish to reduce the gloss. Then I made a sketch on paper for the record.

Relief combined
with stylized wilderness

WOODCARVINGS OF SPECIFIC SCENES and people can be challenging to any carver, because they usually involve foliage, may include water and clouds, and can be expected to achieve at least approximate likenesses. The usual in-the-round treatment of such a subject tends to be a caricature, and a very stiff one at that. A relief panel offers better prospects, but can be difficult as well. Thus, it is advisable to make a series of compromises, possibly arriving at an unusual solution or depiction.

This panel (Fig. 531) will serve as an example. It was a commission, a birthday present for the lady of the carving from her husband. It was to depict them in their canoe, not on Long Island Sound where they commonly paddle, but at an island in northern Maine. No pictures were available of the island, the canoe or its occupants, but the canoe is a standard Grumman® 17 and the occupants are friends, so there was a starting point.

There are several books on canoeing with pictures of two people in a canoe, as well as pictures of this particular canoe, so a rough sketch could be made. Once this was finished, the client made several criticisms: I had seated him too far forward; I had changed the point of view from that in the pictures, raising it slightly so more of the legs of both people were visible; I'd made the paddles too short; instead of the flat shoreline I'd drawn, there should've been a curved one, with a bluff and rocks, and over the bluff a tangle in which birch, an apple and an oak could be distinguished at designated points; there were no pines, and at the left, there should've been an edge with an overhang. There should also have been a slight bow wave and a small wake as well, he suggested.

These alterations were put on the sketch, which was then adapted to a piece of old mahogany ¾ × 12 × 19 in (1.9 × 30 × 48 cm). I arbitrarily decided to lower the ground ½ in (13 mm) around the canoe, leaving wood for the bow wave and wake,

Fig. 531. Mahogany panel, ¾ × 12 × 19 in (1.9 × 30 × 48 cm), is made from a century-old table leaf, so patina is preserved in framing and brush on the shore at top.

as well as for the eddy where the visible paddle enters the water. Only the lower portion was grounded, initially.

Water can be difficult to depict—if you try to be too specific. It is much easier to *suggest* wavelets by leaving the background rough and texturing it with a small-diameter flat gouge, say a ½-in (13-mm) No. 4 or 5. The curvature of the canoe was shaped to clear the visible paddle, show the precise position of bow wave and wake, and to get a proper meeting line between canoe and water. Bad meeting lines, between such objects as a house and the ground in front of it, are a common error in low-relief panels. Here, the curvature of the canoe itself makes the solution obvious. The canoe surface is brought down to the water; there is no step between.

When rough shaping of figures and canoe were completed, it was possible to go back and do the shoreline, indenting it irregularly and establishing the rocks along the shore to match the client's description. Again, the rocks had to be sloped on their lower surfaces so that they met the water without too much step, and cut back near the male figure to help him stand out. Some visible shoreline (where the sand itself meets the water) was also included to establish perspective. To get the effect of an overhang and erosion, the "vertical" portion of the bank was sharply indented along the top. This idea was enhanced by showing a side view of the overhang at the left-hand upper end. This takes some juggling, and requires that you stand back and look at the entire panel frequently as you work.

Because the panel was old mahogany—it had been the center of a small table for over a hundred years—the surface had a dark and attractive patina, which had to be sacrificed for the water area and the principal subject. By trenching in at the edges, I could leave a darker border or frame on three sides, along with a V-tooled, border-defining line I had carved along the top.

It seemed rather absurd to attempt carving a Maine wilderness atop the island when the center of interest should be the canoe. So the bush area was simply stylized with irregular lines, although portions of the boles of the three special trees were made visible in suitable locations and identified by branching and bark texture. The birch, for example, could be carved so that the dark patches indicating one-time small branches could be left while the patina is cut away to lighten the rest. On the oak, there are vertical lines simulating bark markings and high-up branching. On the apple, there is a shorter trunk and a visible crotch. This worked out quite well, and saved a great deal of time, energy and likely disappointment.

The finished piece was given a spray coat of satin varnish as a sealant, followed by two coats of Kiwi® neutral shoe polish. (Conventional waxes tend to load open-grain woods like mahogany and eventually create grey speckles, unless the entire surface is filled.)

High relief permits realistic scenes

HIGH-RELIEF CARVING was, until perhaps 100 years ago, quite commonly done in Europe and Japan, and, by extension, in the United States. It was the common form of carved decoration in palaces and mansions, churches, temples and monasteries. Panels were incorporated in heavy furniture, such as chests and cabinets, applied in overmantels, door frames and ceilings, even on walls. Much of the private decoration was composed of bucolic scenes involving people and animals with a background of trees and shrubbery, but in churches and monasteries it covered a wide range of religious subjects, from depictions of saints to the Stations of the Cross.

High-relief carvings usually incorporate a number of figures, often carved in the round, to depict a scene against a foreshortened background that serves as the equivalent of a stage setting (and which may include medium and/or low relief, as many museum dioramas do). Forced perspective is commonly employed.

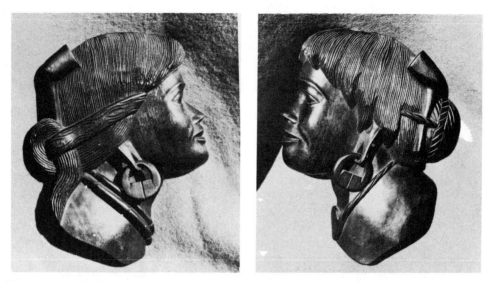

Figs. 532, 533. Philippine women, in mahogany and 2 in (5 cm) thick, are almost half-relief. Each has an integral-carved earring. Because of the depth, modelling is relatively easy.

The most famous English carver, Grinling Gibbons, who commonly carved swags of flowers and fruit, was, in fact, criticized (and still is) for occasionally carving his subject in the round and appliquéing it to a panel. This permitted him to work from both back and front, and lessened the problem of how much undercutting was necessary—a problem which still plagues anyone who undertakes a high-relief carving. His favorite material was limewood, although he also worked in other woods, bronze and stone, and his work has never been surpassed in Europe. Some of his swags, in St. Paul's, London, and other English buildings, tremble at the slightest vibration—and have been trembling for almost 300 years.

The vulnerability of high-relief carving (both during and after carving) may be one of the factors that led to its decline. Others are: changing tastes in decoration, reduced availability of thick wood, and greater consciousness of time. In high-relief carving, a relatively enormous amount of wood must be cut away, unless frontal figures are appliquéd. Also, the completed work is fragile, a real dust-catcher, and has a tendency to

appear florid and overdone by modern standards.

Ken Evans, of Portland, Oregon, owns the unsigned carving (Fig. 535) and has made extensive inquiries about it. It is probably a copy of the painting made in Austria by Franz DeFregger (1835–1921), but the painter was originally a carver who didn't study painting until he was 25 years old, and the painting was made nine years later in Munich. Did DeFregger make the carving, then copy it later in oils, or did some

Fig. 534. Toreador and bull from Ecuador, was pierced and silhouetted, and looks deeper than it is. The 10-in long (25-cm) panel is only ½ in (12.7 mm) thick.

unknown make the carving? Nobody knows, which is at least a minor argument in favor of signing carvings—something that European carver-craftsmen did not do often, because their work was often copied from paintings.

The subject of both painting and carving comes from an actual occurrence in 1809. Josef Speckbacher, the central figure, was a leader under the Tyrolean patriot, Andreas Hoffer. He was meeting with others at an inn when some of his men discovered that his eight-year-old son, Anderl, was actively participating in the fight for Tyrolean freedom against the French and Bavarians, obviously without the advice or consent of his father. In the picture, a *Schutze* (marksman) of the Freedom Fighters is returning the son to his father (Fig. 537). Note, in the carving, the almost free-standing figures, the complexity of the wall decorations, the detail in the "wall painting" of the Madonna and Child (Fig. 536) and the fully carved little wagon at upper right. Which was first, painting or carving? And who carved the panel? The carving is 4 × 24 × 20 in (10 × 61 × 51 cm), and weighs 37 lbs (16.6 kg) with its wide and elaborate frame (not shown). The wood is cembra pine. The carver shows textures on the deer horn and wrinkles on the faces, as well as defining hair and other details.

This is an excellent example of the use of high relief to tell a story, rather than being limited to the depiction of an individual or group, as a three-dimensional single figure normally is. It shows a familiar subject, and the carver was therefore able to base his work on fact—even if his "fact" is only a painting—and he wasn't forced to stylize because his knowledge did not extend to precise details.

Lower relief and modelling

IF HIGH-RELIEF CARVING is accompanied by problems in deciding how much undercutting is necessary, lower-relief carving brings similar problems in modelling.

Most present-day relief carving is quite shallow, with backgrounds sunk as little as ⅛ in (3.2 mm) on small plaques and ½ in (12.7 mm) or 1 in (25.4 mm) on larger ones. The illusion of greater depth is obtained by darkening or texturing the background, by pierce-carving, or by silhouetting the subject so that there is little or no background of the wood itself. This makes modelling and forced perspective extremely important; so important, in fact, that many carvers make mistakes and their panels have a "wooden" look (forgive the pun). Others are extremely intricate, containing so much detail, plus efforts to undercut, that they become fussy and overdetailed, losing their strength in more ways than one.

Here I have attempted to combine a great many widely differing subjects and techniques to provide a sort of index of low and medium relief, and of modelling, and to show how and where they differ from in-the-round, which is quite similar to high-relief carving. Consider, for example, the two silhouette panels in mahogany from the Philippines (Figs. 532, 533), typical of the technique commonly in use there. Each is 10 × 13 in (25.4 × 33 cm), but carved from 2-in (5-cm) wood. This thickness, combined with the silhouetting and modelling, makes the carvings appear almost in-the-round, except for a flat back. The carver actually achieves considerable depth in modelling the face around the eyes and neck, which gives the face a natural look. Further, he carved the earrings free, using the old "chain trick" to achieve an effect.

The high modelling of medium relief is obtained in the woman-and-child panel (Fig. 489) and the bullfighter panel from Ecuador (Fig. 534), as well as in the series of Indians and other figures from the Pátzcuaro area of Mexico (Fig. 538). The Mexican carver was not nearly so skilled in technique, but these figures have a crude strength, nonetheless. The carver let his imagination run free. Some of the full figures are 6 ft tall (1.8 m); all are at least 1 in (25.4 mm) thick, in soft wood. Sharply contrasting in size is the small head of a girl from Ecuador (Fig. 490), with its somewhat

Figs. 535–537. The above unsigned carving is 4 in (10 cm) thick, roughly 20 × 24 in (50 × 60 cm), and includes every detail of the painting from which it was taken. Close-up (below right) of marksman and boy shows how the illusion of depth was obtained. Note the free-standing figures and perspective size-reduction. Other close-up shows detail of antlers and the low-relief miniature of the Madonna and Child.

Fig. 536.   Fig. 537.

Fig. 538. Sketches of primitive Mexican figures from Pátzcuaro.

stylized face (accented nose and eyebrow outline), which is actually in the round in wood 1 in (25.4 mm) thick, framed by the hair at the top and brought to a pointed and thin tress below to provide delicate, balanced support on the base.

In all of these carvings, modelling is not much of a problem because the third dimension is deep. The difficulties increase as thickness is reduced, so that planes and apparent relative elevations become increasingly important. Familiar handlings of this problem are depicted in the little Indian-head pendant from Peru (Fig. 539) and the copy of an antique candle sconce from Spain (Fig. 542). Ruth Hawkins in Brasstown, North Carolina, contrasted her two angels in holly (Fig. 540) by mounting

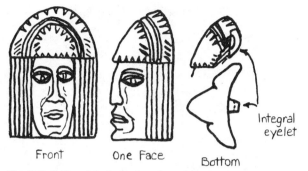

Front   One Face   Bottom

Integral eyelet

Fig. 539. Indian-head pendant from Peru is triangular in cross-section.

Fig. 540. These angels, carved in low relief in holly, would be lost as silhouettes unless placed against a contrasting background.

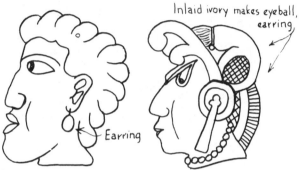

Inlaid ivory makes eyeball, earring

Earring

Fig. 541. Maya profile, contrasted here with one from Haiti, was carved in ebony, with very low relief.

them on a strongly patterned cross section of branch, which ties the composition together and silhouettes the figures.

In working out a design on a surface, or in carving shaped objects and plaques, it may be enough to use very little modelling, leaving much of the surface flat and undisturbed. An excellent case in point is a tabletop which, if carved at all, should have minimum-depth surface carving, so the stability of objects placed upon it will not be imperiled. Also, fewer crevices are thereby provided for the accumulation of dust and dirt. (This, of course, is less important if the carving is to be covered with glass, but some compromise must be arrived at between the amount of wood surface there is to support the glass and its thickness.) The design should be worked out so that any complex or deep carving is away from the

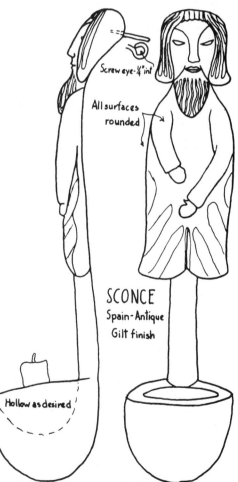

Screw eye-¼"int

All surfaces rounded

SCONCE
Spain-Antique
Gilt finish

Hollow as desired

Fig. 542. The copy of an antique candle sconce was carved in soft wood. Note the exaggerated nose and brow lines.

Figs. 543, 544. Head of Tarahumara Indian (left), in cedar, was trench-carved and is self-bordered. The study of Benito Juarez (right), is in mahogany and has various V-grooves detailing general features.

Fig. 544.

areas where stability is needed. A flat tabletop I saw in Bali had large and flat floral designs at the points where service and salad plates, saucers and centerpiece would normally be placed, while the rest of the surface was actually deep-relief and pierce-carved.

It is not always necessary to work over an entire surface and to blend all lines and model all contours; it may, in fact, be better on occasion *not* to do so. One factor is the grain of the wood. If it is strong and lovely of itself, carving should be subordinated or even omitted. Any effort to subdue a strong grain with even stronger carving usually ends in confusion for both carver and viewer.

Again, if the wood is old and has a desirable patina, minimal carving will help to preserve the patina. If it is a chair back—or, worse still, a chair seat—minimal carving will be appreciated by any sitter.

In addition to the questions raised in the preceding paragraphs, there are those having to do with technique. Should the design have crisp, sharp edges, or should it be

modelled? Should it be trenched, leaving the background high around it, self-framed, or have the background bosted away? Should the lowered visual effect of shallow relief carving be compensated for

Fig. 545. This head of an American Indian was trench-carved by Ted Haag.

by darkening the background or the lines of the carving itself as a scrimshander does? How much should line width be varied, groove-angle changed? Should surface texturing be used, and if so, should it be with veiner, V-tool or knife? Cross-hatched or gouge-scalloped?

Many of the answers to these questions depend upon personal taste, and I find myself varying from panel to panel, often simply to see what effect I can get. Any modelling or texturing breaks up impinging light and changes the apparent tone of what the observer sees. Thus, gouge-scalloping, cross-hatching or parallel-lining will make a surface appear darker because the reflected light isn't beamed as it is from a flat surface. Textured areas tend to sink back, an effect which can be enhanced by "antiquing" them—going over them with a slightly darker stain and immediately wiping most of it away, except in the deepest areas. (This is actually an "instant patina"—because true patina is merely the accumulation of dirt, grease, dust and such over a long period of time, and it is naturally heavier in the grooves and hollows.)

I find that irregular grooving tends to create the effect of slightly wavy hair; regular and precise grooving suggests hair drawn tight to the scalp; fine veiner lines suggest fine hair (except on small figures, when *no* lines suggests even finer hair); and coarser lines suggest a pelt or coarse hair, as in a lion's mane. Tilting a V-tool away from one edge, thus lengthening the other side of the groove, tends to make the sharper side rise visually above the wider one. As the depth of relief is reduced, the effect of even slight variations in surface level and modelling becomes greater, so hollow cheeks and the like can be obtained with very shallow shaping. Also, with very shallow relief, crisp edges will stand out, rounded edges will disappear (an argument against sandpaper also). Trenching does not take away from the carving—see the Indian and Juarez (Figs. 543, 544). It saves a lot of fussing over background and

protects the carving itself. Framing is often confining and more trouble than it is worth.

The answers to others of the preceding questions, and perhaps additional ones, will become apparent by study of the shallow-carved panels. I carved the Tarahumara Indian (Fig. 543) from memory in Mexico, in a piece of cedar, using only a pocketknife. The high-set cheekbones are suggested by shallow hollowing beneath them, the deep-set eyes by sharp brow lines above, the strong jaw and thick lips by the hollowing around them. It is less effective than the Indian by T. E. Haag (Fig. 545), which uses deepened relief. The head of Juarez in mahogany (Fig. 544), also carved in Mexico, but from a Covarrubias sketch, is about 4 × 6 in (10 × 15 cm) and almost the equivalent of a pen-and-ink sketch. Sharp edges define the nose and eyes, the collar and hairdo. Tilted V-grooves raise the lapels above the jacket and project the lips forward from the lower cheek, as well as the hair in front of the forehead. The trench groove around the head is also tilted to give a wider outside edge and visually sets the portrait ahead of the background.

The next example is a breadboard in cherry, carved for a music teacher (Fig. 546). The central clef masks a hanging hole, and the silhouette of the grand piano on the left is matched by a series of children's heads on the right. To separate the figures from the background, and to control the visible grain to a degree, the background is lowered and textured with roughly parallel shallow gouge cuts. Another breadboard (Fig. 547), also of cherry, shows two skate dancers, slightly more modelled. Both examples approach outlining rather than relief carving at all.

The essential in any work like this is a steady and sure hand, as well as a clear and clean design, because every line will show in the finished piece. When used on wood, it becomes more difficult because of the wood grain. Also, because wood is likely to be dark, the filler color should be a white oil

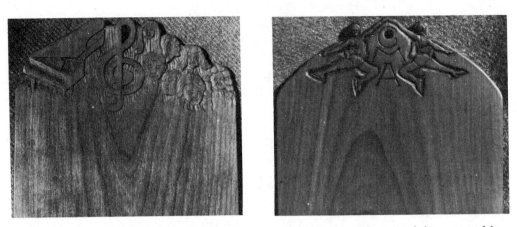

Figs. 546, 547. Two breadboards, in cherry, are 7 × 11 in (17.5 × 27.5 cm). The one at left was carved for a music teacher, the other for a skate dancer.

paint, which is applied in the lines as far as possible, then allowed to dry and sanded off. The problem with wood is that it has surface pores, so the pigment may fill them as well as the carved lines, and may tend to weaken the design.

Intaglio carving is "inside-out"

NEARLY A CENTURY AGO, it was quite common to mould designs in relief on the surface of butter, cookies, cakes and gelatine desserts. This was done with moulds of wood which had the design in reverse; the high spots of the moulded design were the low spots of the mould, and vice versa. In industry, similar moulds were used for rubber, plaster, celluloid (somewhat similar to modern plastics), and other materials. Such designs were achieved by intaglio carving,

which requires the carver to think—and carve—in reverse. It is particularly valuable as training for carving smooth hollows or concavities with gouges; a knife is almost useless as a tool for such work. A power rotary tool can be used, but it tends to leave a rough surface onto which the moulded material will stick, as well as to create unintentional undercuts and make what should be straight lines irregular.

Older cookie and butter moulds had simple geometric patterns, and were usually flat boards which were pressed against the material to be moulded; but as time went on, all sorts of elaborate designs were produced, including coats of arms, initials, and even scenes. For cookie dough, in particular, designs were ultimately carved into a roller similar to a rolling pin, which made

Fig. 548. Springerle cookie-roller with patterns.

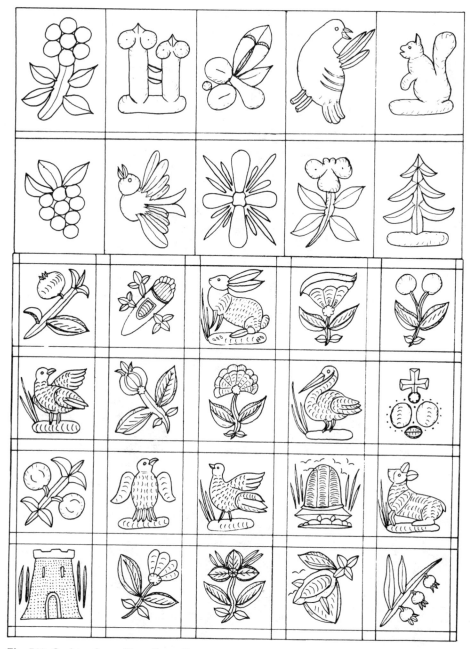

Fig. 549. Springerle cookie-roller patterns.

the impression more uniform. These rollers decorate *springerle*, a lightly spiced German Christmas cookie.

Designs are carved, largely in single cuts, with small, deep gouges, and detailed with the veiner (itself a very small, deep gouge) and V-tool. Short-bent gouges are helpful but not essential for spherical cuts. Best of all, designs really don't have to be too precise, so you can learn to swing the tool and cut from various angles to accommodate grain. Also, the designs can be put on a flat

Fig. 550. The Maoris of New Zealand are particularly adept at low relief carving. This panel in pine by Austin Brasell shows motifs that are usually background or secondary to a principal figure depicting an ancestor. White spots are paua shell; size is ¾ × 15¾ × 15¾ in (1.9 × 40 × 40 cm).

board rather than on a roller, or used individually for decorative panels.

Preferred woods are light-colored ones with dense grain, like maple or birch. Pine can be used, but the grain tends to rise if the piece gets damp (important only if you plan to make cookies or moulded butter pats). Tools must be very sharp to avoid tearing at cut edges, and sanding should be avoided.

If the panels are purely decorative, any wood can be used as long as it isn't too inclined to split. The carving in such a panel can be made more prominent and decorative by "antiquing" with a slightly darker stain. If you plan to do this, first apply a thin coat of matte or satin varnish so the stain doesn't penetrate cross-grain areas unduly and cause undesirable dark areas. If the surface is sealed, stain can be applied and wiped off the surface before it dries, so shading of the color is possible.

Fig. 551. (below) Typical Maori's motifs.

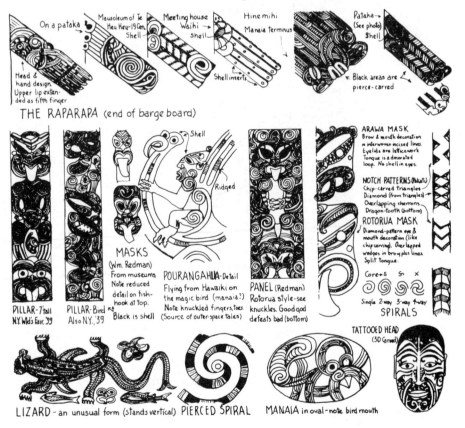

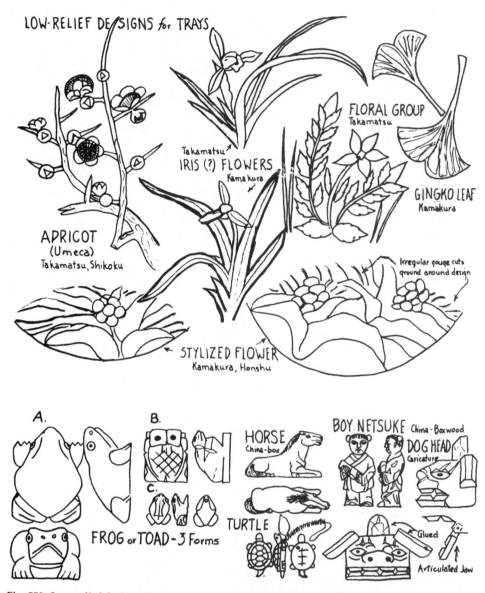

LOW-RELIEF DESIGNS for TRAYS

APRICOT (Umeca) Takamatsu, Shikoku

Takamatsu IRIS (?) FLOWERS Kamakura

FLORAL GROUP Takamatsu

GINGKO LEAF Kamakura

STYLIZED FLOWER Kamakura, Honshu

Irregular gouge cuts ground around design

A.

B.

C.

FROG or TOAD - 3 Forms

HORSE China-box

TURTLE

BOY NETSUKE China-Boxwood

DOG HEAD Caricature

Glued

Articulated Jaw

Fig. 552. Low-relief designs for trays. Amphibians are a favorite gift between Japanese families, wishing long life and good luck. On earlier trays the carving may be tinted and even be partially gold-leafed.

Much more elaborate designs can be carved this way. You've undoubtedly seen some, such as the "gingerbread men" from Williamsburg, Virginia. Incised lettering, trade-marks, logotypes, even inverted portraits, such as those carved in shell in Italy, are also possible. (For shell, a rotary tool with grinding wheels does the heavy work.) Note, incidentally, that ridges are difficult because of the problems of smoothing the surfaces around them. The small lines suggesting feathers on a bird or veins in a leaf are all incised (cut in). This makes leaf veins stand out in a cookie as they do in real life, but the feather divisions will stand out rather than being depressed. Optically,

Fig. 553. A three-dimensional copy of a detail of Picasso's "Dora Marr Seated." This is a low-relief carving in walnut, ¾ × 11 × 12 in (1.9 × 28 × 30 cm). David Peters was the carver.

this is not unpleasant, and therefore nothing to worry about; but if you do tend to worry, such elements as feathers can, of course, be formed by a series of small cuts with a somewhat flatter gouge. It doesn't affect the taste of the cookie.

18

How to Carve Lettering

LETTERING ON A CARVING may have one or more purposes. It can be just a signature and/or date, a title, a dedication, or the major subject of the carving itself. If you carve a likeness, you will almost certainly want to add a title. The Arabic alphabet is cursive (script) and flowing, thus lends itself to endless variations and is easy to incorporate in a design, but our Roman alphabet is rigid and much more difficult to use. Once it consisted only of capitals, and before that simply incised strokes, but the addition of lower-case letters for ease of reading, and of the running-hand, cursive or script forms for easier handwriting, tremendously complicated the job of the carver. Today we have vertical letters and sloping letters (italics), and many alphabets have weighted lines and curves and lines to end each basic stroke. These letter terminals are called *serifs* and are a major problem in relief carving, particularly across grain. Also, letterers add flourishes called *swashes* to the tails of letters—as some penmen do—or make elaborate tails and loops called *uncials*.

All this does not mean that any lettering you do must be elaborate—or boring. You can vary the designs to suit your purpose, as long as the letters are recognizable and legible, and you can finish them in many ways. The effect of raised lettering can be achieved by stamping or otherwise texturing the background around it; letters can be outlined (if they are large enough), inlaid or even carved with channels or grooves in the wider verticals of capital letters. But the easiest form is V-groove incising, particularly if the wood and the tool sharpness permit use of the veiner or V-tool, or you are working in end grain. You *can* go all out and do raised lettering as a continuous cursive strip, as if a ribbon had been laid on the surface to form the letters. If you undertake that, be prepared for trouble, and expect no sympathy from me. It is my firm belief that much lettering on carvings, particularly titles, is unnecessary and looks crude, even if the carving itself is well done. If you must have elegant lettering, have it engraved or etched on a brass or silver appliquéd plate.

Even the simplest lettering is difficult to carve. The difficulties include line width, spacing and depth, and increase with smaller size and more complex letter forms, such as serifs and swashes, as well as if the letters must project rather than be incised, because the eye picks up very small variations in the curve, spacing or width of a line. Further, calligraphy—the design and execution of ornamental lettering—is rising in public favor, so many people are more conscious of letter forms.

It is a paradox that the typewriter and most other forms of commercial type place each letter in a block of uniform width and height, while the calligrapher and the handsetter consider a great many spacing variations essential. Small wonder that carvers go to templates and routers to produce passable lettering!

There are an endless number of rules that the sign painter and the hand typesetter, as well as the calligrapher, follow. Some of the

Fig. 554.   Fig. 555.   Fig. 556.

Fig. 554. Gothic letters in relief, Spanish, 14th or 15th century.

Fig. 555. Incised letters from the Forum at Rome.
Fig. 556. Elizabethan lettering from an incised inscription at North Walsham, Norfolk, England.

Fig. 557 (left). Panel in English sycamore (harewood), about 12 × 16 in (30 × 41 cm), has incised lettering combined with a trenched low-relief of a bird impaled on a thorn, which also provides an initial letter C. Thorn grows from a Celtic interlaced potted-tree design forming the left border. The alphabet is Celtic, with some additions to make it understandable today.

Fig. 558 (right). Serifed and weighted letters provide a pattern for clay impressions. Letters must have sloping sides to pull from the clay. Wood is white pine, and overall size is 2 × 7½ in (5.1 × 19 cm).

simpler ones are: The letters i and l require only ½ space, while the letters m and w require 1½; a punctuation mark requires ½, with a single space between words and at least a double space between sentences. Letters that are very boxy, like capital H, need ½ space between, but rounded ones like O, P and Q can be crowded closer to adjacent letters. Letters like o and c actually look smaller in a line of type than do many others, so they can be made slightly taller. A letter like t, particularly a capital T, can be crowded slightly closer to adjacent letters like o or a because of the projecting crossbar on top. This is also true of the letter f on its right side. Interline spacing can vary widely, from one-half the total line width to more than twice the line width, but line spacing should be widened as line length or letter weight increases, for ease of reading.

There are many other rules, some of which will vary with the particular alphabet being used. For example, in the large plaque pictured (Fig. 554), the t, l, and f are special forms requiring a full space in width. My best suggestion for the beginner at carving letters is to use a simple sans serif alphabet. Gothic, script, italic and archaic alphabets are much harder to carve well.

There are occasions when all these suggestions must be abandoned, as in designing and carving the legend of the bird (Fig. 557). This is the old Celtic story, so it seemed appropriate to design it with an alphabet from *The Book of Kells*, and to use a decorative band from that book as well.

My first idea was a simple carving of the bird suspended from a thorn, the whole composition "white on white" except for a vermilion drop of blood. Then I realized

that the carving might well be meaningless to most people, and the legend itself should be included. This suggested that the plaque take the form of an illuminated manuscript, with the bird as the ornamental initial. It seemed advisable to include some other decoration for the "page" as well, so the idea of including a side band combined with the thorn branch was born. Fortunately, the ancient Celts were fond of designs of vines growing from pots, so the branch could simply be an extension. It could also incorporate some of the complex patterns the Celts used in the bird itself, so I braided the extended tail.

Pick a simple alphabet

PICK A simple alphabet, at least initially. Gothic and flowery lettering is not designed for the carver but for the penman and illustrator, and most woods won't take the detail, even if your eyes and tools will. And incise your lettering, unless you have endless time and patience. Incised letters can be tinted easily for legibility, by simply putting on a stop coat of varnish and flowing a paint or stain into the lettering then wiping off the excess as a scrimshander does on ivory. (If the surface of the piece is tinted by the coloring, it can be lightly sanded to clean it up, but you can't do that with raised lettering!)

Because thin plastic sheet can be molded to almost any form and will pick up even surface roughness and grain lines, some carvers have had commissions to produce patterns for such work. These patterns are often in woods that will display a decided grain, like oak, particularly with a little sandblasting after carving. Sign carvers

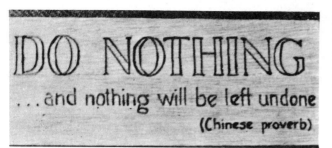

also make use of this characteristic of wood, sandblasting their lettering after completion to give it a weathered look. It is also quite common to batter the sign a bit with a chain or other flexible but hard object to add to the weathering, as well as to do some scorching with a blowtorch (which incidentally removes burrs and feather edges, and makes sanding unnecessary).

The "MDA 7" shown here (Fig. 558) is in this category. It was produced in white pine with raised and serifed lettering to serve as a pattern in clay or Plasticine®. Because it was to be applied directly to the material, which had to read correctly, the pattern had to be in reverse and also had to have slightly sloping sides so it could be withdrawn after it was pressed into the material.

Another problem that you may face on occasion is to produce a monogram. This is usually composed of three letters, but may be two or four, or even more in the case of a company or an individual who carries a "Junior" or "III," for example. The simplest approach is to make the letter of the Christian name dominant, with the other two laced over it. Because so many letters in the English alphabet have vertical and horizontal lines, this is relatively easy. A dominant circular letter like c or o can enclose the others, or one with a space at top and/or bottom, like m, n, or w, can do the same.

Sometimes one letter can serve to complete another, as in the initials AGA, in which the G can tie together the two A's, one over the other, by forming the crossbars as it cuts through both. Of course, modern printers avoid the entire problem by putting the letters in order, vertically, horizontally or diagonally, but the calligrapher interlocks them in one way or another, even if he or she must modify the letter form to do it.

Lettering an award panel

AWARDS OF ONE KIND or another lend themselves particularly to woodcarving, and can range from a simple shaped plaque for a background to something that includes likenesses. Almost always, however, unless the award incorporates an engraved plate, some lettering will be required, and some research will be necessary.

This example (Fig. 561) is one of the more elaborate panels I've done, presented to a man on his 55th birthday. The client suggested the general form: an indication of the subject's college background, indicated by initial letters and mascots, and his professional life to date.

The first step in designing such a panel is to do the research. In this case, I had to find out the shape of the Princeton letter P, the Columbia letter C, and the New York University letter forms as well as its symbol. All involved telephone calls to the college offices. To simplify the design, I decided to use only the heads of the Princeton tiger and the Columbia lion, and only the torch from the circa-1952 NYU symbol, an Olympic runner carrying a torch. (NYU and Prudential now use stylized symbols, but the torch I carved, as well as the Prudential Insurance Rock of Gibraltar, are both older designs—and were in use at the time my subject was there.)

An essential in the design of an award, unless the overall shape is to be symbolic, is

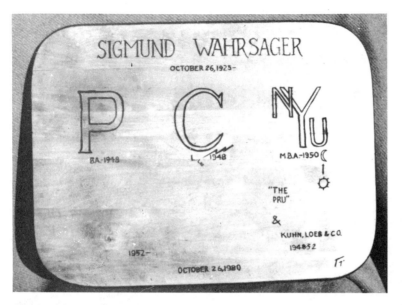

Fig. 560 (above). Lettering was incised with a V-tool on this maple panel, which was then sprayed with two coats of matte varnish. The varnish acted as a stop when stain was put over the surface and then wiped off.

Fig. 561 (below). Finished panel, showing elements glued in their proper locations. All but Goldilocks are mahogany; she is pine. Finish is matte varnish and wax. (See Figs. 629, 630, page 318.)

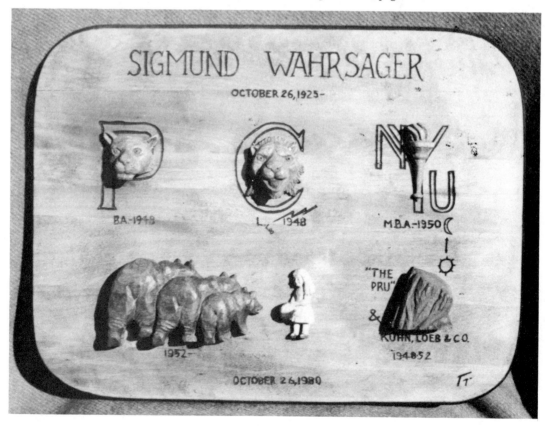

ABCDEFGHIKLMNP
QRSTWY! 1234567890
abcdefghjkmprstuvwxyz

Fig. 562. Engraver's Old English.

ABCDEFGHIJKLM
NOPQRSTUVWXYZ

Fig. 563. So-called Modern initials.

ABCDEFGHIJKLMNOPQRSTU
VWXYZ& 1234567890$
abcdefghijklmnopqrstuvwxyz

Fig. 564. Caslon Old-Style alphabet, the basis for
numerous modern type faces.

ABCDEFGHIJKLMNOP
QRSTUVWXYZ&
abcdefghijklmnopqrstuv
wxyz 1234567890$

Fig. 565. Ultra-Bodoni Italic; note slant and extra-fat
letters.

ABCDEFGHIJKLMNOPQRSTUV
WXYZ& 1234567890$
abcdefghijklmnopqrstuvwxyz

Fig. 566. Sans Serif, which must be carefully spaced
between letters for ease in reading.

the shape and size of the plaque, because other elements must be fitted to it. I had in mind a rectangle of fairly conventional proportions, and was fortunate to have saved the top of a small stand. It was glued up of 1-in (2.54-cm) maple, 13 × 17½ in (33 × 45 cm), with rounded corners and fluted edges, so it required only top sanding to be ready for use. I planned to incise the lettering with a V-tool, and trials on the back of the top showed that it could be carved with a good, clean line, providing, as always, the V-tool was sharp.

The next step was to lay out the plaque and size the elements. The principal employer of the subject turned out to be Bear, Stearns & Co., which immediately suggested another symbol in rebus form—a back view of the three bears and their visitor, Goldilocks. In an animal anatomy book, I found a head-on view of a Malay tiger and a practically tail-on view of a bear. My family crest is a lion head with tongue out, and this seemed appropriate to the occasion because the subject had attended Columbia, but was forced to leave after a few months (as a result of his father's death), so did not earn his intended law degree there. (Hence the lightning bolt and the displaced final letters of LLB.)

To lay out the bear group involved drawing silhouettes of the bear pose in three sizes and shuffling them one over the other to get a shape that fit the space and still emphasized the "bear sterns." Goldilocks was sized to fit.

To get contrast with the maple, I decided to make parts of the units three-dimensional. This would avoid a confusing welter of incised lines and lend some depth to the panel. Also, I could use a contrasting color of wood—in this case mahogany scraps—except for Goldilocks, who wouldn't really have been appropriate in a dark wood. She is of pine. The heads, bear group, torch and Goldilocks were blanked out with a coping saw, then whittled.

Lettering was laid out as simple unserifed letters, except for the subject's name and the college initials, which conform to *their* style. Incising serifs is troublesome, particularly when the lettering is only ¼ in (6.4 mm) tall. Also, all lettering was done in capitals, to get maximum size for carving. Letter carving was done with the V-tool and a light mallet; this gives much better control than carving by hand. It was necessary in some instances, such as periods and short lines running with the grain, to make stop cuts with the knife, and in a few instances to finish an angular meeting point with the knife, but, in general, lettering could be done quite rapidly by this method.

When lettering was completed, the panel was fine-sanded to remove burrs, then given two good sprayed coats of satin varnish. This provides both a surface finish and a stop for the "antiquing." It is very important that the lettering be fully varnished, or the stain will run into the grain at the sides and discolor the surface. (I had this problem in one or two places, which later required scraping of the surface in those areas and respraying.) I used, incidentally, a German Beiz sal-ammoniac, water-based stain, walnut in color.

Once all this is done, the emblems, separately spray-varnished, are glued in place, the assembly given a third coat of varnish, then two coats of wax or clear shoe polish. Sign it, add ring hangers on the back, and it's ready to go.

A lettered panel

A VALUED CLIENT phoned in desperation. Her son was in a dramatic production at his school, and the cast wanted to reward the three teachers who had helped with preparations for it. The play was "Godspell." Only two days were available in which to produce the awards, and the budget was limited, so elaborate designs were out and religious motifs were considered inappropriate for the recipients.

My suggestion was that we award lettered plaques that could be hung or placed on a table as desired. I had incising in mind

Fig. 567. Three steps in carving plaques. Bottom, as routed. Middle, largely set-in (note tab end, which provides a clamping surface during routing). Top, as carved.

Fig. 568. After antiquing, the four plaques in maple, ¾ × 3 × 13 in (1.9 × 7.6 × 33.0 cm).

as being rapid and simple, but the client wanted raised lettering. I had some pieces of maple from which I could squeeze out three ¾ × 3 × 12-in (1.9 × 7.6 × 30.5-cm) blanks, so I designed a sort of scroll with 2-in (5.1-cm) block capital letters. This left room for a roll at the left but merely a curled edge at the right, particularly after a second telephone call that increased the number of panels to four and used the last suitable piece of maple.

I decided to make the letters ¼ in (6.4 mm) deep and to rout the backgrounds as much as possible. This was followed by setting-in around the letters with small chisels and levelling the background. The roll and the curl were done by hand, as was texturing of the background with a small gouge cutting random scallops. (I use a plastic-headed light mallet for setting-in and much of this work; I can control the tools better this way than with the thrust of an arthritic shoulder.) The numerals '82 were placed one above the other in the space created by the final L, and the surface matte-varnished. Then walnut stain was brushed on and immediately wiped out, to create an antiquing effect—and we were done.

The plaques were a great success. In fact, the director of the show, another teacher who had been rewarded with a pair of tickets to a Broadway show, expressed regret that she had not gotten one. My client, who is very fast on her feet, explained that a special plaque was being made . . . then confessed to me what she had done. At the same time, she asked if I couldn't make another plaque as well as a remembrance for her son, who had starred in the school production.

There was no maple of proper size, but I found a piece of cherry and one of oak, and made slightly more elaborate plaques, the one for the son including a star in the space created by the first L. Then the client had a further idea—could I make a small pendant with the word "Godspell" on it as well? The result was a holly carving with curved top and the word "Godspell" angled across it and "1982" incised in the upper right-hand corner. They were received with acclaim. End of commission.

Simple lettering can solve many problems. I would suggest, however, that it be done in a fairly hard and dense wood to reduce the problems of splitting. Incising letters with a V-tool is faster, but raised letters are more dramatic.

19

You Can Whittle Ivory

That is, if you can find it

MAN HAS REVERED IVORY as a symbol of opulence, purity and innocence for over 15,000 years. Ivory is still perhaps the finest carving material for miniatures, but it is unlikely to remain that much longer, for now all of its sources are numbered among the endangered species.

All ivory is essentially like your own teeth. It has an outer layer of very hard enamel, then a much thicker layer of dentine, and finally a core of much softer material that looks like slightly discolored clotted cheese pressed solid. Usual practice is to chip or grind off the enamel, both to remove surface defects and discoloration and to expose the softer and whiter dentine. This is not necessary, however—witness the low-relief animal poses I carved in the enamel layer. Enamel is harder to carve than dentine, but a design of any depth goes through it anyway.

Ivory has so little grain that this is unimportant. It has very little tendency to split, although old ivory does tend to separate in layers as it dries out. Thus, for example, my carvings of the polar bear and puffins (Figs. 569, 570) are mounted on the butts of walrus tusks; partially separated portions of the dentine layer I sawed through and split off. On a conventional walrus tusk, the dentine layer will be perhaps ⅜ in (9.5 mm) thick at the base and go clear through near the tip. Larger pieces, like the walrus (Fig. 571) are carved of cross-slices, so will in-clude some of the core material. This is slightly yellow, with a honeycomb or pebbly pattern, because that's where the blood vessels and nerves were. (The polar bear is mounted on the jaw end of such core material, which is quite dark there.)

Elephant ivory also tends to separate as it grows older, just as some woods do, particularly if the carving is kept in a thoroughly dry place. Large blocks of elephant ivory are sensitive to sudden heat changes. A high-intensity lamp too close to the block, too much concentration with a power burr or a grinder, or even sudden change from a cool storage room to a warm room may cause cracking. (Also, carving ivory with power tools may cause burning, and is likely to cause a smell like that of old bones burning.)

The usual way to work ivory is to saw a blank, then to shape it as much as possible with drills, files and sanding sticks. But surface designs must be put in with an edged tool. For lines, an engraver's burin will work, as well as a V-tool or veiner if the piece can be securely held. (If the tool slips, you'll find that your hand is much softer than ivory.) A hand vise or a sandbag may be helpful, depending upon shape. But I find a pocketknife works very well, or a hook blade, such as is used for leather. The included angle of the edge should be increased, however; sharpening must be frequent. Even then, chips are appallingly small.

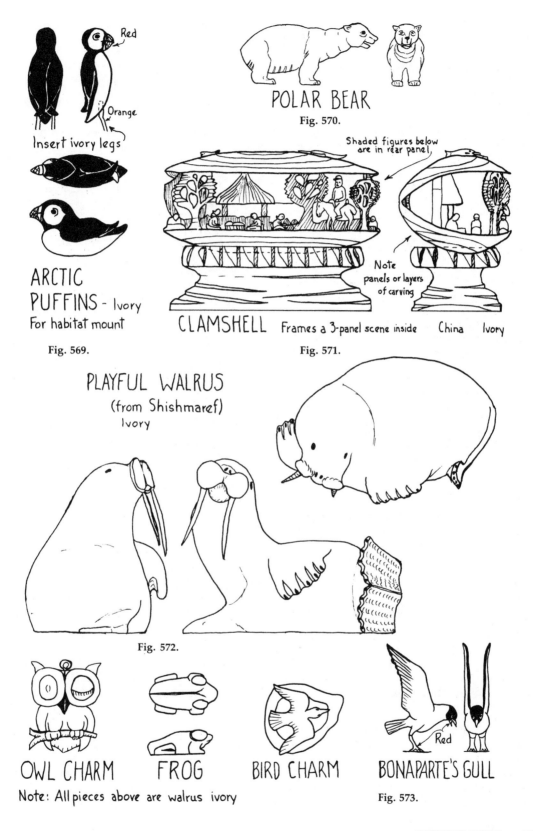

Red

Orange

Insert ivory legs

POLAR BEAR

Fig. 570.

ARCTIC
PUFFINS – Ivory

For habitat mount

Fig. 569.

Shaded figures below
are in rear panel

CLAMSHELL   Frames a 3-panel scene inside   China   Ivory

Note
panels or layers
of carving

Fig. 571.

PLAYFUL WALRUS
(from Shishmaref)
Ivory

Fig. 572.

OWL CHARM   FROG   BIRD CHARM   BONAPARTE'S GULL

Red

Note: All pieces above are walrus ivory

Fig. 573.

Polishing must be done very carefully to avoid scratching and dulling the surface as well as blurring sharp edges. Ivory is such an intense white that blurred edges tend to disappear, leaving nothing visible but an amorphous blob. Very fine sandpaper or emery paper, preferably worn, can be used for rough smoothing, but for finishing, something like jeweller's rouge and a cloth is better. The final polishing, at least among the Eskimos, is with paste silver polish.

After polishing, you will probably find that your carved lines are not visible at a short distance. The Japanese and Chinese speed up the normal antiquing process (deposition of dirt in crevices) by coating the carving with strong tea or bathing it in smoke, then wiping it off. A light-colored wood stain will do the same thing, but be sure to work only small areas and wipe off the surface fast! This leaves darker tones in the crevices. It is also possible to draw in lines with India ink or to fill grooves with ink or pigment. This has a tendency, however, to give the carving a harsh look. A lighter-colored ink of the transparent kind will work better to define detail carving or important lines, but even this must be used with care. In scrimshaw, of course, which is really a form of etching, the technique was to smoke or otherwise darken the surface, then scratch the design in with a knife point, sharpened nail or awl, fill in with ink, then sand or scrape off the surface discoloration, leaving the lines filled. This is possible because ivory does not absorb the ink, as wood would, so it has no tendency to blur or spread. But beware the mistaken line! The ink will reveal *all* lines and depressions.

Bone, stone, shell and nuts

ONCE POSSESSED OF TOOLS, man carved anything that came to hand, from stone and shell to bone, horn, nuts and bark. The principal problem with most of these materials is that they are harder and more brittle than wood, so tools must have a greater included angle and be sharpened more fre-

quently. Files, rasps, abrasives, saws and drills are much more often necessary, and modern rotary tools like hand grinders and flexible-shaft tools are much faster. The bone carvings pictured here were done with a flexible-shaft tool.

Eskimos carve whalebone upon occasion, and various kinds of stone, principally greenstone, a form of soapstone (on the East Coast, gray soapstone was more common), and Alaskan jade. Whalebone and soapstone can be whittled easily, but tend to be brittle. Coastal people of India, Africa, and the Americas have all carved shell, as well as using pieces of it as inlays in wood carvings; one tribe in Mexico even makes mosaics by careful placing of abalone shell in a pitch base. The composition is inlaid in wood and may be a cross, or even a miniature violin or guitar.

My intent in mentioning all these materials is merely to suggest options.

Bone is cheaper than ivory

ANIMAL-BONE CARVING is relatively little known in the United States, although it has been done for centuries by primitive peoples elsewhere in the world. The Balinese are particularly adept at it, carving cow shoulder and leg bones into intricate, usually Hindu, designs. Other South Pacific peoples have carved bone—some of it human, regrettably. Mexicans in and around Guanajuato make a variety of bone carvings from cow bone, ranging from statuettes to small finger rings and pins. It is likely that American carvers will be doing more carving of bone as the controls on ivory increase, or the supply itself diminishes because the animals that provide it are hunted to extinction. Even the Eskimos in Alaska, who still have access to walrus tusk (at inflated prices), are carving whalebone on occasion.

Such bone as I have carved—cow and sheep—is harder than most woods but softer than ivory. It can be whittled with a knife, or carved with chisels if it can be held (beware of hand-holding when you use

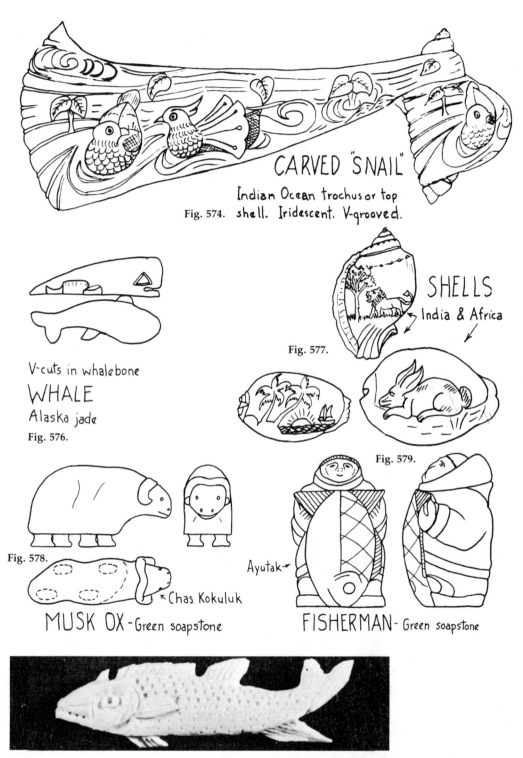

CARVED "SNAIL"

Indian Ocean trochus or top
Fig. 574.   shell. Iridescent. V-grooved.

SHELLS
India & Africa

Fig. 577.

V-cuts in whalebone
WHALE
Alaska jade
Fig. 576.

Fig. 579.

Fig. 578.

Chas. Kokuluk

MUSK OX - Green soapstone

Ayutak →

FISHERMAN - Green soapstone

Fig. 580. This fishpin, an example of power carving of buffalo bones, is by Ruth Brunstetter. Shaping is somewhat restricted by cutters available, but the material takes well to polishing.

Fig. 581. Greenstone, a form of soapstone and relatively soft, is found in Alaska and has been worked there by both Eskimos and Indians. The musk ox at the right and the bear at the left are probably handmade, but the Eskimo with a fish (middle) is probably a product of a "factory" in Seattle, which imports the stone and exports "native art" for tourists in Alaska.

chisels—they may slip). Bone is also more open-grained than ivory and more brittle, so it is a natural candidate for rasps and files and power grinders. It can be polished like ivory, and painted or tinted.

Carve stone and shell

MANY KINDS OF STONE HAVE BEEN CARVED by man, ranging from the soft ones such as soapstone, onyx and alabaster through harder ones such as pipestone, jade, marble and granite on to very hard ones that include emerald, ruby and sapphire. The soft stones can be carved or whittled like wood with a pocketknife or simple wood-carving chisels (except that edge angle should be increased), while the hardest can be cut only with diamond.

I have whittled soapstone, pipestone and onyx. It is a slow process involving frequent sharpening of the knife. Pipestone, incidentally, is one of a variety of stones that are softer when first mined and harden with exposure to air. It is dense and fine-grained, and will support a great amount of detail.

The Turks seem to have a practical monopoly on another and quite different pipe

Figs. 582–584 (above and on facing page). A man's bracelet (wood with bone appliques), a pin and a carved eagle, all in buffalo bone by Ruth T. Brunstetter, Hyde Park, New York. Mrs. Brunstetter, an artist, took up the mounting of animal skeletons some years back, and now has an extensive collection. This bone is from a friend who has a small buffalo herd in New York State.

mineral, meerschaum, because they control its source—Asia Minor. It is anhydrous magnesium silicate, soft, porous, fine-grained and clay-like, but light enough to float in water, and is carved into the finest and most expensive pipes and cigarholders in the world.

Shell is an animal product rather than a mineral, but it carves quite similarly and also has a similar brittleness and lamination. I am speaking primarily of marine shells. The horn is boiled or otherwise heated, then carved while hot; it is brittle when cold and dry. Heat was obviously involved in the Indian shaped pieces, such as the lion (Fig. 600) decorated later by scratching so that the torn surface of the cut shows almost white against the darker horn. In Mexico and India, small in-the-round pieces like pendants are carved from the thicker horn at the tip. The American Northwest Coast Indians shaped mountain-sheep horn into spoons, some with elaborately carved handles. It's enjoyable—if you can find the horn.

Fig. 583.

Fig. 584.

Figs. 585, 586 (above and right). Soapstone and pipestone pieces by Charlie Reed, a Cherokee. The pipestone piece above is only 1 in (2.54 cm) long but contains nine units, in which can be seen a large frog swallowing a human head with a smaller frog atop it. The soapstone piece (right) is 1½ in (3.8 cm) wide and has a number of figures. Shown here is a face and body with upraised arm, which on the back is also the thumb of a hand. Also shown are a bird head, a turtle and a crab-like figure along the bottom.

Fig. 586.

Fig. 587 (right). Simple red pipestone carving by S. Toomi, a Cherokee, is about 2 in (5.1 cm) long and shows an Indian girl bathing beneath a waterfall.

Figs. 588–590 (above, right and below). Two Turkish meerschaum pipes purchased in Jerusalem. The white head of the chieftain at right is much more detailed, and the meerschaum is much higher grade, so it cost five times what the other one did.

Fig. 589.

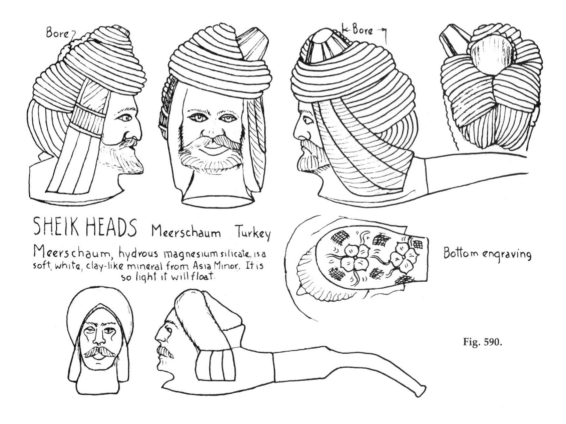

Bore?

Bore

SHEIK HEADS Meerschaum Turkey

Meerschaum, hydrous magnesium silicate, is a soft, white, clay-like mineral from Asia Minor. It is so light it will float.

Bottom engraving

Fig. 590.

Fig. 591. Cameo shell with a finished cameo ready to be cut out.

Fig. 593. Two shell figures from Italy. The larger appears to be the core of a conch shell; the small head of a girl is from a cameo-shell core.

Fig. 592. Pendant and cross from Mexico, with shell fragments set in a black base and polished. Wood in pieces like this is primarily a backing. Fragments are cut with coping saw and files.

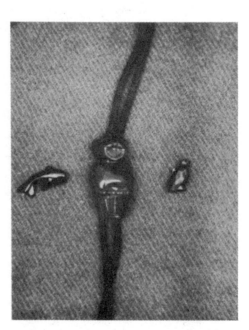

Fig. 594 (right). Alaskan jadeite whale and Billiken bolo slide. The Billiken has a gold nugget in his navel; rubbing it is supposed to bring good luck. The small bird at right is of wood.

Figs. 595, 596 (above and below). Tiny fish, frogs, a cat and other pieces carved from semi-precious stones by Indians in Brazil. The largest is less than an inch (2.54 cm) long.

Fig. 597. Two birds and a fish carved from semi-precious stones by Indians in Mexico. The central bird is about ⅝ in (16 mm) long; the fish at right is a fire opal.

Fig. 598 (right). Tiny onyx fruits and vegetables are on unusual Indian product near Puebla, Mexico. Here are bananas, pineapple, sugar cane, avocado, apple, pepper and other examples, shown full size. They are tinted with dyes.

Fig. 599 (left). This double walrus head is in soapstone, with walrus-ivory tusks. It was carved in Alaska back in the Fifties.

Fig. 600. Carved and shaped horn lion is typical of fine Indian work in this specialized field. It is about 10 in (25 cm) long and dark brown, with lighter scratched decoration.

Fig. 601. Girl figure with basket made from separate cow-horn tip, and horn showing house, fence and mountain, both from Patagonian Chile.

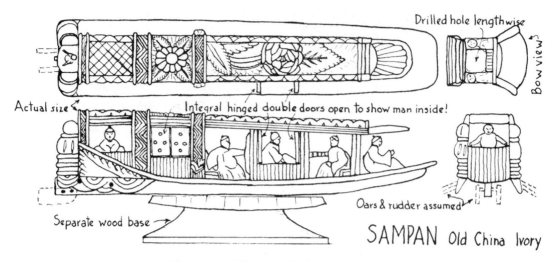

Drilled hole lengthwise

Bow view

Actual size

Integral hinged double doors open to show man inside!

Separate wood base →

Oars & rudder assumed

SAMPAN Old China Ivory

Figs. 602, 603 (above and below). Chinese
ivory carvings tend to be extremely detailed.
This is a complete sampan, with a detailed
structure and even passengers. it is about 4 in
(10 cm) long, with ¼-in (6.4-mm) shutters that
open and close!

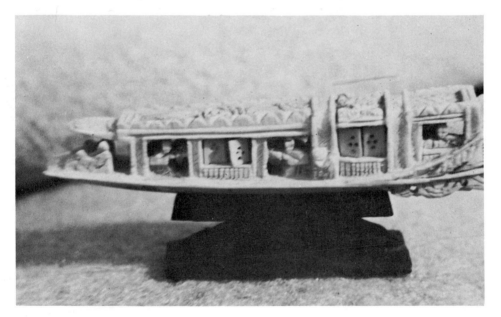

Fig. 604. This walrus tusk, about 15 in (38 cm) long, was given to me by a friend for experimentation. I carved 14 animals on it with pocketknife, hook knife, veiner and V-tool, cutting through the dentine in each case because I didn't know it should be taken off initially.

Figs. 605, 606 (right and below). Devil head carved from horn in Patagonia, Chile. It has a chain for hanging.

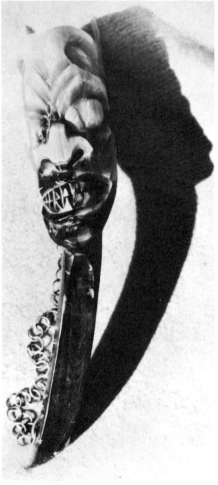

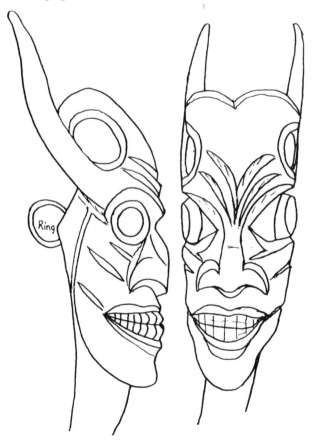

Fig. 607 (above). Polar bear and puffins mounted on the butts of an old walrus tusk, which was laminated and, thus, permitted a front section to be sawed out. The blackish porous central mound is where the blood vessels meet the solid tusk; the thin upper area meets the walrus' upper jaw. Puffins are painted with oils to proper colors. Fig. 608 (below). Two cormorant carvings by Alaskan Eskimos. The taller one is mastodon ivory, and the smaller ones are from King Island and mounted on a whale vertebra.

Fig. 609 (right). Eagle pendant and earrings for the U.S. Bicentennial (1976)—again, whittled.

Fig. 610 (left). Flying goose, from a laminate of walrus tusk 3 in (7.6 cm) long, is mounted on music wire inserted into a California-ironwood base. The cattail at the base of the wire is also walrus ivory.

Fig. 611 (right). Musk ox and 2-in (5.1-cm) duck were blanks sawed out by an Eskimo who deserted them for the pipeline. I found the blanks in an Anchorage shop and whittled them on the way home.

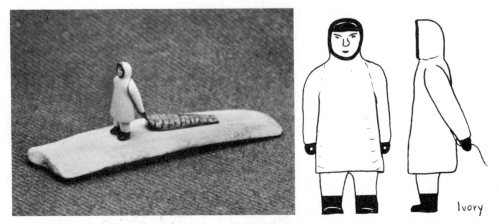

Fig. 612 (above, left to right). From St. Lawrence Island, Alaska, comes this ivory assembly, with a 2-in (5.1-cm) Eskimo drawing a red-tinted sledge of walrus meat. Both are mounted on a piece of fossil ivory 6 in (15 cm) long.

Fig. 613. The Japanese have long produced netsuke—small pieces of wood or ivory once used to pull the drawcords on purses men carried in their kimono sashes. Though many are now made primarily for well-heeled American collectors, they are delightful miniature in-the-round subjects. These are ivory.

Appendix I

Belt buckles

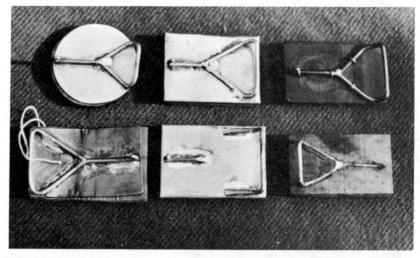

Fig. 614. Varied buckle-back arrangements by John Phillip include soldered clips on stainless (top left) and brass (lower left). At upper right is a clip secured with staples made of 1-in (2.54-cm) bent brads. At lower right, the clip has been glued into a groove. (Neither of these has a backing of metal.) At top center is a two-part clip, while at bottom center the backing of thin stainless has been crimped like a bezel around the wood front. Here, a separate pin and clip are soldered to the backing.

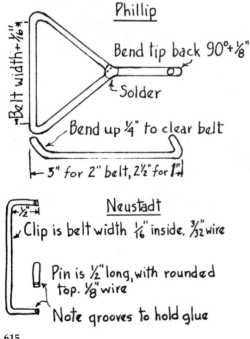

Fig. 615.

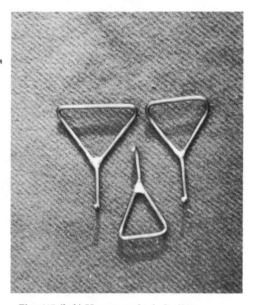

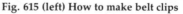

Fig. 615 (left) How to make belt clips

Fig. 616 (above) John Phillip's formed clips to fit 1-, 1½- and 2-in (2.54-, 3.8- and 5-cm) belts. Joints are soldered.

Fig. 617. Top buckle is 1¾ × 3¾ in (4.4 × 9.6 cm), curved, of South American walnut relief-carved with a buck's head. Upper-left buckle is redwood burl 1¾ × 2½ in (4.4 × 6.4 cm), with chamfering only. One at upper right is California walnut burl, 2¼ × 3 in (5.7 × 7.6 cm), with inlaid masks of walrus ivory, hand-carved in relief. At lower left is Australian gum, turned and carved to fit a lady's 1-in (2.54-cm) belt. Lower right buckle is California walnut, 2¼ × 3 in (5.7 × 7.6 cm), with Indian sun design of darkened grooves and gold-stone insert.

Fig. 618. An elaborate clip, hinged in a soldered-on socket to give greater flexibility. The pin is soldered on separately. Face is walnut, incised with a simple initial.

Fig. 619 (left). "His" and "Hers" matching buckles of walnut, curved, with inlaid stainless initials. By John Phillip.

Fig. 620. This walnut facing is carved with a trenched low-relief prairie dog I copied from a photograph.

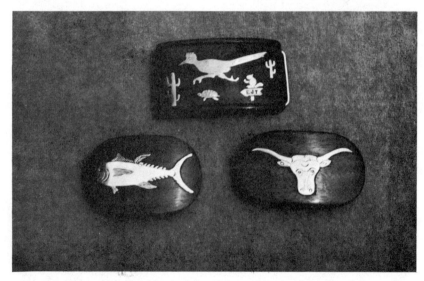

Fig. 621. More walnut buckles by John Phllip. Inserts are brass for upper one and steer head, stainless for fish.

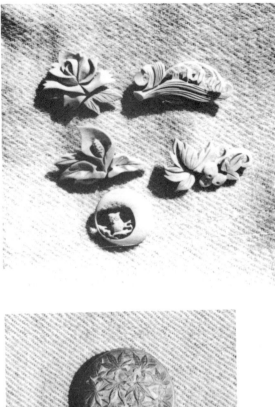

Small pieces

Fig. 622. These silhouette pins of ³⁄₁₆-in (4.8-mm) boxwood are deeply carved and finished in clear lacquer with a shine. They are relatively inexpensive and quite modern in styling. These and other pieces on these two pages were made in Japan.

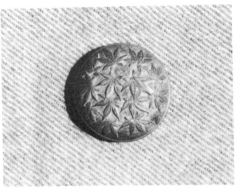

Fig. 623. Japanese or scarlet maple provides the material and the design for this 2¾-in (7-cm) turned box, with all-over design on top. It is from Miyajime.

Fig. 624 (right). Torii, or gate, against a minimalized scenic background adorns the face of this rice-serving paddle of a wood like our basswood. This carving is on a 4 × 5½ in (10.2 × 14.0 cm) surface, and overall height is about a foot (30.5 cm). The mountains and buildings are merely suggested, while the torii is detailed. No color or shading is used.

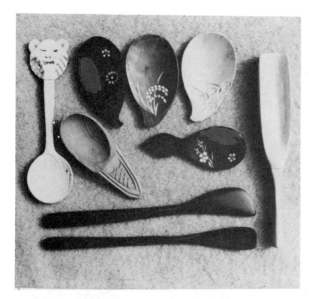

Fig. 625 (left). The short-handled tea scoops, used to put loose tea into pots, and other small pieces may be stained and carved afterward so the base color of the wood contrasts with the stain, or they may simply be clear-lacquered. The lion-head spoon at left and the larger tea scoop at right have no finish, while the tea scoop and butter spreader at bottom are red-lacquered in the traditional way.

Fig. 626. These pendants include a 2½-in (6.4-cm) disc of a stylized thistle (tinted), another with a pert girl face and flower, the third an excellent stylization of a Samurai bust (double-sided) with separately carved legs hinged inside the "waist," and a small hammer suggesting the lucky god, Daikoku.

Fig. 627. The frog and turtle are significant to the Japanese, the horse to the Chinese. Here are small, lucky pieces, the frog and turtle at left only about ½ in (12.7 mm) long, thonged for attachment, plus a stained cryptomeria frog at top and a blocky one on its own base below. The boxwood horse is about 2 in (5.1 cm) long, and is Chinese.

DUSTING BIRD

BEAR Charles Church

CUB

LAMBS Hope Brown

SWAN
Ethel Hogst

DUCKLING Hope Brown

HOUNDS Jack Hall

Fig. 628. Simplicity in animal carvings, typical of the John C. Campbell Folk School, Brasstown, North Carolina.

Fig. 629 (left). Templates can be cut from heavy paper to size elements and test their locations in an applique carving. This was particularly important in posing the three bears and Goldilocks, and in checking that the torch was not too large in an award panel (Fig. 561).

Fig. 630. Finished emblems. These were glued to a maple panel carrying incised lettering to identify them (Fig. 561).

Figs. 631, 632. Farrier's shop and below, sculptor's house and travelling magic show—three of a number of models made from hollow tree trunks by my grandson Robin at age 14–16. Scale is less than 1:12.

Fig. 631.

Fig. 632.

Fig. 633. The Sands barn after re-erection. It is 24 × 41 ft (7 × 12.5 m) and 16 ft (2 m) high at the eaves, with a 45° roof pitch. Of the Dutch type, it was built about 1690.

Fig. 634.

SHINGLING

SPLITTING SHINGLES

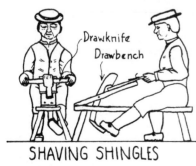

SHAVING SHINGLES

Figs. 634, 635. A 9-in model of the barn above, carved in a left-over portion of a support timber, showing shingling, froe-splitting of shingling (left) and shingle-shaping with a drawknife (right). Figures are ¾ in tall. Trim is pieces of the original pine, hardware hammered from soft iron wire. Shingles are ¼ × ⅜ in-pieces of cedar carbon-dated at 8,500 years old, plus or minus 500.

Skate history decorates a Christmas tree

The particular group shown below was a commission from a lady who is a skate dancer, who has four sons who play hockey, and who wanted something decidedly different for Christmas-tree decorations. The people were made in basswood, jelutong, or Alaska red cedar and tinted with oils; one pair of skates is of mahogany, the other of cherry; all were finished with flat varnish. Skate runners—and in the case of modern skates, the entire skates—are cut from thin metal and shaped by filing. I used aluminum for most, but brass shim stock for two tiny pairs, just for variety.

PAIR SKATING
(Tai Babilonia & Randy Gardner, U.S. 1976)

PAIR SKATING
(Irina Rodnina & Aleksandr Zaitsev, USSR, 1976 champions)

Fig. 637.

Fig. 636.

Fig. 638 (right). Frisian girl wears vintage costume and Wichers de Salis skates, an old type with strap-on wood body and inserted metal blades. Figure in tinted basswood, about 5½ in (14 cm) tall.

Fig. 639. Frisian boys in historic costumes, each of tinted one-piece cedar. Skates had strapped-on wood bodies and inserted blades.

Figs. 640, 641. Crossed hockey sticks with puck (left) are 4 in (10 cm) long; puck is ⅝-in (16-mm) dowel. Sticks are varnished and trimmed, with tape-wound handles. At right, for contrast, are crossed "shinney" sticks whittled from twigs, with miniature soup can for puck—the poor-boy version of hockey.

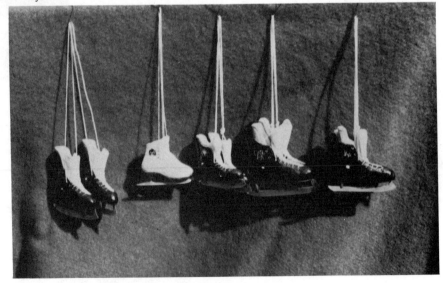

Fig. 642. Four pairs of graduated-size miniature hockey skates and a pair of ladies' dancing skates, the longest about 1¾ in (4 cm), whittled from basswood and tinted. Drilled holes in upper shoe cuffs are laced with thread-braided laces, which provide a method of hanging as well.

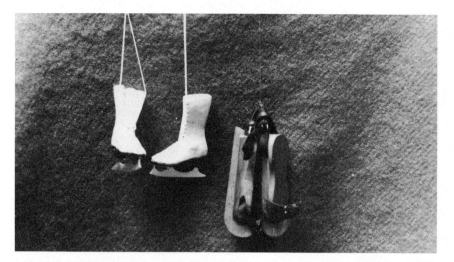

Fig. 643. Ladies' skates circa 1910 came high above the ankle. Beside them is a pair of all-wood skates, the commonest homemade farm variety both here and abroad for centuries.

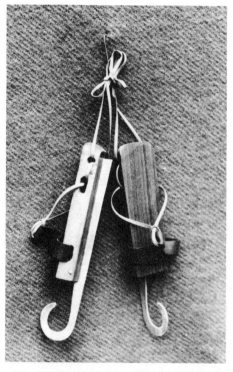

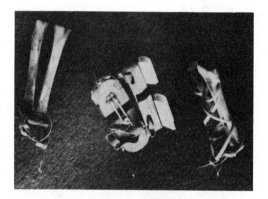

Fig. 645. Three pairs of miniature skates about 2 in (6 cm) long include two of bone, showing earliest single lacing and later multiple-type. At center are antique adjustable-sledrunner beginners' skates with wood body and metal runners.

Fig. 644. The Hollandse (Dutch) skates at left were among the fancier varieties, with ankle thong and double toe-stirrup. These are cherry.

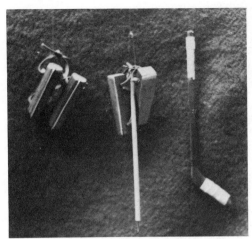

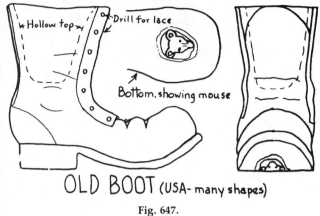

OLD BOOT (USA- many shapes)

Fig. 647.

Fig. 646. First skates after the bone ones were simply blocks of wood held on with thongs. The wearer pushed himself along the ice with a pronged pole (center). Legend has it that an error led to the first skates with a metal plate on the edge, which reduced wear and friction and made skating as we know it possible.

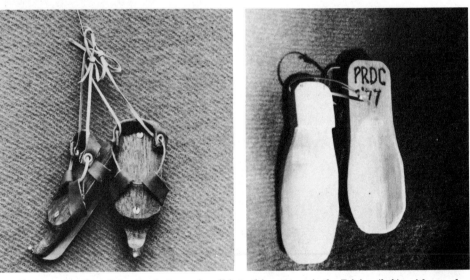

Figs. 648, 649. A rather elaborate skate used well into this century is the Frisian (left), with wood body and metal runner. Straps formed a sort of sandal when laced on. These are mahogany, with gilt beads. Shoe horns at right in the shape of shoe soles are of maple, with incised lettering. About 6 in (15 cm) long, they are mementos for a skaters' committee.

Figs. 650–652. Here are whittled boots in various sizes, two with mice peering through holes in the soles. The small ones and the loafers at top and above were made into pendants.

Fig. 653 (left). This Frisian girl of about 1880 wears Wichers de Salis skates (runners inset aluminum). She is about 8 in (20 cm) high and has a fluted skirt. Skate details are whittled.

Fig. 654 (above). Frisian boy of the same period, wearing Doorlooper (rink) skates of aluminum, has suffered a mishap. He is about 6 in (15 cm) tall and is hung from the upper hand. His jacket buttons are copper nails.

Fig. 655. Frisian boy (at left), companion to the girl, wears Outerkirk skates of aluminum and has copper tacks for buttons. He is 8 in (20 cm) tall. All three of these carvings have been enlarged from mobile elements on preceding pages.

Figs. 656, 657. Girl and boy are enlarged from a skating print of about 1860 set in Central Park, New York. She is 9 in (23 cm) tall, he 10 in (25 cm). His cap tassel is whittled separately and inserted for strength. Skates are aluminum.

Fig. 658 (right). Formal skating couple are also enlarged from an old skating print. Man's coat buttons are round-headed brass nails; lady's muff is appliquéd to get desired grain. Overall height of the pair is 12 in (30 cm).

Circus wagons and carousel horses

A NUMBER OF CARVERS have been making models of circus wagons and carousel horses in recent years, recalling the golden age of the circuses in America from 1870 to about 1915. In 1880, there were more than 50 circuses on the road, each trying to outdo its rivals in the splendor of its parade, which was relied upon to attract crowds to the circus grounds. Larger circuses had extremely ornate and elaborate wagons, spectacles and regalia for the parade, at least one wagon reputedly costing $40,000 alone in those years before inflation.

Biggest and most elaborate of the circus-parade models is that at Shelburne Museum in Vermont, which incorporates over 300 ft (91 m) of 1-in (2.5 cm) scale models, the equivalent of a 2-mile (3-km) parade—which no circus could ever mount alone.

Models were carefully scaled from the originals or from photographs over a 25-year period, largely as the hobby of one man, with the assistance of four others at various times. It includes five bands; 53 band-wagons, tableaux and cage wagons; 400 draft, riding and driving horses; 90 ponies, mules and donkeys; 30 elephants, 33 camels, 14 zebras, 80 animals in cages, 60 lead animals, 20 clowns, 83 musicians, 170 riders, and over 130 other personnel. Wagons are hand-carved and painted; no two horses are alike. Pictured here are the Old-Woman-in-a-Shoe tableau wagon and the African crocodiles in a tank-cage wagon, both drawn by buckskin horses, and a group of the carousel horses which are part of the same display. The parade is housed in a 500-ft (152 m) arcuate building built for it in 1965.

Fig. 659. Carousel horses.

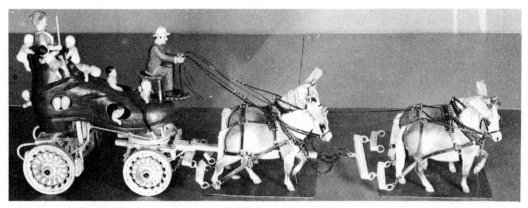

Fig. 660. Wagon with "Old Woman in a Shoe" tableau.

Fig. 661. Circus wagon carrying crocodile tank.

New Guinea pieces are unique

THE TROBRIAND ISLANDS lie perhaps 100 miles (160.9 km) north of the eastern tip of Papua New Guinea, and are part of that relatively new republic. They are visited infrequently by tourists because they are off the beaten track, so the natives have not been strongly influenced by the white man. They live as they always have, almost nude and in grass-thatched shacks, but they produce some of the finest and most original wood carvings available. These are made without power equipment of any sort, and include circular bowls, long hollowed-out drums, and many small objects that we would start on a band saw. Also, the carvers usually work with very hard woods like ebony (black, macassar and striped), kwila (a light tan wood) and garamut (red-brown).

The carving here is distinctly different from the more familiar work along the Sepik River in Papua New Guinea proper, which is more primitive and tends much more to the large, somewhat grotesque depiction of the human face (masks and shields) and utilizes a great deal of color.

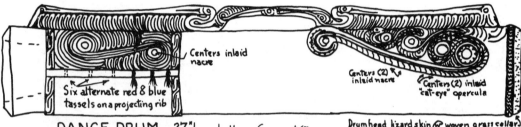

DANCE DRUM — 27" long, hollow. Garamut (?)

Fig. 662.

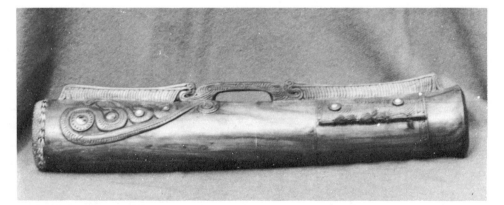

Fig. 663. Elaborate drum of garamut wood is 4 × 26½ in (10.2 × 67.3 cm), plus the projecting handle, which is integral. The drumhead is lizard skin edged by a braided grass collar. Handle and collar at right are patterns of incised lines, with varicolored tassels and inlaid nacre on the collar. The pattern near the head is a pair of snakes in low relief, surrounding circles, two with nacre inlays, the other two with cat-eye opercula inlays. The maker said the hardest job was boring the wood end to end.

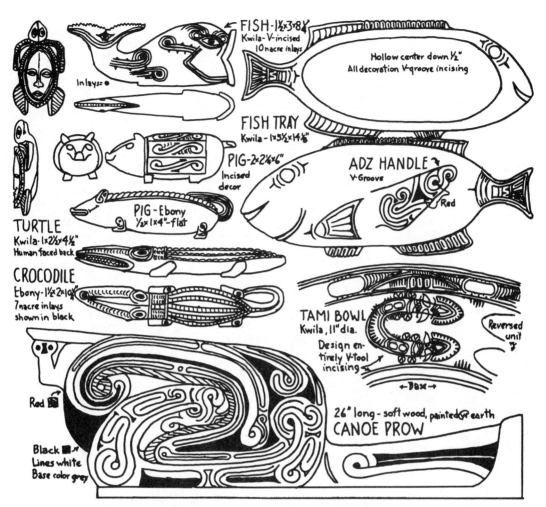

FISH – 1½ × 3 × 8½
Kwila – V-incised
10 nacre inlays

Inlays = ●

Hollow center down ½"
All decoration V-groove incising

FISH TRAY
Kwila – 1 × 5½ × 14½"

PIG – 2 × 2¼ × 6"
Incised decor

ADZ HANDLE
V-Groove
Red

TURTLE
Kwila – 1 × 2½ × 4½"
Human faced back

PIG – Ebony
½ × 1 × 4" – flat

CROCODILE
Ebony – 1½ × 2 × 10"
7 nacre inlays
shown in black

TAMI BOWL
Kwila, 11" dia.
Design entirely V-tool incising

Reversed unit ↗

← Base →

Red ▨ ↗

Black ■ ↗
Lines white
Base color grey

26" long – soft wood, painted & earth
CANOE PROW

Fig. 664. Trobriand Island pieces.

Fig. 665. Seagoing canoes are quite large and fitted with outriggers and a woven reed sail. The formal ones have carved prows (above) backed by a double-eared shield. This prow is 1½ × 8 × 24 in (3.8 × 20.3 × 61.0 cm).

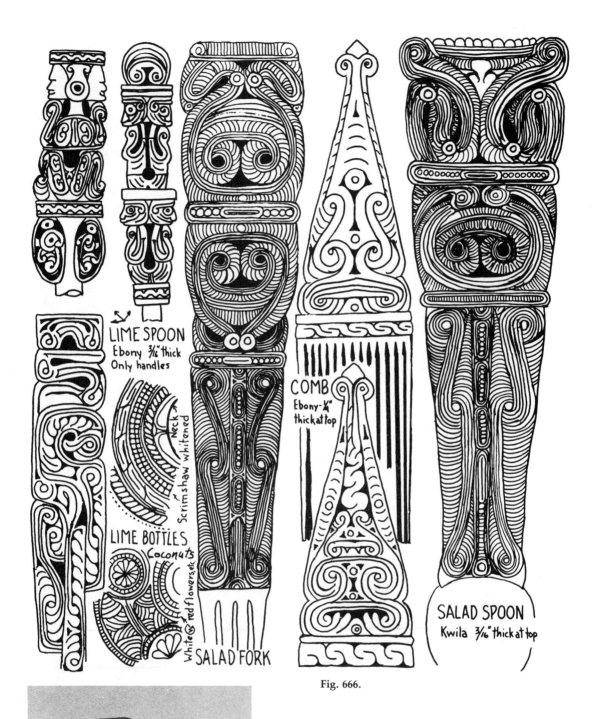

LIME SPOON
Ebony 3/16" thick
Only handles

LIME BOTTLES
Coconuts

Neck

Scrimshaw whitened

White & red flowers etc.

SALAD FORK

COMB
Ebony-1/4"
thick at top

SALAD SPOON
Kwila 3/16" thick at top

Fig. 666.

Fig. 667 (left). The two pigs, one circular in cross section, the other flat, are of ebony with scroll-carved decoration. The smaller is about 3½ in (8.9 cm) long.

Appendix II

Woodworkers' Conversion Tables

Imperial inches	Metric millimetres	Woodworkers' parlance (mm)	Metric millimetres	Imperial inches	Woodworkers' parlance (mm)
$\frac{1}{32}$	0.8	1	1	0.039	$\frac{1}{16}$
$\frac{1}{16}$	1.6	$1\frac{1}{2}$	2	0.078	$\frac{1}{16}$
$\frac{1}{8}$	3.2	3	3	0.118	$\frac{1}{8}$
$\frac{3}{16}$	4.8	5	4	0.157	$\frac{5}{32}$
$\frac{1}{4}$	6.4	$6\frac{1}{2}$	5	0.196	$\frac{3}{16}$
$\frac{5}{16}$	7.9	8	6	0.236	$\frac{1}{4}$
$\frac{3}{8}$	9.5	$9\frac{1}{2}$	7	0.275	$\frac{1}{4}$
$\frac{7}{16}$	11.1	11	8	0.314	$\frac{5}{16}$
	12.7	$12\frac{1}{2}$	9	0.353	$\frac{3}{8}$
	14.3	$14\frac{1}{2}$	10	0.393	$\frac{3}{8}$
	15.9	16	20	0.787	$\frac{13}{16}$
	17.5	$17\frac{1}{2}$	30	1.181	$1\frac{3}{16}$
	19.1	19	40	1.574	$1\frac{9}{16}$
	20.6	$20\frac{1}{2}$	50	1.968	$1\frac{15}{16}$
	22.2	22	60	2.362	$2\frac{3}{8}$
	23.8	24	70	2.755	$2\frac{3}{4}$
	25.4	$25\frac{1}{2}$	80	3.148	$3\frac{1}{8}$
		51	90	3.542	$3\frac{9}{16}$
		76	100	3.936	$3\frac{15}{16}$
		$101\frac{1}{2}$	150	5.904	$5\frac{15}{16}$
		127	200	7.872	$7\frac{7}{8}$
		$152\frac{1}{2}$	300	11.808	$11\frac{13}{16}$
		$177\frac{1}{2}$	400	15.744	$15\frac{3}{4}$
		203	500	19.680	$19\frac{11}{16}$
		$228\frac{1}{2}$	600	23.616	$23\frac{5}{8}$
		254	700	27.552	$27\frac{9}{16}$
		$279\frac{1}{2}$	800	31.488	$31\frac{1}{2}$
		305	900	35.424	$35\frac{7}{16}$
		457	1,000	39.360	$39\frac{3}{8}$
		$609\frac{1}{2}$			
		$914\frac{1}{2}$			

Fig. 668 (above ... tall. That at left s... women graduated ... inlays where the ha... carved with a series ... (Suawesi) and is of m...

Fig. 670. The two outer ... × 4½ in (6.4 × 11.4 cm) ... 5½ in (8.9 × 14.0 cm), are ... of the Papua New Guinea ... arms showing the fish eag... drum. Both have nacre inl... smaller center pendant ha... surrounded by tracery. All ... ebony and are under ⅛ in (... the edges.

...c sizes given for tools and joint parts, etc., cannot work out ... to one or the other there is no difficulty. In the timber ... 25 mm.

Make your own D-adzes

CARVERS IN EGYPT, almost 5,000 years ago, are shown in an ancient wall decoration reproduced by The Metropolitan Museum of Art, New York, already using the chisel, mallet and adze. The mallet was like a small bat, and the pounding surface was the butt of the handle, or the chisel was used alone if the wood was soft enough to permit it. What is most interesting, however, is the use of the adze, which is relatively unknown to most American carvers.

In various forms (see sketches), the adze was the basic woodcarving tool, not only of the Egyptians, but also of the Africans, American West Coast Indians, Eskimos, Polynesians and New Guinea carvers, among others. It is also familiar among Italians, but not among the Germans and English. Some years ago, when I attempted to buy an adze for demonstration purposes, the suppliers in New York were out of stock (although several forms of the tool were shown in their catalogues) and unworried about it, because their specialists felt that the adze was much too dangerous a tool for "amateurs."

Early adzes had heads of the hardest stone available, and it should be pointed out that they had many applications other than carving wood. They were also used for tilling the ground and for squaring timbers; the former need disappeared with the development of the plow and the latter with the ready availability of planed lumber. When bronze, and then steel, became available for blades, the adze became a much more productive tool, although it should be pointed out that even in the early days, work with the adze was often primarily the removal of charcoal—the interior shape of a canoe, for example, was roughed out by burning. Some adzes had interchangeable blades, others were double-bladed. John E. Hendricks (whose Indian name is Wahnadagee) of Bellingham, Washington, wrote to explain to me the making and use

of the modern D-adze, one of several shapes still in use by carvers in his area. His discussion led me to make a couple of D-adzes, which I have found to be excellent tools, easy to control and rapid in chip removal. The American Northwest Coast and Arctic Indians use them for carving totem poles, bowls, spoons, ladles and the like. They also use the elbow-type (regular) adze as well, but the D-adze has been favored for many years because it is easier to master and control. Blades are made from old mill files and rasps, smaller sizes from 6-in (15 cm) files and larger ones from 10-in (25 cm) and 12-in (30 cm) files. But let Wahnadagee tell the story:

"Handles can be plain, or quite ornamental, as shown in the sketches, and should be made of a hard, shock-resisting wood like rock maple. A channel is cut on the striking face (the vertical bar of the D) to fit the blade, a section of old mill file or rasp—for smaller adzes from 6-in files and larger ones from 10- or 12-in ones. The file is bolted in so it has light bearing at the bottom towards the direction of impact. Such a tool just can't be beat for totem carving or milling and sculpting of cedar wood in general. With a little practice, it can do all the shaping of something even as small as a spoon up to the point of final detail. I have one that is metal except for the grip and is a real work-horse.

While I use a hand axe for some roughing, I prefer the D-adze because you face the surface you're working on, rather than viewing it from one side. Also, I've always made my own tools, many of them from old saw steel. I now have many tools, but I still prefer the old ones, as well as the old ways for curing and preparing native woods such as cedar. (I make sewn-leather sheaths for all cutting edges for the sake of safety as well as for edge preservation.)

D-adzes are easy to make to suit the user. The only question that may trouble some makers is how to drill holes in a file or rasp. I

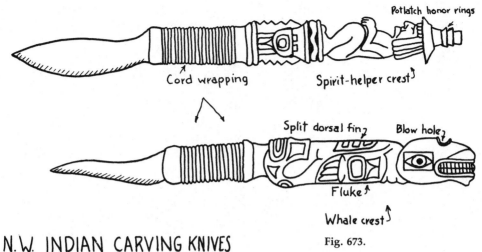

Potlatch honor rings

Cord wrapping

Spirit-helper crest

Split dorsal fin

Blow hole

Fluke

Whale crest

N.W. INDIAN CARVING KNIVES

Fig. 673.

have two methods: On small files, I put a plumber's-torch flame on the exact spot to be drilled, and hold it there until the spot turns bright red—about 30 seconds. Then I let it cool in air (don't quench it in water or you'll harden it again). It will then be soft enough to drill with HSS bits. If the file is smaller, or a fragment for a knife or firmer, I wrap a wet cloth around the knife end before heating. [A setup for controlling annealing is sketched—Author.]

I anneal larger files or rasps in my trash-burner stove, putting the piece to be annealed on top of the ashes and building my regular morning woodfire on top of it. I take the annealed piece out the next morning before I re-start the fire, and drill as before. This is followed by grinding off the serrations or file pattern, and cutting the blade to desired length.

The temper is tested with a file at the cutting edge; it should file about like a good axe does. One doesn't want a flint-hard edge, which is likely to shatter or break off. If the blade is too soft, it can be re-tempered before sharpening. I do that, on the few occasions when it is necessary, with the plumber's torch, heating the cutting edge until it is bright red and quenching in bear's grease or old cylinder oil. (If old cylinder oil is used—which is more readily available than bear grease for most of us—be sure it is free of gasoline by pretesting a small quantity of it for flare-up.) Actually, in this case, the blade is slightly case-hardened.

Some tribes do not bolt the blade, but bind it on as on the knife pictured. This is somewhat harder to do than bolting, and in my opinion not worth the trouble. It is also

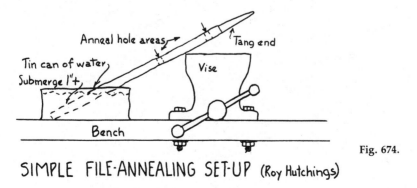

Anneal hole areas

Tang end

Tin can of water, Submerge 1"+

Vise

Bench

Fig. 674.

SIMPLE FILE-ANNEALING SET-UP (Roy Hutchings)

possible to install a screw-clamp arrangement, but that is usually bulky and clumsy. With the bolt method, the holes in file and handle can be matched, and the only problem is some wear on bolt holes after a lot of hard use. By the way, the bolts should be of the countersunk type, so they don't project from the face of the blade.

I make blades for carving knives from worn-out carpenter's handsaws, particularly Craftsman® (Sears) or Disston® brands. To use such steel, remove the handle, then clamp the blade in a wide-jaw machinist's vise so about a 3-4-in. (19 mm) width of the blade is between the jaws. Start at the front or outer end of the saw. Now, beat along the blade at the top of the vise with a heavy ballpeen hammer. This will start a break along the vise line. Move the saw along a vise width and reclamp, then hammer it to continue the crack. The resulting strip can be ground or broken into desired lengths and shaped by grinding. The toothed-edge strip, by the way, can be made into short saws for rough-shaping soapstone (steatite), bone or other carving materials. The steel can also be formed into so-called "crooked knives" by beating a section carefully on and over an iron rod, pipe or mandrel.

To secure a blade into the handle, grind a slot in the handle end, then put epoxy glue (I use Elmer's®) into that slot and the slot sawed in the handle, assemble in position, and bind temporarily with cord. When the glue has set, replace the cord with a rawhide, bearhide, or fishline wrapping. Coat the wrapping with a mixture of two-thirds spar varnish and one-third turpentine or equivalent. This preservative prevents fraying or chafing. (In the old days, the preservative was a special pitch.) I prefer to sharpen such blades from one side only; this lengthens edge life and the tool cuts more like a draw-shave.

The beads and colors on knives and adzes have definite traditional meanings. Black is the decorative color for tools, which are not ceremonial. Ceremonial colors are related to the spirit language. Red denotes blood, the life giver for animals and fish. Blue denotes the Great Spirit and the Sky People, the Thunderbird's house and other spiritual things. Dark blue denotes bravery and courage; the voice of horror is in its tone. Green, yellow and brown honor our Mother the Earth; they suggest gracious giving to sustain life and the rhythm and beauty of growing things. They suggest annual renewal, the chain of life.

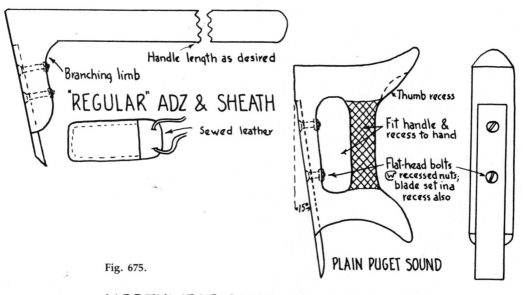

Handle length as desired

Branching limb

"REGULAR" ADZ & SHEATH

Sewed leather

Thumb recess

Fit handle & recess to hand

Flat-head bolts w/ recessed nuts; blade set in a recess also

PLAIN PUGET SOUND

Fig. 675.

NORTHWEST COAST INDIAN D-ADZES

Sharpening methods

I WILL DESCRIBE one new power-sharpening method in some detail—that of H. M. Sutter, Portland, Oregon, who is an expert on the subject. His equipment is relatively inexpensive and mostly homemade. (You can buy setups from several makers.) The first and primary machine is a belt grinder which takes a 1 × 42-in (2.5 × 106.7-cm) belt and is available from a number of companies, including Sears or Montgomery Ward. A series of backing blocks is added just above the table, the shape conforming to the sweep or curvature of the tool being ground. For rough grinding, Mr. Sutter uses a 60-grit belt. He finish-shapes with a 150-grit, and does final whetting with a 320-grit or crocus cloth. He feels that this produces a better and straighter edge than most people can obtain on handstones.

He produces the micro-bevel on the inside of gouges with a slip, by hand, and finishes it with a leather or plastic wheel and tin oxide. These wheels are mounted on a ball-bearing arbor mounted vertically and operated at 250-300 rpm. He has an assortment of wheels 6 in (15.2 cm) in diam-

eter, with edges of various curvatures and V's to fit his tools. Some of the plastic discs are made very thin to fit inside small veiners and fluters, so they tend to bend. These are supported near their centers by thin plywood discs. Leather discs are made of old belting glued together and shaped with harness tools.

Wheels are coated with a very thin mixture of tin oxide in kerosene. An alternative is to mix the powder with water to which a few drops of detergent have been added. Another is to use the very fine abrasive used in polishing eyeglasses, or to use very fine rouge or some other abrasive oxide. Both sides of the cutting edge should be polished to a mirror finish—it reduces drag. The final operation is further polishing with a cloth-buffing wheel and tripoli wax. In normal carving of soft woods, the buffing operation will usually keep the tool sharp. Incidentally, a fine-grit 6-in (15.2-cm) wheel on this slow-speed mandrel will grind straight edges on firmers and V-tools without the danger of burning created by the typical high-speed modern grinder—it acts like an old-fashioned grindstone.

Fig. 676. Commercial belt sander adapted to include a short arbor that will take a buffing wheel. It is, in effect, an extension of the belt-driving pulley.

The necessity for resharpening and the danger of edge-nicking can be reduced by proper tool care. Keep tools on the bench or workplace side by side with their sharp edges towards you so you can select your next tool easily. Store them in slots so their sharpened edges touch nothing, and when you carry then, put them in a roll that covers but does not touch the ends. It is advisable to strop each tool after you have carried them in a roll—in fact, some pros strop each tool before they use it, as a barber does; a tool can lose feather-edge alignment just from sitting. Keeping tools from rusting goes without saying, but I will say it anyway.

Make carver's screws

THROUGH ALL MY YEARS OF WOODCARVING, I have never used a carver's screw; clamps or a wood vise have always served my purposes. Besides, carver's screws are not stocked by some suppliers and are now very expensive, at least for this one-time machinist. However, my boyhood friend, John Phillip, now of Whittier, California, presented me with several screws of his own design recently. They are simple, inex-pensive, easy to use and even to make, because the components are available in hardware stores.

To begin with, threaded stock is available, usually in 2-ft (61-cm) lengths, from stores such as Sears. They also sell lag screws of various sizes. If you have the tools available, you can drill and tap the end of a piece of threaded stock to take a ¼- or ⁵⁄₁₆-in (6.3- or 8-mm) lag screw with the head cut off and the shank threaded. Even simpler is to get a long lag screw of the desired diameter, cut off the head and thread the shank. Either of these designs can be equipped with spacers cut from pipe (⅜- or ½-in [9.6- or 12.7-mm] diameter) washers and double nuts. The double nuts are necessary to screw the screw into the wood blank, but after that only a single one is needed. Beyond that, all you need do is to drill a hole of suitable diameter in your bench or other work table, and you're ready to go.

It is even simpler, in the absence of threading tools, to buy a lag screw of suitable length (about 4 in [10 cm] for the usual 2-in [5-cm]-thick bench top), and simply use it directly as a carver's screw. If it is too long, washers can be added beneath the bench top.

Figs. 677, 678 (above) and 679 (below). Leather and plastic wheels (above) are homemade and used on an arbor made by connecting an old washing-machine motor to a pulley-driven shaft, as shown below. Discs are shaped to fit the interiors of various gouges and the V-tool.

Fig. 679.

An adjustable open-end wrench tightens and loosens either lag screw or single nut on the designs first mentioned. It is possible, of course, to be more elaborate and to make a wing nut like those commonly supplied with a carver's screw, or you may find a conventional wing nut with suitable thread. An alternative is to drill two opposed flats of a hexagonal nut and drive in short pins to make a wing nut of sorts, but I find it more secure to tighten the screw with a wrench so it will withstand fairly strong blows at the upper end of a blank.

The depth a carver's screw is driven into the blank depends upon the height of the blank and the amount of force you expect to exert at the top. Too short a screw will pull, especially in soft woods like pine or bass. Too long a screw may project through the base on small carvings. (As a matter of fact, I have seen small German carvings with integral bases—say, of a deer or a dog in woodland—in which a stump is carved beneath the animal's body. It is there to cover what would otherwise be a hole from the carver's screw.) Also, the carver's screw should be inserted in a drilled pilot hole to reduce the danger of splitting, and the screw itself should be large enough to avoid being bent when it is driven in or under stress of carving. I have found that by drilling the hole for the screw near the outer corner of the bench enables me to work around the piece well enough so that frequent adjustments of the screw are not required. A short carver's screw can also be used to hold a panel for relief carving.

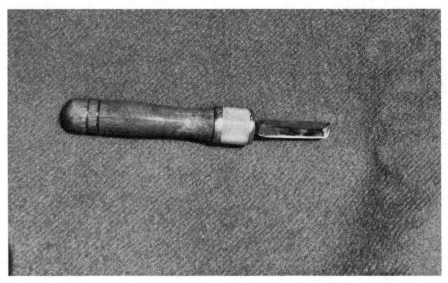

Fig. 680. Mr. Phillip made this knife from a cut-off high-speed-steel lathe tool bit. It is unusual in that it is sharpened on both sides and on the end, so it can be used as a chisel. It is similar to a tool the Chinese make for carving ivory.

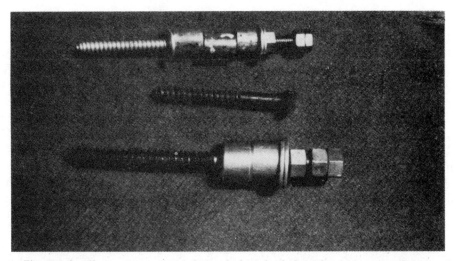

Fig. 681. Small carver's screws can be made from lag bolts either by cutting off the head and rethreading the shank for standard hex nuts (top and bottom) or by using the lag screw without change. Pipe spacers (top) should be flanked by washers to increase bearing surface.

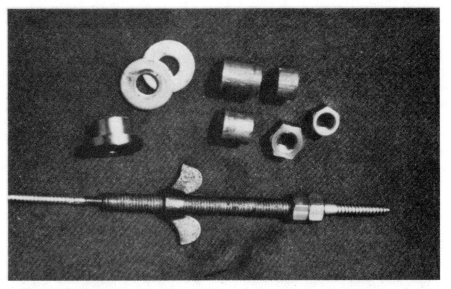

Fig. 682. Threaded stock, in this case ½-in (12.7-mm), can be drilled and tapped for ¼-in- (6.3-mm)-diameter lag screws with heads cut off and shanks threaded. It may also be possible to get wing nuts to fit. The screw shown was cut in half to make two.

More on gold-leafing

SUPPLIERS OF GOLD LEAF can provide a simple procedure, or it can be done as explained to me by Gardner Wood, who has gold-leafed many temple carvings over the past fifteen or more years.

Gardner Wood advises beginning with a relatively dense wood, such as basswood, that requires no filler (oak is obviously a bad choice). If filling is necessary, use a lacquer sealer like Prime®, following the directions on the can. When it dries, sand lightly with very fine or worn sandpaper to get rid of any raised wood fibres. Then cover the surface with gold size, available from the gold-leaf supplier and most paint stores. It is a slow-drying, oil-base size (one brand is Swift's®), and should be brushed on in a thin coat and left overnight. The surface is ready for application of the leaf when tacky—when a dry finger touched to it comes away with a pinging sound, and without picking up any size. (The surface will stay in this state for a day or more under normal conditions.) The gold leaf is simply laid over this tacky surface and pressed down with dry fingertips. Transfer sheets have a blank corner, so the sheet can be picked up without touching the gold. When rubbed down, the transfer tissue can then be readily lifted off. Inevitably, some gold will be wasted, and some missed areas will have to be filled in. To prevent gold adhesion in unwanted areas, dust them with a little talcum powder; to remove it, just use an ordinary ink eraser.

When covered, the surface must be burnished to remove jeweller's rouge that held the gold to the transfer sheet and to seal it. This is best done with balls of combed cotton rubbed over the surface in a circular polishing motion. If done properly, the surface will immediately show a higher gloss. Following burnishing, any areas that are likely to be abraded—such as the shank of a candlestick or the pushing surface on a door—should be protected. A finish like McClosky® Heirloom varnish will do the job nicely.

A gold-leafed surface is basically ultra-smooth, though it may sometimes be desirable to have a textured surface. Mr. Wood achieves the latter by using a product called Liquid Steel, basically an epoxy containing powdered steel, which can be brushed on the wood surface before gold-leafing. This creates a black surface that can be raked, combed or otherwise textured as desired. It is lightly sanded when dry. Because of the texturing, it is obvious that the application of gold leaf would cause bridging and holes that would show the black surface. To avoid this, the textured surface is sprayed with bronze or another tone. Then gold leaf is applied, rubbed in and burnished. It will leave some voids because of the texturing, but these create an antiqued look.

Gold leaf alone tends to be flat and uniform, so it may be desirable to antique it to bring out depths and shadows. There is available a heavy paste called Rub'n Buff® (American Art Clay Co., Inc., PO Box 68163, Indianapolis, Indiana 46286) available in many art-supply stores in 18 tones of brass, bronze, copper and gold. The paste will stick to any surface, and can be applied by rubbing or by thinning with turpentine and using a brush in difficult areas. Various tones can be applied one over the other to get special effects. It is particularly effective over textured areas, and the more the surface is rubbed the better it gets. The virtue of such texturing is that the surface color can range from a yellow gold to a green in recessed areas. As before, the treated surface should be protected with a good polyurethane varnish if subjected to frequent handling or other unusual wear. Otherwise, gold leaf will stand years of atmospheric wear, requiring only occasional washing with water and a mild soap to remove smog and grime deposits.

On old gunstocks you will find a form of inlay that could be more widely used because it is relatively simple to do. It can be done with silver, brass or copper flat wire or strip, or combinations, and usually takes

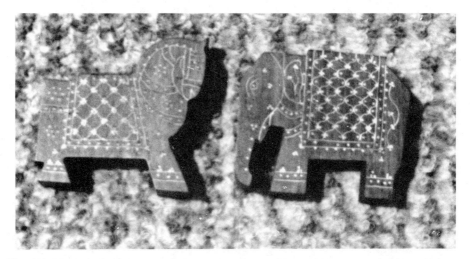

Fig. 683. Horse and elephant are of teak, decorated with brass inserts. The horse, for example, is ¾ × 3 × 3 in (1.9 × 7.6 × 7.6 cm), and wire inserts are ⅟₆₄ × ⅟₃₂-in (.40 × .79-mm) ribbon. Even the larger spots are made from bits of the same wire, curled up.

Fig 684. Camel and two bullocks are also of teak with brass inserts. Pieces such as these, as well as those in Fig. 683, were made in India years ago, but are probably too costly to produce at today's tourist prices.

the form of long cyma curves or scrolls—sometimes with added accents produced by endwise inlay of "spots" of round wire. In India, it was common to decorate small stylized figures of horses, elephants and the like with brass inlay in this way (Figs. 142 and 143), and examination indicates that the brass was formed to desired shapes, simply driven into a wood such as teak, then sanded off until the crushed fibres of wood at the surface and any projecting brass were removed. The entering edge of the brass was slightly wedge-shaped for penetration.

The conventional method of inserting silver and gold is more considerate of the wood. The desired design is laid out on the surface or transferred to it after all but final sanding has been done (so metal dust sanded off later will not penetrate surface crevices). Then a narrow trench is produced along the lines of the design by driving in a thin blade sharpened from both sides like a firmer. These can be made from any thin tempered steel, such as straight X-acto® chisel blades. Blade widths can vary from ¼ in (6.4 mm) down to ¹⁄₁₆ in (1.6 mm), the latter for following curves. These blades should be driven into a depth corresponding with wire or strip width and leave a V-shaped groove as wide at the top as the metal is thick. The metal ribbon is then cut off, formed to shape and driven in progressively, using a light hammer and a dowel. The wire should be just about level with the surface, so light sanding will smoothe it at surface level. If the wire buckles during driving, cut out and replace the buckled portion, since flattening out buckled ribbon and attempting to redrive it usually results in failure and added complication from enlargement of the trench.

In woods such as walnut and teak, the sides of the trench will close in and grip the wire with no problems; but you can use thinned glue in the slot to make sure, or rough the side of the wire ribbon slightly with a file. Make sure that any two pieces of wire that butt together are a good joint, because any gap will be very visible when the work is finished. It may be helpful to file the end of the ribbon at a slight angle in such a case, so the upper portion actually wedges in place as it is driven down. Once the wire is in place, the surface is final-sanded, metal filings brushed and dusted away and the piece is ready for finishing. And any finish will include some moisture that will cause the sides of the trench to swell back and grip the insert tightly.

INDEX

(Numbers in italics refer to illustrations)

Action figures, 206–209, *207–209, 321*
Adzes, *15,* 16, 336–338, *339*
Africa, 35, 222
Alabaster, 300
Alaskan jade, 298, *299, 304*
Alder, 33, 34
Alpacas, *90, 113*
Alphabets, *see* Lettering
Alto-relievo, 240
Amboina, *34*
Andersen, Hans Christian, 189
Angels, children as, 214, *214–215*
Angling cut, 21
Animal bone, 298–300, *299–301*
Animals, carving, 65–125
  birds, *see* Birds
  butterfly mobiles and ornaments, 117–120, *118, 119*
  caricaturing, 71, 72–73, *72, 73,* 90–93, *91, 93, 97, 105*
  cats, 95–98, *96–98, 334*
  dinosaur mobile, 106–112, *107–108*
  dogs, *67,* 71–72, *72,* 98–104, *99–103*
  fish, *see* Fish
  gold-leafing, *345*
  horses, *77, 98, 99,* 104–106, *110, 345*
  in ivory, 296, *297, 310, 311*
  miniature, *35, 84, 85, 86, 87, 317, 318, 332*
  in own design, 120–122, *121, 122*
  panels of, 81, *81, 106, 123, 262*
  in relief, *106, 266, 267*
  of South America, 112–114, *112–114*
  in stone, *305, 306*
  stylizing, *90–95, 92, 94*
  to suit client needs, 124–125, *124–125*
  variations in, 65–84, *65–84*
  see also specific animal

Anteater, *114*
Antiquing, 55, *55,* 56
Apple (wood), 33
Argentina, 91, 93, 186
"Arkansas," 24
Armadillo, 82, *83, 90,* 91, *114*
Ash, (wood), 13, 34
Ashtray, fish, *110*
Atlas, 201–206, *203–206*
Austria, 180
Award plaque, 124, *124–125*
Axe, hand, 16

Back-bent tools, 15
"Bad wood," 38
Bali, 8, 35, 37, 45, 66, 77, 81, 84, 200, 298
Bark, thick, carving, 40, *41*
Base, 53–54, *52, 53*
Bas-relief, 240
Basso-relievo, 240
Bass viol player, *181*
Basswood, 13, 32, 34, 54
Bears, *66, 67,* 73–74, *73, 78, 79, 248, 297*
Beaver award plaque, 124, *124–125*
Bebek (dragon duck), 83–84, *84*
Beech, 34
Beef wood, 35
Bee tree, 32
Belt buckles, 62–64, *63–64, 313–315*
Belt sander, *340*
Benches, 16–17, *17*
Berruguete, Alonso, *John the Baptist, 252*
"Bill," 98, *99*
Birch, 34
Birds
  designs, *121, 122*
  panels, *262*
  varieties of, *33,* 68–69, *68, 69, 70,* 71, 72–73, *73,* 74–76, *74–76,* 84–90, *84–90,* 94, *94, 111, 297, 306*
  see also specific bird
Black bear, *248*
Black cottonwood, 40
Black walnut, 33–34, *33*
Blinding wood, (blind-my-eyes), 35
Block stool, *55, 267*
Boar, *81,* 82
Boat(s)
  models, 168–169, *169*
  panel, 163–168, *164–167*

Bolivia, 113
Bolo patterns, 60, *61*
Bone, animal, 298–300, *299–301*
Book of Kells, The, 289
Bosting, 23
Bowls, *134, 249, 254*
Boxes, *265, 316*
Boxwood, 36
Brasell, Austin, *284*
Brazil, 90, 209, 305
Breadboards, *266, 282*
Bronzing, 57
Brooch, 80, *80*
Brown, Hope, 95, *98*
Bruegel, Eleanor, *211–212*
Brunstetter, Ruth T., *299, 300*
Bubinga, 35
Buckeye, 34
Buildings, *see* Doors; House
Bulls, *35, 66, 67, 92, 93*
Bunyan, Paul, *196*
Burgees, 168, *169*
Burins, *16,* 18
Busts, *199, 241*
Butterfly mobiles and ornaments, 117–120, *118–119*
Butternut, 33, 34, 74

Cabinet maker's shop model, *170, 171*
Calipers, 31
Camels, *51,* 91, *93, 345*
Cameo, 242, *304*
Candle sconce, *279*
Canoe, *331*
Card holders, *74, 75,* 80, *80*
Caricatures
  animal, 71, 72–73, *72, 73,* 90–93, *91, 93, 97, 105*
  human, *181,* 185, *185, 187, 197*
Carousel horses, 328, *328*
Carver's bench, 16–17, *17*
Carver's screws, 340, *342, 343*
Carving personality, 9
Carving tools, *see* Tools
Catalpa, 40
Cats, 91–92, *93,* 95–98, *96–98, 334*
  card holder, 80, *80*
Cavo-relievo, 240
Cedar, *33, 33*
Celtic birds, 80, *80*
Centaur and oread, *39*
Chair, 55
Chamfer, *12*

Chapman, Kenneth M., *Evolution of the Bird in Decorative Art*, 120
Charms, *250, 297*
Checks, in wood, 37–38
Cherry wood, 33, *34*
Chess knight, *77*
Chestnut, 34
Child angels, 214, *214–215*
Chile, 42, 90, 186, 241, 307, 309
China, 105, 146, 265, 308, 317
Chips, 21
Chisels, 14–15, *16*, 18
  shapes, *13, 14*
  sharpening, 27
  using, *19*
  vs. knives, 18–20, *19*
Christmas tree decorations, 124, 168–169, *169*
Circus wagons, 328, *329*
Clark, Fred, *74, 75*
Clasp knife, 11
Clouds and sheep panel, 270, *270–272*
Cocobola, 35, *36*
Coconut shell, 41, *43*
Coelanglyphic sculpture, 240
Comb, *334*
Constellations, *206*
Conversion tables, *335*
Cookie roller, 282–283, *282–283*
Coppering, 57
Costa Rica, 253
Cottonwood, 34
  black, 40
  bone, 87
  skeleton, 82, *82*
"Cowboys," South American, *186*
Crane, *66*
Creatures
  dragons, *68*, 146–151, *146–151*
  statuettes, 152–155, *152–155*
  unicorns, 141–145, *141–145*
Cryptomeria, 40
Crystal ball, in carving, 188, *188*
Curl cut, *12*
Cutting with knife, *12*, 13–14, *19, 20*, 21
Cypress, 33, *34*

D-adzes, 336–338, *339*
Daisy, *22*
Dance drum, *330*

Dance mask, miniature, *248*
Dancers, 46–47, *47*
Decoys, 71
Deer, *70*
"Deer Dancer," *45*
DeFregger, Franz, 275–276
Denmark, 197
Designs, original, 120–122, *121, 122*
Devil head, *309*
Dinosaur mobile, 106–112, *107–108*
Disk, *264*
Dog-leg tools, 15
Dogs, *67*, 71–72, *72*, 98–104, *99–103*
  skeleton, 82, *82*
Dogwood, 34
Doors, 160–162, *161, 162*, 251
  relief carving on, *239, 268–269*
Doorstop, 72
Doves, 87, *87, 89*
Dragon duck, 83–84, *84*
Dragons, *68*, 146–151, *146–151*
Draw cut, *12, 19*
Driftwood, 45, *46*
Drill cut, *12*
Drums, 82, 83, *330*
Dry rot, 33, *38*
Ducklings, *88*
Ducks, *79, 80, 86, 87*, 90
Dürer, Albrecht, "Praying Hands," 210, *210*

Eagles, 66–67, *66*, 75–76, *75, 76, 86, 88, 121*, 122, *122*
Eaglets, *111*
Earrings, *69*
Easter Island, 8, 254
Ebony, 36, *37, 332–334*
Ecuador, 41, 42, 50, 83, 113, 114, 184, 253, 275
Elephants, *345*
Elephant tusk, 296
English oak, 36
English sycamore, 36
English walnut, 36
Enlarging methods, 29, 30–31
Eriksen, Edvard, 189, *190*
Eskimos, 250, 298, 310, 311, 312
Eternal knot, *129*, 132
Evans, Ken, 275

Faces and heads, carving, 172–188
  caricatures, *173, 174*, 185, *185*, 187
  ears, 183
  eyes, 178–179
  face, 173, *175*
  and facial variations, *177*
  head, 172, *175–176, 178*
  jaws, 183
  nose and profile, *177*, 179–183
  portrait, 183–185
  South American heads, *186*, 187
Fawn, 92, *93*
"Feather Dancer," 46–47, *47*
Figa, *209*
Fiji, 161
Finishing pieces, 44–57
  with antiquing, 55, *55*, 56
  with a base, 53–54, *52, 53*
  with gold-leafing, 56–57, *344–346, 345*
  with machine-roughing, 51–52, *51*
  with modelling, 49–50, *50*
  and surface textures, 44–49, *44–48*
  with texturing, 48–50, *50*
  with wood showing, 54–56
Firmer chisel, 14, *14*
Fish, 69–70, *69*, 83, *83*, 94, *94*, *112*, 116–117, *116–117, 306*
  ashtray, *110*
  jointed, 115–116, *115*
  spoon, *110*
Fixed-blade knives, 10–11, *12*, 20
Flaws, in wood, 33, 37, 38–40, *38, 39*
Fleming, Peggy, *209*
Flowers, carving, 126–140
  door panel, *268–269*
  exercises in, *129–134*, 131–134
  pendants, *127*
  and pine tree, 138–140, *137–138*
  and polyglot panels, 135–138, *135–136*
  in relief, *236, 268*
  simple, *126–127*, 128–131
  tools for, 128
  variety in, 134–135, *134–135*
  whittling, *22*, 128
Fluteroni chisel, 15

Forness, Bruce T., 37
Fox, *78*, 79, 84, *85*, *110*
Frogs, 39, 40, *74*, *75*, *297*, *317*
Frame, picture, *239*
Fruitwoods, 33, 34
Furniture, miniature, *170*, *171*
Galapagos Islands, 71, 83
Garamut, 34
Gibbons, Grinling, *36*, 128, 275
Gilding, 56–57
Giraffe, 91, *93*
Gnomes, whittling, 58, *58–59*
Goat, 67, *67*
Goetz, Gunther, *135*
Gold-leafing, 56–57, *57*, 344–346, *345*
Gouges, 14, *14*, 17, 18, 23
Gourds, carving, 41–43, *43*
Grain, cutting with, 11, 13, 21
Granadillo wood, 74
Greek peasant carvings, 115–116, *115*
Greenheart, 35
Greenstone, 298, *300*
Grounding, 23, 255–257, *255*
Guillotine cut, *19*
Gum, 34
Gypsy seer, *188*
Haag, T. E., 84, *134*
  Adder and Eve, 91, *92*
  Cat and the Fiddle, 91, *92*
  relief carvings, *233*, *240*, *262*, *280*, 281
  stylized animals, 91, *92*, *92*, *93*, 94
  stylized human figures, *213*
Haiti, 45, 253, 279
Half relief, 240, *241*
Hand axe, 16
Hand routers, 16
Hands, 210
Hansa, 79, *79*
Hard woods, 33, 54
  see also specific wood
Harewood, 35, 36
Hatchet, shingling, 16
Hawkins, Ruth, 214, *214–215*
Headdress, *41*
Heads, *41*, *309*
  caricatures, *173*, *174*, *185*
  carving, 172, 175–176, *178*, *182*
  relief carving of, *235*, *275*, *279*, *280*
  see also Faces and heads, carving

Hedgehog, *78*, 79
Hendricks, John E., 336
Hercules vs. the Nemean Lion, *152–153*
Hickory, 34
Hickory nuts, 41, 43
High relief, *239*, 240, *241*, 242, 274–276, *275*, 274–276
Hoch, Sheldon, 121
Hoffer, Andreas, 276
Holland, 266
Hollow cut, *12*
Hollow relief, 240–241
Holly, 34
"Honey Girl," 98, *99*
Honing, 24, 25, *26*
Horn, *307*
Horses, 77, 98, *99*, *104–106*, *110*, *317*, *345*
  head, *8*
House, carving "portrait" of, 156–160, *157–160*
House posts, *114*
Human figure, carving, 189–215
  in action, 206–209, *207–209*, *321*
  children as angels, 214, *214–215*
  hands, 210–212, *210–212*
  male musculature, 201–206, *203–206*
  proportions of, 197–200, *198*
  stylized, 213, *213*
  torso, *198*, 200–201
Hutchings, Roy, *337*

Ibex, 79, *79*
Ibis, 79, *80*
India, 104, 260
Insect panel, *269*
Insignias, *61*
Intaglio carving, 241–242, 282–286, *282–283*
Intaglio-relevato, 240
International Wood Collectors Society, 37
Ironwood, 34, 36, 94
Israel, 52, 68, 70, 78, 79, 254
Italy, 304
Ivory, whittling
  animals, 296, *297*, *310*, *311*
  miscellaneous examples of, *308–312*
  types of, 296
  working with, 296, 298
Ivorywood, pink, 35, 36–37

Jade, Alaskan, 298, *299*, *304*
Jaguar, *65*
Japan, 40, 48, 67, 95, 224–226, 248, 285, 312, 316, 317
Jelutong, 32, 34
Jewelry, *69*, *316*
  see also Pendants
Juarez, Benito, 223, *280*, 281
"Justice," *257*

Kashimir, 260
Kerosene, 34
Kittens, *98*
Knife cuts, *12*, *19*, *20*, 21
Knives
  vs. chisels, 18–20, *19*
  cutting with, 13–14
  types of, 10–11, *11*, *12*, *337*, *342*
  for whittling, 20–21
Knots, in wood, 37, 38
Kokkinakes, Spyros, *115*
Krishna, *259*
Kubbestol, *55*, 267
Kwila, 34

Lacewood, 36
Lacquer, 55
Lettering, 287–295, *290*
  an award panel, 290, *291*, 293
  on plaques, 293–295, *294*
  and selecting an alphabet, *288*, 289–290, *289*, *292*
Lignum vitae, 35, 36
Lime, 36, *36*
Linden, 36
Lions, 76, *77*, 91, *91*, *110*, *307*
  head, *38*
Little Mermaid, 189, *190*
  miniature, 189–195, *191–195*
Llamas, *90*, 91, *91*, *113*
Log, carved, *255*, *256*
Lohs, Martin, 210
Low relief, *127*, 240, 250, *262*, *284–286*

Macadamia, 34
Macaroni chisel, 15
Machine-roughing, 51–52, *51*
Madonna and Child, 39, *184*
Magnolia, 34
Mahogany, 13, 32, 34, 36
Mallets, 15–16, *15*
Maple, 34
Martin, Wade, *8*

Masks, 222–230
  African, 222
  Japanese, 224–226,
    224–225
  Mexican, *223*
  miniature dance, *248*
  relief carving, *254, 264, 265*
  step-by-step carving,
    226–230, *226–230*
  tools for, 223–224
Meerschaum, 301, *303*
Mexico, 37, 40, 41, 46, 66, 67,
  70, 71, 77, 81–90, 96,
  105, 110–112, 223, 298,
  304, 306
Mezzo-relievo, 240
Michelangelo, 198
Miniatures
  animals, *35, 84, 85, 86, 87,
    317, 318, 332*
  carving, 28
  dance mask, *248*
  furniture, *170, 171*
  of Little Mermaid, 189–195,
    191–195
  oil bowl, *249*
  totem pole, *243–247*
  see also Models; Small
    pieces; specific piece
Minton, Hugh, Jr., 101, *101*
Minton, Hugh C., 146
  self-portrait, 216–218,
    216–217
Mobiles
  butterfly, *118*, 119
  dinosaur, 106–112, *107–108*
Modelling, 49–50, *50*
  and low relief, *275,
    276–282, 277–280, 282*
Models, *319, 320*
  boat, 168–169, *169*
  of cabinet maker's shop,
    170, 171
  of carousel horses, 328, *328*
  of circus wagons, 328, *329*
Monkey, 82–83, *83*
Moonstone, 260
Moorish carved door, 161,
  162, 251
Morgan, Neil, 7
Motifs, *123, 250, 284*
Myrtle wood, 34, 101

Napkin rings, *60, 67, 134*
Neckerchief slides, 60–62,
  60, 61
Nepal, 260, 262
Nereid, *240*
Netsuke, *312*

Neustadt, Harrison, 62–63,
  64, *313*
Newel posts, 123
New Guinea, 45, 330,
  330–334
New Zealand, 284
Nighthawk, *33*
Noah's ark, 67, *68*
Noh masks, 224–226,
  224–225
Nudes
  Atlas, 201–206, *203–206*
  female, *200, 233*
  Little Mermaid, 189–195,
    191–195
  male, 202
  relief carving, 240
Nuts, carving, 41–43, *42*, 298

Oak
  Austrian, 36
  Eastern white, 34
  English, 36
  red, 34
Oil bowl, *249*
Oiling, 55
"Old Man of the Sea," 45–46,
  46
Olive pits, 41, *42*
Olive wood, 52
Onyx, 300, *306*
Osage orange, 34
Owls, 67, *67*, 81–82, *81, 86,
  87, 91, 91, 111, 115*, 116

Panels, *33, 34, 52*
  of animals, 80, *81, 106, 123,
    262*
  boat, 163–168, *164–167*
  of clouds and sheep, 270,
    270–272
  door, *251, 268–269*
  floral, 135–138, *135–136,
    236, 268–269*
  insect, *269*
  lettered, 293–295, *294*
  pine tree, *137–138,
    138–140*, 234
  polyglot, 135–138, *135–136,
    237–239, 237, 238*
  of scenes and people,
    273–274, 273
Pantographs, *30, 31*
Panza, Sancho, *174*, 175
Parakeet, *115*, 116
Paring cut, *12*
Paulownia, *33*
Peach pits, 41, *42, 43*
Pear (wood), *33*
Pecan (wood), *33*, 34

Pelicans, *111*
Pendants, *69, 76, 77, 86, 87,
  127, 279, 304, 311, 317,
  333*
Penguins, 73, *73*, 92, *93, 94,
  114*
Penknife, *11, 12*
Personality of carver, 9
Peru, 43, 91, 113, 114, 161, 279
Philippines, 76, 77, 199, 275
Phillip, John
  belt buckles, 62, 63–64,
    313, 315
  knife, *342*
Picasso, Pablo, "Dora Marr
  Seated," *286*
Picture frame, *239*
Piercing, 50, *50*, 242
Pig, *332*
Pine
  ponderosa, 40
  sugar, 32
  white, 13, 32, 34, 54
  yellow, 32
Pine cone panel, *234*
Pine tree panel, *137–138,
  138–140*
Pink ivorywood, 35, 36–37
Pins, *316*
Pipe, *303*
Pipestone, 300, *302*
Pits, carving, 41–43, *42*
Place card holder, *74*, 75, 80,
  80
Planes, 16
Plaques
  award, 124, *124–125*
  floral, *135*
  letters on, 293–295, *294*
Pochote, 34
Pocketknife, 10, 11, *11*, 20
Pointing cut, *12*
Polyglot panels
  floral, 135–138, *135–136*
  relief carving, 237–239,
    237, 238
Ponderosa pine, 32, 40
Poplar, 32–33, 34
Portraits, 183–185, 216
  and self-portraits, 216–220,
    216–217, 219–220
Power tools, 16, 18
Praying girl, *258*
Prepackaged hand carvings,
  7–8
Proportioning dividers, *30, 31*
Purpleheart, 35, 109
Puzzle box, *265*
Pyrography, 48–49

Quail, *111*
Quixote, Don, *173, 174,* 175,
185

Rabbits, *42,* 84, *85*
Raddha, *259*
Raleigh, Sir Walter, *202*
Red alder, 34
Red oak, 34
Reed, Charlie, *302*
Relief carving, 231–286
  animals, *106, 266–267*
  clouds and sheep panel,
    270, *270–272*
  door panels, *268–269*
  Far-Eastern, 258, 260–261,
    259–265
  flowers, *236*
  grounding in, 255–257, *255*
  half relief, 240, *241*
  high relief, 240, *241,*
    274–276, *275*
  hints on, 257–260
  hollow relief, 240–241
  and inlaying, 242–243
  intaglio, 241–242, 282–286,
    282–283
  lower relief, and
    modelling, *275,*
    276–282, *277–280, 282*
  low relief, *127,* 240, 250,
    262, 284–286
  miscellaneous examples of,
    233–236, 248–257, 277
  painting on, 250
  polyglot panels, 237–239,
    237, 238
  of scenes, and people,
    273–274, *273*
  and "setting in," 23, 232
  tools for, 18, 23, 232–233
  on totem pole, *242–247*
  wood for, 231–232
Riffler file, 16, 18
Rimachi, Domingo
    Fernandez, *91*
Road runner, 88, *88, 89,* 90
Rocking cut, *12*
Rooster, 76, *76*
Rosewood, 34–35, 36
Rowan, J. O., *249*
Russian bowl, *254*

Salad bowl, *134*
Salad set, *334*
Sandalwood, 36
Sanding, 21–22, 44, 55
Satinwood, 35, 36

Saws, 16
Sayers, Charles M., 18
  The Book of Wood Carving,
    133
Scrapers, 16
Seal, *112*
Seeds, carving, 41
Self-portraits
  of E. J. Tangerman,
    218–221, *219–220*
  of Hugh C. Minton,
    216–218, *216–217*
Serifs, 287
"Setting-in," 23, 232
Sharpening tools, 24–27, *25,
    26,* 339–340, *340, 341*
Shavings, 8
Sheep and clouds panel, 270,
    270–272
Shellac, 44, 55
Shells, carving, 41, 43, 298,
    299, 300–301, *304*
Shingling hatchet, 16
Shoe, wooden, *242*
Shoe horn, *115*
Silhouetting, 50, *50, 254, 275,*
    276
Silvering, 57
Simons, Richard J., 211
Sisso, *262*
Siva, *35*
Size of piece, 28–31
  and enlarging methods,
    29, *30–31*
  miniatures, 28
  and reducing methods, 31
Skates and skaters, *322–324,
    326–327*
Skeletons, *42, 82*
Skew chisel, 14, *14*
Skin diver, *111*
Skowhegan Indian, *348*
Slicing cut, *12*
"Slips," 24
Small pieces
  gnomes, 58, *58–59*
  miscellaneous, *316–319*
  neckerchief slides, 60–62,
    60, 61
  skates and skaters,
    322–324, 326–327
  see also Miniatures; specific
    piece
Snail, 76, *77*
Snake, *66*
Soapstone, 298, *299, 300,
    302, 306*
Soft woods, 32–33, 54–56
  see also specific wood

South American
  animals, 112–114, *112–114*
  "cowboys," *186*
  heads, *186,* 187
  see also specific country
Spain, 93, 162, 252, 279
Speckbacher, Josef, 276
Spoons, *110, 317, 332*
"Squash player," *53*
Sri Lanka, 79, 97, 258, 259,
    260, 261, 264, 265, 347
Stab cut, *12*
Stains, 55–56
Stations of the Cross, The,
    211–212
Statue, *348*
Statuettes, 152–155, *152–155,
    208, 333*
Stiacciato, 240
Stones, carving, 298, 300–301
  animals, *305, 306*
Stones, for sharpening tools,
    24, *25–26*
Stool, 55, *267*
Stop cuts, *19, 20,* 21
Street orchestra, *180*
Stropping, 24, *26*
Stylizing
  animals, 90–95, *92, 94*
  human figure, 213, *213*
Sugar pine, 32
Surface textures, 44–49,
    44–48
Sutter, H. M.
  designs for neckerchief
    slides, 60, *61,* 62
  flower carving lessons,
    129–133, *131–134*
  tool sharpening method,
    339
  tools, 18, 232–233, *233*
Swamp oak, 34
Swans, *42,* 84–85, *85,* 89, 90
Swashes, 287
Swedish sloyd, *12*
Sycamore, 34, 36

Tagua nuts, *42, 42*
Tahiti, 7
Tangerman, E. J.
  Carving Birds in Wood, 84
  self-portrait, 218–221,
    219–220
  Whittling and Woodcarving,
    98
Teak, *13,* 35, *35,* 55
Temple carvings, 94, *95*
Textures, surface, 44–49,
    44–48

Texturing, 48–50, *50*
Thumb push, *12*
Thuya, 35
Tibet, 260, 263
Tiki, 7
Tlingit oil bowl, *249*
Toad, *39*, 40, *74*, *75*, *297*, *317*
Tools, 10–23
    adzes, *15*, 16, 336–338, *339*
    auxiliary, 16
    and benches, 16–17, *17*
    care of, 20
    carver's screws, 340, 342,
        343
    for carving flowers, 128
    for carving masks, 223–224
    chisels, *13*, 14–15, *14*, 16,
        27
    chisels vs. knives, 18–20,
        19
    choosing, 11
    and cutting with grain, 11,
        13
    gouges, 14, *14*, 17, 18, 23
    hints on using, 20
    knives, 10–11, *11*, *12*, 18, 20
    mallets, 15–16, *15*
    nicking self with, 20
    pocketknife, 10, 11, *11*
    power, 10, 11, *11*, 16, 18
    for relief carving, 23,
        232–233
    sharpening, 24–27, *25*, *26*,
        339–340, *340*, *341*
    sizes, 17–18
    and vises, 16–17, *17*
    for whittling, 20–21
    see also specific tool
Toomi, S., *302*
Toreador and bull, *50*, *275*,
    276
Tortoise, 71, *71*, *83*, *114*
Totem poles, *242*, *246*
    miniature, 243–247
Trays, *48*, *49*, *263*, *285*
Trench carving, 240–241, 281
Trobriand Islands, 330,
    330–334

Trolls, 73–74, *73*
Trout, 116–117, *116–117*
Tupelo, 34
Turkey, 300–301, *303*
Turtles, 71, *71*, *83*, *114*

Ulysses and Cyclops,
    154–155, *155*
Ulysses and Polyphemus,
    152–154, *154*
Uncials, 287
Unicorn, 141–145, *141–145*

Varnish, 40, 44, 54, 55, 56
Veiner chisel, 18
Veiner gouge, 14, *14*
Veneers, 36
Vermilion, *34*, 35, 80
Virgin of Soledad, 46, *46*
Vises, 16–17, *17*
V-tool, *14*, 15, 18, 27

Wahnadagee, 336
Walking stick, *333*
Walnut, 13
    black, 33–34, *33*
    English, 36
    Italian, 36
    shell, 41, 43
Walrus, *297*, *306*
Walrus tusk, 296, *297*, *310*,
    311
"Washita," 24
Waxing, 55
Weasels, *75*, 76
West Germany, 51–52
Whale, *299*
Whalebone, 298, *299*
Whetting, 24, *25*, *26*
White oak, 34
White pine, 13, 32, 34, 54
Whittling, 20–22
    and bases, 53
    and chips, 21
    cutting methods, 22–23
    flowers, *22*, 128

gnomes, 58, *58–59*
ivory, 296–298, *297*,
    308–312
mistakes, 8
neckerchief slides, 60–62,
    60, *61*
and sanding, 21–22
and size of piece, 29
skates and skaters,
    321–327, *322*, *325*, *326*,
    327
and stop cuts, *20*, 21
tools for, 20–21
wood for, 33–34
Willow, 33, 34
Windswept, 38
Winery doors, 161, *161*
Wood, 32–41
    "bad," 38
    and bark, 40, *41*
    checks in, 37–38
    dry-rotted, *33*, 40
    with flaws, 33, 37, 38–40,
        38, *39*
    and gourds, 41–43, *43*
    grain, cutting with, 11, 13,
        21
    hard, 33, 54
    imported, 35–37
    knots in, 37
    local availability of, 34
    and nuts, 41–43, *42*, 298
    and pits, 41–43, *42*
    for relief carving, 231–232
    and seeds, 41
    soft, 32–33, 54–56
    what to start with, 37
    for whittling, 33–34
    see also specific wood
Woodchucks, *75*, *75*
Wooden shoe, *242*

Yellow pine, 32.
Yugoslavia, 76, 255, 256

Zebrawood, 35, 36
Zimmerman, Eric, *105*
Zivkovic, Bogosav, 255, *256*